W9-DJN-931

CORWIN & PELTASON'S

Understanding
the
Constitution

CORWIN & PELTASON'S

Understanding
the Constitution

TENTH EDITION

J. W. PELTASON

Holt, Rinehart and Winston
New York   Chicago   San Francisco   Philadelphia
Montreal   Toronto   London   Sydney   Tokyo
Mexico City   Rio de Janeiro   Madrid

Cover photo by P. Miller/Image Bank.

Library of Congress Cataloging in Publication Data

Corwin, Edward Samuel, 1878–1963.
  Corwin & Peltason's Understanding the constitution.

  Bibliography: p. 292
  Includes index.
    1. United States—Constitution. 2. United States—Constitutional law.
  I. Peltason, J. W. (Jack Walter), 1915-   . II. Title. III. Title: Corwin
  and Peltason's Understanding the constitution. IV. Title: Understanding
  the constitution.
  KF4528.C67 1985   342.73   84-28982
  ISBN 0-03-071176-2   347.302

CBS COLLEGE PUBLISHING
Holt, Rinehart and Winston
The Dryden Press
Saunders, College Publishing

Contents

Preface

The Constitution of the United States, the supreme law of the land, is by no means self-explanatory. In an attempt to make it understandable, this book sets forth the main features of the Constitution and the practical significance of its most important provisions as they are construed and applied today. Attention is also given to the immediate historic origins of the Constitution and its basic principles.

The central core of the Declaration of Independence and of each Article of the Constitution are discussed section by section, amplified, and interpreted in nontechnical terms. Because the constitutional system—the fundamental rules by which government power is organized and limited—includes, in addition to the documentary Constitution, those basic practices and customs that we have developed during the last 200 years, these features of our government are discussed to some extent. In addition, there is a brief essay that points up the basic features of our constitutional system: federalism, separation of powers, and judicial review.

An attempt has been made to avoid legal detail and over elaborate citations. The absence of extensive documentation and the attempt to simplify may give an impression of dogmatism that I should here like to disavow. The author is well aware that there is no such thing as "the interpretation" of the Constitution; the reader is warned that others would find different meaning in the words of the Constitution and in the opinions of the judges who interpret it.

If this volume gives its readers an understanding of the document itself and an appreciation of the important role that constitutional interpretation plays in the conduct of our government, it will fulfill its purpose.

This revision covers all relevant decisions of the Supreme Court through the end of the 1983 term, that is, all decisions through July 1984. By the early 1980s, the transition from the Warren to the Burger Court was long over. With the first Reagan appointment to the Court, a new era of decision-making was well under way. Our Constitution has felt the impact of Watergate and the trauma of Vietnam. The two hundredth anniversary of the signing of the Declaration of Independence has passed. Now the bicentennial of the ratification of the Constitution is almost upon us. There are times of national soul-searching about the adequacy of our constitutional system. For these reasons and others, I think it appropriate to add a few words about these events and to comment about the course of constitutional development, most especially about the interaction between the electoral process in particular and the political process in general and our constitutional system.

*   *   *

On April 29, 1963, all who revere the Constitution of the United States suffered a major loss with the death of Professor Edward S. Corwin. I think it may be said without exaggeration that "the General," as he was affectionately known by his thousands of students, knew more about the Constitution of the United States than any person who ever lived. At least those of us who had the privilege of studying under him knew that Chief Justice Hughes was in error when he said that the Constitution is what the Supreme Court says it is—we knew that the Constitution is what Corwin said it is.

Professor Corwin combined his mastery of knowledge about the Constitution with wisdom and powerful analytical skills so that his major works, many of which were written almost a half century ago, are still as fresh and important today as when he wrote them.

This volume was among the least of his books. Although many of the views expressed and the words used are those of Professor Corwin retained from earlier editions, the responsibility for this revision is mine. It is more than the usual cliché, however, for me to acknowledge that whatever is its merit is attributable to the teacher; the errors to his student.

I wish to thank Prentice-Hall, Inc., for permission to quote occasional sentences from previous publications.

Special thanks are owed to Sheldon Steinbach, who, drawing upon his great knowledge of the copyright law, wrote the several pages on the Copyright Act of 1978. I also want to thank Christopher Byrne for his help in getting for me the most recent decisions of the Supreme Court almost at the moment they were issued.

Professor Grier Stephenson of Franklin and Marshall College gave generously of his time, and his comments have been very useful in this revision. I am especially indebted to Professor Stephen Wasby of the State University of New York at Albany. He is an outstanding critic with an authoritative knowledge of our Constitution and the work of our courts. He patiently went through the manuscript during its several drafts, brought to my attention errors of fact and interpretation, and suggested many ways to make the presentation of the materials more coherent and useful.

Margaret Teasley deserves an extraspecial thanks for extraspecial proofreading.

J. W. P.

Irvine, California
January 1985

A Note on Case Citations

The number of cases mentioned in the text has been kept to a minimum. The case citations, although more extensive, have not been as exhaustive as is the practice in legal journals and political science articles. It is more important for most people to know what the Supreme Court has said about what the Constitution means and to have some feeling for the issues involved than to know the names of the cases. Nevertheless, there are some cases of such significance that knowledge of them is part of a liberal education, and still others are cited for those who wish to inquire further.

Cases that came to the Supreme Court before 1875 are cited by the name of the official court reporter. Thus *McCulloch* v. *Maryland,* 4 Wheaton 316 (1819), means that this case can be located in volume 4 of Wheaton's *Reports of cases argued and adjudged in the Supreme Court of the United States* on page 315 and that the case was decided in 1819. Cases after 1875 are cited by the volume number of *United States Reports,* a publication of the Government Printing Office that records the cases adjudged in the Supreme Court. Thus the case of *United States v. Nixon* is cited 418 U.S. 683 (1974) and is, therefore, found in volume 418 of the *United States Reports* beginning on page 683 and was decided in 1974.

For the special use of lawyers and scholars, commercial publishers make Supreme Court decisions available more quickly than does the United States Government Printing Office (GPO); even the GPO's Preliminary Prints now are not available until several years after a decision has been handed down. For this reason, cases decided in more recent years will be cited as follows: *Firefighters* v. *Stotts,* 81 L Ed 2d 483 (1984), meaning that this case can be found in volume 81 of the Lawyers Cooperative Publishing Company, second series, on page 483, and it was decided in 1981.

I call special attention to the comprehensive annotation of the Constitution published by the Library of Congress, a complete revision is scheduled every ten years, but a cumulative supplement to keep the volume current is available every two years. The most recently available edition of *The Constitution of the United States: Analysis and Interpretation* (Washington, D.C.: Government Printing Office, 1973) was prepared under the editorship of Lester S. Jayson. This monumental work builds on the first edition published in 1952 under the editorship of Professor Corwin.

Background of
the Constitution

The Constitution can best be understood within the historical situation in which it was written and has been applied. By placing the Constitution in the context of history, we learn of the conditions and conflicts that produced it and continue to give it meaning. We therefore begin with a brief consideration of the Declaration of Independence and the Articles of Confederation, the two most important documents affecting the background of the Constitution.

The Declaration of Independence is the first formal American state paper. It is not judicially enforceable, and it establishes no legal rights or duties. But the Declaration has had a decisive impact on the development of our governmental system. It sets forth the ideals and reflects the standards of what might be called the American Creed. This Creed, with its stress on the rights of people, equality under the law, limited government, and government by consent of the governed, infuses the structures and practices of the Constitution. The Declaration remains the American Conscience: a constant challenge to those who would subvert our democratic processes or deny persons their inalienable rights.

THE DECLARATION OF INDEPENDENCE

In Congress, July 4, 1776, by the Representatives of the United States of America, in General Congress assembled.

This was the first time that "the United States of America" was officially used. Previous practice was to refer to the "United Colonies."[1]*

We celebrate our independence on the anniversary of the day it was proclaimed. The actual deed, however, was approved by the Second Continental Congress two days before, when it adopted by a narrow vote Richard Henry

* Superior figures refer to notes found at the back of the book.

1

Lee's resolution "to declare the United Colonies free and independent states." Thomas Jefferson, John Adams, Benjamin Franklin, Roger Sherman, and Robert R. Livingston were appointed to draft a declaration to accompany this resolution of independence. It was Jefferson who did most of the work.

Jefferson had the task of rallying both American and world sentiment to the cause of independence. As he later wrote, "Neither aiming at originality of principles or sentiments, nor yet copied from any particular and previous writing, it was intended to be an expression of the American Mind."[2] Jefferson drew on precedents that were known to all educated Englishmen and Americans, especially on John Locke's often-quoted *Second Treatise of Civil Government,* written in 1689. This volume was thought to be an authoritative pronouncement of established principles. Locke's ideas provided ready arguments for the American cause, and they were especially embarrassing to an English government whose own source of authority was based on them.

The Preamble

When in the Course of human events, it becomes necessary for one people to dissolve the political bands which have connected them with another,

---

One of the points at issue between the colonists and the English government was whether Americans and English were one people or two. Here the Americans asserted that they formed a separate entity, previously connected with the English people but not an integral part of them.

---

and to assume among the powers of the earth, the separate and equal station to which the Laws of Nature and of Nature's God entitle them,

---

Equality of sovereign nations was stated as a requirement of the law of nature; today this would be called "international law."

---

a decent respect to the opinions of mankind requires that they should declare the causes which impel them to the separation.

The favorable opinion of mankind was a military necessity. The demand for independence was slow in developing, and many Americans continued to hope for reconciliation with the mother country even as late as the summer of 1776. As long as the revolution remained a purely internal quarrel between England and her colonies, foreign governments were reluctant to give military assistance; and assistance was desperately needed if the Americans were to make successful their revolutionary acts. The French were especially anxious to support any move that would weaken English power, but they first wanted assurances that the Americans meant business. The Declaration of Independence notified the world that the Americans were serious, and it was both an appeal to the conscience of mankind and a call for military help.

The American Philosophy of Government

We hold these truths to be self-evident, that all men are created equal, that they are endowed by their Creator with certain unalienable Rights, that among these are Life, Liberty, and the pursuit of Happiness.

These ringing words introduced the American philosophy of self-government. About six weeks before, Virginia had adopted a constitution that contained the first American bill of rights. In it the same concepts that are found in the Declaration were stated as follows: "That all men are by nature equally free and independent, and have certain inherent rights, of which, when they enter into a state of society, they cannot by any compact deprive or divest their posterity; namely, the enjoyment of life and liberty, with the means of acquiring and possessing property, and pursuing and obtaining happiness and safety."

It did not necessarily follow that independence from England would lead to republican institutions in the United States. It is, therefore, highly significant that the Americans based their revolutionary acts on constitutional principles. The revolution was not justified so that one group of Americans could impose their will on other Americans free of English control, but so that Americans could govern themselves. The Declaration is not just a declaration of independence; it is also a defense of free government.

Many have scoffed at the assertion that all are created equal. They argue that such a statement flies in the face of the obvious facts—some have brains, talent, and virtue, and others do not. The Declaration, however, does not assert that people are equal in all things. It proclaims that people are equally endowed with certain inalienable rights, among these being a right to their own lives, liberties, and pursuits of happiness. These are a person's birthrights; they are not secured by an act of governmental grace or received as a gift from others. As John Adams—a member of the drafting committee that wrote the Declaration, a believer in equal rights but not in natural equality—wrote in 1814,

That all men are born to equal rights is true. Every being has a right to his own, as clear, as moral, as sacred, as any other being has. This is as indubitable as a moral government in the universe. But to teach that all men are born with equal powers and faculties, to equal influence in society, to equal property and advantages through life, is as gross a fraud, as glaring an imposition on the credulity of the people, as ever was practiced by the monks, by Druids, by Brahmins, by priests of the immortal Lama, or by the self-styled philosophers of the French Revolution.[3]

In 1776 people spoke of inalienable or natural rights; today we speak of human rights, the rights that distinguish men and women from the other creatures who inhabit the earth, the rights that make for the "humanness" of human beings. To some, the dignity of all individuals and their inherent worth grow out of the belief that all are the children of God and are created in His image. To others, the equal right of all to be treated as unique, inviolable beings is based on humanistic grounds. But for whatever reason, these truths that were self-evident to the men of 1776 underlie the culture and civilization of the free world.

How inalienable are inalienable rights? Such rights may be forfeited by wrongdoing. The government may call upon persons to sacrifice their lives and liberty in defense of the nation. But that some should be called to make the sacrifice and others favored arbitrarily, or that the innocent should be made the tools of others' happiness, are actions contrary to the concept of the equal right of each person to life and liberty.

How is the existence of slavery to be explained in a nation whose leaders proclaimed the doctrine of inalienable rights? The Declaration makes no distinction between black and white; in 1776, most Americans believed that slavery was an evil institution that sooner or later had to be abolished. In his original draft, Jefferson blamed the Crown for the establishment of slavery in the United States and condemned the King for waging "cruel war against human nature itself, violating its most sacred rights of life & liberty." This clause offended some of the delegates from slaveholding states; in the midst of their crisis the Americans decided to fight one evil at a time, and Congress deleted this passage in order to secure united support against England. It was to be another eighty-seven years before the practices of the nation started to conform in this respect to the professions of the Declaration.

That to secure these rights, Governments are instituted among Men, deriving their just powers from the consent of the governed,

---

People create government for the purpose of securing their preexisting natural rights. That the rights come first, that government is created to protect these rights, and that government officials are subject to the natural law were not novel ideas in 1776. These ideas were based on the concepts of a state of nature, natural law, natural rights, and the social compact. As John Locke wrote, before the establishment of society people lived in a *state of nature.* Thomas Hobbes, an antidemocratic philosopher, had insisted that in the state of nature, where there was no government to make and enforce laws, people made war on each other and life was "solitary, poore, nasty, brutish and short." But Locke argued that even in a state of nature there was a law governing conduct—there was the *natural law,* comprising universal, unvarying principles of right and wrong, and known to people through the use of reason. For example, if an Englishman were to meet a Frenchwoman on an uninhabited and ungoverned island, he would not be free to deprive her of her life, liberty, or property. Should he attempt to do so, he would violate the natural law and could rightly be punished.

Although the state of nature was not, according to Locke, a lawless condition, it was an inconvenient one. Each had to protect his or her own rights, and there was no agreed-upon judge to settle disputes about the application of the natural law to particular controversies. Realizing this, people decided to make a *compact* with one another in which each would give to the community the right to create a government equipped to enforce the natural law. Thereby each agreed to abide by the decisions made by the majority and to comply with the laws enacted by the people's representatives, provided they did not entrench upon each's fundamental rights. The power of government was thus limited.

Modern social scientists and historians agree with Aristotle that people are social animals and have never lived in a presocial and pregovernmental state of nature. Government, rather than being a consciously created institution, has developed as naturally as the family. But to reject the belief that government originated through a social compact does not invalidate the belief that men and women are primary and governments secondary, and that governments derive their coercive authority from the consent of the governed. The moral primacy of the individual remains. It is on the philosophical and ethical, rather than the historical, concept of priority of men and women over governments that Americans base their insistence that governments are to be evaluated by how they improve the well-being and protect the rights of individuals. Hence,

---

That whenever any Form of Government becomes destructive of these ends, it is the Right of the People to alter or to abolish it, and to institute new Government, laying its foundation on such principles, and organizing its powers in such form, as to them shall seem most likely to effect their Safety and Happiness.

In other words, the people may abolish their government whenever it ceases to protect natural rights and becomes destructive of the ends for which it was established. In a free society where the consent of the governed is regularly expressed through open debate and free elections, it is not likely that revolutionary action will be necessary in order to alter the foundations of government. The colonists tried first to use constitutional devices to adjust their grievances. Finally, they felt compelled to revolt and, in the eyes of English law, to become traitors.

The doctrine of revolution pronounced in the Declaration is not a legal doctrine; there is no constitutional right to engage in revolutionary conduct. Nor should the doctrine proclaimed by the Declaration be confused with that of those who espouse change by the use of violence. Jefferson did not defend the right of a fraction of the civic community to seize the government and use it to suppress the rights of others. The conservative nature of the revolutionary right asserted is underscored by the next sentence.

Prudence, indeed, will dictate that Governments long established should not be changed for light and transient causes;

Without denying that the people have the right to change government whenever a majority of them think it destructive of their rights, the writers of the Declaration counsel caution.

---

and accordingly all experience hath shown, that mankind are more disposed to suffer, while evils are sufferable, than to right themselves by abolishing the forms to which they are accustomed. But when a long train of abuses and usurpations, pursuing invariably the same Object, evinces a design to reduce them under absolute Despotism, it is their right, it is their duty, to throw off such Government, and to provide new Guards for their future security. Such has been the patient sufferance of these Colonies; and such is now the necessity which constrains them to alter their former Systems of Government. The history of the present King of Great Britain is a history of repeated injuries and usurpations, all having in direct object the establishment of an absolute Tyranny over these States.

Charges Against the King

The Declaration makes no mention of Parliament. It directs its accusations at the King. The colonists were asserting the constitutional theory that their allegiances were to the Crown, not to Parliament, and that they were bound to England through the King. They were contending that Parliament had no authority over them and had no right to regulate their affairs. (To concentrate the attack on the King was also good political tactics. Quite a few members of Parliament sympathized with the colonists, and there was no point in unnecessarily alienating them.) This colonial view of the nature of the British Empire eventually triumphed over the eighteenth-century English view that the English Parliament had authority to legislate for all the dominions.

The details of the specific charges leveled by the Declaration against the King are of less significance today than are the other parts of that document. The fact is that as kings go, especially those ruling in the eighteenth century, George III was not all that bad. The several charges against him are listed without additional comment. It is interesting to note, however, that when it came time to write the Constitution steps were taken to guard against some of the abuses charged to the King, such as making sure judges were not dependent upon the will of the President for the tenure of their offices and the amount of their salaries, making the military dependent on and inferior to civil authorities, guaranteeing trials by juries in the jurisdiction in which criminal offenses were alleged to have taken place, and establishing fixed dates for the election of the members of the House of Representatives.

To prove this, let Facts be submitted to a candid world.

He has refused his Assent to Laws, the most wholesome and necessary for the public good.

He has forbidden his Governors to pass Laws of immediate and pressing importance, unless suspended in their operation till his Assent should be obtained; and when so suspended, he has utterly neglected to attend to them.

He has refused to pass other Laws for the accommodation of large districts of people, unless those people would relinquish the right of Representation in the Legislature, a right inestimable to them and formidable to tyrants only.

He has called together legislative bodies at places unusual, uncomfortable, and distant from the depository of their Public Records, for the sole purpose of fatiguing them into compliance with his measures.

He has dissolved Representative Houses repeatedly, for opposing with manly firmness his invasions on the rights of the people.

He has refused for a long time, after such dissolutions, to cause others to be elected; whereby the Legislative Powers, incapable of Annihilation, have returned to the People at large for their exercise; the State remaining in the mean time exposed to all the dangers of invasion from without, and convulsions within.

He has endeavoured to prevent the population of these States; for that purpose obstructing the Laws for Naturalization of Foreigners; refusing to pass others to encourage their migration hither, and raising the conditions of new Appropriations of Lands.

He has obstructed the Administration of Justice, by refusing his Assent to Laws for establishing Judiciary Powers.

He has made Judges dependent on his Will alone, for the tenure of their offices, and the amount and payment of their salaries.

He has erected a multitude of New Offices, and sent hither swarms of Officers to harass our People, and eat out their substance.

He has kept among us, in times of peace, Standing Armies without the Consent of our legislatures.

He has affected to render the Military independent of and superior to the Civil Power.

He has combined with others to subject us to a jurisdiction foreign to our constitution, and unacknowledged by our laws; giving his Assent to their acts of pretended Legislation:

For quartering large bodies of armed troops among us:

For protecting them, by a mock Trial, from Punishment for any Murders which they should commit on the Inhabitants of these States:

For cutting off our Trade with all parts of the world:

For imposing taxes on us without our Consent:

For depriving us in many cases, of the benefits of Trial by Jury:

For transporting us beyond Seas to be tried for pretended offences:

For abolishing the free System of English Laws in a neighbouring Province, establishing therein an Arbitrary government, and enlarging its Boundaries so as to render it at once an example and fit instrument for introducing the same absolute rule into these Colonies:

For taking away our Charters, abolishing our most valuable Laws, and altering fundamentally the Forms of our Governments;

For suspending our own Legislatures, and declaring themselves invested with Power to legislate for us in all cases whatsoever.

He has abdicated Government here, by declaring us out of his Protection and waging War against us.

He has plundered our seas, ravaged our Coasts, burnt our towns, and destroyed the lives of our people.

He is at this time transporting large armies of foreign mercenaries to compleat the works of death, desolation and tyranny, already begun with circumstances of Cruelty & perfidy scarcely parallel'd in the most barbarous ages, and totally unworthy the Head of a civilized nation.

He has constrained our fellow Citizens taken Captive on the high Seas to bear Arms against their Country, to become the executioners of their friends and Brethren, or to fall themselves by their Hands.

He has excited domestic insurrections amongst us, and has endeavoured to bring on the inhabitants of our frontiers, the merciless Indian Savages, whose known rule of warfare, is an undistinguished destruction of all ages, sexes and conditions.

In every stage of these Oppressions We have Petitioned for Redress in the most humble terms: Our repeated Petitions have been answered only by repeated injury. A Prince, whose character is thus marked by every act which may define a Tyrant, is unfit to be the ruler of a free People.

Nor have We been wanting in attention to our British brethren. We have warned them from time to time of attempts by their legislature to extend an unwarrantable jurisdiction over us. We have reminded them of the circumstances of our emigration and settlement here. We have appealed to their native justice and magnanimity, and we have conjured them by the ties of our common kindred to disavow these usurpations, which, would inevitably interrupt our connections and correspondence. They too have been deaf to the voice of justice and consanguinity. We must, therefore, acquiesce in the necessity, which denounces our Separation, and hold them, as we hold the rest of mankind, Enemies in War, in Peace Friends.—

Conclusion

We, Therefore, the Representatives of the United States of America, in General Congress, Assembled, appealing to the Supreme Judge of the world for the rectitude of our intentions, do, in the Name, and by Authority of the good People of these Colonies, solemnly publish and declare, That these United Colonies are, and of Right ought to be Free and Independent States; that they are Absolved from all Allegiance to the British Crown, and all political connection between them and the State of Great Britain, is and ought to be totally dissolved; and that as Free and Independent States, they have full Power to levy War, conclude Peace, contract Alliances, establish Commerce, and to do all other Acts and Things which Independent States may of right do.—And for the support of this Declaration, with a firm reliance on the protection of Divine Providence, we mutually pledge to each other our Lives, our Fortunes and our sacred Honor.

Did the Americans declare their independence on behalf of the United States or on behalf of each of the thirteen sovereign states? The language is ambiguous. In later years these questions became important as arguments arose about the nature of the federal system, and especially about the source of the national government's authority in the field of external affairs.

The Supreme Court has taken the view that in 1776 all powers in the field of foreign affairs previously vested in the English Crown passed to the United States, so that the states never did have power to make war and peace or deal as sovereign nations with other governments. Other Americans have insisted that it was the separate colonies that declared their independence and that all powers of the Crown passed to each state. It was these states, so it is argued, which in turn created the central government, first by informal acquiescence and then more formally in the Articles of Confederation and the Constitution.

Whatever the original intent, the former view had the support of the North's victory in the Civil War, the growth of national sentiment, and the sanction of the Supreme Court.

The men who signed the Declaration of Independence probably gave little thought to the matter; they had more immediate problems to solve. With full recognition of the gravity of their acts and their individual property, they pledged their lives, their fortunes, and their sacred honor. John Hancock of Massachusetts, president of the Continental Congress, was the first to so pledge with his famous bold signature.

THE ARTICLES OF CONFEDERATION

Although the Second Continental Congress, which had assembled in May 1775, had no formal governmental authority, it raised an army, appointed a commander in chief, negotiated with foreign nations, coined money, and assumed all powers that, it claimed, belong to an independent and sovereign nation. However, it seemed desirable to legalize these practices and place Congress's operations on a more formal basis of authority. Accordingly, even before the Declaration had been proclaimed, Congress appointed a committee, headed by John Dickinson of Maryland, to draft Articles of Union. In 1777 Congress submitted these Articles to the state legislatures, but not until March 1781 did all the states approve—Maryland, acting in behalf of the six states with no land claims, held out until the seven states with claims to western lands agreed to cede them to the Union—and our second national government began to function.

The Articles of Confederation did not materially alter the structure or powers of the government that had unofficially but effectively been governing the United States since 1775. They established a league of friendship, a "perpetual Union" of states, resting expressly on state sovereignty. The state legislatures promised to treat each other's citizens without discrimination, to give full faith and credit to each other's legal acts and public proceedings, and to extradite fugitives wanted in another state.

The structure of the central government was quite simple. There was only a single-chamber Congress. There was no executive, although a committee consisting of one delegate from each state managed affairs when Congress was not assembled. There was no judiciary, although Congress acted as a court to resolve disputes among the states.

Each state had one vote in the Congress and each state legislature selected its own representatives to cast that vote, paid them, and could at any time recall them. The only restrictions on a state's choice were that it could send no less than two nor more than seven members and no person could be a delegate for more than three years in six or serve at the same time as an officer under the United States.

The powers of Congress were limited. The Second Article stated, "Each State retains its sovereignty, freedom and independence, and every power, jurisdiction and right, which is not by this confederation expressly delegated to the United States, in Congress assembled." In short, Congress had only those powers that were expressly delegated.

Congress could determine peace and war, send and receive ambassadors, enter into treaties—except that it could not deprive states of the right to tax imports or prohibit exports—deal with prizes taken by United States forces, coin money, fix standards of weights and measures, regulate affairs with Indians not members of any state, establish a postal system, appoint military officers in the service of the United States above the rank of colonel, and decide certain disputes that might arise among the states. Decisions on these matters required the approval of at least nine states, and the Articles themselves could not be amended without the approval of all thirteen states.

Congress did *not* have the power to collect taxes from individuals, to regulate commerce, or to prohibit the states from coining money. To secure funds it determined how much each state should pay, but it was up to each state to collect taxes from its citizens and turn the money over to the national treasury. If a state refused to do so, there was little that Congress could do. Likewise, Congress could negotiate treaties with foreign nations, but it had no way of making states comply with the obligation thus assumed. Resembling an international organization composed of sovereign nations rather than a national government, Congress could not impose obligations directly on individuals or enforce its legislation through its own agencies. In order to enforce congressional commands, it would have been necessary to apply sanctions against the offending states as such.

TOWARD A MORE PERFECT UNION

In retrospect, it may appear that the Americans lacked vision when they failed to establish a more tightly knit Union and to create a strong central government. But it must be remembered that they had just fought a war against centralized authority and, with limited communications and transportation facilities, they had good reason to believe that there could be no self-government except through local government. Nor should the accomplishments of the government under the Articles of Confederation be overlooked. It successfully brought the war to a conclusion; negotiated the Treaty of Paris of 1783, which gave the United States *de jure* status as a nation; established an enduring system for the development of western lands; and refined the practices of interstate cooperation that gave Americans further practical experience in handling national problems.

And there were plenty of these. The English refused to withdraw their troops from western lands until the states lived up to their treaty obligations to indemnify British subjects for property confiscated during the war, and Congress was powerless to make either the British or the states comply. The Spanish threatened to close the mouth of the Mississippi to American trade; foreign commerce languished. The Americans, having ceased to enjoy the privileges of membership in the British Empire, were unable to secure treaty advantages from other nations, who had no desire to make agreements with a nation that could not enforce them.

Once the fighting stopped, pressure to cooperate was reduced, and the states started to go off in their several directions. Some printed worthless paper money, while some failed to contribute their share to support the central government. Trade barriers were established by some states in an attempt to give their own merchants special privileges, and the seaboard states levied taxes on goods going inland. Within the states, conflicts between debtors and creditors were often bitter—defaulting debtors resented the harsh laws that caused them to lose their property or go to jail; creditors resented the acts passed giving debtors longer time to pay off debts or permitting them to use inflated paper currency.

Attempts were made to amend the Articles in order to give Congress authority to collect taxes and to regulate interstate commerce. In 1781 Congress submitted an amendment to the state legislatures that would give it power to collect taxes, but another flaw in the Articles was made apparent when the amendment failed because a single state, Rhode Island, refused to agree. Two years later New York vetoed a similar amendment. What could be done?

A relatively small group of important and articulate Americans had been agitating for a more vigorous national government, but general sentiment was against any drastic changes. The nationalists had to move carefully. They needed an opportunity to present their proposals to the country. Interstate conferences to discuss navigation and commercial matters gave them such a chance. After successfully negotiating an agreement with Maryland, some nationally minded Virginians proposed that all the states send delegates to Annapolis in September 1786 to discuss the establishment of a uniform system of commerce for the entire nation. But only five states sent commissioners to the Annapolis Convention.

Although disappointed by this apparent lack of interest, Alexander Hamilton of New York and James Madison of Virginia persuaded the delegates who did come to try to salvage something. They adopted a report urging the states to send delegates to another convention to be held the following May in Philadelphia. It was further stated that such delegates should be authorized not only to discuss trade matters but also to examine the defects of the existing system of government, and "to devise such further provisions as shall appear to them necessary to render the constitution of the Federal Government adequate to the exigencies of the Union."

Even before Congress authorized a convention, several of the state legislatures, following Virginia's lead, selected delegates. Distinguished men were chosen and the country was notified that the approaching Philadelphia Convention was to be taken seriously. After hesitating, Congress gave its consent, carefully stipulating, however, that the delegates should meet "for the sole and express purpose of revising the Articles of Confederation and reporting to Congress and the several legislatures such alterations and provisions therein as shall when agreed to in Congress and confirmed by the states render the federal constitution adequate to the exigencies of Government & the preservation of the Union." Ultimately all the states except Rhode Island selected delegates.

THE CONSTITUTIONAL CONVENTION

Seventy-four persons were appointed delegates to the Philadelphia Convention, but only fifty-five attended, of whom only thirty-nine took a leading part in deliberations. This distinguished group was not interested in mere political speculation but, above everything else, in establishing a government that would work; they were well equipped for the task. Seven of the delegates had served as governors of their respective states, thirty-nine had served in Congress, eight had had previous experience in constitution making within their own states. Despite this wealth of experience, the Convention was composed mainly of young men. The youngest was only twenty-six, six were under thirty-one, and only twelve were over fifty-four. They were men of consequence—merchants, manufacturers, planters, bankers, lawyers. The small farmers and city mechanics were not represented; the back-country rural areas were greatly underrepresented, although this was not the case in several of the state ratifying conventions.

Conspicuous in their absence from the Convention were Patrick Henry, Samuel Adams, John Adams, John Hancock, Tom Paine, and Thomas Jefferson—the fiery democratic leaders of the Revolution. Henry had been appointed but refused to attend; he was not in favor of revising the Articles of Confederation. "I smelt a rat," he is reported to have remarked. Jefferson and John Adams were abroad, representing the United States in a diplomatic capacity, Paine had returned to England, and Hancock and Samuel Adams had not been chosen delegates.

Six men stand out as leaders of the Convention: George Washington, James Madison, Edmund Randolph, Benjamin Franklin, James Wilson, and Gouverneur Morris—three from Virginia, three from Pennsylvania.

Washington, first citizen of Virginia and of the United States, was unanimously selected to preside over the Convention. He had been extremely reluctant to attend and had accepted only when persuaded that his prestige was needed to assure the success of the Convention. Although he seldom spoke, his influence was vitally felt both in informal gatherings and in the Convention sessions. The universal assumption that he would become the first President under the new government inspired confidence in it.

Madison, only thirty-six at the time, was one of the most learned and informed of the delegates. He had been a member both of the Congress and of the Virginia Assembly. Foreseeing the future significance of the Convention, Madison always sat in the front of the room, where he could hear all that was said; he kept a detailed record of the proceedings. Even today, Madison's notes, although he edited them in the 1820s, almost 40 years after the event, remain our major source of information concerning the Convention.

Edmund Randolph, thirty-four, was governor of Virginia, and a member of one of Virginia's first families. Although he declined to sign the Constitution, he later advocated its ratification.

Benjamin Franklin, at eighty-one, was the Convention's oldest member. Second only to Washington in the esteem of his countrymen, Franklin had a firm faith in the people. Despite his great age, Franklin played an active role. At critical moments, his sagacious and humorous remarks broke the tension and prevented bitterness.

Most of Franklin's speeches were read to the Convention by his fellow delegate James Wilson. This Scottish-born and Scottish-trained lawyer had signed the Declaration of Independence and represented his state in Congress. He was a strong supporter of Madison; his work on the Convention's Committee on Detail, although inconspicuous, was very important.

In sharp contrast to Franklin, the third Pennsylvania delegate, Gouverneur Morris, was strongly aristocratic in his sympathies. He was an eloquent and interesting speaker and addressed the Convention more often than any other member, and his facility with the pen is shown by the fact that he was chosen to write the final draft of the Constitution. Years later he began a letter, "The hand that writes this letter wrote the Constitution."

Besides these six, there were others of outstanding prominence at the Convention: George Mason, Charles Pinckney, Roger Sherman, Alexander Hamilton, Luther Martin, to mention a few. Hamilton, representing New York, did not play as important a role as one might expect; his influence was nullified to a great extent by his associates from New York, who opposed the Constitution. Hamilton lost influence, also, through his advocacy of a strong and completely centralized national government. At the opposite extreme was Luther Martin from Maryland, who was an ardent and fearfully boring champion of the small states. As soon as it was apparent that his views were in the minority, Martin went back to Maryland.

Convention Debates and Procedures

The Virginia delegates, who were anxious to establish a strong central government, took advantage of an eleven-day delay in the opening of the Convention—a delay due to the failure of a sufficient number of delegations to appear at the time the Convention was scheduled to open—to prepare a series of proposals. This gave the nationalists time to prepare a plan that imparted to the debates a general direction that the less nationalistically inclined delegates were never able to reverse. Eventually the Virginia Plan, with modifications, became the Constitution.

Immediately after Washington was chosen to preside and rules of procedures were adopted—of which the rule of secrecy was perhaps the most significant—Randolph introduced Virginia's fifteen resolutions. The Virginia Plan contained some startling proposals. The Convention's mandate from Congress and most of the delegates' instructions from their state legislatures restricted them to the consideration of amendments to the Articles of Confederation. The Virginians, however, proposed a completely new instrument of government differing fundamentally from the Articles. They proposed that a central government be established with power to pass laws and with authority to enforce these laws through its own executive and judicial branches. They proposed that Congress be a bicameral (two-house) legislature in which states should be represented on the basis of wealth or population; that this Congress be given all powers vested in the existing Congress plus the authority "to legislate in all cases to which the separate states are incompetent, or in which the harmony of the United States may be interrupted by the exercise of individual legislation."

For the first two weeks, the Convention discussed the Virginia Plan. Delegates from the less populous states were afraid that their interests would be overlooked by a national legislature dominated by representatives from the large states. They favored a less powerful national government with more independence of action by the states. They counterattacked on June 14 when Paterson of New Jersey introduced nine resolutions, the New Jersey Plan, as an alternative to Virginia's scheme. Although proposing that Congress be given the power to regulate commerce and levy taxes, Paterson's proposals would not have significantly altered the Articles of Confederation. All states were to have the same weight in a single-chambered national Congress, a plural executive was to administer the law, and a single national Supreme Court was to supervise the interpretation of national laws by the state courts. Although some of its provisions were incorporated in the Constitution, the New Jersey Plan was ultimately rejected and the delegates resumed discussion of the Virginia Plan.

Small-state delegates grew increasingly discontented with the deliberations, and there were threats of withdrawal. Presently the Convention became dead-locked over the crucial issue of representation in the upper house of the proposed Congress. Finally, a committee of eleven, one delegate from each state (Rhode Island had refused to send delegates to the Constitutional Convention, and much of the time New York was unrepresented), was appointed to work out a compromise. Three days later, on July 5, the committee presented its report, known to history as the Connecticut Compromise. The nationalists conceded that in the upper house each state should have equal representation, but on the condition that money bills originate in the lower chamber. Furthermore, slaves were to be counted as three-fifths of the free population both in determining representation in the lower house and in apportioning direct taxes among the states according to population. Delegates from the less populous states, being thus mollified, were then ready to support the establishment of a strong central government.

However, there remained many other differences still to be reconciled: questions about suffrage, the structure and authority of federal courts, and the procedures for selecting the President. But on many basic issues the delegates were in general agreement. All supported the idea of a republican form of government; all agreed that the powers of the national government should be distributed among a legislative, an executive, and a judicial branch. Without extended debate, it was decided to impose limits on the power of the states to coin money or interfere with the rights of creditors. By the end of the summer, the delegates had a document to present to the nation.

The document the framers had prepared was not merely a revision of the Articles of Confederation. Rather, they ignored their instructions and called for an entirely different structure of government. Moreover, contrary to their instructions from the Congress and the provisions of the Articles of Confederation, they called for the direct submission of their work for ratification to the states, rather than via the Congress, for ratification by special conventions within the states, rather than by state legislatures, and for the new Constitution to go into effect when approved by three-fourths of the states, rather than to wait for the unanimity called for by the Articles before the Articles could be amended. In summary, the framers called upon the nation to engage in another, the Second American Revolution.

Final Day

On September 17, 1787, after four months of debate, the delegates took their seats. General Washington called the meeting to order. The secretary began to read the final copy of the Constitution. When he finished, Dr. Franklin rose; too feeble to speak for himself, the good doctor turned to his fellow delegate James Wilson and asked him to read a speech that he had prepared for the occasion. The delegates stirred in their seats. "Mr. President," said Wilson, his strong voice giving emphasis to the wisdom of one of America's sages:

I confess that there are several parts of this constitution that I do not at present approve, but I am not sure I shall never approve of them. . . . The older I grow, the more apt I am to doubt my own judgment, and to pay more respect to the judgment of others. . . . On the whole, Sir, I cannot help expressing a wish that every member of the Convention who may still have objections to it, would with me, on this occasion doubt a little of his own infallibility—and to make manifest our unanimity, put his name to this instrument.

At the conclusion of his speech, Franklin shrewdly moved that the Constitution be signed by the members in the "following convenient form, viz., 'Done in Convention by the unanimous consent of the States present the 17th of Spr. &c—In Witness whereof we have hereunto subscribed our names,' " This ambiguous form had been drawn up by Gouverneur Morris in order to gain the support of those members who had qualms about giving their approval to the Constitution. It was introduced by Franklin so that it might have a better chance of success.

The roll was called on Franklin's motion. The results: ten ayes, no nays, and one delegation divided—the motion was approved.

The delegates then moved forward to sign. Only three persons present at this historic meeting refused to place their names on the Constitution—others who had opposed the general drift of the Convention had already left Philadelphia. As the last member came forward to sign, Franklin, Madison's notes tell us,

. . . looking towards the president's chair, at the back of which a rising sun happened to be painted, observed to a few members near him, that painters had found it difficult to distinguish, in their art, a rising from a setting sun. "I have," said he, "often and often in the course of the session, and the vicissitudes of my hopes and fears as to its issue, looked at that behind the president, without being able to tell whether it was rising or setting; but now, at length, I have the happiness to know that it is a rising, and not a setting sun."

Their work over, the delegates adjourned to the City Tavern to relax and celebrate a job well done.

Ratification Debate

The Constitution was not ratified without a bitter struggle within the states, especially in Virginia, Massachusetts, and New York. Both in the campaign for the election of delegates to the ratifying conventions and in the conventions themselves, the Constitution was subjected to minute and searching debate.

By the end of June 1788, ten states had ratified, one more than was needed. But New York still had not acted, and because of its central geographic location, ratification by New York was essential for the success of the new government. All during the previous winter and spring the debate had been intense. Hamilton, fearful of the outcome, had secured the assistance of James Madison and John Jay to write a series of articles to win over the people of New York. The influence of these articles, since known as *The Federalist Pa-*

pers, on the outcome of the ratification struggle is sometimes exaggerated, but that they did help bring about the final favorable verdict is undoubted. Written under pressure and for partisan purposes, they nevertheless quickly became the most important contemporary comment on the Constitution; because of their penetrating discussion of the basic problems of government and their profound analysis of our constitutional system, they remain today one of America's outstanding contributions to the literature of political science.

Basic Features
of the Constitution

The provisions of the Constitution are best understood within the context of certain basic features that underpin the entire document and establish the character of the American system of government: federalism, separation of powers, and judicial review.

FEDERALISM

A federal government is one in which a *constitution* divides governmental power between a central and subdivisional governments, giving to each substantial functions. In contrast, the unitary systems are ones in which a constitution vests all governmental power in a central government. In a unitary system, the central government may delegate authority to local units; what it gives, however, it has the constitutional authority to take away. In a federal system, the constitution is the source of both central and subdivisional authority; each unit has a core of power independent of the wishes of those who control the other level of government. Examples of governments that are federal in form and practice are those of Switzerland, Australia, and Canada.

American federalism is only one variant of the many forms of federalism. In Canada, the Constitution reserves to the central government powers not given to the provinces. In the United States we do it the other way around and reserve to the states powers not given to the national government. Federal systems create tension over questions about where authority resides. In the United States we have resolved that tension by tilting toward the supremacy of the national government. Other federal systems, Switzerland, for example, tilt in the other direction—toward the subdivisional governments, or what the Swiss call the cantons.

Constitutional Basis of American Federalism

1. The Constitution grants certain legislative, executive, and judicial powers to the national government.

2. It reserves to the states powers not granted to the national government.

3. It makes the national government supreme. The Constitution, all laws passed in pursuance thereof, and treaties of the United States are the supreme law of the land. American citizens, most of whom are also state citizens, owe their primary allegiance to the national government; officers of the state governments, of course, owe the same allegiance.

4. The Constitution denies some powers to both national and state governments, some only to the national government, and still others only to the state governments.

Conflicting Interpretations of American Federalism

Throughout our history, political conflicts have generated debates about the nature of nation-state relationships. Can slavery be outlawed in the territories? Does the national government have the power to regulate railroad rates or forbid racial discrimination? Who owns the oil under the seas offshore of the United States, the state or the national government? Does the national government have any responsibility to support institutions of higher education? Frequently, the groups supporting particular interpretations of the national-state relationship have switched positions, depending on the immediate issue. As issues and times have changed, so also have the details of the arguments. It is, however, a useful oversimplification to classify the arguments into two broad schools—the states' rights and the nationalist positions.

The states' rights interpretation rests on the basic premise that the Constitution is a compact among the states. The states, it is argued, created the national government and gave it certain limited powers. In case of doubt as to whether a particular function has been given to the national government or reserved to the states, the doubt should be resolved in favor of the principal parties to the constitutional contract—the states—and against their agent—the national government. Hence, the national government's powers should be construed narrowly and should not be expanded by interpretation. The clause conferring on Congress the power to legislate when "necessary and proper" to carry into execution the powers assigned to the national government (see page 78) confers only the authority to legislate if it is *absolutely* necessary to effect one of the national government's express powers.

According to the states' rights interpretation, the existence of the national government does not in any way curtail the full use by the states of their reserved powers. However, the existence of the reserved powers of the states does restrict the scope of the national government's granted powers. For example, because the power to regulate agriculture is one of the powers reserved to the states, the national government may not use its enumerated powers in such a way as to regulate agriculture. And suffusing the states' rights orientation toward our federal system is the assumption that state governments are closer to the people and so more accurately reflect their wishes than does the national government. The national government has to be watched carefully to make sure that it does not deprive the people of their liberties.

Nationalists, on the other hand, reject the whole idea of the Constitution as a compact among the states and deny that the national government is an agent of the states. Rather, they argue, the Constitution is a supreme law coming from "We the people of the United States." It was the people, not the state governments, who created the national government, and they gave it sufficient power to accomplish the great objectives listed in the Preamble. The national government is not a subordinate of the states. In order not to frustrate the people's intentions, the powers of the national government should be construed liberally. In addition to construing broadly each of the powers expressly given to the national government, a liberal construction of the "necessary and proper" clause gives Congress the right to adopt any means that are convenient and useful in order to carry into effect expressly delegated powers. The national government should not be denied power unless its actions clearly conflict with express constitutional limits or clearly have no constitutional basis.

The nationalists also deny that the reserved powers of the states set limits to the national government's use of its delegated authority. The national government, for example, may exercise to the fullest its power to regulate commerce among the states. The fact that such regulation may touch upon matters otherwise subject to the reserved powers of the state is without constitutional significance, except if it interferes with functions "essential to the separate and independent existence" of state governments.[1] Furthermore, states may not use their reserved powers—for example, the power to tax—in such a way as to interfere with programs of the national government. The national government represents all the people, each state only a part of the people.

In 1819, the Supreme Court had its first of many occasions to choose between these two interpretations of our federal system when the great case of *McCulloch* v. *Maryland* came before it.[2] Maryland had levied a tax against the Baltimore branch of the Bank of the United States, which McCulloch, the cashier, refused to pay on the ground that a state could not tax an instrumentality of the national government. Maryland's attorneys argued that the national government did not have the power in the first place to incorporate a bank, but even if it did, the states had the power to tax it.

John Marshall, speaking for the Supreme Court, gave his full support to the nationalist position. Although the power to incorporate a bank is not among the powers expressly delegated, it is a necessary and proper—that is to say, convenient and useful—means of carrying into effect such delegated powers as caring for the property of the United States, regulating currency, and promoting interstate commerce.

"Let the end be legitimate, let it be within the scope of the Constitution, and all means which are appropriate, which are plainly adapted to the end, which are not prohibited, but consist with the letter and spirit of the Constitution, are constitutional." Moreover, although the states have the power to tax, they may not tax instruments created by the national government, inasmuch as "the power to tax involves the power to destroy."

McCulloch v. *Maryland* to the contrary notwithstanding, many continued to champion the states' rights interpretation. Among the spokesmen for this view, albeit with varying emphases, have been Thomas Jefferson, Chief Justice Roger B. Taney (Marshall's immediate successor), John C. Calhoun, the Supreme Court majority of the 1920s, and Ronald Reagan. In addition to John Marshall, the nationalist interpretation has been supported, again with varying emphases, by Abraham Lincoln, Theodore Roosevelt, Franklin Roosevelt, and throughout most of our history by the Supreme Court. That the nationalist interpretation has been dominant most of the time can be seen from the following description of national and state powers.

Classification of National Powers

By Constitutional Source

1. *Enumerated powers* are those that the Constitution expressly grants—for example, the power to raise and support armies and navies.

2. *Implied powers* are those that may be inferred from power expressly granted—for example, the power to draft people from the express power to raise armies and navies.

3. *Resulting powers* are those that result when several enumerated powers are added together—for example, the authority to make paper money legal tender for the payment of debts results from adding together the enumerated powers to coin money, to regulate commerce among the several states, and to borrow money.

4. *Inherent powers* are those powers in the field of external affairs that the Supreme Court has declared do not depend upon constitutional grants but grow out of the very existence of the national government.

By Relation to State Powers

1. *Exclusive powers* are those that only the national government may exercise—for example, the power to conduct foreign relations and to establish uniform rules of naturalization. In some cases the Constitution explicitly gives the national government exclusive power or expressly denies the states the right to act; in others the nature of the national power involved is found by the Supreme Court to rule out state actions.

2. *Concurrent powers* are those that the national government shares with the states—for example, the power to tax. Whenever action by the national government conflicts with state action, the former prevails.

3. *Expressly forbidden powers* are those the Constitution denies to the national government in relation to state governments—for example, the national government may not tax states' exports. (Remember here we are describing the limitations on national powers in the context of nation-state relations. There are other limitations on national powers designed to protect civil liberties.)

4. *Implied limitations on national power* are those limitations that grow out of the nature of the federal system created by the Constitution in which states are integral units. The national government may not use any of its powers, the power to tax, for example, in such a way as to destroy the states or make it impossible for them to govern themselves.

Reserved Powers of the States

The reserved powers of the states may be classified according to the nature and subject of the power.

1. To tax and to spend. This power, like all powers reserved to the states, may not be used to place a burden on the national government, to frustrate its activities, or to conflict with national regulations.

2. To regulate persons and property in order to promote the public welfare, known as the *police power*. This power, like all state powers, must be exercised in a manner consistent with constitutional limitations. It is the Supreme Court—an agency of the national government—that makes the determination in case of an alleged conflict between a state's exercise of its powers and a national constitutional limitation which is to prevail.

3. To regulate intrastate (local) commerce and those aspects of interstate commerce that in the opinion of Congress (or in the case of Congress's silence, in the judgment of the Supreme Court) are appropriate for state regulation.

4. To take private property, the power of eminent domain. Under the Constitution (see page 202) the states as well as the national government may take property only for public purposes and must compensate the owners.

5. To establish a republican form of state and local government. Subject only to the constitutional requirement that each state is to have a republican form of government (see page 123), each state is free to establish whatever kind of state and local governments it wishes. Moreover, the people of each state, through their own state constitution, may impose limitations on state officials beyond those contained in the national Constitution. They cannot, however, deprive state officials of the responsibilities the Constitution gives them—to illustrate, the power to ratify or reject constitutional amendments is vested by the Constitution under certain conditions in state legislatures, and the people of a state cannot take that power from the legislature and vest it in the electorate.

Federalism Today

Speaking precisely and technically, Congress has no general grant of authority to do whatever it thinks necessary and proper in order to promote the general welfare or to preserve domestic tranquility. But as a result of the emergence of a national economy, the growth of national allegiances, and a world in which total war could destroy us in a matter of minutes, our constitutional system has evolved to the point where the national government has ample constitutional authority to deal with any national or international problem.

As recently as the Great Depression of the 1930s, constitutional scholars and Supreme Court justices seriously debated whether Congress had the constitutional power to regulate labor, business, education, housing, social security, and welfare. Only a decade or so ago there were constitutional questions about the authority of Congress to legislate against racial discrimination. Despite an occasional "flashback" to prior more restrictive interpretations, nowadays there are only a few subjects that the Supreme Court might consider to be beyond the scope of national regulation, for example, regulation of the hours and pay of state employees (see page 132), and perhaps the regulation of marriage and divorce. In fact it is accurate, even if technically incorrect, to make the generalization that Congress has the power to do whatever it believes is necessary and proper to promote the general welfare. Today the national government is involved with the hospitals in which we are born, the families in which we grow up, the schools we attend, the places where we work, the ways in which we travel, the places where we keep our money, the conditions under which we are buried. In fact, one is hard put to think of anything we do that is not in some way affected by a rule, regulation, or program of the national government.

The principles of federalism no longer impose serious constitutional restraints on the powers of Congress, the President, or the federal courts, most especially on Congress. As Justice Rehnquist commented, not altogether with approval, "It is illuminating for purposes of reflection, if not for argument, to note that one of the greatest 'fictions' of our federal system is that the Congress exercises only those powers delegated to it, while the remainder are reserved to the States or to the people."[3] (See the Tenth Amendment.) There are significant restraints on the powers of the national government, but today these are the ones that stem from constitutional provisions designed to protect the liberties of the people rather than from those parts of the Constitution designed to preserve the powers of the individual state governments.

SEPARATION OF POWERS AND CHECKS AND BALANCES

Another basic feature of the Constitution is the distribution of national powers among three departments that are given constitutional and political independence of each other. The President's power, for example, comes not from Congress but from the Constitution. And most important, the personnel of each of the three branches are chosen by different procedures and hold office independently of the other branches. It is this independence of the three branches, not just the distribution of functions, that is the central feature of our system of separation of powers. England also has executive, legislative, and judicial branches, but the English government is not established according to the principle of separation of powers, inasmuch as the legislature chooses the prime minister and her cabinet and the executive depends on the legislature both for retention of office and for authority.

The framers of the Constitution feared concentration of powers in a single branch. To them, separation of powers and checks and balances were desirable to prevent official tyranny and, even more important, to prevent a single segment of the population—majority or minority—from gaining complete control of the government. It was hoped that by making each branch accountable to different groups, a variety of interests would be reflected. Hence compromises and a balancing of interests would result.

In addition to separate functions and considerable political and constitutional independence, each branch has weapons with which to check the others. The President has a qualified veto over laws enacted by Congress, the courts interpret the laws, but the President and the Senate select the judges; the President is commander in chief of the armed forces, but Congress provides them, and so on.

The doctrine of separation of powers is more accurately described as a "sharing of powers by separated institutions." Each department is given a voice in the business of the others, and each is made dependent on the cooperation of the others in order to accomplish its own business. It is through this blending of powers by politically independent branches that the doctrine of checks and balances is made effective.

The blending of duties beyond that specifically authorized by the Constitution is often necessary to accomplish the business of government. This fact has resulted in a considerable straining of the constitutional doctrine that what the Constitution gives to each department, it should not give away, and that each department should stick to its own last. For example, the Constitution vests the legislative power in Congress; what the Constitution gives to it, Congress is not supposed to delegate to others. The Supreme Court has recognized, however, that, in view of the complexity of the conditions that Congress is called upon to regulate, it is impossible for that body to make all policy decisions. As a result, the Court has approved considerable delegation of discretion. In fact, the Supreme Court has been willing to tolerate so much delegation of policymaking by Congress to executive agencies that Justices Marshall and Brennan consider the doctrine against the delegation of legislative power to be obsolete. They wrote: "The notion that the Constitution narrowly confines the Congress to delegate authority to administrative agencies, which was briefly in vogue in the 1930s, has been virtually abandoned by the Court for all practical purposes, at least in the absence of delegation creating the danger of overbroad, unauthorized, and arbitrary application of criminal sanctions in the area of constitutionally protected freedoms."[4]

Justices Marshall and Brennan are correct insofar as the Supreme Court's actually declaring congressional delegation unconstitutional is concerned. Only in the 1930s and only in two cases was any legislation set aside for being an unconstitutional delegation of legislative power. But legislation continues to be challenged on this ground, and as recently as 1974 the Supreme Court narrowly construed an act of Congress giving to independent regulatory agencies the right to levy fees against those they regulate in order to avoid any suggestion that Congress had given such agencies the power to levy taxes, a power presumably only Congress may exercise.[5] Despite such occasional reminders that Congress should not delegate away its essential legislative powers, the Court continues to sustain legislation delegating considerable policymaking authority to executive agencies.

Indeed, nowadays it is sufficient if Congress sets down a general policy. Once it has done this, it may authorize administrative officials to make rules to carry the general policy into effect. By so doing, Congress, the Court has ruled, maintains the form of constitutional propriety: it retains its "essential" legislative duties and merely delegates what the Court has labeled "quasi-legislative" power. Thus the Supreme Court has sustained congressional delegation of authority to the Interstate Commerce Commission to establish "fair and reasonable" interstate railroad rates, to the Federal Trade Commission to make regulations to prevent "unfair methods of competition" in interstate commerce, to the Federal Communications Commission to regulate radio and television in "the public interest, convenience, and necessity," and to the Secretary of Labor to promulgate nationwide standards governing health and safety in the workplace, including standards for use of toxic materials "which most adequately assures, to the extent feasible, on the basis of the best available evidence, that no employee will suffer material impairment of health or functional capacity even if such employee has regular exposure to the hazard dealt with by such standard for the period of his working life."[6] This standard was too broad for Justice Rehnquist who argued that Congress had set no standard at all and had left the crucial policy choices in the hands of the Secretary of Labor. But it was Justice Rehnquist who spoke for the Court in upholding the delegation to the Secretary of the Treasury of the discretion to prescribe regulations imposing on banks requirements to keep certain records and to report to federal officials certain transactions. He commented, "While an Act conferring such broad authority over transactions such as these might well surprise or even shock those who lived in an earlier era, the latter did not live to see the time when bank accounts would join chocolate, cheese, and watches as a symbol of the Swiss economy."[7] Congress, however, always retains the power to rescind its delegation or to alter the policies enacted by those to whom it has given quasilegislative discretion. Furthermore, congressional delegation of legislative authority to private associations or individuals remains unconstitutional.[8]

The doctrine of separation of powers has other corollaries, although they seldom become objects of judicial discussion. Yet the Court did declare unconstitutional a provision of the Federal Election Campaign Act of 1974 for interfering with presidential appointing powers (see page 102). The doctrine of executive privilege was featured in the debates over Watergate which produced a leading Supreme Court decision (see page 90). And also out of President Nixon's resignation came litigation that resulted in a Supreme Court essay on the doctrine of separation of powers.

This litigation resulted when Congress, acting quickly to prevent ex-President Nixon from taking custody of his presidential papers (as had every other President), placed these papers under the charge of the Administrator of the General Services Administration. Nixon challenged the law for, among other things, violating the doctrine of separation of powers. He argued that Congress had improperly delegated the power to decide when and how to disclose presidential materials to a subordinate officer of the President. Such a delegation, he contended, encroached upon the President's powers over his own files and reversed the presumption of confidentiality of such materials. The Court majority, however, rejected Nixon's argument as resting upon "an archaic view of separation of powers as requiring three airtight departments of government." The majority placed considerable reliance on the fact that President Ford had signed the 1974 act, that President Carter had not sought to intervene in the lawsuit in behalf of presidential prerogatives, and that the papers had been placed in the custody of an executive official, the General Services Administrator. Chief Justice Burger in dissent wrote: "Whether there has been a violation of separation-of-powers principles depends, not on the identity of the custodians, but upon which branch has commanded the custodians to act. Here, Congress has given the command. If separation-of-powers principles can be so easily evaded, then the constitutional separation is a sham."[9]

The constitutional separation of powers has been altered by two other constitutional developments: the growth of national political parties and the increased legislative influence of the President. National parties, however, are such loosely organized political instruments that even when the President and a majority of the Congress belong to the same party, they are often ineffective devices for coordinating governmental action. More significant has been the President's expanding role as chief legislator. Today, the President is expected to have a legislative program of his own and to use his powers and prestige to secure its adoption by Congress. The growth of presidential leadership has brought the legislative and executive branches into closer relationship than many of the Founding Fathers anticipated, and undoubtedly many of them would be surprised to discover that the President has been able to take over so many and such important legislative responsibilities. At the same time, the traditional independence of Congress has remained intact; the President is frequently compelled to deal with legislators whose political security is greater than his own.

Separation of powers is of special importance in the case of the federal judiciary's independence. Both the mores of our politics and the design of the Constitution give judges a large measure of independence. Although this independence is relative, the Founding Fathers took special precautions to isolate the judiciary from executive and legislative influence. They did not wish the judges to be subject to executive dominance because they remembered how certain English kings had used judges to punish enemies and reward friends. They were also afraid that there might be times when Congress and the President might respond to political and social convulsions and act hastily and oppressively. The judges, it was hoped, with their independence and political security would be more likely to withstand transitory gusts of popular passion and to take a more detached and long-range view. The relative independence of the judges from political influences takes on additional significance because they have the important power of judicial review.

JUDICIAL REVIEW AND JUDICIAL POWER

Judicial review is the authority of judges to interpret the Constitution and to refuse to enforce those measures that, in their opinion, are in conflict with the Constitution; the ultimate authority is that of the justices of the Supreme Court. It is because judges are official interpreters of the Constitution that a study of the American Constitution is in such large measure a study of judicial decisions and opinions.

The Constitution does not specifically grant the courts the power to interpret the Constitution, but it furnishes sufficient verbal basis for the power. The first assertion of the power against an act of Congress was made in Chief Justice John Marshall's famous decision, in 1803, in the great case of *Marbury* v. *Madison.*[10] The case arose out of the following situation.

The Federalists had lost the election of 1800, but before leaving office they succeeded in creating several new judicial posts. Among these were forty-two justice of peaceships for the District of Columbia, to which the retiring Federalist President, John Adams, appointed forty-two Federalists. The Senate confirmed these appointments and the commissions were signed and sealed, but Adams' Secretary of State, John Marshall, failed to deliver certain of them. When the new President, Thomas Jefferson, assumed office, he instructed his Secretary of State, James Madison, not to deliver seventeen of these commissions, including one for William Marbury. Marbury decided to take action, and consulting the law he found that Section 13 of the Judiciary Act of 1789 declared: "The Supreme Court . . . shall have the power to issue . . . writs of mandamus, in cases warranted by the principles and usages of law, to . . . persons holding office, under the authority of the United States." (A writ of mandamus is a court order directed to an officer requiring the officer to perform a certain "ministerial" duty, that is, a nondiscretionary act as required by law.) Without further ado, Marbury, through his attorneys, went before the Supreme Court and asked the justices to issue a writ of mandamus to Secretary Madison ordering him to deliver the commission. The Court, speaking through

Marshall, who was now Chief Justice, held that Section 13 of the Judiciary Act of 1789 was repugnant to Article III, Section 2 of the Constitution inasmuch as the Constitution itself limited the Supreme Court's original jurisdiction to cases "affecting ambassadors, other public ministers and consuls, and those to which a state is party." Since Marbury fell in none of these categories, the Court declined to take jurisdiction of his case, Section 13 to the contrary notwithstanding.

Where did the Supreme Court derive the authority thus to contradict Congress? Marshall reasoned that the Constitution is law, that it is the duty of courts to interpret the law in order to decide cases in accordance with it, and that therefore the Supreme Court had the authority and indeed was duty-bound to interpret the Constitution, and of course to prefer it to any other law. He also pointed out that the Constitution enjoins the courts to enforce as the supreme law of the land only those acts of Congress that are "in pursuance of the Constitution" (Article VI, Section 2). Therefore, the Court must first determine whether a law is in pursuance of the Constitution before it is entitled to enforce it as the "supreme law of the land."

Although the argument sounds plausible, Marshall's logic and the basic political philosophy on which his contentions rest have been continually questioned over the years. To this day a heated debate rages about whether the consequences of judicial review are favorable or unfavorable to the maintenance of our democratic system. Critics, including several Presidents, have argued that the Constitution is "supreme law" because it emanates from the people. Therefore, the most politically accountable and responsive agencies—Congress and the President—who, like the justices, have also sworn to uphold the Constitution, have a better claim to interpreting its meaning than does the least politically accountable agency—the Supreme Court.

Also questioned is Marshall's logic, his assertion that the Constitution is a law of the same kind and character as ordinary law, and therefore that the judges have a superior claim to interpret it. The Constitution, it is argued, is not ordinary law but political law. The Constitution is the prime political document of the nation.

Other facets of Marshall's argument are also attacked. He assumed that Article III and Section 13 were in conflict, but this is not obvious. It is perfectly reasonable to construe Article III as not restricting the Supreme Court's original jurisdiction to the types of cases listed. Or the Court could have construed Section 13 as authorizing the Supreme Court to issue writs of mandamus if it had jurisdiction. Moreover, in order to rule as he did, Marshall had to violate several canons of constitutional interpretation, including deciding an issue not necessary to dispose of the case. Once the Court had concluded it lacked jurisdiction it need not have gone on to deal with the other issues.

Finally, critics of judicial review have not accepted the argument that it is a necessary check on Congress and the President. They argue that Congress and the President are checked by the voters, whereas the only regular check on the judges is their own self-restraint, which seems at times to be lacking.

Most of the criticism of judicial review is directed, it should be noted, against review of acts of Congress, although it is today infrequently exercised adversely to such acts. That there must be a central review of state action by the Supreme Court is generally conceded. As Justice Holmes once put the matter: "I do not think the United States would come to an end if we lost our power to declare an Act of Congress void. I do think the Union would be imperiled if we could not make that declaration as to the laws of the several states."[11]

RESTRICTIONS ON JUDICIAL REVIEW

John Marshall's successful assertion in *Marbury* v. *Madison* that constitutional questions are justiciable, that is, appropriate questions for judges to decide, has meant that the Supreme Court has played the central (but not exclusive) role in constitutional interpretation. It has also meant that litigation is often as important a means for policymaking as legislation is.

As important as litigation is to our policymaking processes, judges do not have a roving commission to make policy or to interpret the Constitution whenever and however they wish. Courts operate within a prescribed setting and are subject to certain limitations. First, they can only decide real legal cases and controversies. Moreover, individuals are not free, by filing a lawsuit, to invoke judicial power whenever they have a grievance they want the judges to decide. They must have standing and present the judges with the proper kind of justiciable, that is, nonpolitical question. These doctrines and others that have grown up around the limitations set on courts—real case and controversy, standing, mootness, ripeness, political questions—"relate in part, and in different though overlapping ways, to an idea, which is more than an intuition but less than a rigorous and explicit theory, about the constitutional and prudential limits to the powers of an unelected, unrepresentative judiciary in our kind of government."[12]

Three of the limits flowing from the doctrine of separation of powers are of special importance: the standing to sue requirement, the political doctrine limitation, and the canons of judicial interpretation.

Standing to Sue

Before a person, an organization, a corporation, or a group of persons may invoke judicial power, they must have *standing*, that is, be able to show past or immediate concrete threat to a legal right or that they are in real jeopardy of losing such a right. A speculative or abstract interest is not sufficient; a mere wish to vindicate one's preferences will not do. Nor is it enough to show a general desire to prevent Congress from acting unconstitutionally or to keep the President from exceeding his authority. No matter how qualified an organization may be in evaluating a problem, such qualification does not give it standing to invoke judicial power.[13] The question is "whether the party seeking relief has alleged such a personal stake in the outcome of the controversy as to assure that concrete adverseness which sharpens the presentation of issues upon which the Court so largely depends for illumination of difficult constitutional questions."[14]

In recent years, the Supreme Court and Congress have broadened and "modernized," in a variety of ways, the concept of standing to permit a wider range of persons to resort to the courts. First, the Court has slightly lowered what was previously an absolute barrier to suits by persons whose only claim to standing is they are taxpayers who believe a federal appropriation is unconstitutional (see page 60). In addition, "economic interests that at one time would not have conferred standing have been reexamined and found sufficient: . . ."[15] Data processing firms were permitted to challenge regulations that allow banks to compete with them, and tenant farmers were allowed to challenge regulations of the Secretary of Agriculture affecting their economic status.[16]

Some noneconomic interests have also been recognized. Persons who claimed that damage to the environment limited their enjoyment of nature were granted standing to challenge some regulations of the Interstate Commerce Commission.[17] Black "testers," who had no intention of moving but who inquired whether housing were available in order to see if landlords were complying with provisions of the Fair Housing Act and were told no when such housing was available to whites, had standing because they were injured by being denied the statutorily created right to truthful housing information. White testers who were told that housing was available had no standing as testers, but they did have standing as persons who had been injured by being denied "the right to the important social, professional, business and economic, political and aesthetic benefits of interracial associations that arise from living in integrated communities free from discriminatory housing practices."[18] In fact "The concept of particularized injury has been dramatically diluted" so that consumers have been allowed standing to challenge regulations issued by regulatory commissions, for example, those of the Interstate Commerce Commission governing railroads.[19]

One additional exception to the standing rule needs to be mentioned. Under what is known as the "overbreadth doctrine," the Court has permitted persons whose own conduct may be unprotected nonetheless to challenge broadly written laws affecting the rights of expression that may have a deterrent effect on protected expression. Such a statute may be challenged on its face value even though a more narrowly drawn statute would be valid as applied to the party in the case before it. This exception from the general rule of standing is predicated on "a judicial prediction or assumption that the statute's very existence may cause others not before the court to refrain from constitutionally protected speech or expression."[20]

Despite its liberalization, the doctrine of standing retains its validity, and the Court is again raising the barriers. Although a developer seeking to build in a suburb would have standing to challenge its zoning ordinance, neither low-income minority persons nor taxpayers living in a central city were allowed to challenge such laws that they claimed made it difficult for them to move to the suburb.[21] A person who had been stopped by the Los Angeles police, who offered no resistance but was rendered unconscious by a "choke hold," was allowed to sue for damages for that particular incident. However, because it was so speculative that he might be stopped and subjected to the same practice again, he was denied standing to challenge the constitutionality of the practice and seek an injunction ordering the police not to use such tactics again except in life-threatening situations.[22]

Another case, *Allen* v. *Wright,* makes it clear that the Burger Court is placing more restraints on federal judicial action. The Court ruled that black parents whose children were attending public schools in districts undergoing desegregation had no standing to challenge Internal Revenue Service regulations relating to the conditions under which private schools are entitled to tax exemption. The parents alleged that the IRS regulations were allowing schools that discriminated against blacks to retain their tax exemption improperly. The existence of these private schools, the parents argued, made it difficult to integrate the public ones, and thus deprived them and their children of their constitutional right to attend integrated public schools. Justice O'Connor, writing for the Court, stated that judges should not decide how the IRS enforces the tax laws. She wrote, "The Constitution assigns to the Executive Branch, not to the Judicial Branch, the duty to take care that the laws be faithfully executed."[23] Justice Brennan, who along with Stevens, Marshall and Blackmun dissented, wrote rather angrily, "Once again, the Court 'uses' standing to slam the courthouse door against plaintiffs who are entitled to full consideration of their claims on the merits."[24]

Clearly, the Court has retreated a long way from the view of Justice Douglas who would have given standing to trees and other inanimate objects "about to be despoiled, defaced, or invaded by roads and bulldozers."[25] Chief Justice Burger has pointed out,

> That the Constitution does not afford a judicial remedy, does not, of course, completely disable the citizen who is not satisfied with the "ground rules" established by the Congress . . . Lack of standing . . . does not impair the right of [a citizen] to assert his views in the political forum or at the polls. Slow, cumbersome, and unresponsive though the traditional electoral process may be thought at times, our system provides for changing members of the political branches when dissatisfied citizens convince a sufficient number of their fellow citizens that elected representatives are delinquent in performing duties committed to them.[26]

Despite Chief Justice Burger's warning and the fact that during the last several years the Supreme Court has raised the standing-to-sue barrier to the federal courthouse door, the increasing recourse to the courts for dealing with political issues has not been stemmed because of what many believe to be the unresponsiveness of the other branches of government. The doctrine of political questions, to which we now turn, is still alive, but the number of questions not considered justiciable becomes fewer and fewer.

The Doctrine of Political Questions

Even if persons have standing to sue, the question they present to a court must be a justiciable, not a political, one. Political questions are those the Constitution clearly directs to the Congress or the President; that lack judicially discoverable standards for resolving; that cannot be decided without an initial policy determination of a kind clearly for nonjudicial discretion; that would be impossible for a court to handle without expressing lack of respect due to the Congress or the President; that involve an unusual need for unquestioning adherence to a policy decision already made; or that could create embarrassment by leading to conflicting pronouncements by Congress, the President, and the Courts.[27] For example, it is for the President to determine which foreign government is to be recognized by the United States, for Congress to determine if a sufficient number of states have ratified a constitutional amendment within a reasonable time to make the ratification effective, for Congress and the President to determine in case of conflicting claimants which government of a state is the legitimate one, for Congress to determine whether states have the republican form of government required by the Constitution,[28] for Congress and the President to decide if a state's National Guard is being properly trained and disciplined (the issue was raised by a legal challenge to the way the Guard had been used at Kent State). Since the Supreme Court decides which are justiciable and which are political questions, this limitation on the authority of the courts is a self-defined one.

In 1962 the Supreme Court significantly contracted the scope of the doctrine of political questions. Prior to that time it had refused to allow federal judges to get involved in the "political thicket" of determining what kind of legislative districting schemes were constitutional. State courts followed suit. Voters living in urban areas who objected to arrangements that gave rural counties a disproportionate number of representatives had no judicial recourse. The only redress available was from the legislatures themselves. Since the legislatures were the product of the allegedly discriminatory district arrangements, and since the rural voters who benefited from the status quo had no desire to alter the existing pattern of representation, appeals by city voters for more equitable representation were ineffective.

In *Baker* v. *Carr* (1962), the Supreme Court ruled that schemes for determining the boundaries of legislative districts and for apportioning representatives among these districts do raise justiciable questions under the equal protection clause of the Fourteenth Amendment.[29] Since then, the Supreme Court has expanded its ruling to cover the drawing by state legislatures of congressional district boundaries,[30] unit-voting schemes for choosing state officers,[31] and local governmental legislative or policymaking units such as county commissioners.[32]

Canons of Judicial Interpretation

Throughout its history, the Supreme Court has developed certain rules of interpretation to guide federal judges. Among the rules—sometimes ignored but generally followed—are these:

1. Do not decide a constitutional issue unless it is absolutely necessary in order to dispose of a case.
2. Whenever there is a choice, interpret a law in such a way as to render it constitutional.
3. If it is necessary to make a constitutional ruling, restrict it as narrowly as possible and do not anticipate or decide issues not immediately before the Court.[33]

Many critics contend that judges pay little attention to these canons, but they are part of the conventions and environment in which judges work.

As a result of the doctrine of political questions, the standing-to-sue requirements, and the fact that judges decide only real cases and controversies, there are some constitutional questions for which there are no judicial answers. The nature of the President's responsibility to formulate legislative programs, the constitutional authority of the President to send munitions to our allies without congressional authorization or prohibition, or the extent of the President's power to abrogate treaties are not the kinds of questions that can readily be raised in the form of a lawsuit. Even those questions that can more readily be formulated into lawsuits are often not brought before the courts for many years, if at all. There was no authoritative judicial interpretation until 1926, for example, of the President's authority to remove executive officers,[34] or until 1969 of each congressional chamber's authority to determine the qualifications of its members,[35] or until 1974 of the prerogative of the President to withhold information,[36] or until 1981 of the question whether Congress had the authority to require a male-only registration for a possible draft.[37]

Congress members, Presidents, governors, legislators, school boards, sheriffs, police officers, and all public officials have a duty to act constitutionally. Often they have to measure their actions against their own reading of the Constitution, most especially if there is no Supreme Court decision that is relevant. Judges are the authoritative, but not the only, interpreters of the Constitution.

Courts in the Political Process

Courts are deliberately isolated from political battles and partisan conflicts; in a free society, however, they can never, at least over a period of time, interpret the Constitution in a manner at variance with the desires of most of the people. Judges have the power of neither the sword nor the purse, and in order to make their decisions meaningful they have to have the support of most of the people most of the time. Whenever they hand down rulings that arouse the hostility of significant numbers, it is not at all certain that the rulings can be made to stick; sometimes they do not.

Judges, unlike congress members and even the President, are not immediately accountable to the electorate. But in time, as judges resign, retire, or die, the President, who is elected by a national majority, nominates and the Senate confirms new judges to fill vacancies. The views of these new judges will probably reflect the demands of contemporary majorities. At times, congressional majorities and the President, and the groups they represent, have been so strongly opposed to certain Supreme Court decisions that they have changed the laws to alter the structure or size or jurisdiction of courts in order to secure decisions more consistent with their wishes. Time after time, new judges—sometimes even the old ones—have found it necessary to reinterpret the Constitution to adjust it to changing demands. Judges interpret the Constitution, but they, like all other public officials, are servants, not masters, of the electorate.

Failure to recognize that the judges' power is limited may lead people to believe that the Supreme Court can guarantee, for example, freedom of speech, or insure the preservation of our constitutional system. Judges both lead and respond to the values of the nation. But only insofar as they reflect the views of most of the people can they guarantee free speech or preserve republican government. If most of the people are strongly opposed to freedom of speech, the chances are we shall not have it. If most desire it, the chances are that the

Supreme Court will hand down decisions protecting it. In short, the Constitution ultimately is not "what the judges say it is," but what the people want it to be.[38]

THE POLITICAL PROCESS AND CONSTITUTIONAL DEVELOPMENT

For fifteen eventful years before the 1968 election, the Supreme Court under Chief Justice Earl Warren did not hesitate to participate actively in the political process. Among other things, the Supreme Court declared racial segregation in all its forms unconstitutional, enlarged the authority of Congress to legislate against racial discrimination, expanded the protection of the Bill of Rights to apply to state and local officials, enlarged the scope for political speech, limited the authority of states to regulate obscenity, raised higher the wall of separation between church and state, and insisted that legislative bodies be apportioned to reflect equal voting power among voters regardless of where they live.

The Warren Court's involvement in our political life was not unique. The Supreme Court has always been in the center of our major domestic political battles. And since interpretation of the Constitution is in the highest sense a political matter—that is, a choice among conflicting political values—the justices have frequently been attacked by those who differ with their decisions. Until the Warren Court, however, the more usual pattern was for the Supreme Court to reflect conservative views and for the criticism to come from those of liberal persuasion. This was not so in the case of the Warren Court. It reflected the attitudes of the less conservative members of our society. Its critics tended to be those who believe that justices should show more restraint about imposing their own values on the society, who charged that the Court had moved too quickly, had opened too widely the opportunities for persons to distribute "offensive" materials, had imposed too many restraints on police and prosecutors, and had forced on the nation the justices' own ideas of how best to establish representative legislative bodies.

In the 1968 presidential campaign, candidate Nixon made it quite clear that he agreed with the critics of the Supreme Court. He promised that if he were elected, he would fill judicial vacancies with persons who shared his own "strict-constructionist" constitutional views. Once in office a somewhat unusual combination of circumstances made it possible for him to select four justices during his first term. To replace the retiring Earl Warren, he selected Warren Burger, a judge from the Court of Appeals for the District of Columbia. The Senate rejected his first two choices to replace the resigning Justice Fortas, but finally confirmed his third choice, Harry A. Blackmun, another circuit judge and close friend of the Chief Justice. In the fall of 1971 Justice Black died and Justice Harlan retired. To replace them, President Nixon nominated Lewis Franklin Powell, Jr., a veteran of private practice and bar leadership from Virginia, and William Hubbs Rehnquist, an Arizonan who had served the Nixon Administration in the Department of Justice. In December of 1971 the Senate finally confirmed both appointees, although Justice Rehnquist faced considerable opposition because of his conservative views, especially with respect to civil liberties and civil rights issues.

Then, in November of 1975, illness finally forced Justice Douglas, who many thought was trying to hold on until 1977 when a Democrat might be in the White House, to retire after 35 years of service, the longest of any jurist in our history. President Ford replaced him with John Paul Stevens, from the Court of Appeals for the Seventh Circuit.

President Carter was the first full-term President who did not select at least one Supreme Court justice. However, soon after he took office Congress created 117 new districts and 35 new courts of appeals positions which, along with normal vacancies created by deaths, retirements, and resignations, gave President Carter the unprecedented opportunity to appoint over 300 federal judges. He selected substantially more blacks and women than had ever been appointed to sit on the federal courts. These Carter-selected judges, reflecting in general the perspective of the administration that appointed them, will influence the course of judicial decision-making well into the next century. Moreover, they make it likely that in the years ahead the lower federal courts will be more liberal and activist than their superiors on the Supreme Court, most of whom have been appointed by Nixon, Ford, and Reagan.

During his first term President Reagan appointed about 180 federal judges, most of whom share his views with respect to opposition to busing, affirmative action quotas, and greater powers for prosecutors, and disagree with Supreme Court decisions on the death penalty, abortion, and prayer in schools. Most of Reagan's appointees to the lower federal courts are white males.[39] During his first term Reagan had a chance to appoint only a single member of the Supreme Court, despite the fact that when he came to office six sitting justices were over age seventy-two.

When Justice Stewart retired at the end of the 1980 term, President Reagan lived up to his campaign promise to appoint women and justices committed to a more conservative judicial orientation when he nominated Sandra Day O'Connor from the Arizona Supreme Court. Justice O'Connor, a graduate of Stanford Law School, (the same class as Justice Rehnquist and a close friend of his), has, in her early years on the Court, often voted with the conservative wing.

The differences between the Warren and Burger Courts, although subject to exaggeration, are significant and have grown increasingly so in recent years. The Burger Court is more reluctant than was the Warren Court to use judicial power to set aside legislative decisions or to interfere with administrative arrangements, and is more apprehensive about judges participating so actively and openly in the political process. The Burger Court has recently moved to a less rigorous stance on separation between church and state, been more favorable toward interpretations of the Constitution that strengthen the hands of the police and be less protective of the rights of the accused, and has indicated a less positive stand with respect to affirmative action programs. It gives state governments more leeway in determining how justice should be administered and which movies should be considered obscene.

However, the differences between the Burger and Warren Courts should not be exaggerated. The Burger Court issued the decision declaring most state laws against abortion unconstitutional, perhaps the greatest example in recent years of judicial intervention in the political process. In *INS* v. *Chadha* (see page 55) it called into constitutional question more acts of Congress than all of its predecessors combined.[40] It has approved affirmative action programs in hiring and education, especially those established by Congress. It has not reversed outright any of the major initiatives of the Warren Court, but it has eroded some of those initiatives, particularly in the area of criminal procedure.

Nor should it be assumed that on all issues the Nixon-Ford-Reagan appointees vote as a bloc against all the judges from the days of the Warren Court. For example, all participating justices (Justice Rehnquist abstained because of his prior involvement in the question while working in the Department of Justice) agreed that the President has no constitutional authority to allow warrantless wiretapping in order to protect the nation against domestic insurrection;[41] and all participating justices agreed that the President has no absolute privilege to withhold information from courts.[42] In recent years the Court has split five to four on many important decisions. The Chief Justice and Justice Rehnquist hold down the conservative end of the Court, with Justice Rehnquist being the most articulate and conservative justice. Justice O'Connor frequently votes with them. Justices White, Powell, Blackmun, and Stevens now serve as the "swing men." Justice White is tending more toward the conservative side, but Justice Blackmun has become more moderate. Justices Brennan and Marshall along with Justice Stevens represent the diminished liberal wing and have become the Court's most frequent dissenters.

With the Court so evenly divided on so many important issues, the next few judicial appointments are going to make a significant difference. As 1985 begins Justice Brennan is seventy-eight, Chief Justice Burger is seventy-six, as are Justices Powell, Blackmun and Douglas. Justice White is sixty-six, but he has already served more than twenty-one years. Justice Stevens is sixty-three, Rehnquist is fifty-nine, and Justice O'Connor is fifty-three. On Inauguration Day 1985, five of the nine justices were seventy-six or older, and it is unlikely that all of them will be able to remain active for another four years. (If they follow the precedent of some previous justices, they are going to do their best to hold off retiring or dying until there is a president in the White House congenial to their constitutional views. In the past, many justices have successfully outlived their political opponents. Oliver Wendell Holmes served until he was ninety, Roger Taney and Hugo Black until eighty-five, and another five, including Louis Brandeis, served beyond their eightieth birthdays.)

The process of constitution-making does not stop: It is a process in which the voters participate. Although it is doubtful whether many voters cast their ballots for presidential candidates on the basis of constitutional issues, it was an issue in the 1984 and earlier elections. Walter Mondale declared, "Above all we must win to save the Supreme Court. If that Court is replaced by Mr. Reagan, it could well be that our great cause of justice will be doomed for the lifetime of everyone in this room."[43] Republicans, on the other side, reminded their followers that with the Court so evenly balanced and showing signs of moving in a conservative direction, Reagan's reelection could change what the Court decides the Constitution means in many major areas.

It could well be that the most important consequence of the 1984 election will be that the voters, in choosing Reagan, chose the person who will nominate the members of the Supreme Court who will control that Court's decisions for the next decade or so and shape the contours of the Constitution that will last beyond his administration. In picking Reagan the voters are likely to ensure that the Burger Court will move even more dramatically toward the constitutional orientation of Ronald Reagan and away from that of the Warren Court. This vital link between the electorate and the appointing authority helps to ensure that what the Supreme Court decides does not vary too often, for too long, or by too much from what most of the people want it to decide.

The Constitution of the United States

THE PREAMBLE

We the People of the United States, in Order to form a more perfect Union, establish Justice, insure domestic Tranquility, provide for the common defence, promote the general Welfare, and secure the Blessings of Liberty to ourselves and our Posterity, do ordain and establish this Constitution for the United States of America.

The Preamble is the prologue of the Constitution. It proclaims the source of the Constitution's authority and the great ends to be accomplished under it. It does not, however, by its own terms create any governmental powers or vest any rights in the people.[1]

The phrase "We the People of the United States" is ambiguous. It is probably historically more accurate to say that it was not the people collectively who created the Constitution in 1789, but the people of each individual state. The states established the voting requirements for delegates to the ratifying conventions and administered the election machinery; it was a vote of the ratifying conventions of nine states, irrespective of the total popular vote in all of the states, that was essential for ratification. But whatever the historical case, there has since developed a national community of the people of the United States.

From the Preamble we learn that the Constitution claims obedience, not simply because of its intrinsic excellence or the merits of its principles, but also because it is ordained and established by the people. "The government of the Union," said Chief Justice Marshall, "... is emphatically and truly, a government of the people. In form, and in substance, it emanates from them. Its powers are granted by them, and are to be exercised directly on them, and for their benefit."[2] The people are the masters of the Constitution—not the reverse.

ARTICLE I: THE LEGISLATIVE ARTICLE

Section 1

All legislative Powers herein granted shall be vested in a Congress of the United States

It is significant that of the three branches of the national government the legislative branch is mentioned first. The framers of the Constitution desired "a government of laws and not of men,"[3] and expected Congress, except in time of war or emergency, to be the central and directing organ of the government.

With one very important exception, Congress has no legislative power except those "herein granted" by the Constitution. Powers not granted or powers that cannot reasonably be implied from the granted powers are denied to Congress and reserved to the states (see the Tenth Amendment). By way of contrast, the British Parliament has complete legislative powers over all matters. But this contrast between the scope of authority of Parliament and that of Congress should no longer be given too much significance. Today Congress's legislative powers are very liberally construed. So long as its actions do not violate specific constitutional rights of individuals, there is little that Congress wants to do that it lacks constitutional authority to do.

The field of foreign relations provides the principal exception to the general rule that Congress has only those legislative powers granted to it by the Constitution. As a necessary concomitant of nationality, the Congress, along with the President, has full power to deal with the external relations of the United States. Congress has the power to authorize the acquisition of territory by discovery and occupation and to adopt legislation denying certain kinds of aliens entrance into the United States, even though these are not among the legislative powers specifically granted by the Constitution to the Congress. For the source and scope of such powers, one must turn to international law and practice, not to the Constitution. As a member of the society of nations, the Congress, along with the President, who speaks for the United States in this field, has the same powers as do those who act for any other nation in the field of external relations.[4]

Section 1

[continued] which shall consist of a Senate and House of Representatives.

By granting legislative powers to two distinct branches of Congress, the framers created a bicameral legislature, as contrasted with a single-chamber, or unicameral, legislature. Of the framers, only Benjamin Franklin favored a single-chamber legislature. The others felt that two chambers were needed so that representation in one might be based on population, whereas in the other the states would be represented as states and hence equally. Also, it was thought, the two chambers would serve as a check on each other and prevent the passage of ill-considered legislation. Bicameralism also conformed to the framers' general belief in balanced government, a government that would represent the interest of all parts of society. The House, it was thought, would reflect the attitudes of the popular or democratic elements, and the Senate would reflect the views of the aristocratic elements.

Section 2

1. The House of Representatives shall be composed of Members chosen every second Year.

Some of the framers favored annual terms, believing that "where annual terms end, tyranny begins"; Madison and others favored a three-year term. The framers compromised on a two-year term. The House has several times proposed an amendment to extend the terms of its members to four years; the Senate has refused to concur. Those who oppose such an amendment argue that the present midterm elections provide a desirable check on the popularity of the presidential party. They also contend that if the terms of House members coincided with a presidential election, congressional elections would become so submerged in presidential politics that representatives would be overly subject to presidential influences.

Section 2

1. [continued] by the People of the several States.

In the Great Compromise, the framers agreed that while senators were to be chosen by the state legislatures, representatives were to be elected by the people. In 1963, the Supreme Court, in *Wesberry* v. *Sanders,* gave this tenet additional significance by holding that a state legislature is also required to establish congressional districts consisting as nearly as practicable of an equal number of people. Said the Court, "One man's vote in congressional election is to be worth as much as another's."[5]

Since then the Court has laid down very stringent standards to ensure the application of what it now, along with the rest of the nation, calls "the one-person, one-vote principle" concerning congressional districts: A state legislature, in drawing congressional districts, must justify any variance from precise mathematical equality by showing that it tried in good faith to come as close as possible to absolute mathematical equality. Even minor population deviations are not permissible unless a state can demonstrate they are absolutely necessary to achieve some legitimate goal "such as making districts compact, respecting municipal boundaries, preserving the cores of prior districts, avoiding contests between incumbent Representatives."[6] So far no state has been able to justify to the Supreme Court's satisfaction any variance from mathematical equality for congressional districts even for these legitimate goals: The Supreme Court set aside New Jersey's reapportionment plan in which the difference between the largest and smallest districts was only 0.6984 percent of the average district.[7]

State legislators are subject to less stringent standards when apportioning their own chambers, as are city councils, county commissioners, junior college districts, and other policy-making state and local government units. Here the standard is only the equal protection clause of the Fourteenth Amendment (see page 229), and the allowing of a greater divergence in numbers of people among electoral districts in order to accommodate other legitimate governmental objectives. The Court has established the guideline that an apportionment plan for a state legislature with a maximum population deviation under ten percent falls within the category of a minor deviation requiring little, if any, justification. A plan with larger disparities creates a *prima facie* case of discrimination and must be justified, as, for example, by its nondiscriminatory adherence to giving to each county one representative regardless of population. However, "there is clearly some outer limit to the magnitude of the deviation that is constitutionally permissible even in the face of the strongest justifications."[8] The Court has hinted that outer limit may be around seventeen percent.

Section 2

1. [continued] and the Electors in each State shall have the Qualifications requisite for Electors of the most numerous Branch of the State Legislature.

The word "electors" in this paragraph means voters. In the original Constitution, representatives were the only members of the national government to be chosen directly by the voters. In 1787, the qualifications for voting varied widely from state to state. In the Constitutional Convention, a majority of the delegates believed that the suffrage should be limited to those who possessed some kind of property; as they could not agree about the amount or kind of property that should be required, they finally left it to the individual states to determine the qualifications of voters for representatives.

Although this clause gives states authority to determine suffrage qualifications for voting in congressional elections, including primaries, the right to vote in such elections is one conferred by the Constitution. Accordingly, the national government may protect the voter in the exercise of this right against either private violence or state discrimination.[9]

The above clause should be read in connection with Section 4 (see page 46), which permits Congress to supersede suffrage regulations set by the states so far as voting for congress members, senators, and presidential electors is concerned.

Section 2

2. No person should be a Representative who shall not have attained to the Age of twenty five years, and been seven Years a Citizen of the United States, and who shall not, when elected, be an inhabitant of that State in which he shall be chosen.

In other words, persons who are twenty-five years old or older, who have been citizens of the United States for seven years, and who are citizens of the state that they represent are constitutionally eligible for membership in the House of Representatives. Neither the House of Representatives nor the Congress nor any state legislature may add to these constitutional qualifications.

Persons who lack the age and duration of citizenship qualifications at the time of election may nevertheless be admitted to the House (or to the Senate) as soon as they become qualified.

Although the Constitution does not require members of Congress to reside in the district they represent, politically it is almost essential that they be residents, since the voters normally refuse to elect a nonresident. By way of contrast, under British practice, members of Parliament are often elected to represent districts other than those in which they live. Our insistence upon local residence reflects and supports the prevalent belief that representatives' primary obligation is to their own districts rather than to the country as a whole.

Section 2

3. Representatives and direct Taxes shall be apportioned among the several States which may be included within the Union, according to their respective Numbers,

After each decennial census (see below), Congress apportions representatives among the several states.

Direct taxes are not defined in the Constitution but are generally thought to be limited to taxes on property and a head tax, so much per person. The requirement that direct taxes be apportioned among the states according to population is of little significance today because of the Sixteenth Amendment. Other than income taxes—which the Supreme Court once ruled to be a direct tax[10]—Congress does not levy any such taxes (see Article I, Section 9 and Amendment Seventeen).

Section 2

3. [continued] *which shall be determined by adding to the whole Number of free Persons, including those bound to Service for a Term of Years*, and excluding Indians not taxed, *three fifths of all other Persons* [emphasis added].

The term "other persons" meant slaves. Because of the Thirteenth and Fourteenth Amendments, the emphasized words are obsolete.

The term "Indians not taxed" has also been rendered obsolete. States may not collect income taxes from the income earned by Indians working on reservations, but Indians do pay federal income taxes and state and local taxes on activities conducted outside tribal reservations. All Indians today, in one way or another, pay taxes. They are citizens and voters. They are now counted in the census and are included in determining the number of representatives to which each state is entitled in the House of Representatives.

Section 2

3. [continued] The actual Enumeration shall be made within three Years after the first Meeting of the Congress of the United States, and within every subsequent Term of ten Years, in such Manner as they shall by Law direct. The Number of Representatives shall not exceed one for every thirty Thousand,

This restriction of the size of the House of Representatives is now meaningless. After the 1980 census, our population (excluding the District of Columbia), at that time, was 224,843,423. The constitutional limit would allow for 7,495 members (224,843,423 divided by 30,000). Obviously, a chamber this size would be of little value; Congress, by law, has limited the number of representatives to 435, approximately one representative for every 517,000 persons.

Congress, after determining the number of representatives to which a state is entitled, has left it primarily up to the state legislatures to divide their respective states into congressional districts, each of which elects one representative. Subject only to *Wesberry* v. *Sanders,* the state legislatures are under no constitutional restraints in drawing these districts. The party in control may carve up the state in such a way that the voters of the opposing party are concentrated in as few districts as possible, a practice known as gerrymandering. The *Wesberry* requirement that congressional districts be composed, as nearly as is practicable, of an equal number of people makes this kind of gerrymandering a little more difficult but not impossible.

Section 2

3. [continued] but each State shall have at Least one Representative;

After the 1980 census, three states, Alaska, Wyoming, and Vermont had fewer than 517,000 inhabitants; each, however, was given its constitutional minimum. Delaware, North Dakota, and South Dakota, even though their populations are above the national average for one representative, also have only one representative since their numbers are not sufficient to win for them an additional seat. Because of this requirement, even the House of Representatives cannot provide that every person in the United States has equally weighted voting power with every other person; one person in the least populous states has more voting power than a person in more populous states.

Section 2

3. [continued] and until such enumeration shall be made, the State of New Hampshire shall be entitled to chuse three, Massachusetts eight, Rhode-Island and Providence Plantations one, Connecticut five, New York six, New Jersey four, Pennsylvania eight, Delaware one, Maryland six, Virginia ten, North Carolina five, South Carolina five, and Georgia three.

This was a temporary provision until a census could be taken to determine the basis of representation. It has no significance today.

Section 2

4. When vacancies happen in the Representation from any State, the Executive Authority shall issue Writs of Election to fill such Vacancies.

The chief significance of this clause is the insurance that vacancies in the House of Representatives are not filled by gubernatorial appointment, as is the case with vacancies in the Senate. In many instances, when the next election is less than a year away, governors do not call special elections.

---

5. The House of Representatives shall chuse their speaker and other Officers;

In form, the Speaker of the House is chosen by the House of Representatives; in fact, he is chosen by the majority party, or more precisely, by a majority of the majority party. The duties and powers of the Speaker and of the other officers are determined by the rules and practices of the House. Curiously enough, the Constitution does not specify that the Speaker must be a member of the House. The framers simply assumed that the examples of the British House of Commons and of the state assemblies would be followed.

---

5. [continued] and shall have the sole Power of Impeachment.

It is a common error to think that the power to impeach means the power to remove a person from office; in fact, it is only the first step in that direction. It is the power to accuse and to initiate formal charges.

The House ordinarily exercises its authority in a two-step process: After an investigation and a report from the House Judiciary Committee the House first considers a resolution of impeachment; if this carries then the House votes detailed articles of impeachment. The House has adopted impeachment resolutions against thirteen persons, one of whom then immediately resigned so that articles of impeachment have actually been prepared and voted on only twelve times. Those involved were one senator, one President, one Supreme Court justice, and the rest judges of the lower federal courts.

In recent years the most celebrated impeachment considerations were those against President Nixon. Although the House Judiciary Committee recommended to the House that it impeach the President, he resigned before the matter was brought to the floor of the House. The House then dropped the matter. It need not have done so, since resignation does not necessarily prevent the House from acting or the Senate from trying a person impeached by the House, but in the Nixon case, as in every other similar one in our past, resignation terminated the matter.

---

1. The Senate of the United States shall be composed of two Senators from each state, *chosen by the Legislature thereof,* for six Years; and each Senator shall have one Vote [emphasis added].

The emphasized portion of this paragraph has been superseded by the Seventeenth Amendment. The framers adopted equal representation of all states in the Senate at the insistence of the smaller states, who made it their price for accepting the Constitution. As a result of this victory, the 400,000 inhabitants of Alaska and the 470,000 inhabitants of Wyoming have the same number of representatives in the Senate as the 17.5 million inhabitants of New York and the 23.5 million inhabitants of California. This means that, on the one hand, the New England states, with 5 percent of the total population, have 12 percent of the Senate seats; the mountain states, with only 5 percent of the total population, have 16 percent. On the other hand, the Middle Atlantic states, with 16 percent of the total population, have only 6 percent of the Senate seats; the east north-central states, with 18 percent of the total population, have only 10 percent. These figures account for the disproportionate influence that the mining and agricultural interests, and especially the former, have sometimes exerted through the Senate on legislation.

Section 3

2. Immediately after they shall be assembled in Consequence of the first Election, they shall be divided as equally as may be into three Classes. The Seats of the Senators of the first Class shall be vacated at the Expiration of the second Year, of the second Class at the Expiration of the fourth Year, and of the third Class at the Expiration of the sixth Year, so that one third may be chosen every second Year:

As a result of this original division of senators into three classes, the Senate has been a continuous body. Only one-third of the senators' terms expire at the same time; hence at least two-thirds of its members at any time have been members of the preceding Congress.

The fact that the Senate is a continuing body whereas the House is not sometimes has constitutional significance. The Supreme Court, for example, has pointed out that while a Senate subpoena issued five years earlier is still clearly valid, a subpoena issued by the House at the same time may not be valid because "the House . . . is not a continuing body" and thus the subpoena comes from a prior Congress.[11]

A contentious question, answered differently by different Vice-Presidents and different sessions of the Senate, is whether the fact that the Senate is a continuing body means that in each new Congress a majority of the senators is bound by the Senate rules carried over from the prior Congress, including the rule that an extraordinary majority of the Senate is required in order to terminate debate. If the Senate is bound, a minority may filibuster (see page 58) attempts by a majority of the senators to alter the rules making it easier to terminate debate. If the Senate is not so bound, a simple majority of the senators could at the beginning of a new session alter the previous session's rules.

Section 3

2. [continued] and if Vacancies happen by Resignation, or otherwise, during the Recess of the Legislature of any State, the Executive thereof may make temporary Appointments *until the next Meeting of the Legislature, which shall then fill such Vacancies* [emphasis added].

This clause was modified by the Seventeenth Amendment, which provides for the direct election of senators.

---

3. No Person shall be a Senator who shall not have attained the Age of thirty years, and been nine Years a Citizen of the United States, and who shall not, when elected, be an Inhabitant of that State for which he shall be chosen.

You have to be a little older and live in the United States a little longer to be eligible to serve as a Senator than as a member of the House of Representatives.

---

4. The Vice-President of the United States shall be President of the Senate, but shall have no Vote, unless they be equally divided.

The Vice-President has much less control over the Senate than the Speaker has over the House. In fact the Vice-President seldom presides over the Senate. He is more inclined to do so when the issue before the Senate is controversial and there is an expectation of a close vote. The first Vice-President, John Adams, exercised his "casting vote" some twenty times, a record that still stands.

---

5. The Senate shall chuse their other Officers, and also a President *pro tempore,* in the Absence of the Vice President, or when he shall exercise the Office of President of the United States.

The President *pro tempore* of the Senate is chosen by the majority party. This officer is normally the member of the majority party with the longest continuous service in the Senate. Unlike the Vice-President, the President *pro tempore* can, being a senator, vote on any matter before the Senate.

---

6. *The Senate shall have the sole Power to try all Impeachments.*

When the House of Representatives impeaches a federal officer, the officer is tried before the Senate.

---

6. [continued] When sitting for that Purpose, they shall be on Oath or Affirmation.

See page 134.

Section 3

6. [continued] When the President of the United States is tried, the Chief Justice shall preside.

This provision disqualifies the Vice-President who might be personally involved because he or she is in the line of presidential succession.

Section 3

6. [continued] And no person shall be convicted without the Concurrence of two-thirds of the Members Present.

Of those impeached by the House, the Senate has convicted four, all judges of the lower federal courts. Others have resigned before Senate trial. The most celebrated Senate impeachment trials were those of Supreme Court Justice Samuel Chase in 1802 and President Andrew Johnson in 1868. In neither case did the Senate sustain the impeachment charges, although in Johnson's case the vote was only one shy.

Section 3

7. Judgment in Cases of Impeachment shall not extend further than to removal from Office, and disqualification to hold and enjoy any Office of honor, Trust, or Profit under the United States:

Despite its ambiguous language, the Constitution has always been construed to make removal from office automatic upon conviction by a two-thirds vote of the Senate. Disqualification, however, is not mandatory. Of its four convictions the Senate voted for disqualification in only two. In each of these cases, the vote on disqualification was by majority vote.

Section 3

7. [continued] but the Party convicted shall nevertheless be liable and subject to Indictment, Trial, Judgment, and Punishment, according to Law.

This provision clearly says that it is not double jeopardy to subject an officer of the United States both to trial before the Senate on impeachment charges and to trial before the courts on criminal charges.

What of a related issue: May an officer of the United States be brought to trial before being removed from office through impeachment? In the case of judges the answer is probably "yes."

In the case of the Vice-President the answer is probably also "yes." Vice-President Spiro T. Agnew resigned after pleading no contest to certain criminal charges. In the case of the President, the answer is probably "no". The difference is that whereas the business of government would not be seriously jeopardized if one judge were brought to trial or even if the Vice-President were forced to defend himself or herself in a criminal court, the entire business of government could be endangered if the President were brought to trial. Fortunately, only once has the issue involving a President been a serious one. The grand jury investigating Watergate did name President Nixon as an unindicted coconspirator. The jury did not indict him, largely in order to avoid the thorny question of whether or not he could be forced to trial while still serving as President.

The President can be criminally tried for actions undertaken while he was serving as President, but probably only after he has left the White House. Individuals, however, cannot sue the President, while he is in or out of office, for damages for any injury he might have caused them. This "absolute presidential immunity from damage liability extends to all acts within the outer perimeter of the President's official responsibility." The Court has very strongly suggested that presidential immunity stems from the Constitution itself. "We consider this immunity," wrote Justice Powell for the Court, "a functionally mandated incident of the President's unique office, rooted in the constitutional tradition of separation of powers and supported by our history."[12] Justice White, speaking for three other dissenting justices, responded, "Attaching absolute immunity to the office of the President, rather than to particular activities that the President might perform, places the President above the law. It is a reversion to the old notion that the King can do no wrong."[13]

Judges and prosecutors have this same absolute immunity from civil suits for damages, but may be and have been subjected by Congress for payment of attorneys' fees for persons who have secured injunctions to prevent these officials from depriving persons of their constitutional rights (see page 220). Cabinet members and presidential assistants have only a qualified (or good faith) immunity from civil suits for damages: It is not clear if they are subject to payment of attorneys' fees for injunctions against their practices depriving people of their civil rights.

Section 4

1. The Times, Places, and Manner of holding Elections for Senators and Representatives, shall be prescribed in each State by the Legislature thereof;

Subject to congressional revision (see below) this clause confers on the legislature in each state "authority to provide a complete code for congressional elections, not only as to times and places, but in relation to notices, registration, supervision of voting, protection of voters, prevention of fraud and corrupt practices, counting of votes, duties of inspectors and canvassers, and making and publication of election returns; in short, to enact the numerous requirements as to procedure and safeguards which experience shows are necessary in order to enforce the fundamental rights involved."[14]

Section 4

1. [continued] but the Congress may at any time by Law make or alter such Regulations, *except as to the Places of chusing Senators.*

The emphasized portion has been modified by the Seventeenth Amendment.

The clause covers primaries and preprimaries in which candidates for the Senate and House are nominated, if such primaries effectively. control the choice or are state-required.[15] Congressional power as to times, places, and manner consequently extends to such primaries.

Congress has established the first Tuesday after the first Monday in November in the even-numbered years as the date for the election of representatives, except where other times are prescribed by state constitutions. Now that Maine has amended its constitution to abandon its September elections, all states hold these elections on the same day, and all states now elect senators on that same date.

Congress requires that the district system be used for the election of representatives and that elections be by secret ballot. Also, Congress has placed a limit on contributions to candidates seeking election to Congress and has adopted rather extensive regulations to prevent corrupt and fraudulent practices in connection with these elections.

In *Oregon* v. *Mitchell* (1970) the Supreme Court, by five-to-four, ruled that Section 4 authorizes Congress to set aside state age requirements for voting for Congress and for presidential electors, but *not* for state and local officials.[16] However, with the addition of new members to the Court since that decision, it is doubtful if a majority would now agree that the times-places-manner clause even authorizes Congress to set aside state suffrage requirements to vote for national officials. But so far as the eighteen-year-old vote is concerned, the Twenty-sixth Amendment settled the issue.

Section 4

2. The Congress shall assemble at least once in every Year, *and* such Meeting shall be on the first Monday in December, unless they shall by Law appoint a different Day.

The Twentieth Amendment has superseded this paragraph. Congress now convenes in January (see page 260).

Section 5

1. Each House shall be the Judge of the Elections, Returns and Qualifications of its own Members,

---

Does this section authorize each chamber to add to the stipulated constitutional qualifications or does it merely authorize each house to determine if a particular member has these qualifications? Prior to 1969 both the House and the Senate had adopted the former construction, and on occasion each chamber had denied duly elected persons their seats because they were morally or politically objectionable to a majority of the respective chambers. For example, in 1900 the House refused to admit Brigham H. Roberts from Utah because he was a polygamist. These precedents, which spring in the first instance from the practice of the British Parliament and the early state legislatures, were relied on by the House of Representatives in 1967 when it excluded Adam Clayton

Powell, Jr., because of his alleged misconduct and for being held in contempt by a court for refusing to pay a judgment against him for slander. The Speaker ruled that since the question was whether Powell should be excluded rather than expelled (see below), only a majority was necessary, although in fact the vote on exclusion was passed by more than two-thirds.

Powell and thirteen voters from his district asked the District Court for the District of Columbia for a declaratory judgment saying that the House had acted unconstitutionally, and for an order requiring House officers to pay Powell his salary. Both the District Court and the Court of Appeals (including Chief Justice Burger, then a sitting judge on the Court of Appeals) dismissed Powell's complaint, arguing that the question was a political and not a justiciable one and that for the judges to rule would violate the doctrine of separation of powers.

By the time the case was before the Supreme Court, Powell had been reelected and admitted to Congress. Many observers felt that the Court would avoid handling such a politically ticklish issue by holding the question to be moot, or that if it did accept the case, it would rule either that the issue raised a "political question" or that the long historical practice of Congress had settled the construction in favor of allowing each chamber to add to constitutional qualifications. However, Chief Justice Warren, with only Justice Stewart dissenting, held that Section 5 merely authorizes the House to determine if its members meet the qualifications prescribed in the Constitution.[17] Since Congressman Powell met these qualifications, the House had been without power to refuse to admit him to its membership.

Subject only to this limitation that it may not add qualifications for membership beyond those stipulated by the Constitution, each chamber determines finally which person is entitled to be seated, for example, when there is a challenge to the validity of the election (such as on grounds of vote fraud).[18] Each chamber may, if it wishes, refer a disputed matter elsewhere, and a state can recount votes in a senatorial or congressional race in the event of a challenge. But a state's verification of the accuracy of returns or a court's decision relating to an election contest are subject to revision by the chamber involved.

Ordinarily each chamber prefers to settle its own election contests. In 1975, however, when the New Hampshire Ballot Law Commission certified that the Republican candidate, Louis C. Wyman, had 110,926 votes and the Democratic candidate, John A. Durkin, had 110,924 votes, the Senate, after almost a year of trying, was unable to choose between them. It finally declared the seat vacant and returned the matter to New Hampshire, where a special election was held in which Durkin was elected.

Section 5

1. [continued] and a Majority of each [house] shall constitute a Quorum to do Business; but a smaller Number may adjourn from day to day, and may be authorized to compel the Attendance of absent Members, in such Manner, and under such penalties as each House may provide.
2. Each House may determine the Rules of its Proceedings, punish its Members for disorderly Behaviour, and, with the Concurrence of two thirds, expel a Member.

Although it takes only a majority—that is, the majority of a quorum—to prevent a member-elect from being seated, it takes two-thirds of a quorum to expel a member once he or she has been admitted to membership, or "seated." Since congress members are not liable to impeachment, expulsion by their respective chambers is the only way they may be unseated—except, of course by defeat at the polls.

Section 5

3. Each House shall keep a Journal of its Proceedings, and from time to time publish the same, excepting such Parts as may in their Judgment require Secrecy; and the Yeas and Nays of the Members of either House on any question shall, at the Desire of one fifth of those Present, be entered on the Journal.

This requirement is consistent with the belief that in a republic the proceedings of the legislature should be published except in unusual circumstances.

The *Journal* should not be confused with *Congressional Record.* The *Journal* is the official record of congressional acts, resolutions, and votes, whereas the *Record* purports to be a report of what is said in each house. In fact, because of the practice of freely allowing members to "revise and extend their remarks," as well as to print articles, speeches, poems, and so on by nonmembers, much appears in the *Congressional Record* that was never said on the floors of Congress.

By the parliamentary device of resolving itself into a Committee of the Whole, the House of Representatives can avoid the constitutional necessity of a roll-call vote on the demand of one-fifth of those present.

Section 5

4. Neither House, during the Session of Congress, shall without the Consent of the other, adjourn for more than three days, nor to any other Place than that in which the two Houses shall be sitting.

This clause has little significance. Nowadays, although the two chambers take "recesses," they do not "adjourn" but remain in continuous session. Moreover, there is never any question about holding meetings of the entire House or Senate in any place except the Capitol building in Washington, D.C.

Section 6

1. The Senators and Representatives shall receive a Compensation for their Services, to be ascertained by Law, and paid out of the Treasury of the United States.

Although elected by the people of the states from congressional districts, congress members must look to the national treasury for their compensation. During the struggle for ratification of the Constitution, many persons had objected to this provision because it permits congress members to determine their own salaries. In practice, congress members have been somewhat reluctant to increase their salaries for fear of public displeasure. When in 1815 Congress abandoned a $6 per diem stipend and voted itself a raise to $1,500 per year, the outcry was so great that nine members resigned and numerous others were defeated at the polls. In recent years Congress has tried without success to decrease the political liability of members of Congress for increasing their own salaries. In 1969 Congress provided for a quadrennial review by a top level Commission on Executive, Legislative, and Judicial Salaries of the salaries of the Cabinet Officers, members of Congress, and federal judges. Its recommendations are submitted to the President who in turn submits the report with his recommendations to Congress. Each House of Congress must vote on the President's proposal within sixty days, and if both Houses approve, the adjustment takes effect at the start of the first pay period beginning thirty days thereafter. But in most instances Congress has refused to go along with the recommendation, for fear of giving challengers an issue at the next congressional election. Nor has Congress been more successful in trying to bracket congressional salaries in with those of other federal employees. In 1975 Congress subjected the salaries of Cabinet Officers, members of Congress, and federal judges, to the recommendation of the Advisory Committee on Federal Pay. These recommendations were subject to presidential modification and to veto by either chamber. (*INS* v. *Chadha* may call for some alteration in such practices, although the Court, prior to *INS* v. *Chadha* but as recently as 1980, treated congressional vetos of the Advisory Committee's recommendation as effective—see page 110). In almost every instance, Congress set aside the proposed increases, not only for itself but for top-level federal civil servants, Cabinet Officers, and federal judges as well (see page 110 for the special problems relating to judicial salaries that require they be treated separately).

Section 6

1. [continued] They shall in all cases, except Treason, Felony, and Breach of the Peace, be privilege from Arrest, during their Attendance at the Session of their respective Houses, and in going to and returing from the same;

The words "breach of the peace" are construed not in the limited sense of a particularly defined crime, but to cover all criminal offenses; the exemption extends only to arrest for civil offenses while engaged in congressional business. With the abolition of imprisonment for civil offenses, this clause has lost its significance. As the Supreme Court recently reemphasized by quoting approvingly from Jefferson. "Legislators ought not to stand above the law they create but ought generally to be bound by it as are ordinary persons."[19]

Section 6

1. [continued] and for any Speech or Debate in either House, they shall not be questioned in any other Place.

The protections of the speech and debate clause extend not only to members, but to those who are acting as their authorized agents. State legislators obtain no protection from this provision.[20] They may have equivalent protection under their respective state constitutions so far as actions in their state courts are concerned. Still undecided is whether or not members of Congress can waive their rights under this clause, or even if the Congress could do so.[21]

The speech and debate clause exempts members of Congress from arrest, prosecution, or suit for anything they say on the floor of Congress, in committee, or in committee reports. What they say with respect to these legislative matters cannot be introduced as evidence in any criminal prosecution, nor may there be a judicial inquiry into motives for making a speech related to the legislative process, or for how or why a member of Congress has cast a particular vote.[22] The protection extends, however, only to a legislative act that has been performed. A promise to deliver a speech, to vote, or to solicit others to vote, or to introduce a bill at some future date are not "speech or debate" and matters relating to such may be introduced in trials of members of Congress for bribery or conspiracy to commit bribery.[23]

Nonlegislative functions—issuing news releases, making speeches outside of Congress, performing errands for constituents, and keeping voters informed, for example—are not protected by congressional immunity. Although a senator, or his assistants, could not be compelled to respond to any questions or in any way be questioned about his introduction before a Senate subcommittee of the famed but classified "Pentagon Papers," he had no such immunity from questioning about arrangements he had made for the subsequent publication of these papers by a private publisher or about questions as to how the papers had come into his possession. Introducing materials to a committee is a legislative function; having the materials published by a private publisher is not.[24] Nor was Senator Proxmire protected by the speech and debate clause and he had to stand trial for libel for issuing press releases and making telephone calls in which he accused a scientist of wasting public funds in a project for which the Senator granted his famous—or some would say "infamous"—"Golden Fleece Award."[25] Members of a House of Representatives committee and their staff were immune from suit for the publication of a committee report of use by members of Congress that allegedly violated rights of privacy (the report told of the grades and disciplinary problems of named students). But no such immunity protected the Superintendent of Documents, even though he acted in response to a congressional request, who distributed the same report to the general public. Distribution of a committee report inside the Congress is a legislative function; distribution of the same report outside of Congress is not.[26]

The speech and debate clause only prevents a congressman from being questioned about speeches and debates in "any other Place," making it quite clear that the clause does not limit the power of each chamber to discipline its own members, for example, for defaming others under a cloak of congressional immunity. This is a responsibility that the chambers understandably have been reluctant to exercise.

Although this clause extends only to members of Congress, as we have noted, the separation of powers principle confers upon Presidents absolute immunity for anything they say or do that has any remote connection with their official responsibilities (see page 46). In fact Presidents have more immunity from lawsuits for what they have said and done than do members of Congress (see page 46). With the Supreme Court having determined that judges have an absolute immunity when acting in their judicial capacities, they, including state judges, probably have more immunity than their colleagues in the national legislative branch.

---

2. No Senator or Representative shall, during the Time for which he was elected, be appointed to any civil Office under the Authority of the United States, which shall have been created, or the Emoluments whereof shall have been increased during such time.

The ineligibility clause has resulted in little litigation. A taxpayer tried to challenge Justice Black's appointment to the Supreme Court on the grounds that as a senator, he had voted for legislation improving the retirement benefits of members of the federal judiciary. The Court ruled that the taxpayer lacked standing to raise the issue.[27] Justice Black, although serving for thirty-four years, died while in office and never received any benefits of the Retirement Act.

The issue was raised again after President Carter nominated Representative Abner Mikva, a liberal Democrat from Illinois, to the Court of Appeals for the District of Columbia. Some senators challenged Mikva's nomination as a violation of this clause because a judicial pay raise had gone into effect during his term, but after he had resigned his House seat. Shortly after his nomination was confirmed, Congress passed a law granting members of Congress standing to contest such judicial appointments on eligibility grounds. Senator McClure, a conservative Republican from Idaho, in a suit financed by the National Rifle Association raised this challenge. A three-judge district court ruled, however, that despite the law, a senator lacked standing to challenge a nomination confirmed by the entire Senate. The Supreme Court affirmed that ruling without comment.[28]

---

2. [continued] and no person holding any Office under the United States, shall be a Member of either House during his Continuance in Office.

The incompatibility clause stems from the doctrine of separation of powers. It contrasts sharply with the British system, in which most high executive ministers are also members of Parliament. It makes members ineligible to serve in the executive branch while retaining membership in Congress. It does not, however, prevent the appointment of members of Congress as temporary representatives of the United States at international conferences. Senators have sometimes served temporarily as members of the United States delegation to the United Nations General Assembly.

Does the clause prevent members of Congress from serving in the military reserve forces? Some reservists who opposed our involvement in Vietnam thought so, and as taxpayers and citizens they sought a judicial order to require the Secretary of Defense to strike congressional members from the reserve lists and to declare that service by members of Congress in the reserves is prohibited by the incompatibility clause. The Supreme Court dodged the issue by holding that those who raised the question lacked standing to sue.[29]

---

1. All Bills for raising Revenue shall originate in the House of Representatives; but the Senate may propose or concur with Amendments as on other Bills.

This provision, based on the theory that the House is more directly responsive to the will of the people than the Senate, was inserted at the insistence of the more populous states in order to relate taxation to representation. It has not, however, kept the Senate from originating revenue measures in the guise of amending House bills, by striking out an entire measure except the title and the enacting clause. This paragraph, moreover, does not have the same significance that it had in 1787, when senators were chosen by state legislatures.

---

2. Every Bill which shall have passed the House of Representatives and the Senate, shall, before it become a Law, be presented to the President of the United States; if he approve he shall sign it, but if not he shall return it, with his Objections to that House in which it shall have originated, who shall enter the Objections at large on their Journal, and proceed to reconsider it. If after such Reconsideration two thirds of that House shall agree to pass the Bill, it shall be sent, together with the Objections, to the other House, by which it shall likewise be reconsidered, and if approved by two thirds of that House, it shall become a Law. But in all such Cases the Votes of both Houses shall be determined by yeas and Nays, and the Names of the Persons voting for and against the Bill shall be entered on the Journal of each House respectively. If any Bill shall not be returned by the President within ten Days (Sundays excepted) after it shall have been presented to him, the Same shall be a Law, in like Manner as if he had signed it, unless the Congress by their Adjournment prevent its Return, in which Case is shall not be a Law.

Although the framers expected Congress to be the dominant branch of the government, they did not wish it to be in a position to arrogate to itself all powers. So they gave the President a qualified veto both to prevent Congress from overstepping its boundaries and to enable him to influence the actual course of legislation.

After a bill has been passed in *identical* form by both houses of Congress it is presented to the President, who can do one of three things:

First, he can sign the bill and it becomes the law of the land.

Second, he can return it to the house in which it originated, stating the reasons for his disapproval. If the bill is then repassed by a two-thirds vote of *both* houses, which means two-thirds of a quorum of the members thereof, it becomes law despite the President's veto. On the other hand, if the bill does not secure the approval of two-thirds of a quorum of the members of *both* houses, the veto is sustained and the bill does not become law.

Third, the President can refuse to sign the bill but retain possession of it.

It then becomes law at the end of ten days (excluding Sundays) after its presentation to him, provided Congress is still in session.

As the Constitution says, "If *Congress by their adjournment prevent its* [a bill's] *Return, in which Case it shall not be a law.*" The bill is thus subject to what is called the "pocket veto." The pocket veto applies differently to the three different kinds of adjournments. It probably does not apply to the first; there is a dispute about the second, and it clearly applies to the third.

First, in which it probably does not apply, are the recesses that Congress frequently takes for short periods, for example, over Christmas. In 1970 President Nixon tried to pocket veto a health bill during such a recess. Senator Kennedy argued that the pocket veto could not be used for such adjournments and took the question to federal courts. The Court of Appeals for the District of Columbia agreed with him. The Department of Justice decided not to take the matter to the Supreme Court.

Second, there are the intersessional congressional adjournments. (In the early days of the Republic, Congress used to go home during the summer and not start its second session until December of the next year.) These days Congress does not end its first session until November or December, and then starts the second session the following January. There continues to be a debate between Congress and the President whether the pocket veto can be used between sessions. In 1976 President Ford, in response to another suit by Senator Kennedy, agreed that as long as the House and Senate designated officers to receive veto messages during such between-session recesses, he would not use a pocket veto. President Reagan, however, abandoned that policy and vetoed measures during intersession adjournments, including one that tied aid for El Salvador to its compliance with certain human rights conditions. Thirty-three House Democrats and the Senate have filed a suit charging that these pocket vetoes are unconstitutional. A federal district judge has sided with the President. The matter is likely to end up before the Supreme Court.

The third type of adjournment comes at the end of the second session, the so-called adjournment *sine die,* in which a particular Congress adjourns never to return again (see page 43 about the Senate which, in one sense, has never adjourned). Everyone agrees that the pocket veto applies to such adjournments.

Unlike many state governors, the President cannot approve parts of a bill and veto other parts; he must give approval or disapproval to the bill as a unit. Because the President does not have an "item veto," Congress has been able to get measures past the President by using "riders," provisions that are not germane to the main purpose of a bill. Riders are most effective when tacked on to appropriation bills, thus forcing the President to accept them in order to secure funds for the operations of the government. President Reagan is only the most recent of many Presidents who have urged Congress either to grant the President an item veto or to propose a constitutional amendment that would do so.

Not only has Congress been unwilling to give the President such authority, but in the Budget and Impoundment Control Act of 1974, as a reaction to President Nixon's refusal to permit the spending of funds that Congress had appropriated, imposed a "legislative veto" (see below) over presidential "rescissions" and "impoundments." In the aftermath of the *Chadha* case (see below) and in the face of major budget deficits of recent years, Congress may ease up on its controls over presidential rescissions as a substitute for a presidential item veto.

3. Every Order, Resolution, or Vote to which the Concurrence of the Senate and House of Representatives may be necessary (except on a question of Adjournment) shall be presented to the President of the United States; and before the Same shall take Effect, shall be approved by him, or being disapproved by him, shall be repassed by two thirds of the Senate and House of Representatives, according to the Rules and Limitations prescribed in the Case of a Bill.

Despite the inclusive language of what has come to be known as the *presentment clause,* there are, in addition to questions of adjournment, certain orders, resolutions, and votes that require the concurrence of both houses but are not presented to the President for his action.

First, when a constitutional amendment is proposed by a two-thirds vote in both houses of Congress—that is, by a vote of two-thirds of a quorum thereof—it is submitted immediately for ratification without being sent to the President for his approval or disapproval. Congress does not exercise ordinary legislative powers when it proposes constitutional amendments. It operates under the powers given it in Article V. This is a self-contained, complete statement of methods for amending the Constitution, and it omits the President from the procedure.

The second exception to the requirements of the presentment clause used to be the "legislative veto." Congress started to use the legislative veto in a small way in the 1930s, and in a big way beginning in the 1970s until the Supreme Court in *INS* v. *Chadha* (1983), in what may be the most significant decision of this decade, called the practice to a halt.

Beginning in 1932 Congress started to condition its more general delegations of powers to the President and to executive departments on the approval of a particular exercise of that power by Congress, or by one house. (Sometimes, it even gave a veto to a legislative committee.) These resolutions of one chamber or concurrent resolutions of both were not submitted to the president.

The "legislative veto" came in many forms. In some laws Congress stipulated that what the President did was to be effective unless disapproved by either or both chambers within a certain number of days. In others Congress provided that what the President did was effective only if approved by both houses of Congress within a certain time period. For example, under the 1973 War Powers Act, unless Congress adopts a concurrent resolution of approval within sixty days, troops sent into combat by the President are to be withdrawn. Under the Impoundment Control Act of 1974 if the President withholds funds temporarily, a "deferral," he must report this to Congress, and his action is effective unless overturned by a resolution of either chamber. If the President wishes to impound funds permanently, a "rescission," his act rescinding the appropriation is *in*effective unless both the House and Senate approve within forty-five days.

Since 1932 when the first veto provision was adopted, more than two hundred pieces of legislation have carried some form of congressional veto; about half of these bills were enacted after 1972.

The use of the congressional veto sparked criticism of it as an evasion of "the presentment clause," and as a violation of the doctrine of separation of powers. The one-house veto was also subject to the charge that it violated the bicameralism provisions of Article I. Most scholars, however, supported the practice, at least in the form calling for action by both chambers.

Presidents of both parties, felt otherwise. Often when presented with legislation delegating powers to them and their agents but subjecting such delegations to a legislative veto, presidents complained that these provisions were an unconstitutional invasion of presidential powers. Nonetheless they had little choice. Congress looked upon the legislative veto as an essential means of exercising oversight of the executive departments to ensure that they were carrying out the intent of Congress. Without the legislative veto, Congress could only overturn the actions of the President and executive officials by enacting overriding legislation, which would have to be presented to the president for his approval or veto. Congress was not about to give up the practice.

The Supreme Court kept out of the battle for half a century, but in a sweeping decision, *INS* v. *Chadha* (1983),[30] ruled the legislative veto unconstitutional. The particular provision in question granted the Attorney General authority to suspend the deportation of certain aliens, but he had to report all such suspensions to Congress. Either chamber had an opportunity in the current session (or in the next one) to veto the suspension of deportation by passing a resolution of disapproval. If Congress did nothing, then the alien's status was adjusted to that of a lawful resident. The Court could have limited its decision to this particular use of the legislative veto, or to one-house vetos, but the language of the Court is so broad that it sounded "the death knell for nearly 200 other statutory provisions,"[31] more laws than the Supreme Court has declared unconstitutional in our entire history.

What are Congress's options as it reviews the more than 200 provisions for the legislative veto? It can refuse to delegate the authority. It can be more precise in its delegations. It can delegate for brief periods of time thereby alerting the executive officials that if they act in such a fashion that aggravates enough congressmen, the law delegating authority to them is not likely to be reenacted. It can stipulate in the original legislation delegating authority that the actions will not become effective for a certain period of time, and that they must first be reported to Congress, giving Congress time to enact overriding legislation. (Such legislation, of course, would have to be presented to the President under the provisions of the presentment clause.) Clearly the *Chadha* decision is one of great importance, and will alter the balance between Congress and the President in ways yet to be determined.

Congressional Organization and Procedure: The Unwritten Constitution

The Constitution provides the barest outline of congressional organization and gives a partial description of how Congress operates. Other basic practices have developed over the last two hundred years. Of special importance are the role of political parties, the selection of committee leaders, and the rules governing debate.

Political Parties in Congress

The nature of the party system is as significant as the formal Constitution in determining how a governmental institution operates. The Soviet one-party system, for example, makes meaningless the formal constitutional discretion of the Soviet legislature. The constitutional structure of the English and French parliaments is much the same, yet the French multiparty system leads to a kind of legislature very different from the English three-party system.

If political parties are so important, why is our Constitution silent about their organization and operation? The Founding Fathers considered parties divisive and baleful influences. Although they knew that "factions," as they called parties, might develop, they hoped that the constitutional arrangements would curtail party influences and make it difficult for them to operate. To a considerable extent, they were successful. Parties have not been decisive organizations in determining the outcome of legislative struggles nor have they served as important agencies in coordinating the executive and legislative branches. They have, however, always played a role of some significance in the operation of Congress. Congressional candidates are nominated by parties, they run in elections as representatives of a party, and the majority party in each house "organizes" that chamber.

Prior to the opening of a Congress,* each party in each chamber holds an organizing meeting. (The Republicans call their meetings a conference, the term also used by Senate Democrats; House Democrats still keep the older name "caucus.") At these meetings, the parties nominate their candidates for the various congressional and party offices, the most important in the case of the representatives being the Speaker of the House, and in the case of the senators, the majority leader. These party conferences also confirm the assignments of their own party members to the standing committees of the Congress (the formal appointment is made subsequently by the chamber); elect the floor leaders and their assistants, known as "whips"; and select policy committees to mold strategy during the coming sessions. In recent sessions, these party agencies, especially the Democratic caucuses of the House, have strongly asserted their authority. The Democratic caucus in the House has taken some vigorous stands on policy issues—it even went so far as to remove from office some senior committee chairmen (see below).

Each party may also hold conferences during the course of the sessions, but only the recommendations of the organizing conferences receive the united support of party members. All Democratic House members, for example, support their party's candidate for Speaker; all Republicans support their conference's candidate. Thus the party with the most members selects the Speaker and other House officers. The Vice-President, who presides over the Senate, may belong to the minority party in the Senate, but the President pro tempore who presides in his absence is always a member of the majority party in the Senate.

---

* We have a new Congress every two years that inaugurates its first session in January of odd-numbered years. The second session meets the following January; unless the the party lineup in the chamber has changed because of deaths, resignations, or special elections, the organization does not change.

Despite attempts to build the parties into organizations to coordinate legislative actions within Congress (and between Congress and the President), the parties do not necessarily dominate or determine legislative policy. Senators from Michigan, to cite one example, are likely to support legislation favorable to the automobile industry irrespective of party affiliation or of the desires of party leaders. On many votes, members of both parties can be found on both sides. Nevertheless, on many key issues, party affiliation is important. Parties also provide the primary organization in Congress for the development of legislative programs.

Selection of Committee Chairpersons

The standing committees and subcommittees process bills, hold investigations, and recommend legislative action. They are composed of members of both parties, each party being represented in approximately the same ratio as its strength in the entire chamber.

The chairpersons of committees and subcommittees are influential leaders. For decades they were picked by strict seniority—the member of the majority party who had the longest continuous service on the committee became chairperson. No matter how much he or she might differ with party colleagues, no matter how much an idea might be out of tune with those of the President, even if both belonged to the same party, the senior member became chairperson. But, beginning in 1971, Democrats and Republicans in both the House and the Senate began to make changes in their procedures. The custom of seniority still prevails, but it is now merely a presumption that the senior member will be chosen as chairperson, no longer an automatic guarantee that it will be so. The chairpersons of all committees and subcommittees now know that if they displease a majority of their fellow party members, they may be voted out of their posts.

Rules and Debate

With so many members and so many issues, the time of the House is carefully controlled. The House Rules Committee, except for certain privileged matters, normally stipulates the amount of time and the conditions under which the House may debate legislation (the Rules Committee merely recommends, but its recommendations are almost aways accepted by the House). Representatives may be ruled out of order if their remarks are not pertinent to the topic at hand and they speak subject to rigorously enforced time limits. In the Senate, however, debate is practically unlimited. Once senators gain the privilege of the floor, they can talk on any subject for as long as they can stand. This rule of unlimited debate and the right to talk about anything even if it has no connection to the subject at hand, permits a few determined senators to tie up the business of the Senate by filibustering—talking to delay or to prevent the Senate from voting. Senators who strongly object to a measure seldom have to engage in a filibuster. Merely by threatening to do so, they are normally able to deter the Senate leaders from attempting to bring the objectionable measure before the Senate for consideration.

Once a filibuster is begun, it is difficult to stop. It takes a vote of three-fifths of the senators duly chosen and sworn in—in most instances sixty senators—to apply *cloture,* or closure as it is called. (It requires two-thirds of those present and voting to close debate on a motion to amend Senate rules.) Although the Senate in recent years has been more inclined than in the past to invoke cloture, the power to talk and talk and talk remains a significant weapon of senate minorities. At one time it was the favorite weapon of southern senators to keep the Senate from adopting civil rights bills. More recently, it has been used by liberal senators to force compromises or forestall legislation or appointments they do not want.

Enumeration of Congressional Powers

Section 8 enumerates the legislative powers granted to Congress. In interpreting these powers, we should, as Chief Justice Marshall put it, never forget that it is a Constitution we are reading, a Constitution "intended to endure for ages to come, and consequently to be adapted to the various crises of human affairs.[32] Furthermore, each separately enumerated grant should be read as if the necessary and proper clause (see page 78) were part of it.

Section 8

1. The Congress shall have Power to lay and collect Taxes, Duties, Imposts and excises, to pay the Debts and provide for the Common Defense and general Welfare of the United States;

This paragraph grants to Congress the important powers of the purse: the power to collect taxes, pay debts, and spend money for the common defense and general welfare.

The power to pay debts is not restricted to the payment of the legal obligations of the national government. On the contrary, Congress may pay off obligations which are merely moral or honorary, and when this power is tied to the power to spend for the general welfare, it results in the power of Congress to decide who shall receive dollars from the federal treasury.

A word of caution—the "general welfare" clause is tied to the power to tax and to spend: There is no general power granted to Congress to legislate for the general welfare. But as we have noted in discussing federalism, as a result of the liberal construction of congressional powers and the demands of our times, there are no longer serious constitutional limits on the ability of Congress to do what it considers necessary and proper to promote the general welfare.

James Madison argued in vain that Congress could tax and spend only in order to carry out one of its other granted powers—that is, Congress could tax and spend to establish post offices and post roads (Section 8, paragraph 7), to regulate commerce with foreign nations (Section 8, paragraph 3), and so on. From the first, nevertheless, the power of Congress under this clause has been interpreted as being in *addition* to its other powers and, hence, as exercisable in its own right without reference to them. Today, Congress taxes and spends hundreds of millions of dollars every year to aid agriculture, education, and business, to alleviate conditions of unemployment, and to take care of the poor, the aged, and the disabled, despite the fact that none of these things is specifically within its other delegated powers.

Approximately 25 percent of the money that the states and the local governments spend comes nowadays from the federal government. Some of it is in the form of revenue sharing in which the national government merely turns dollars over to local units with relatively few strings; other dollars come in the form of block grants for such purposes as education or manpower training, in which the state and local units have considerable flexibility as to how they will use the dollars, or as "categorical grants" in which there are rather specific conditions which state and local governments must follow if they wish to receive the federal funds, sometimes including the requirement that the state match from its own resources federal grants. By tying conditions to the funds it makes available Congress has been able to regulate vast areas—everything from how highways will be built, through how the national guard should be trained, to how universities and colleges shall assign faculty to do research or, to protect their privacy, how to post the grades of their students.

When Congress acts under the spending power and intends to impose conditions on the grants it makes to the states, Congress must act "unambiguously" so that when the state accepts the federal funds it does so with an understanding of the federally imposed conditions.[33]

It is difficult, and until recently impossible, to secure a judicial hearing on the constitutionality of a federal grant-in-aid. In 1923 the Supreme Court told Massachusetts that it lacked standing to challenge the constitutionality of a federal grant program because a state may not stand between the national government and the national government's own citizens.[34] At the same time the Supreme Court told a private taxpayer, Mrs. Frothingham, that her interest in avoiding an increase in tax liability did not give her sufficient standing to challenge the Maternity Act of 1921 on the grounds that Congress had invaded the legislative province of the states.[35] For forty-five years these decisions were construed as an absolute bar to taxpayer suits challenging the constitutionality of federal expenditures. Then in 1968 the Supreme Court in *Flast* v. *Cohen* modified the *Frothingham* decision by permitting federal taxpayers to challenge the constitutionality of those provisions of the Elementary and Secondary School Act of 1965 that channel federal funds for instructional materials to religious and sectarian schools. The establishment clause, Chief Justice Warren explained, operates as a specific constitutional limitation upon the exercise by Congress of the taxing and spending power. Unlike Mrs. Frothingham, who had merely argued that Congress had exceeded its general authority, in *Flast* v. *Cohen* the taxpayers contended that Congress had breached a specific limitation upon its taxing and spending authority. Here they had standing to raise the issue.[36]

The difference between the *Frothingham* and the *Flast* cases is difficult to discern, and the line between permissible and impermissible taxpayer suits is hard to explain. Nor has the Supreme Court's subsequent elaboration been very helpful. The Court has explained that before taxpayers have standing to sue they must show (1) a logical link between their taxpayer status and the challenged legislative enactment and (2) a "nexus" between this status and a specific constitutional limit on the taxing and spending power. Furthermore, taxpayer standing covers only challenges to the exercise of congressional power under the tax and spending clause because only such legislative actions directly affect the rights of taxpayers.[37] In addition, the Court has distinguished between a permissible challenge to a federal expenditure that arguably conflicts with a specific constitutional prohibition, and on the other side impermissible suits that challenge a federal spending act on grounds that it violates more general constitutional principles. "Any doubt that once might have existed concerning the rigor with which the *Flast* exception to the *Frothingham* principle ought to be applied should have been erased by this Court's recent decisions," wrote Justice Rehnquist for the Court, which is judicial language meaning *Flast* did not change things very much. In fact, the *Flast* decision may well be a "sport" in the stream of constitutional development.

Since the *Flast* decision, the Supreme Court has reaffirmed several times the *Frothingham* principle "precluding a taxpayer's use of a court as a forum in which to air his generalized grievances about the conduct of government or the allocation of power in the Federal system."[38]

Not only can Congress spend for regulatory purposes, it can also tax for such purposes. Although in the past ostensible tax laws have been struck down because of the contention that they were really regulations of subjects reserved to the states, today, if the measure is a tax on its face, judges are not likely to inquire into congressional motives or to set aside the tax because it is actually an attempt to regulate subjects reserved to the states. And Congress can heavily tax activities—for example, dangerous white phosphorus matches or bank notes issued by state-chartered banks; the fact that the impact of the tax makes the activity uneconomic raises no constitutional problems.

Of course Congress may not use its authority to tax in such a fashion as to deprive persons of specific rights secured by the Constitution. For example, Congress has attempted to regulate gamblers and gambling, the sale of narcotics, and traffic in dangerous weapons through some rather elaborate tax laws. To the extent that in order to comply with such laws gamblers, narcotics peddlers, and sellers of dangerous weapons, in effect, have to produce evidence that they are engaging in illegal activities, the measures violate the guarantees against compelling persons to testify against themselves.[39]

The power to tax and to spend has become one of the two major sources—the other is the power to regulate commerce among the states—of the so-called national police power, the power to regulate persons and property for the safety, health, and welfare of society. Congress has no general grant of police power, but it may and does use its delegated powers for police-power purposes.

Section 8

1. [continued] but all Duties, Imposts and Excises shall be uniform throughout the United States;

The uniformity clause does not require Congress to levy only taxes that fall equally on each state nor does it prevent Congress from defining a tax in geographic terms. It means that Congress may not make *unreasonable* geographic classifications. Thus a unanimous Court upheld the Crude Oil Windfall Profit Tax Act of 1980 levying a new and higher tax on all oil except that produced from wells located in a northerly section of Alaska. The exemption was not drawn on state political lines. It reflected a congressional judgment that the unique climactic and geographic conditions that make drilling wells in that region so much more costly than elsewhere justified exempting this oil from the windfall profit tax in order to encourage further exploration in that area.[40]

[In all subsequent paragraphs of Section 8 the words, *"The Congress shall have the power"* are understood.

Section 8

2. To Borrow Money on the Credit of the United States.

Congress borrows money by authorizing the sale of government securities to banks, business, and private individuals. The most important forms of government securities are bonds, treasury certificates, and treasury notes.

Section 8

3. To regulate Commerce with foreign Nations,

Congress's power to regulate commerce with foreign nations is contained in the same clause as is its power to regulate commerce among the states (see below). In fact, Congress's power over foreign commerce is greater than its power over commerce among the states, although nowadays its power over commerce among the states is so expansive that this distinction between the two kinds of commerce is of no significance.

More to the point, the foreign commerce clause places greater restraints on a state government's power than does the interstate commerce clause. Taxation of foreign commerce is subject to closer scrutiny than taxation of interstate commerce. A state tax of foreign commerce is unconstitutional if it either "creates a substantial risk of international multiple taxation" or "prevents the Federal Government from speaking with one voice when regulating commercial relations with foreign governments."[41] State taxation of *property* owned by a foreign corporation is especially protected from state taxation. For example, a state can tax a domestic airplane or railroad car if the airplane or railroad car is in the state for a certain number of days, if the tax is proportioned to the time in the state, if the tax rate does not discriminate against interstate commerce, and if the tax is related in some way to services provided by the state. But such a test will not justify a state tax on the ship of a foreign nation that may be docked in its ports.[42]

The Supreme Court's bold language against state taxation of foreign commerce should not be taken too seriously. The Court takes its cue on these matters from the President and Congress. Unless the executive branch vigorously intervenes to object that a state tax on the *income* of a corporation may affect the income of its foreign subsidiaries, the Court is not likely to set these taxes aside merely because they might lead to multiple taxation. Said Justice Brennan, "This Court has little competence in determining precisely when foreign nations will be offended by particular acts, and even less competence in deciding how to balance a particular risk of retaliation against the sovereign right of the United States as a whole to let the states tax as they please. The best that we can do, in the absence of explicit action by Congress, is to attempt to develop objective standards.[43]

---

3. [continued], and among the several States,

The commerce clause is another important basis on which Congress has developed a national police power. It is also an excellent demonstration of the fact that the vague words and phrases of certain sections of the Constitution have enabled a document written in 1787 in the days of the oxcart to be adapted to the needs of modern industrial society.

"Commerce," in the sense of this clause, includes not only buying and selling (traffic), but all forms of commercial intercourse, of transportation, and of communication. Congress's power extends to commerce if it is carried on with foreign nations or "*affects* more states than one." The power of Congress over such commerce is the power to govern it. In the words of Chief Justice Marshall in *Gibbons* v. *Ogden,* this power "is complete in itself, may be exercised to its utmost extent, and acknowledges no limitations other than are prescribed in the Constitution."[44]

Congress is not obliged, when regulating "commerce among the states," to consider the effect of its measures on matters that have been generally regulated by the states. Indeed, it may regulate intrastate activities (those within a state) when these substantially affect interstate or foreign commerce. And, although Congress's measures are usually intended to benefit commerce, they are not required to do so. Congress may even prohibit or greatly restrict commerce in order to promote the national health, safety, and welfare, and for humanitarian purposes. From 1808, it proscribed the African slave trade. Many years later, it prohibited the transportation of lottery tickets between the states and, still later, the transportation of liquor into states having "dry laws." Since 1920, Congress has made it a federal crime to use the channels of interstate commerce for the shipment of stolen automobiles or impure foods or in the traffic of white slavery, for use by "loan sharks," or for travel in order to commit certain specified crimes. Congress has also closed the channels of interstate commerce to goods of enterprises engaged in commerce or production for commerce that do not pay all employees minimum wages and overtime pay as prescribed by federal law. To make this law effective, Congress not only has banned the interstate transportation of goods so produced, but has also made it a federal offense to produce goods under such conditions when the goods are "intended" for sale in interstate commerce (Fair Labor Standards Act). To safeguard interstate commerce from interruption by strikes, Congress may regulate employer–employee relations in business and industries that "affect" such commerce, and has in fact done so (the Wagner and Taft-Hartley Acts).[45] Congress has also used the commerce clause to justify comprehensive federal regulations as to how coal may be mined, including requirements for restoring lands and for protecting farmland.[46]

The commerce clause is also the constitutional peg for the 1964 Civil Rights Act forbidding discrimination because of race, religion, or national origin in places of public accommodation and because of race, religion, national origin, and sex in the case of employment. As the Supreme Court said (*Heart of Atlanta Motel* v. *United States*), "Congress' action in removing the disruptive effect which it found racial discrimination has on interstate travel is not invalidated because Congress was also legislating against what it considers to be moral wrongs."[47] Congress may also extend its laws to remote places of public accommodation, since its power over interstate commerce extends to the regulation of local incidents that might have a substantial and harmful effect on that commerce. Congress has authority to enact such laws because discrimination restricts the flow of interstate commerce, and because interstate commerce is being used to support the discrimination.

In 1969 the Supreme Court sustained the application of the Civil Rights Act to what Justice Black in dissent characterized as "this country people's recreation center, lying in what may be, so far as we know, a little 'sleepy hollow' between Arkansas hills miles away from any interstate highway" because the park leased its paddle boats from an Oklahoma company, its juke box was made outside of Arkansas, and it played records manufactured outside the state. Ingredients served in the snack bar were obtained from out-of-state sources, and as the Court majority speaking through Justice Brennan wrote, "it would be unrealistic to assume that none of the 100,000 patrons actually served by the Club each season was an interstate traveler." Justice Black did not question that Congress could bar racial discrimination under its powers stemming from the Fourteenth Amendment, but he felt the commerce clause should not be stretched "so as to give the Federal Government complete control over every little remote country place of recreation in every nook and cranny of each precinct and county in every one of the 50 states."[48] But he dissented alone.

Although Justice Rehnquist and Chief Justice Burger have warned, "it would be a mistake to conclude that Congress's power to regulate pursuant to the Commerce Clause is unlimited," and they would require Congress to show that its regulatory activity is "substantially" related to interstate commerce,[49] the fact is "the task of the Court in reviewing congressional commerce clause regulations is exceedingly narrow." A court may invalidate legislation enacted under the Commerce Clause only if it is clear that there is no rational basis for a congressional finding that the regulated activity affects interstate commerce, or that there is no reasonable connection between the regulatory means selected and the asserted ends."[50] In reality, the Supreme Court has turned over to Congress the interpretation of the scope of its powers under the commerce clause. Congressional regulations when based on the commerce clause are seldom challenged: When challenged the Court, with cohesion that is rare, has no difficulty in concluding that Congress may regulate such purely local transactions as fees charged by real estate brokers and lawyers, or the mining of farmland.[51]

From the commerce clause, Congress also derives its full powers over the "navigable waters of the United States," including the waters that may be made navigable by "reasonable improvements." These waters are subject to national planning and control; the authority of Congress over them "is as broad as the needs of commerce," including flood protection, watershed development, and the recovery of the cost of improvements through utilization of power.[52]

The commerce clause is important, moreover, not only as a grant of power to Congress but also as a limit on the power of the states. In giving this power to the national government, the Constitution took it away from the states, at least in large part. Therefore, whenever a state, in professed exercise of its taxing power or police power, passes a law materially affecting interstate or foreign commerce, the question necessarily arises whether this is not really an unconstitutional regulation of foreign or interstate commerce. Of course, if the state law conflicts with a federal regulation, the federal regulation supersedes.

Not only does a congressional regulation supersede a conflicting state regulation, but an act of Congress conferring power on states under the commerce clause preempts judicial judgments. "Courts are final arbiters" of the negative implications on states' powers "under the Commerce Clause only when Congress has not acted. . . . When Congress has struck the balance it deems appropriate, the courts are no longer needed to prevent states from burdening commerce, and it matters not that the courts would have invalidated the state tax or regulation under the Commerce Clause in the absence of congressional action."[53] If Congress ordains that the states may regulate an aspect of interstate commerce, any action taken by a State within the scope of the congressional authorization is rendered invulnerable to commerce clause challenge. (The state action, however, may violate other provisions of the Constitution, the equal protection clause, for example.)

When, however, Congress is silent, the Supreme Court determines whether a state regulation that affects commerce is permissible. In the exercise of this great power, the Court has handed down hundreds of decisions, some of which involved vast commercial interests. It has laid down scores of rules about which volumes have been written. There is, naturally, no space for such matters in a book like this but, in essence, what the Court does is to weigh the local interest against the general commercial interest, and then give the right of way to the interest the Court deems, all things considered, to be the more important one.

First, the Court looks to ensure that a law purporting to protect the public is not merely a disguise behind which a state is favoring its own local commerce. "Where simple economic protectionism" is found, "a virtual per se rule of invalidity has been erected."[54] A law may be struck down either for a discriminatory purpose against out-of-state commerce or for a discriminatory effect on such commerce.[55] Even if a state regulates local and interstate commerce even-handedly, and imposes only incidental burdens on interstate commerce, the Court may strike down such a law if the burden is, in the justices' judgment, excessive in relation to local benefits.

Second, in recent years the Court has made a distinction between state and local governments when they enter the market as participants and when they act as regulators of commerce. When they are acting as participants in the market, they are not subject to the restraints of the commerce clause. Thus Boston could require those to whom it gave construction contracts to perform the work on the contract by a force consisting of at least fifty percent of Boston residents. South Dakota could give preference to in-state buyers for the cement it produced, and Maryland could favor in-state processors in getting rid of abandoned automobiles.[56] However, what a city may do without violating the commerce clause, may violate the privileges and immunities clause—the one in Article IV, not the one in the Fourteenth Amendment—by limiting the ability of out-of-state residents or businesses to participate in that particular business (see page 119).

Of the hundreds of examples of how the Supreme Court, when Congress is silent, has performed this balancing role with respect to state police power laws (those passed to promote the public health, welfare, and safety), here are a few: Florida could not ban out-of-state banks from engaging in investment advisory services.[57] Arizona was not allowed to impose a fourteen passenger or seventy freight car limit on interstate trains, nor could it require interstate trains to carry a "full crew as defined by the state legislatures."[58] Minnesota could ban the sale of milk in disposable plastic bottles.[59] Illinois could not require interstate trucks to be equipped with specific kinds of contoured mudguards.[60] Wisconsin and Iowa could not ban trucks longer than fifty-five feet because such a ban placed a substantial burden on interstate commerce, and the evidence did not support the states' contentions that such regulations made the highways safer.[61] Washington could not ban supertankers from Puget Sound, but it could require those without certain kinds of safety equipment to use tugboats.[62] New Jersey could not prohibit the importation of solid or liquid waste which originated or was collected outside the state since this imposed on out-of-state commercial interests the full burden of conserving the state's remaining landfill space and it was a freeze on the flow of commerce for protectionist reasons.[63] Arizona could not require a California company to process cantaloupes in Arizona, for the burden imposed was excessive in relation to the state's minimal interest in regulating their packaging.[64] North Carolina could not require Washington apple growers to use only U.S.D.A. grades or no grades at all on apples shipped into North Carolina and thereby have to forego using the superior-grade levels established by the state of Washington.[65] Maryland could bar companies producing and refining oil from operating retail service stations.[66] Illinois could not require persons wishing to buy up shares and take control of one of its corporations to register with the state's secretary of state. Not only would this lead to a direct regulation of commercial activities outside of Illinois, but, in the Court's judgment, the burden on interstate commerce outweighed any local benefits.[67] Arkansas could regulate the wholesale electric rates charged by rural power cooperatives to its member retail distributors.[68]

At one time states were allowed to prohibit the export of wildlife on the grounds that the animals belonged to the people of the state, but the Supreme Court has reversed this line of holdings.[69] A state can no longer deny access to its local goods "be they animal (minnows), vegetable (cantaloupes), or mineral (natural gas).[70] However, as we have noted, if the state enters the market and *manufactures* products, it may, like a private business, decide to whom it is going to sell and restrict what it produces to its own citizens. Thus South Dakota could confine the sale of the cement it manufactured to its own citizens.[71] Note, however, that South Dakota could not have restricted access to its limestone, from which the cement is manufactured, for that would fall under the line of precedents as applied to resources and wildlife.

As difficult as the issues are when it comes to deciding whether or not a state law enacted to promote the public well-being should be applied to interstate commerce, questions relating to the application of state taxes to interstate commerce are even more complicated. (These questions also get combined with due process considerations: Under the due process clause a state may not tax that which is not within its jurisdiction and over which it has no control and confers no benefits.)

The Supreme Court in *Complete Auto Transit Inv.* v. *Brady,* has attempted to clarify the apparently conflicting precedents it has spawned. It adopted the following four-pronged test to measure the constitutionality of state taxes as they relate to interstate commerce: (1) Is the tax applied to an activity with a substantial nexus with the taxing state? (2) Is it fairly apportioned? (3) Does it not discriminate against interstate commerce? and (4) Is it fairly related to the services provided by the state? If the answer to all four questions is yes, the tax is constitutional.[72]

There has been considerable controversy in recent years over the adoption by more than twenty states of the "unitary business" principle, taxing the income of corporations that do business around the world. The Supreme Court has said this principle does not violate either the commerce or due process clauses. It has given its approval as well to the three-factor formula used by the states: the proportion of a unitary business's total payroll, property, and sales which are located in the taxing state. The Court's action means that in some instances two states will tax the same income. The justices have told Congress that if it wishes to limit state taxation beyond that required by the Constitution, it should do so because the rule regarding how taxes should be apportioned to an interstate business is "essentially a legislative task."[73]

Here are some other examples of decisions relating to state taxation as applied to interstate commerce: Louisiana could not tax natural gas taken from the Gulf of Mexico, processed in that state, but on its way to ultimate consumers, while at the same time effectively exempting from the tax the natural gas used within the state.[74] West Virginia could not levy a gross receipts tax on business selling at wholesale (from which local manufacturers were exempt) even though those manufacturers are subject to a higher manufacturing tax.[75] Montana could levy a substantial severance tax on each ton of coal mined in the state even though 90 percent of the coal is shipped to other states.[76] Montana, unlike Louisiana, taxed equally the coal that was to be used locally. (Justice White voted with the majority in the Montana case, but expressed his discomfort with the decision. He suggested that Congress might want to use its power to protect interstate commerce from undesirable burdens to overturn the Montana tax.) Illinois could not require a mail-order house that owned no property in Illinois—and did not advertise there or have any agents in the state—to collect a use tax from Illinois consumers who purchased goods via catalogs.[77] On the other hand, California could require a mail-order business to collect use taxes even though the sales went directly from California consumers to the business in the District of Columbia, but the business did maintain offices in California which solicited advertising for its magazine.[78] Alabama could collect a tax on a traveling photographer, but states may not levy taxes on sellers from out of state who come into a state merely to solicit orders for subsequent interstate shipment.[79]

There is certainly no field in which the Court's reviewing power has been more valuable than this one. Although we have fifty state legislatures, we have one national economic and industrial system—one prosperity. Nor is there any field in which the Court has, on the whole, done better work in maintaining the national authority "in full scope without unnecessary loss of local efficiency."[80] In interpreting the due-process clause of the Fourteenth Amendment, the Court has frequently been lured into questionable positions by that will-o'-the-wisp word *liberty,* but commerce clause cases are generally down-to-earth cases, well seasoned with facts and figures.

---

3. [continued] and with the Indian tribes;

This clause has been broadly construed to confer plenary power on Congress to deal with the special problems of the Indian tribes. Since 1871, when Congress declared that henceforth there would be no more treaties negotiated with Indian tribes, this clause has been the primary source of federal authority over Indians. The clause also "singles Indians out as a proper subject for separate legislation."[81]

It is because of both the power conferred on Congress by this clause and the special historical relationship that has always existed between the national government and the Indian tribes that the Supreme Court sustained an act of Congress giving Indians belonging to federally recognized tribes preference in employment by the Bureau of Indian Affairs. "The preference . . . is granted to Indians not as a discrete racial group, but, rather, as members of quasi-sovereign tribal entities whose lives and activities are governed by the BIA in a unique fashion. . . . The legal status of the BIA is truly *sui generis.* . . . As long as the special treatment can be tied rationally to the fulfillment of Congress's unique obligation toward the Indians, such legislative judgments will not be disturbed."[82]

The national government, acting through the Bureau of Indian Affairs in the Department of Interior, counts 280 Indian tribes, pueblos, and groups within the continental United States. There are also slightly more than 200 Native Alaskan communities served by the Bureau.

Of the 1,418,195 people who designated themselves as Indians for the 1980 Census, about 680,000 live on reservations or nearby (this includes all Indians in Alaska and those in Oklahoma who live on or near the former reservations in that state). Nonreservation Indians—any Indian is free to move anywhere he or she wishes—are entitled to be treated like any other citizen.

To be eligible for most benefits provided by the Bureau of Indian Affairs, one must live on or near a reservation. Reservation Indians, like those living off the reservation, are American citizens by act of Congress. Today, by act of the states in which the reservations are located, reservation Indians have the right to vote.

The clause conferring authority on Congress to regulate commerce with Indian tribes also places limits on the power of the states to do so. State laws of a general nature may be applied on reservations only if their application does not impair a right granted or reserved by federal law, and does not interfere with the self-government Congress has reserved for the tribes. State regulation of the commercial activities of Indian tribes is allowed only if the state overcomes two independent but related barriers: A state may not act if its authority has been pre-empted by federal law, or if its actions interfere with a tribes' ability to exercise its sovereign functions.[83] For example, a state may not apply its general rules relating to hunting and fishing on reservations to either Indians or non-Indians, even if there is no specific federal pre-emption since such state regulations are "incompatible with federal and tribal interests reflected in federal law and there is no state interest at stake sufficient to justify overriding tribal regulations."[84]

Congress has also stipulated that only federal and tribal criminal laws are to apply on reservations, except where Congress has specified to the contrary. Federal jurisdiction encompasses the more serious crimes, while states have limited rights to assume jurisdiction over some crimes committed on reservations, and most states have done so.

Laws relating to the sale of alcoholic beverages on Indian reservations are treated in a special way. Congress has prohibited such sales unless the tribe wishes to exercise local option. Seventy tribes have chosen to do so, and this delegation has survived a constitutional challenge that Congress had unconstitutionally delegated its legislative powers to a nongovernmental agency.[85] But Congress delegated power over these sales to tribes, subject to conformity with state regulation. The general canon that "State laws generally are not applicable to tribal Indians on an Indian reservation except where Congress has expressly provided . . . does not apply to liquor sales. . . . Congress has divested the Indians of any inherent power to regulate in this area. . . ." Unlike the power to tax and other governmental powers, the power to regulate liquor sales is not a fundamental attribute of sovereignty which the tribes retain."[85]

The Indian commerce clause does not of its own force bar all state taxation of matters that indirectly affect the economic interests of the tribes, but only prevents undue discrimination against or burden on Indian commerce. Thus Washington was allowed to collect a sales tax on sales of cigarettes to nontribal members, including nontribe Indians, in stores operated by the tribes on reservations.[86] (Tribes also collected their own taxes on these same transactions.) On the other hand, states may not levy taxes that fall even indirectly on reservation Indians or tribal activities unless Congress, by express authority, has conferred such powers on them. A state may not, for example, collect taxes on income earned by Indians on reservations, collect a fuel tax from a non-Indian firm that cut trees on a reservation and transported them to a tribal sawmill, or collect a sales tax on tractors delivered to an Indian tribe.[87] New Mexico was told that federal law pre-empted its collecting a tax from the receipts that a non-Indian construction company received from a tribal school board for building a school on the reservation. (New Mexico could collect the same tax from the contractor for work he did for the federal government.)[88]

These limitations on the power of states to tax Indian activities on reservations do not extend to off-reservation activity. New Mexico could collect a sales tax on a ski resort operated by the Mescalero Apache tribe off the reservation, although it could not tax the property the tribe owned and used in operating the resort.[89]

Indian tribes have only the jurisdiction over non-Indians living on reservations conferred on them by Congress, but with Congress's approval they may exclude nonmembers from reservations.[90]

The tribes have inherent powers to govern themselves and their own people. They are "domestic, dependent nations."[91] In governing themselves the tribes are unconstrained by the Bill of Rights or the Fourteenth Amendment. Although by the Indian Civil Rights Act of 1968 Congress imposed restraints on tribal governments similar, but not identical, to those contained in the Bill of Rights and the Fourteenth Amendment, federal courts have only limited power to review tribal actions for conformity with this law. The Supreme Court refused to permit federal courts to consider the claim of a female member of a Santa Clara pueblo, and of her daughter, challenging as illegal and unconstitutional a tribal regulation denying membership to children of women who marry outside the tribe, but not to children of men.[92]

---

4. To establish a uniform Rule of Naturalization,

"Naturalization" is the legal process by which a foreigner is admitted to citizenship. In view of the inherent power of any sovereign nation to determine its own membership, the naturalization clause must today be reckoned superfluous.

By virtue of this same inherent power, Congress has the right to determine which foreigners may enter the United States, for what purposes, and on what conditions. " 'Over no conceivable subject is the legislative power of Congress more complete' than the admission of aliens."[93] This power extends even to granting the Attorney General discretion to determine which, if any, aliens who advocate "the economic, international and governmental doctrine of world communism" should be admitted to the United States.[94]

This grant of power to Congress over naturalization includes within it the power to regulate immigration, and it gives to Congress considerably greater authority to regulate the conduct of aliens within the United States than have the state governments. Moreover, aliens are in the United States at the sufferance of the national government and may be removed through administrative procedures. Even so, while they are here this grant of authority does not permit Congress to deprive aliens, any more than it may citizens, of such rights as freedom of worship, speech, fair trials for criminal prosecutions, or other fundamental rights protected by the Constitution. Furthermore, congressional power to regulate the admission of aliens includes authority to preempt conflicting state laws. For example, "Congress has broadly declared as federal policy that lawfully admitted resident aliens who become public charges for causes arising after their entry are not subject to deportation; and that as long as they are here they are entitled to the full and equal benefit of all state laws for the security of persons and property."[95]

---

4. [continued] and uniform Laws on the subject of Bankruptcies throughout the United States;

Bankruptcy laws enable debtors to obtain release from their obligations upon surrender of their property to their creditors. Thus are the "wholly broke made whole again." Congress has passed several such laws, each successive one marking a wider application of the rights of debtors.

One of the issues revolves around the priority of rights among creditors, including federal and state governments. Congressional enactments take priority over conflicting state laws. For example, after a federal court had discharged a bankrupt person from all debts, a state law could not be applied that called for forfeiture of a driver's license for failure to satisfy an earlier judgment resulting from an automobile accident.[96]

Another set of issues relates to the kinds of obligations that may be set aside through bankruptcy proceedings. A controversy recently surfaced about to what extent an employer, by going into receivership, that is, putting the firm under the control of a judge on the grounds that without some relief from its creditors (including its employees), the firm will go out of business, may get out of obligations under a collective bargaining contract. Congress resolved the issue by requiring that prior to seeking court approval for modification of a collective bargaining agreement, a company in financial difficulty that files under Chapter 11 (the part of the bankruptcy statute that allows financial reorganization) must first make a good faith effort to get the union to change the agreement. Only when this fails may a judge order a revision in the contract, if the judge determines a modification is necessary to save the firm.

Congress's power under this clause is wide, but not unlimited. "The bankruptcy power is subject to the Fifth Amendment's prohibition of taking private property without just compensation." There is substantial doubt that Congress could, by bankruptcy legislation, retroactively destroy a creditor's ownership in property sold to a debtor.

In 1973 when Congress designed a special law to deal with the bankruptcy of eight northwestern and midwestern railroads, the act was challenged for violating the uniformity requirement of the bankruptcy clause. The contention was that this highly complicated act applied to only parts of the country and dealt with those subject to its provisions differently from bankrupt railroads in other parts of the nation. The Court responded that the uniformity requirement does not call for geographic uniformity. It requires only uniform treatment for all creditors and debtors covered by the law. Furthermore, during the time the act was in effect the only bankrupt railroads were those covered by it.[97]

A decade later, however, the Supreme Court seemed to give the uniformity provision a somewhat different interpretation. When the Rock Island Railroad was in the midst of bankruptcy proceedings, Congress enacted a law ordering the trustee to provide up to $75,000,000 as a priority item to pay the unemployment benefits of workers who might not find jobs with the successor organization. The bankruptcy court refused to implement this act because it amounted to an unconstitutional taking of the railroad's property without just compensation. Congress then reenacted the act with the additional provision that if the railroad's property were taken to pay for the unemployment benefits to its workers, the railroad had a right to bring an action against the federal government for compensation. On review the Supreme Court, ignoring the taking of property issue, held that because the act applied only to one railroad, it was not uniform and therefore exceeded the authority of Congress.[98]

Section 8

5. To coin Money, regulate the Value thereof, and of foreign Coin, and fix the Standard of Weights and Measures;

This power, in conjunction with the power to borrow money on the credit of the United States, gives Congress the authority to issue paper money and to make it legal tender for the payment of all debts.

---

6. To provide for the Punishment of counterfeiting the Securities and current Coin of the United States

---

It would seem that Congress has this power even without this clause as a result of the necessary and proper clause.

Pursuant to this authority Congress has enacted two statutes designed to make it more difficult to counterfeit money by restricting photographic reproductions of currency. The first, enacted during the Civil War to combat the surge in counterfeiting caused by the great increase in government obligations, makes it a criminal offense for any person to print or in any manner publish a likeness of currency. The second, adopted in a 1958 codifying Treasury practice, permits the printing or publishing of the likeness of any security for certain purposes and for those purposes only, namely, "for philatelic, numismatic, educational, historical or newsworthy purposes." In addition, the publication must be in articles, books, journals, newspapers, or albums"; the illustrations must be in black and white; the reproduction must be undersized by at least three-fourths or oversized by at least one and one-half, and the negatives used in making the illustrations must be destroyed after their final use.

The Supreme Court in 1984 declared the purpose requirement to be an unconstitutional violation of the First Amendment because it is not a content-neutral time, place, and manner regulation and would require the government to determine whether the message being conveyed is newsworthy or educational (see page 152). The Court assumed that the requirement that the illustration must be in a publication is unconstitutional, but left this issue open for final determination for another day. (Time, Inc. was the party to the suit and since the publication requirement caused it no problems, the Court ruled that Time lacked standing to raise the issue.) The Court upheld the constitutionality of the size and color requirement, and said nothing about the one requiring the negatives to be destroyed.[99]

---

7. To establish Post Offices and post Roads;

This clause, combined with the power to regulate interstate commerce and to spend for the general welfare, permits Congress to subsidize airlines, railroads, and shipping companies and to grant money to the states for road building and maintenance. But the fact is that through its powers to tax and to spend for the general welfare, Congress could perform these same functions even in the absence of this grant. Today this provision is superfluous, but when the framers wrote it they resolved any doubts about the ability of the national government to establish a postal system. Of course the founding fathers could not have anticipated the liberal interpretation of the necessary and proper clause (see page 78).

---

8. To promote the Progress of Science and useful Arts, by securing for limited Times to Authors and Inventors the exclusive Right to their respective Writings and Discoveries;

The Constitution limits congressional power to granting these exclusive rights only for limited times.

Congress has secured to authors, musicians, and artists the protection of copyrights, and to inventors the protection of patents.

Copyright protection is afforded to "original works" including books, plays, musical works, pantomimes, sculptural works, motion pictures, and sound recordings. The owner of a copyright is given certain exclusive rights with respect to such works, including the right to reproduce the copyrighted work and to license its sale. The copyright law, however, does not protect ideas or principles, but rather protects the particular manner in which they are expressed or described.

Works are protected from the moment of creation, whether published or unpublished, and do not need to be registered or identified with a copyright notice. Registration with the Register of Copyrights is, however, a prerequisite for bringing suit for infringement; in the case of works published without the copyright notice, registration must occur within five years of publication or copyright protection is lost. The protection extends through the life of the author plus fifty years. For anonymous works and works prepared by an employee at the request of an employer, the protection is for seventy-five years from the date of first publication or one hundred years from the year of creation, whichever expires first.

Notwithstanding the exclusive right of copyright owners, there are certain circumstances under which it is permissible to reproduce or display copyrighted works without the permission of the copyright owner. Traditionally the courts have considered copying for purposes such as criticism, comment, news reporting, teaching, scholarship, and research to be fair use. The standards of "fair use" described in the law include (1) the purpose and character of the use, including whether it is for commercial or educational purposes; (2) the nature of the copyrighted material, i.e., periodical, film, book, videotape; (3) the amount of materials used in relation to the whole; and (4) the effect of the use on the potential market for or value of the copyrighted work.

A five-to-four Court decided that manufacturers of videotape recorders could not be sued for damages by owners of copyrighted television programs. Many copyright holders who licensed their works for broadcast had no objection to having their broadcasts taped, and the evidence indicated that the largest use of videotapes was for "time-shifting purposes" to allow the viewer to see the materials at a time different from that in which it was telecast, and thus there was little evidence that copyright owners suffered financial harm. Four justices contended that taping a copyrighted television program is infringement and that time-shifting is not fair use, and that the recording manufacturers were guilty of inducing infringements.[100] Congress could override this decision, but in view of the millions of people with videotape machines in their homes this seems unlikely.

Penalties for copyright infringement include injunctions against infringing actions, the impounding and destruction of infringing copies, awards of actual or statutory damages, and the assessment of costs and attorneys fees. Statutory damages may range from $250 to $10,000 per infringement. If the infringement is found to be willful, a court may increase the statutory damages to $50,000. There are also criminal penalties for willful infringements undertaken for personal or commercial advantage or for financial gain. On the other hand, an innocent infringer who is defined as one who was not aware and had no reason to believe that his acts constituted an infringement is protected by a provision that allows the court in its discretion to reduce statutory damages to $100.

Although the new law is more specific than the previous law in many areas, there remain numerous ambiguities which will eventually have to be clarified through judicial determinations.

Persons who invent or discover any new and useful art, machine, manufacture, composition of matter, certain types of plants, including man-made microorganisms,[101] and so on, may secure a patent from the Patent Office located in the Department of Commerce. A patent gives the patent holder the exclusive right to the invention or discovery for seventeen years and, like a copyright, may be sold, assigned, or willed. Litigation growing out of conflicting patents may be appealed to a special court—the U.S. Court of Appeals for the Federal Circuit in Washington, D.C.

> The clause is both a grant of power and a limitation. This qualified authority . . . is limited to the promotion of advances in the "useful arts." . . . The Congress in the exercise of the patent power may not overreach the restraints imposed. . . . Nor may it enlarge the patent monopoly without regard to the innovation, advancement or social benefit gained thereby . . . Innovation, advancement, and things which add to the sum of useful knowledge are inherent requisites . . . in a patent system which by constitutional command must "promote the Progress of . . . useful Arts." This is the *standard* expressed in the Constitution, and it may not be ignored.[102]

Although the copyright power is governed by the same introductory and limiting phrase as the patent power, the Supreme Court has not insisted on the same standards for copyrights as for patents. To secure a copyright, it is not necessary to establish that the materials are useful, innovative, and beyond the state of the art—originality is sufficient.

Under this clause, Congress does not have power to protect trademarks, which are words, letters, or symbols used in connection with merchandise to point out the ownership and origin of the product; it does, however, have power under the commerce clause to protect trademarks used in interstate commerce. Trademarks that are registered with the Patent Office need not be original, but they must be distinctive. Registration of a trademark grants the right to its exclusive use in interstate commerce for twenty years with unlimited rights of renewal.

Obviously, no state can adopt any regulation that conflicts with federal patent or copyright laws, but the Constitution does not totally exclude states from protecting certain kinds of material. A state may provide copyright protection for records and tapes not covered by federal law.[103] A state may enforce its trade secret acts to provide protection for processes that are either nonpatented or even nonpatentable.[104]

---

9. To constitute Tribunals inferior to the Supreme Court;

All federal courts, except the Supreme Court, rest exclusively on acts of Congress. Any court, except the Supreme Court, can be abolished by act of Congress. It is not clear whether Congress must provide for the judges of the courts it abolishes. In 1802, when Congress first exercised its power to abolish a federal court, no provision was made for the displaced judges. But in 1913, the only other time Congress has exercised this power, when the commerce court was abolished, Congress redistributed the commerce court judges among the circuit courts.

---

10. To define and punish Piracies and Felonies committed on the high Seas, and Offenses against the Law of Nations;

Congress can make any crime under international law a crime under national law. In the past, this has not been important because international law has dealt chiefly with governments rather than individuals. Recent developments in the direction of placing *individuals* under the obligations of international law may give this paragraph unexpected importance.

---

11. To declare War, grant Letters of Marque and Reprisal, and make Rules concerning Captures on Land and Water;

The purpose of this clause was to transfer to Congress a power that in Great Britain belonged to the King, or the executive branch. This purpose has not been realized. Especially because of his initiative in the direction of our foreign relations, the President has been primarily responsible for our participation in all our great wars, although the role of Congress has recently been enhanced (see page 97).

Letters of marque and reprisal formerly authorized private individuals to prey upon the shipping and property of enemy nations without being considered pirates. The Pact of Paris of 1856 bans this practice.

---

12. To raise and support Armies,

Under conditions of total war this and the following clause, plus the inherent powers of the national government in the field of foreign relations, confer greater powers than the entire remainder of the Constitution. These include the power to draft people and materials for the armed forces; to establish price ceilings; to requisition property; to allocate and ration materials; to direct the production, marketing, and consumption of all products; and to do whatever is "necessary and proper" to further the successful prosecution of a war. In the words of Chief Justice Hughes, "The power to wage war is the power to wage war successfully."[105] One must have a wide-ranging imagination to comprehend the full scope of these powers. It was under these powers that Congress, in 1946, passed a law giving the federal government control of materials, plants, and information dealing with atomic energy—a statute that has been termed "the most remarkable exercise of governmental power" in the entire history of the country.

The power to raise and support armies, along with the companion clause, "To provide and maintain a Navy" and the "necessary and proper clause" give Congress the power to register and conscript men, during war or peacetime, including the power to register and draft men but not women. When the question was presented to the Supreme Court in 1981, the majority concluded that since women as a group are not eligible for combat, Congress could choose, if it wished, to order only men to register. The dissenting justices did not challenge the power of Congress to exclude women from combat positions, but argued that their exclusion from registration contravened the "equal protection component of the Due Process Clause of the Fifth Amendment" (see page 246).[106]

Section 8

12. [continued] but no Appropriation of Money to that Use [raise and support armies] shall be for a longer Term than two Years;

This limitation is to ensure the dependence of the army on Congress and is a reflection of the framers' belief in civilian supremacy and their fear of standing armies.

Section 8

13. To provide and maintain a Navy;

The navy was not thought to be a threat to liberty, and no limitations were placed on appropriations for it. Moreover, a two-year limitation would not be feasible, as the construction of naval vessels often takes longer than two years and appropriations have to be pledged in advance.

Inasmuch as the framers did not foresee the development of air power, the 1947 act of Congress creating the air force as an independent element of national military power rests on the general *inherent* power of the national government in the fields of foreign relations and national defense.

14. To make Rules for the Government and Regulation of the land and naval Forces;

The power here conferred is, in wartime, shared by the President in his capacity as commander in chief. Congress's power under this section, like all its powers, is subject to specific constitutional limitations. Persons in the land and naval forces do not have precisely the same constitutional freedoms as do those not subject to military jurisdiction, but the Supreme Court has narrowed the definition of who is subject to the rules for the regulation of the armed forces (see page 182).

Congress may legislate for those in the armed forces with more flexibility than is allowed for civilians. The standards used to determine whether the military codes are unconstitutionally vague or overbroad are more like those used to determine the constitutionality of regulations that apply to economic matters—"unfair competition," "excessive profits," and so on. Thus the Court has upheld against the charge of vagueness and overbreadth Article 133, which punishes "conduct unbecoming an officer and a gentleman," and Article 134, which proscribes "all disorders and neglects to the prejudice of the good order and discipline in the armed forces."[107]

15. To provide for calling forth the Militia to execute the Laws of the Union, suppress Insurrections and repeal Invasions:

From an early date, the President has been authorized by Congress to employ not only the state militias but also the armed forces of the United States against "combinations of persons too powerful to be dealt with" by the ordinary judicial processes. Presidents have used their authority under these statutes to dispatch troops to break up combinations of persons interfering or threatening to interfere with the execution of federal court orders. Presidents have even "federalized" a state's militia, now know as the National Guard, just to take it away from the command of a governor. When the President calls the National Guard into federal service, he exercises the same control over it as he does over any unit of the armed forces of the United States.

In the exercise of these powers, the President may, in case of "necessity," declare "martial law." Of this there are various degrees and kinds, the most extreme being that in which military courts temporarily take over the government of a region.

16. To provide for organizing, arming, and disciplining, the Militia, and for governing such Part of them as may be employed in the Service of the United States, reserving to the States respectively, the Appointment of the Officers,

and the Authority of training the Militia according to the discipline prescribed by Congress;

Congress and the states cooperate in the maintenance of the National Guard. Normally, it operates under the direction of the states, subject to provisions made by Congress. When called into the service of the United States, the National Guard becomes a part of the United States military forces and is subject to government by Congress and the President. When the National Guard is not in federal service, Congress can still exercise a considerable degree of control through conditions attached to grants of money to the states for the National Guard.

Section 8

17. To exercise exclusive Legislation in all Cases whatsoever, over such District (not exceeding ten Miles square) as may, by Cession of particular States, and the Acceptance of Congress, become the Seat of the Government of the United States and to exercise like Authority over all Places purchased by the Consent of the Legislature of the State in which the Same shall be for the Erection of Forts, Magazines, Arsenals, dock-Yards, and other needful Buildings;—And

After many years in which Congress exercised direct authority over the District of Columbia, with the District having only appointed officials, the District of Columbia Self-Government Act of 1973 finally brought a considerable measure of home rule to the District. The citizens of the District now elect their own mayor, city council, and school board; the council has limited authority to legislate and to levy taxes, but Congress still retains ultimate legislative authority. A National Capital Service Area provides a federal enclave within the District, consisting of the principal federal buildings.

Despairing of securing ratification of the proposed D.C. Constitutional Amendment (see page 270), the D.C. council authorized a constitutional convention. The council adopted the proposed new constitution and petitioned Congress to admit the District, except for a small portion that would remain as "the seat of Government of the United States," as a new state to be called, New Columbia. Although it is unlikely to do so, Congress could create the fifty-first state of New Columbia by a simple majority of both chambers.

Section 8

18. To make all Laws which shall be necessary and proper for carrying into Execution the foregoing Powers, and all other Powers vested by this Constitution in the Government of the United States, or in any Department or Officer thereof.

As is the case with the general welfare clause, this clause (variously known as the "necessary and proper clause," "elastic clause," and "coefficient clause") is subject to misunderstanding. Congress is not here granted the power to make all laws that shall be necessary and proper for any purpose whatsoever, but only to make laws necessary and proper in order to execute its enumerated powers or to execute powers vested by the Constitution in the President, the Senate, or the courts. However, because of the expansive interpretation given to the several enumerated powers and the generous interpretation of the necessary and proper clause, nowadays there is hardly any subject that Congress cannot deal with. Thus to be precise and "technically" accurate in noting that this clause is not a general grant of power is to convey the wrong impression (see page 2). This may be one of those rare instances when those who are wrong are more accurate than those who are right, and a classic example of how a little learning can be a dangerous thing.

As we have noted, in the famous case of *McCulloch* v. *Maryland*, Chief Justice Marshall construed the word *necessary* to mean convenient or useful and rejected the narrow interpretation "indispensable." As an example: The authority to establish a Federal Reserve Banking System is not among the enumerated powers of Congress, but Congress can so act because establishing such a system is a "necessary and proper" (that is, *convenient*) way of executing its powers to lay and collect taxes, to borrow money on the credit of the United States, and to regulate interstate commerce.

"Inherited" Powers: The Power to Investigate

In addition to specifically vested powers, each house of Congress enjoys important powers by inheritance, as it were, from the English Parliament and the early state legislatures. One important inherited power is that of conducting investigations in order to gather information needed to legislate, to propose constitutional amendments, or to perform other constitutional functions.[108] As a necessary adjunct to its investigating power, each house may subpoena witnesses and punish those who refuse to produce documents or answer questions. As we have noted, the speech and debate clause precludes courts from interfering in advance with the enforcement of a congressional subpoena. Each chamber may itself determine a witness's guilt and have that witness held in custody for as long as it is in session. The more common practice is to turn the recalcitrant witness over to the federal prosecutor for action under a federal law making it a crime to refuse to answer pertinent questions or produce pertinent testimony when ordered to do so by a congressional committee.

What, then, are the constitutional limits to Congress's investigating authority? Or to be more precise, what are the limits on the authority of Congress to compel persons to furnish materials or to answer questions? Congress is not supposed to use its investigatory powers, any more than its legislative powers, to abridge the freedoms protected by the First Amendment. Despite the fact that the Supreme Court has warned Congress that the First Amendment sets boundaries to its investigatory authority, as yet a majority of the justices has never been mustered to sustain an actual claim that compelled testimony, even about political beliefs and activities, did in fact abridge rights secured by the First Amendment.

The doctrine of separation of powers also limits Congress's investigatory power. As the Supreme Court stated it, "The power to investigate must not be confused with any of the powers of law enforcement; those powers are assigned under our Constitution to the Executive and Judiciary." Congress "has no power to expose for the sake of exposure."[109] It may compel answers only if the information sought is needed by Congress in the pursuit of its legitimate business. However, few limits have been placed on what constitutes such pursuit. For example, legislative investigations need not be justified by the development of proposals for new legislation; investigations to determine whether and how government programs are functioning are appropriate.

Since witnesses before congressional committees are not on trial in a formal sense, the committees are not required to give witnesses the same rights they would have in a court of law. Committees, however, must comply with whatever procedural rules they choose to adopt.[110] In addition, witnesses have a right under the Fifth Amendment to refuse to answer questions if the answers would expose them to the risk of criminal prosecution.

By far the most important restraint on congressional investigations has been the Supreme Court's insistence on a strict construction of the federal law defining the offense of contempt of Congress. Contempt of Congress, as defined by the law, is the refusal to answer *pertinent* questions. Before the Supreme Court is willing to permit convictions it insists: (1) that the parent chamber has clearly authorized the committee to make the particular investigation (in the case of investigations by committees of the House of Representatives, since neither the House nor its committees are continuing bodies, the authorization must occur during the term of Congress in which the investigation takes place); (2) that the committee has authorized the investigation; (3) that the committee has made clear to the witness the subject under investigation, the pertinence of the question to the subject, and why the committee has insisted that it be answered; (4) that the grand jury indictment has specified what subject was under committee investigation and which pertinent questions the defendant has been charged with refusing to answer.[111]

In short, despite the Supreme Court's warning to the Congress that it must exercise its investigatory authority within the confines of the Constitution, so far the Court has not placed any substantive restriction on the scope of congressional investigations. It has, however, insisted on scrupulous procedural compliance.

Limitations on Congressional Powers

Whereas Section 8 enumerates the legislative powers of the national government, Section 9 limits them. Section 9, and Section 10 which restricts the powers of the state governments, were originally looked on as a kind of bill of rights.

Section 9

1. The Migration or Importation of such Persons as any of the States now existing shall think proper to admit, shall not be prohibited by the Congress prior to the Year one thousand eight hundred and eight, but a Tax or duty may be imposed on such Importation, not exceeding ten dollars for each person.

This paragraph refers to the importation of slaves into the United States and is of historical interest only.

2. The Privilege of the Writ of Habeas Corpus shall not be suspended, unless when in Cases of Rebellion or Invasion the public Safety may require it.

The writ of habeas corpus—known to the eighteenth century as the Great Writ—was primarily a remedy against executive detention. By this writ a judge could inquire of an arresting officer or jailer why a particular person was in custody. If no proper explanation could be given, the judge could order the prisoner's release. But once it was determined that a person was being held as the result of a sentence imposed by a court with proper jurisdiction, that ended the matter. Since then Congress has expanded the use of the writ to permit federal courts to review the actions of state courts to determine not merely the fact that a person is being detained as the result of a judicial sentence, but whether or not that sentence was obtained as the result of a constitutionally proper trial.[112]

The writ that is protected against suspension except during times of rebellion and invasion "is the writ known to the framers, not as Congress may have chosen to expand it."[113] Congress has the proper authority to order the suspension of the privilege, although in situations in which the President can validly declare martial law he can also suspend the writ. The greater power includes the lesser.

State courts may not inquire into the reasons why persons are held under the authority of the United States; federal courts do have jurisdiction to determine if persons are being improperly held by federal or state authorities. Prior to seeking a federal habeas corpus writ—or the one similar to it that Congress now provides—to review the actions of state courts, a person must first exhaust state remedies, including a petition for review by the Supreme Court. In recent decades the habeas corpus business of federal district judges has grown tremendously, causing considerable resentment among state judges; and partly in response to that criticism, when persons have already had a hearing in a state court on their allegation that evidence has been taken from them in an unconstitutional manner, the Supreme Court has limited the authority of federal district judges to once again review such allegations. In a very important decision, *Stone* v. *Powell,* the Court decided that any time persons have had a hearing in a state court on the allegation that evidence has been extracted from them in violation of their rights under the Fourth Amendment, the matter can no longer be looked into by federal courts via a habeas corpus petition.[114] The Supreme Court also ruled that if defendants fail to raise constitutional claims in state proceedings, they are not to be given any relief via a writ of habeas corpus in the federal court house unless they "demonstrate cause and actual prejudice." The mere proof that state courts committed an error will not suffice.[115]

3. No Bill of Attainder [shall be passed]

A bill of attainder is the infliction by the legislature of punishment. Congress by general law may determine what conduct shall be considered a crime, but it may not impose punishment; this must be done by a court of law.

At common law a bill of attainder was a death sentence, but early in our history we departed from this restrictive definition. Imprisonment, banishment, confiscation of property, denial of jobs, or other kinds of punishments are now recognized as attainders forbidden by this clause.

In the last four decades the Court has entertained challenges under this clause, twice holding that Congress had violated it. The first time was a provision of an appropriation bill that named three federal employees and declared that they should receive no compensation from the federal treasury other than for military or jury services, unless reappointed to office by the President with the consent of the Senate (*United States* v. *Lovett*).[116] The second time was a provision that no member of the Communist Party should be allowed to serve as a trade union officer.[117] In both instances, Congress was found to have passed a bill of attainder in that it inflicted punishment, i.e. loss of job, without trial on named individuals or on members of a specific political group.

The third serious challenge was by former President Nixon who argued that the Presidential Recordings and Materials Preservation Act of 1974, which took control of his presidential papers away from him and vested it in the Administrator of General Services, was a bill of attainder. As Justice Stevens said: "The statute before the Court . . . singles out one, by name for special treatment. Unlike all other former Presidents in our history [and subsequent ones], he is denied custody of his own presidential papers. The statute implicitly condemns him as an unreliable custodian of his papers. Legislation which subjects a named individual to this humiliating treatment must raise serious questions under the Bill of Attainder Clause." But seven members of the Court ruled that this was not a bill of attainder. Nixon, they argued, was a legitimate "class of one"; Congress was not motivated by a desire to punish, but rather to provide an appropriate process for disposing of presidential papers. Justice Stevens in concurrence stated that the decisive fact was that Nixon had made himself a class different from all other Presidents in that he had resigned under unique circumstances and had accepted a pardon. But it was precisely because of these facts, the dissenters contended, that Congress had "punished" Nixon and passed a bill of attainder.[118]

Some male students charged that Congress had imposed a bill of attainder when, via what has come to be known as the Solomon Amendment, it required all men who wish to apply for federal student financial aid in order to go to college to indicate that they have complied with the registration requirements of the Military Selective Service Act. Although a federal district judge agreed with the students, the Supreme Court did not. Rather, Chief Justice Burger, speaking for the Court, pointed out that any student who wishes to apply for aid at any time may become eligible for it by registration. The Solomon Amendment, in addition to lacking the singling out of an identifiable group characteristic of a bill of attainder, was also said not to impose punishment, the sanction, therefore, being a mere denial of a noncontractual governmental benefit. "It imposed no affirmative disability approaching the kinds of disabilities historically associated with punishment."[119]

3. [continued] or ex post facto Law shall be passed.

An ex post facto law is a retroactive *criminal* law that works to the disadvantage of an individual; for example, by making a particular act a crime that was not a crime when committed, or by retroactively reducing the proof necessary to convict, or by increasing punishment retroactively.[120] The prohibition does not prevent passage of retroactive penal laws that work to the benefit of an accused—a law decreasing punishment, for instance.[121]

Although the due process clause imposes some barriers to retroactive *civil* laws, the ex post facto clause imposes none, not even to civil laws that work against individuals—say, an increase in income taxes applied to income previously earned.[122]

"So much importance did the Convention attach [to the ex post facto prohibition] that it is found twice in the Constitution":[123] here as a limitation on the national government and in Section 10 as a limitation on the states.

4. No Capitation, or other direct, Tax shall be laid, unless in Proportion to the Census or Enumeration herein before directed to be taken.

A capitation tax is a poll or head tax. The precise meaning of the term *direct* tax is today uncertain (see page 40).

5. No Tax or Duty shall be laid on Articles exported from any State.

Although Congress cannot tax articles exported from states, it can, under its power to regulate commerce with foreign nations, prohibit these exports by such means as embargoes.

6. No Preference shall be given by any Regulation of Commerce or Revenue to the Ports of one State over those of another; nor shall Vessels bound to, or from, one State, be obliged to enter, clear, or pay Duties in another.

By giving to Congress the power to regulate interstate and foreign commerce, the states were prevented from discriminating against the commerce of other states. This section prevents Congress, in regulating such commerce, from discriminating against the trade of a single state or of a group of states.

7. No Money shall be drawn from the Treasury, but in Consequence of Appro-priations made by Law; and a regular Statement and Account of the Receipts and Expenditures of all public Money shall be published from time to time.

It is this clause that, more than any other, gives Congress control over the acts of the other branches of government—the President, the courts, the mili-tary, and so on—since all depend on Congress for money to carry out their functions. Congress, and not the courts, determines with what specificity execu-tive agencies are to account for their expenditures. Taxpayer suits cannot be maintained to force Congress or a federal agency to comply with this clause. Thus a taxpayer was denied the right to challenge before the courts the consti-tutionality of an act of Congress that permits the Central Intelligence Agency to account for its expenditures "solely on the certificate of the Director."[124]

8. No Title of Nobility shall be granted by the United States: Section 10 im-poses the same limitation on the states.

One wonders how our lives might have been enriched if the Constitution had not prohibited the national government and the states from granting titles of nobility: Babe Ruth might have become not just the Sultan of Swat but the Duke of Swat, and Lindbergh the Earl of Flight, not to mention that Elvis Presley might have become the Prince of Memphis, and who knows who might have become the Duke of Dupont Circle or the Marquis of Irvine. But then again, it could have gone the other way. Titles might have been passed out by the national government and the states not in recognition of outstanding public service but for patronage purposes.

8. [continued]; And no Person holding any Office of Profit or Trust under them, shall, without the Consent of the Congress, accept any present, Emolument, Office, or Title, of any kind whatever, from any King, Prince, or foreign State.

Acquainted with the history of previous republican governments, and aware of the ability of foreign sovereigns to bribe and corrupt republican offi-cials, the framers took precautions to prevent any foreign state from securing undue influence within the executive agencies of the national government.

Limitations on States

1. No State shall enter into any Treaty, Alliance, or Confederation;

When the government of the United States was formed, the individual states lost their international personalities, if, in fact, they ever possessed them.

Constitutionally the states can neither negotiate with foreign states nor have any direct relations with them. The national government possesses a monopoly over the foreign affairs of the United States. States may not exercise their reserved powers in such a way as to intrude on the national government's exclusive right to deal with international affairs. For example, states traditionally regulate the distribution of estates, but these regulations must give way if they impair the effective exercise of the nation's foreign policy by conflicting with agreements between the United States and other nations.[125]

Section 10

1. [continued] grant Letters of Marque and Reprisal;

This power was given to Congress in Section 8, 11 (see page 75) and this Section makes it clear that states are not to have any authority over such matters.

Section 10

1. [continued] [No state shall] coin Money; emit Bills of Credit; make any Thing but gold and silver Coin a Tender in Payment of Debts; pass any Bill of Attainder, ex post facto Law, or Law impairing the Obligation of Contracts; or grant any title of nobility.

After the Revolution, the thirteen states, operating under the weak and ineffective Articles of Confederation, passed through a difficult period of readjustment as a result of the economic and political dislocations of the war's aftermath. Many citizens were in debt; the farmers who had speculated freely in land while prices were rising were especially burdened. Property and debtor laws were extremely harsh. Defaulting debtors were thrown into jail and deprived of all their holdings. In many states, the legislatures, responsive to the pressure of the farmers, passed laws to alleviate the lot of debtors. Paper money was made legal tender for the payment of debts, bankruptcy laws were passed, and sometimes the courts were closed to creditors. These laws, in turn, aroused the creditor classes, who, feeling that their rights had been infringed, demanded action to put a stop to such "abuses" of power by the state legislatures. Creditors, in fact, were foremost among the groups that brought the Constitutional Convention about; the prevention of such interferences with private rights by the state legislatures was one of the major purposes of the Convention. As James Madison put the matter in a speech to his fellow delegates, meddlings with private rights by the state legislatures "were evils which had, more perhaps than anything else, produced this Convention." The paragraph above was the principal result of this concern.

The framers, when they spoke of "contracts" whose obligations could not be impaired by state law, had in mind the ordinary contracts between individuals, especially contracts of debt. However, the meaning of the word was early expanded by judicial interpretation to include contracts made by the states themselves, including franchises granted to corporations. As a result, the "obligation of contracts" clause became, prior to the Civil War, the most important defense of the rights of property in the Constitution. States were prevented from passing any law, whether in the interest of the public welfare or not, that might materially disturb rights secured by contract.[126] In the late 1830s, however, the Supreme Court began to restrict the application of the obligation of contracts clause. By the 1890s,[127] it had been established that all franchises should be narrowly construed in favor of the states and that all contracts implicitly recognized the general police power of the states to regulate property (including contract rights) for the public welfare.

By the 1930s the contract clause had ceased to be a serious limitation upon state powers. It came to mean no more than that a state could impair the obligation of contracts, provided it did so to promote the general welfare and not "in a spirit of oppression" and "without reasonable justification." The clause receded into "comparative desuetude." Then after more than forty years, in 1977 and, to show that it was not a fluke, again in 1978, in the words of the dissenters, the Court "dusted off" the contract clause and declared two state laws unconstitutional. In 1977 the Court declared that New Jersey had violated the contract clause when it set aside a provision of an earlier law enacted to protect bondholders. Justice Blackmun wrote for the Court, "Whether or not the protection of contract rights comports with current views of wise public policy, the Contract Clause remains a part of our written Constitution."[128] And in the 1978 decision Justice Stevens reiterated, "The Contract Clause remains part of the Constitution. It is not a dead letter." The Court declared unconstitutional the application of a Minnesota law that imposed additional pension obligations on employers beyond those they had previously contracted about with their employees.[129]

Despite these two holdings, more recent decisions make it clear that the contract clause is not likely to once again become a major limitation on the power of the states to regulate property. A unanimous Court upheld the application of an Alabama law prohibiting oil producers from passing on to purchasers any increase in severance taxes, despite preexisting contracts stipulating that purchasers were to absorb such increases. The Court pointed out that the Alabama law, unlike those involved in the 1977 and 1978 decisions, did not "prescribe a rule limited to contractual obligations or remedies, but imposed a generally applicable rule of conduct designed to advance a broad societal interest." Alabama was attempting to shield consumers from the burdens of tax increases, and its prohibition applied to all oil and gas producers, regardless of whether they happened to be parties to contracts providing for tax increases to be passed on to purchasers.[130] The Court also ruled that Kansas could regulate natural gas prices, even if it slightly impaired the contractual rights of an energy company because the company was operating in a highly regulated industry, and the state's interest in protecting consumers is a significant and legitimate one.[131] In short, if states avoid singling out contracts, laws passed to promote the general welfare are not likely to run afoul of this clause even if they do incidentally impair the obligations of a contract.

---

2. No State shall, without the Consent of the Congress, lay any Imposts for Duties on Imports or Exports, except what may be absolutely necessary for

executing its inspection Laws: and the net Produce of all Duties and Imposts, laid by any State on Imports or Exports, shall be for the Use of the Treasury of the United States; and all such Laws shall be subject to the Revision and Control of the Congress.

Without the express consent of Congress, but subject to its revision, states may levy an inspection tax on imports and exports. (Inspection laws are concerned with quantity and quality.) Congress, not the courts, decides whether or not the inspection tax is more than "what may be absolutely necessary for execution . . . inspection laws."

The ban on duties and imposts on imports and exports used to be construed to forbid taxation of imports until removed from their original package, and on exports which had begun to move to a foreign country. The Court has now removed such rigid limitations on state taxation. The clause forbids only imposts and duties and not other kinds of taxation. And in deciding whether a financial exaction by a state is an impost or duty, the exaction should be analyzed in terms of the three policy considerations that lead to the adoption of the prohibition against imposts and duties. The clause is designed to prevent (1) state exactions that interfere with the exclusive power of the federal government to regulate foreign commercial relations; (2) state exactions by seaboard states that might disturb the harmony among the states if they are allowed to tax goods that flow through their ports; (3) and in the case of imports (Congress cannot tax exports either), state exactions that interfere with the exclusive power of the federal government to raise revenues from tariffs. Short of these limitations a state may collect nondiscriminatory taxes, as for example, a general property tax applied to imported tires, even though in their original package,[132] or a tax on the gross income from stevedoring activities for loading and unloading cargo ships.[133]

Section 10

3. No State shall, without the Consent of Congress, lay any Duty of Tonnage,

A duty of tonnage is a charge on a vessel, according to its tonnage, for entering or leaving a port or navigating in public waters.

3. [continued] keep Troops, or Ships of War in Time of Peace,

A state has the constitutional right, without the consent of Congress, to provide for and maintain a militia; it may not keep a standing army or maintain its own navy.

3. [continued] enter into any Agreement or Compact with another State,

"Read literally, the Compact Clause would require the states to obtain congressional approval before entering into any agreement themselves. . . . But it has never been so interpreted. Congressional assent is required only for agreements that enhance the political power of states in relation to the national government."[134] An agreement between New Hampshire and Maine "locating an ancient" boundary did not require congressional assent.[135] Nor was congressional approval required for the agreement among twenty-one states to establish an administrative headquarters to audit multistate taxpayers and to facilitate the collection of state taxes from such taxpayers.[136]

When congressional consent is required, Congress may give it in advance, as it has done many times, for example, when it authorized states to make civil defense compacts to be effective sixty days after such agreements have been transmitted to Congress, unless Congress disapproves by concurrent resolution. Sometimes congressional consent is granted in more general terms—as when it gave approval for two or more states to enter into agreements for the cooperative enforcement of their respective criminal laws.

Congressional approval of an interstate compact makes such compact federal law subject to construction by federal rules rather than the rules of a state.[137] Disputes over the interpretation of such compacts are disputes between states and thus are subject to the original jurisdiction of the Supreme Court.[138]

---

3. [continued] or with a foreign Power,

The framers made it very clear in every way possible that the states have no right to negotiate with foreign countries.

---

3. [continued] or engage in War, unless actually invaded, or in such imminent Danger as will not admit of delay.

States have no power whatsoever to declare war. This belongs to Congress alone. As to engaging in hostilities, any invasion of any state is an invasion of the United States. This clause reflects conditions in the eighteenth century when it was possible that a state government might have to assume some responsibility for repelling a foreign invasion until the national government became mobilized to do so.

ARTICLE II: THE EXECUTIVE ARTICLE

Section 1

1. The executive Power shall be vested in a President of the United States of America.

What is the significance of the fact that the words *herein granted* that appear in the Legislative Article are omitted in the Executive Article? Does Section 1 confer "the executive power" on the President or does it merely designate the title of the person who is given certain specified duties by the rest of the article? The more general view, and the one that conforms to presidential practices, is that this section gives the President a power that has never been defined or enumerated and, in fact, cannot be defined since its scope depends largely upon circumstances. Although not so broad, this executive power is akin to the prerogative formerly claimed by the English Crown to act for the public good "without the prescription of the law" and "sometimes even against it."[1] The President can issue proclamations of neutrality, remove executive officials from office, make executive agreements with foreign nations, and take emergency action to preserve the nation, although such powers are not specifically granted him by the Constitution.

> When the President acts pursuant to an express or implied authorization from Congress, he exercises not only his powers but also those delegated by Congress. In such a case the executive action would be supported by the strongest of presumptions and the widest latitude of judicial interpretation, and the burden of persuasion would rest heavily upon any who might attack it. . . . When the President acts in the absence of congressional authorization he may enter a zone of twilight in which he and Congress may have concurrent authority, or in which its distribution is uncertain. . . . In such a case the . . . validity of the President's action, at least so far as separation of powers principles are concerned, hinges on a consideration of all the circumstances which might shed light on the views of the Legislative Branch toward such action, including congressional inertia, indifference, or quiescence. . . . Finally, when the President acts in contravention of the will of Congress, "his power is at its lowest ebb," and the Court can sustain his actions "only by disabling the Congress from acting upon the subject."[2]

During the Korean War, President Truman ordered the Secretary of Commerce to take temporary possession of the steel mills in order to avoid a strike that would disrupt production of steel desperately needed to produce the weapons of war. No law authorized this action. The Taft-Hartley Act gave the President the authority to seek an eighty-day court injunction against strikes that jeopardized the national safety, but the President refused to do so because the union had previously agreed to postpone the strike for a much longer period.

Where did the President secure his authority to order this seizure? From his power as chief executive and commander in chief, argued the attorneys for the government. But the steel companies challenged this contention and the Supreme Court held that the President had acted unconstitutionally.[3] Although Justice Black announced the opinion of the Court, only he clearly denied that the President had any general executive powers. Five other justices joined with him to reject the President's claim to act in this particular instance, but did so because Congress had indicated by the Taft-Hartley Act that the President should not seize property to avert strikes. In the absence of this legislation, a different question would have been presented. Moreover, it is possible that if the justices had been convinced the emergency action was necessary, they would not have interfered even in the face of the Taft-Hartley Act. When it is remembered that three justices agreed with the President, and four carefully limited their concurrence to the particulars of the immediate case, the steel seizure decision does not appear to undermine the general position that the President has authority to act without prescription of law and, perhaps in desperate situations, even against the law, to preserve the national safety, subject, however, to the peril of subsequent judicial reversal, of impeachment, or of political defeat.

Since the steel seizure case, the Supreme Court has four times specifically acknowledged that the President has inherent executive authority, although in each instance it rejected the assertion that inherent presidential power applied in that particular case. In the first, a majority of the Court ruled that because of the presumption against prior restraint of publications (see page 151), the executive authority of the President did not, in that particular instance, justify a court's acceding to his request to restrain a newspaper from publishing secret documents that had fallen into its hands.[4] In the second case, a unanimous Court, one justice not participating, held that the executive authority of the President does not extend to authorizing electronic surveillance of conversations of persons suspected of engaging in domestic subversion.[5]

The third instance was the celebrated case of *United States* v. *Nixon* (1974).[6] The Supreme Court rejected President Nixon's claim that he had an inherent power growing out of the doctrine of separation of powers to have an absolute say about what information he would withhold and what he would release to a court. There is no such absolute executive privilege. The responsibility to decide what information should be released and under what conditions is a judicial and not an executive one. The President, like other persons, is subject to a subpoena of materials needed for criminal prosecutions. In this particular case the Supreme Court held that the tapes in President Nixon's possession were needed for a criminal prosecution and thus sustained the order of the trial judge to the President to release the materials to the court.

The Supreme Court also ruled, however, that the President does have a *limited executive privilege* stemming both from the doctrine of separation of powers and from powers granted him by Article II. This claim of an executive privilege is something that most Presidents have long insisted vests in their office, but this was the first time the Supreme Court had acknowledged that it existed, albeit in a limited fashion. The President does have the right to claim confidentiality of executive communications, especially if he claims that their disclosure would reveal military or diplomatic secrets. Faced with such assertions, the courts are to show "utmost deference." And even outside these areas, the President's "singularly unique role" requires that great efforts be made to ensure that his communications be kept confidential. To this end, the trial judge was instructed to look at the subpoenaed materials in camera (in secret) and to release only that information which he thought related to the trial. Other material was to be returned to the President and "restored to its privileged status." In short, the President has the right to claim executive privilege for materials under his control, subject only to the limitation that if they are needed for a criminal trial and do not reveal military or diplomatic secrets, a trial judge may have limited access to them.

Left unanswered by the Supreme Court, since the issue was not before it, is the right of the President to withhold information from the Congress. The principles of *United States* v. *Nixon* would seem to suggest that under certain circumstances—for example, when the House of Representatives or one of its committees is carrying out its responsibilities under the impeachment clause—the doctrine of executive privilege would not justify the President's refusal to submit materials in response to a congressional subpoena. When President Nixon refused to do so in connection with the House Judiciary Committee's investigation into his possible impeachment, the House chose not to take the issue to the courts; rather the President's failure to respond to the congressional subpoena became one of the grounds of impeachment charged against him by the committee.

The fourth case grew out of the negotiations by President Carter, confirmed by President Reagan, with the Iranian government that led to the release of the American hostages. The President signed an executive agreement with Iran under which the United States agreed to terminate all legal proceedings in the United States by our nationals against the Iranian government, and to transfer such claims to a specially created Iran-United States Claims Tribunal for binding arbitration. In addition, one billion dollars of the assets of Iran held by the U.S. banks were transferred to English and Algerian banks to be held to cover the settlement of claims by American nationals. The rest of the Iranian assets held by American banks were returned to Iranian control. A unanimous Court upheld the President's power to act. The Court stressed the long-standing exercise by the President of the power to enter into executive agreements to settle claims, the long-standing acquiescence by Congress in the exercise of such presidential powers, and in this specific instance the fact that Congress had taken no action to disapprove of what the President did. The Court cautiously concluded: "While it is not concluded that the President has plenary power to settle claims, even against foreign governmental entities, nevertheless where, as here, the settlement of claims has been determined to be a necessary incident to the resolution of a major foreign policy dispute between this country and another, and Congress has acquiesced to the President's action, it cannot be said that the President lacks the power to settle such claims."[7]

Section 1

1. [continued] He shall hold his Office during the Term of four Years, and together with the Vice President, chosen for the same term, be elected, as follows.

See also the Twenty-second Amendment, which limits the President's tenure, and the Twenty-fifth Amendment, which provides for replacement of the vice-president when one succeeds to the presidency.

Section 1

2. Each state shall appoint, in such Manner as the Legislature thereof may direct, a Number of Electors, equal to the whole Number of Senators and Representatives to which the State may be entitled in the Congress: but no Senator or Representative, or Person holding an Office of Trust or Profit under the United States shall be appointed an Elector.

At various times some state legislatures have directed the selection of electors by the legislature itself, by voters in districts, by voters of the entire state, and by a combination of these methods. At the present time, except for Maine which elects two of its four electors by congressional districts (see page 223), all electors in all states and in the District of Columbia are elected by voters on a statewide ticket.

In exercising this power, state legislatures are subject to all constitutional commands. In addition to the obviously applicable Fifteenth and Nineteenth Amendments, other clauses that most especially apply are the First Amendment and the equal protection clause of the Fourteenth. In addition to the clearly unconstitutional denial of the right to vote because of race or sex, a legislature cannot enforce a scheme that would give the voters in one part of a state more electoral votes than voters in another district. A state may not use procedures for nominating electors that make it too difficult for minor parties to get their presidential electoral candidates on the ballot,[8] or that impose greater demands on city folks than on country people in order to get the candidates they favor on a ballot,[9] or that set too early a deadline for filing and make it difficult for independent candidates to run for president.[10]

Section 1

3. [This paragraph has been superseded in its entirety by the Twelfth Amendment.] The Electors shall meet in their respective States, and vote by Ballot for two Persons, of whom one at least shall not be an Inhabitant of the same State with themselves. And they shall make a List of all the Persons voted for, and of the Number of Votes for each: which List they shall sign and certify, and transmit sealed to the Seat of the Government of the United States, directed to the President of the Senate. The President of the Senate shall, in the Presence of the Senate and House of Representatives, open all the Certificates, and the Votes shall then be counted. The Person having the greatest Number of Votes shall be the President, if such Number be a Majority of the whole Number of Electors appointed; and if there be more than one who have such Majority, and have an equal Number of Votes, then the House of Representatives shall immediately chuse by Ballot one of them for President; and if no Person have a Majority, then from the five highest on the List the said House shall in like Manner chuse the President. But in chusing the President, the Votes shall be taken by States, the Representation from each State having one Vote; A quorum for this Purpose shall consist of a Member or Members from two thirds of the States, and a Majority of all the States shall be necessary to a Choice. In every Case, after the Choice of the President, the Person having the greatest Number of Votes of the Electors shall be the Vice President. But if there should remain two or more who have equal Votes, the Senate shall chuse from them by Ballot the Vice President.

The framers of the Constitution had a great deal of difficulty in working out the procedures for selecting the President and the Vice-President. Selection by Congress was rejected on the theory that it would make the President dependent on Congress and would violate the doctrine of separation of powers. Election by the state legislatures was rejected because of lack of confidence in these bodies, which "had betrayed a strong propensity to a variety of pernicious measures."[11] Direct popular election was rejected because the less populous states felt that the more populous states would always elect the President, and because most of the delegates thought that the extent of the country rendered "it impossible that the people can have the requisite capacity to judge of the respective pretensions of the Candidates."[12] So, for lack of something better, the framers devised the system set forth in Section 1, paragraph 3, which they expected would work in somewhat the following fashion: The several state legislatures would prescribe procedures to select the most eminent persons in the states—electors—who would then cast their electoral ballots for the two persons they considered the most qualified to serve as President. When the votes of the electors of the various states were collected, the person with the most votes, provided they were a majority of those cast by the whole number of electors, was to be declared President; the person with the second highest vote was to be Vice-President. It was expected that almost every elector would cast one vote for a candidate from his own state, and the votes would be so dispersed that often no person would have a majority. In this case, the House of Representatives, voting by states, would make the final selection from among the five candidates receiving the highest electoral vote.

But the framers reckoned without political parties, which, by completely changing the operation of the electoral system, made the original provision for it unworkable. The failure became apparent in the election of 1800, when Jefferson and Burr tied in "the Electoral College" for first place. It was the first major breakdown of the constitutional system and the Twelfth Amendment was needed to repair the breach.

Section 1

4. The Congress may determine the Time of chusing the Electors, and the Day on which they shall give their Votes; which Day shall be the same throughout the United States.

Congress designated the first Tuesday after the first Monday in November in presidential election years as the day for the selection of electors. Since electors are now pledged to cast their ballots for the candidates of their party (see page 221), the November election in effect determines who will be the next President and Vice-President. The electors do not give their votes, however, until the first Monday after the second Wednesday in December. On that date, the electors assemble at such place as their respective state legislatures direct (normally the state capitol), give their votes, and certify six lists, which are distributed as follows: one is sent by registered mail to the President of the Senate, two are delivered to the Secretary of State of their respective states, two are sent by registered mail to the Administrator of General Services, and one is delivered to the federal district judge of the district in which the electors have assembled. No chances are taken of losing these precious documents, which usually record a foregone certainty. Then in January (see the Twentieth Amendment) the President of the Senate, in the presence of the Senate and the House of Representatives (see the Twelfth Amendment), opens the certificates and the electoral vote is "counted"; the winners are formally proclaimed "elected."

Electors constitutionally remain free to cast their ballots for any person they wish. There are examples, including recent elections (see page 221), of maverick electors ignoring the wishes of the voters who chose them, but in no case has it affected the outcome of an election. The Supreme Court has upheld the right of a state to allow a political party to require electors to take a pledge in advance that they will vote for the party candidate,[13] but it remains unsettled what could be done to enforce such a pledge.

That states "appoint" electors means in effect that states determine how electors will be selected. Congress counts the electoral votes. Most of the time this is routine, but in 1876 when Congress came to count the electoral votes it found that Rutherford B. Hayes, the Republican candidate, had 165 uncontested electoral votes, and Samuel J. Tilden, the Democrat, had 184 clear votes, one less than necessary, and there were disputes about which was the right slate of electors from Florida, South Carolina, Louisiana, and about one electoral vote in Oregon. How these disputes would be resolved would determine who would become president. The House was controlled by the Democrats, the Senate by the Republicans. The practice up to that time had been that the consent of both houses was required to validate the electoral count.

To break the deadlock, Congress by an act approved by the President created an Electoral Commission consisting of five members of the House chosen by the House, five senators chosen by the Senate, and five justices of the Supreme Court, four of whom were designated in the act, with the fifth to be chosen by these four. The Electoral Commission ended up with eight Republicans and seven Democrats and by a vote of eight to seven the Commission resolved the disputes in favor of Hayes.

As a result of this disputed election, Congress has enacted a provision that if the vote of a state is not certified by the governor, it shall not be counted unless both Houses of Congress concur.

Section 1

5. No Person except a natural born Citizen, or a Citizen of the United States, at the time of the Adoption of this Constitution, shall be eligible to the Office of President;

This clause contains the only constitutional distinction between naturalized and natural-born citizens. Whether a person born abroad of American parents is a natural-born citizen within the meaning of this section has not yet been decided. There is a considerable body of opinion that such a person would be "natural-born" even if perhaps not native-born. The issue is likely to be resolved only if a political party nominates a person born outside of the United States to American citizens and he or she is elected. The answer will come from the electorate.

Section 1

5. [continued] neither shall any Person be eligible to that Office who shall not have attained to the Age of thirty five Years, and been fourteen Years a Resident within the United States.

The Twelfth Amendment states explicitly that the same qualifications are required for eligibility to the Vice-Presidency.

Before the election of President Hoover, there was some question whether the fourteen-year-residence requirement meant any fourteen years or fourteen consecutive years immediately prior to election. Although a legal resident, Hoover had been abroad a good part of the fourteen years immediately preceding his nomination. His election settled any doubts; the interpretation of this requirement came from the most authentic source—the same source that created the Constitution—the people.

---

6. In Case of the Removal of the President from Office, or of his Death, Resignation, or Inability to discharge the Powers and Duties of the said Office, the Same shall devolve on the Vice President, and the Congress may by Law provide for the Case of Removal, Death, Resignation or Inability, both of the President and Vice President, declaring what Officer shall then act as President, and such Officer shall act accordingly, until the Disability be removed, or a President shall be elected.

This clause is supplemented by the Twenty-fifth Amendment. The Twenty-fifth Amendment confirms the precedent established by John Tyler when he succeeded to the presidency on Harrison's death. He signed all state papers, "John Tyler, President of the United States," and established that on the death or resignation of the President, the Vice-President becomes President, not merely Acting President. In the event of the President's disability, the "powers and duties" of the presidency devolve on the Vice-President; he serves only as Acting President.

If there is no Vice-President (a contingency less likely to occur with the adoption of the Twenty-fifth Amendment), by act of Congress the line of succession is the Speaker of the House, the President *pro tempore* of the Senate, the Secretary of State, and on through the list of cabinet officers in the order in which their departments were created. No one, however, may act as President unless he or she possesses the constitutional qualifications of a President; cabinet members serve only until either a Speaker or President *pro tempore* becomes qualified.

The Twenty-fifth Amendment provides procedures to determine who shall judge whether the President is unable to discharge his duties.

---

7. The President shall, at stated Times, receive for his Services, A Compensation, which shall neither be increased nor diminished during the Period of which he shall have been elected.

To preserve the President's independence, Congress is prohibited from increasing or diminishing his salary during the period for which he is elected. Of course, today Presidents are likely to have considerable income through investments they have acquired prior to moving to the White House

7. [continued] and he shall not receive within that Period any other Emolument from the United States, or any of them.

This provision was inserted to prevent the President's own state from compensating him and to ensure his independence of any state. He is totally dependent on the federal government for his salary, which is now $200,000 per year. He also receives the use of the White House, free secretarial and executive assistance, and $90,000 annually for travel and official allowances. He, however, spends much more, the funds coming from other accounts.

8. Before he enter on the Execution of his Office, he shall take the following Oath or Affirmation:—"I do solemnly swear (or affirm) that I will faithfully execute the Office of President of the United States, and will to the best of my Ability, preserve, protect and defend the Constitution of the United States."

The Chief Justice of the United States normally administers this oath or affirmation, but any judicial officer may do so. Calvin Coolidge's father, a justice of the peace, administered the oath to his son.

1. The President shall be Commander in Chief of the Army and Navy of the United States, and of the Militia of the several States, when called into the actual Service of the United States.

This is another provision to ensure civilian supremacy over the military. A civilian, the President, is commander in chief of our armed forces. (Although the Air Force is not mentioned in the Constitution, the President's status as commander in chief of that branch of the armed forces is not in question.) The President appoints all military officers with the consent of the Senate. He governs hostile territories subjugated by our armed forces until their disposition is determined by Congress or by treaty. As commander in chief, he makes the ultimate decisions on all matters of strategy.

The President's "war powers" are vastly more than purely military ones. During the Civil War, President Lincoln, as a "war measure" and without congressional authorization, in the Proclamation of Emancipation declared all slaves in areas in rebellion to be "free." Moreover, the President's powers as commander in chief are augmented by his "executive powers" and by such powers as Congress may delegate to him. Under conditions of total war, when the distinction between soldier and civilian may be blurred, the resulting "aggregate of powers" may be very great, although not unlimited. Outside the theater of war, the courts will review presidential acts.

During World War II, President Roosevelt authorized the army to create "defense zones" on the west coast; under his order, supported by an act of Congress, 112,000 persons of Japanese ancestry, (two-thirds of whom were citizens of the United States) were forced out of their homes and put into relocation camps. These measures were sustained by the Supreme Court on the general ground of military necessity.[14] But the President's order establishing martial laws in Hawaii after the attack on Pearl Harbor was held by the Court to have lacked such justification, to have been contrary to statute and, therefore, to have been illegal.[15]

Congress shares with the President authority over the armed forces: It supplies the money and makes regulations for their governance. While Congress has the power to "declare war," the President is able to give orders to the Army, Navy, and Air Force that may lead to hostilities, as well as to direct our foreign relations to that end. President Polk, by sending troops into disputed territory, deliberately precipitated the Mexican War. President Truman ordered American forces to resist communist aggression in Korea; President Johnson used military power to intervene in Santo Domingo; Presidents Eisenhower, Kennedy, and Johnson ordered American forces into Vietnam, although before the major escalation of our military effort in Vietnam, President Johnson secured from Congress a resolution to support his action. President Reagan invaded Grenada and told Congress about it afterwards. He also ordered troops into Beruit. An example of the President's power over the armed forces that had amusing rather than serious consequences occurred when President Theodore Roosevelt sent the Navy halfway around the world after Congress had threatened to withhold appropriations for a global tour. Congress was then presented with the choice of appropriating money to bring the fleet home or leaving it where it was.

Throughout our history Congress has resisted, but only recently with some success, the President's predominant role in controlling our military forces. Whenever it chooses to do so, Congress clearly has the constitutional authority to refuse to grant funds for military uses or to place conditions on how the funds it does grant may be used. As a practical political fact, however, it has been difficult for Congress to resist the President or to limit the way in which he exercises authority as commander in chief of the armed forces. But as the result of the Vietnam War, and near its end, Congress became increasingly assertive of its authority.

Beginning in 1969, Congress passed a number of resolutions aimed at reasserting its war powers. In 1970 it stipulated that no funds should be used to send ground troops into Cambodia or Laos, an unprecedented restraint on the President's discretion to send the armed forces wherever he thinks necessary. Then came the War Powers Act of 1973.

In the War Powers Act of 1973 Congress stipulated that henceforth, in every possible instance, before the President commits the armed forces of the United States he should consult in advance with Congress and that he should commit forces (1) only pursuant to a declaration of war by Congress, or (2) by specific statutory authorization, or (3) in a national emergency. After committing the armed forces under this third condition, the President is to report within forty-eight hours to Congress; and the troop commitment to be terminated within sixty days unless Congress concurs with the presidential action, with the President being allowed another thirty days if he certifies to Congress that unavoidable military necessity involving the safety of United States forces requires continued use of the troops.

By 1985 the President had used this act seven times. In the case of Lebanon, there was a considerable debate between the President and Congress about whether the Act should come into play. President Reagan insisted that the American military forces had not been committed to engage in hostile actions and therefore the War Powers Act did not apply. Congress insisted that it did. Congress adopted a resolution, and the President signed it. The resolution superseded the War Powers Act and set a time limit for the involvement of our troops in Lebanon.

In more celebrated instances—when President Ford sent Marines to free the ship *Mayaquez* which had been captured by the Cambodians, when President Carter sent a rescue mission into Iran to attempt to free our hostages, when President Reagan sent troops into Grenada to overthrow a hostile regime and to protect American citizens, and when Marines were sent into Lebanon as part of a peace-keeping mission—many felt the President had the constitutional authority to take these actions without regard to the War Powers Act. Others criticized the Presidents for failing to consult with Congress before committing the troops (the Presidents merely informed congressional leaders of their intentions).

Perhaps as significant as these new congressional limits on presidential discretion to deploy the armed forces as he thinks best are the growing political restraints. As recent history in Korea and Vietnam illustrates, a President runs a serious risk of defeat in the next election if he uses the armed forces, with or without congressional approval, as an instrument of foreign policy, and the result is a substantial number of American casualties over an extended period of time.

Section 2

1. [continued] he [the President] may require the Opinions, in writing, of the principal Officers in each of the executive Departments, upon any Subject relating to the Duties of their respective Offices.

Although there is no mention of the Cabinet in the original Constitution, that body came into existence as early as 1793; from the beginning, the President's power over the heads of the major executive departments has extended beyond merely requiring written reports upon subjects relating to the duties of their respective offices. Cabinet members serve at the President's pleasure and his control over their official acts is complete. The executive departments, and usually their duties, however, are created by law, and the money needed for their operation comes from Congress. The Cabinet has never been a prominent feature of American government and its collective advice is seldom significant. With the adoption of the Twenty-fifth Amendment, the Cabinet has been given a constitutional role of importance (in deciding whether the President is disabled), but one which we hope will not have to be used (see page 268).

Section 2

1. [continued] and he shall have Power to grant Reprieves and Pardons for Offenses against the United States, except in Cases of Impeachment.

A reprieve postpones punishment. There have not been many requests for reprieves since the federal death penalty was abolished. A full pardon restores persons to all civil rights and revises their legal status in all respects. In most instances, however, the President merely grants a more limited pardon and restores civil rights on a case-by-case basis. The President can pardon persons before they have been brought to trial, during the trial, or after conviction. (He cannot pardon people before they commit an offense, for no one can be excused from obeying the law.) The power extends only to offenses against the United States, not to those against the laws of a state.

The President's power to pardon extends to persons held in criminal (but not civil) contempt of court by a federal judge. "The power flows from the Constitution alone . . . and . . . it cannot be modified, abridged, or diminished by the Congress."[16] The President may reduce or commute sentences and impose conditions even though the conditions are not provided by statute. The President may not, however, set conditions that offend the Constitution or that make the sentence more rather than less severe.

The most celebrated presidential pardon was President Ford's pardon of former President Richard M. Nixon. Nixon had not been charged with any crime, but President Ford pardoned him for any crimes that he might have committed while President.

President Carter used the power when he first came into office to grant "full, complete and unconditional pardon" to all persons, whether or not they had been formally convicted, who had violated the draft laws during the Vietnam era, except those who had violated the draft laws through force or violence, military deserters, and employees of the Selective Service System. Americans who had left the United States to avoid the draft and had become citizens of another country were permitted to return freely and apply for their citizenship. Congress angrily reacted to this use of the presidential pardon by barring the use of certain supplemental appropriations for the administration of the amnesty program, but since expenses were minimal and other funds were available, the congressional protest was symbolic.

Most of the time presidential pardoning power is routinely exercised. Each year about 400 people petition the President for executive clemency, asking for a reduced prison term or a pardon. Those requested are processed by a pardon attorney according to guidelines established by the President. President Reagan adopted more stringent guidelines, for example, extending the time period in which persons convicted of nonviolent federal crimes could apply for a pardon from three to five years after their sentence ended, and for those convicted of more serious crimes from five to seven years. "Executive clemency is a very personal thing. Each President handles it differently."[17]

Section 2

2. He shall have Power, by and with the Advice and Consent of the Senate, to make Treaties, provided two-thirds of the Senators present concur;

The Senate as a body has provided the President with very little formal advice beyond votes approving or disapproving of treaties. The President nevertheless seeks advice from senatorial leaders from time to time, especially members of the Senate Committee on Foreign Relations. In general, the President negotiates a treaty and then presents it to the Senate for approval. The final step in the making of a treaty is its ratification, which is the President's act.

There are several explanations for the two-thirds vote requirement. The southern states were afraid the northern states—which were in a majority—would negotiate treaties disadvantageous to them. They remembered that John Jay of New York, Secretary of Foreign Affairs under the Confederation, had proposed a treaty with Spain conceding the right to close the mouth of the Mississippi at New Orleans in return for concessions to northern merchants. The two-thirds rule gives sectional groups the power to veto such treaties. In addition to being international compacts, treaties are "supreme law of the land," so that their self-executing provisions are enforced by courts like any other law (see page 131); this fact, too, is sometimes urged in favor of the two-thirds requirement.

Now that the United States is continuously involved in international negotiations, the process of treaty making has achieved considerable significance. At the same time, the two-thirds rule makes it possible for a few senators representing perhaps a minority of the electorate to block treaties desired by the majority, and many have suggested that ratification be by a simple majority of *both* houses of Congress. There are, however, some senators who think that the treaty-making procedures should be made more difficult. Adherents to this view have proposed that, in addition to the two-thirds requirement, the approval of both houses be required before a treaty shall operate as law. In point of fact, since the House of Representatives must approve any appropriations or any legislation necessary to carry out the terms of the treaty, it already enjoys considerable power in this area.

Securing a two-thirds vote of the Senate for treaty ratification has imposed obstacles to the adoption of programs, and it is not surprising that various ways have been devised to get around these obstacles. One is the joint resolution of Congress—an ordinary legislative procedure. Texas was annexed in this fashion after the Senate refused to do so by treaty. Another device is the executive agreement, of which there are two types: (1) Inasmuch as Congress and the President have cognate powers in the field of foreign affairs, it is constitutionally permissible for Congress to delegate to the President larger powers than would be allowable in domestic affairs. Thus, the President is often empowered by Congress to make executive agreements—for example, reciprocal tariff agreements. (2) As part of his undefined executive powers, growing out of his authority to appoint and receive diplomatic officials, and as the nation's official spokesman, the President has the power to negotiate agreements with foreign nations that do not require the consent of Congress. As long as these agreements are not countermanded by Congress they, like treaties, become "law of the land." It was once thought that executive agreements differed from treaties in that they were concerned with affairs of less importance; in fact, executive agreements have sometimes dealt with highly important matters. For example, in September 1940, President Roosevelt handed over to Great Britain fifty naval vessels in exchange for certain leases of military bases. The Atlantic Charter in 1941, the Yalta Agreement of 1944, and the Potsdam Agreement of 1945 are other examples of executive agreements. In 1970 President Nixon signed an "Agreement of Friendship and Cooperation" with Spain that constitutes a significant security guarantee. And in most years there are about five times more executive agreements implemented than formal treaties ratified.

As part of its reassertion of congressional authority in the field of foreign affairs, Congress in the Case of 1972 required the Secretary of State to notify Congress within sixty days of any executive agreement. If the agreement has national security considerations, notification may be done on a classified basis, with only members of the House and Senate Foreign Affairs Committees being told of the agreement.

Since the adoption of the Case Act, there has been considerable conflict between the President and the Department of State on one side and congressional leaders on the other over the definition of what constitutes an executive agreement. The President and the Department of State define executive agreements as those reached with another nation under the President's constitutional powers to conduct foreign relations or as commander in chief, or under authority granted to him by Congress. Administration spokespersons maintain that a mere exchange of understandings between the President and the head of another nation are not covered by the Case Act, not even the European Declaration signed in Helsinki in 1975, in which the heads of many nations indicated their agreement not to interfere with the existing boundaries in Europe. Not only do some congressional leaders take issue with this narrow definition of what constitutes an executive agreement, but they are pressing for legislation that would require the President to submit executive agreements for congressional review and possible veto.

Who has the power to abrogate treaties? The Constitution is silent. After President Carter terminated a mutual defense treaty with Taiwan as part of the agreements that led to recognition of the Peking government, Senator Goldwater and several other senators filed a suit asking a federal judge to set aside the presidential action. They charged that the President could not abrogate a defense treaty without the consent of the Senate or Congress. The Supreme Court dismissed the case: Four justices balked on the grounds that the issues were political—a dispute between Congress and the President in which courts should not intervene; the fifth, Justice Powell, balked on the grounds that the issue was not ready for judicial disposition since neither the Senate nor the House had chosen to confront the President on the matter; Justice Marshall, although giving no reason, also voted in favor of staying out of the matter. Justices Blackmun and White would have taken the case and heard the arguments. Only Justice Brennan went to the merits, and he was of the view that abrogation of the defense treaty with Taiwan was a necessary incident to executive recognition of the Peking government and was part of the presidential power to recognize and withdraw recognition from foreign governments.[18]

Section 2

2. [continued] and he [the President] shall nominate, and by and with the Advice and Consent of the Senate, shall appoint Ambassadors, other public Ministers and Consuls, Judges of the Supreme Court, and all other Officers of the United States, whose Appointments are not herein otherwise provided for, and which shall be established by Law; but the Congress may by Law vest the Appointment of such inferior Officers, as they think proper, in the President alone, in the Courts of Law, or in the Heads of Departments.

Officers who are appointed by the President, by and with the advice and consent of the Senate (only a majority vote is required), are known as "superior," or senatorial, officers. Officers who can, if Congress permits, be appointed by the President alone, by the courts, or by heads of departments are known as "inferior" officers.

Congress violated the appointments clause and the principle of separation of powers when it provided in the 1974 amendments to the Federal Election Campaign Act of 1971 for the appointment of two members by the President, two by the Senate, and two by the House, with confirmation of all six members by both the House and the Senate. It would have been different if the commission had been merely an advisory body such as the Civil Rights Commission, some of whose members are selected by the Speaker, some by the President *pro tempore* of the Senate, and some by the President. But the only way "officers of the United States" exercising significant authority to administer government programs and enforce the law may be appointed is in the manner prescribed by the appointments clause.

The 1974 procedures for the selection of members of the Federal Election Commission also violated the Constitution because they called for the confirmation of the officers by the House and the Senate. The Constitution permits confirmation only by the Senate, not by the Senate and the House.[19]

Congress perhaps violated the appointments clause in the Bankruptcy Amendments and Federal Judgeship Act of 1984 when it provided that bankruptcy judges in office on the date of enactment, July 10, 1984, would continue to serve until October 1, 1986, or four years from the date of their last appointment or reappointment, whichever was later. Thereafter, the courts of appeals are authorized to appoint successors for full fourteen-year terms. This provision raises several constitutional issues, including whether there were any bankruptcy judges in office on July 10, 1984, since the legislation under which they had been operating had terminated on June 27, 1984—the most obvious issue concerns Congress having no power to appoint federal officers, and by this act it, in effect, appointed 242. At the time President Reagan signed the new law, he expressed his constitutional concerns, and has urged Congress to take remedial action.

The Senate has normally refused to accept federal appointments over the objection of the senator from the state in which the office is located, provided the senator is of the same party as the President. This practice, known as "senatorial courtesy," permits a senator to veto presidential appointments and gives each senator extensive control over federal patronage in his or her state. Because of this custom, senators from the state in which the appointment is to be made are usually consulted by the President before he sends the appointments to the Senate for confirmation.

Section 2

3. The President shall have Power to fill up all Vacancies that may happen during the Recess of the Senate, by granting Commissions which shall expire at the End of their next Session.

The word "happen" here has come to mean "happen to exist." The clause allows the President to fill temporarily *any* vacancies while the Senate is recessed, no matter how or when they occurred.

This clause provides an interesting example of the fact that after two hundred years, there are still questions about the meaning of what would appear to be uncomplicated constitutional language. From 1789 to 1984, 307 federal judges were appointed by Presidents under this clause, and no one questioned the validity of such appointments. Then in 1983 the Court of Appeals for the Ninth Circuit, in a decision that will most likely be reviewed by the Supreme Court, sent a case back for retrial because it had been heard by a judge, Walter Heen, serving under a recess appointment made by President Carter. The appellate judges wrote: "A judge awaiting confirmation by political figures will scarcely be oblivious to the effect his decision may have on the vote of these officials."[20] Judge Heen had first been nominated by President Carter on February 26, 1980, but the Senate recessed without having confirmed him and sixteen other Carter nominees. Then on December 31, 1980, while the Senate was still in recess and after he had lost the election, President Carter gave Mr. Heen a recess appointment. He sat for 50 weeks after that before his nomination was withdrawn by President Reagan. The appellate court's action draws into question all the decisions he made during the time he sat under the recess appointment. The Supreme Court will now have to decide if this clause permits a President to make a recess appointment of a person the Senate has failed to confirm, a different question than a recess appointment of a person whom the Senate has rejected.

Section 3

He shall from time to time give to the Congress information of the State of the Union, and recommend to their Consideration such Measures as he shall judge necessary and expedient.

The opening address of the President at each annual session of Congress is known as the State of the Union Message. George Washington and John Adams gave their addresses in person, but Jefferson sent his in writing. President Wilson revived the practice of personally delivering the speech.

At the beginning of each session, the President is now also required by law to send to Congress a budget message and an economic report. From time to time he sends messages, addresses Congress on specific subjects, and makes recommendations for legislation. In this manner he is able to focus national attention on national problems. As an extension of this practice, the executive branch develops many legislative proposals which are then formally introduced by members of Congress.

Section 3

[continued] he may, on extraordinary Occasions, convene both Houses, or either of them

---

Whenever the President thinks it necessary, he can call special sessions of Congress. Once in session, Congress has full powers. In contrast, more than half of the state legislatures, when called into special session, are limited to discussion and action on the particular matters laid before them by the governor.

The Senate has been called into special session by itself, while the House has never been. The reason for the difference is that the Senate has been summoned to ratify treaties and appointments, which it does without the concurrence of the House.

[continued] and in Case of Disagreement between them, with Respect to the Time of Adjournment, he may adjourn them to such Time as he shall think proper;

The President has never been called upon to exercise this duty.

[continued] he shall receive Ambassadors and other public Ministers;

The President is the only officer who can speak officially for the United States to foreign governments. Equally, foreign governments may speak to the United States only through the President, usually via his agent, the Secretary of State. The President's power to receive ambassadors includes the power to recognize new states or governments.

The nature of the problems of foreign policy requires that the initiative and general direction be in the President's hands. The increasing importance of foreign relations during the last several decades accounts in no small part for the increasing power of the President in all fields.

[continued] he shall take Care that the Laws be faithfully executed,

---

The President's duty to see that the laws are enforced is supported by his powers as commander in chief. As already pointed out, Congress very early authorized the President to use the armed forces when necessary to overcome combinations too powerful to be dealt with by judges, federal marshalls, and the regular federal police forces.

The President is constitutionally obliged by this clause to enforce all the laws of the United States, whether or not he approves or disapproves of them, including all federal court decisions and regulations of federal agencies, as they apply to all the people all the time. But there are so many laws and regulations that the President, of course, has great discretion in deciding which particular laws and regulations will receive the priority attention of his administration. The Reagan Administration, for example, has given less attention to and has been less vigorous in its enforcement of the many laws and regulations relating to the civil rights of minorities, women, and the disabled than was the Carter Administration, but has given more attention to the laws and regulations relating to the civil rights of children and fetuses.

[continued], and shall Commission all the Officers of the United States.

This clause, and the one above, plus the undefined executive power clause, give the President unrestricted power to remove all *executive* officers. He is charged with the duty of faithfully executing the laws and therefore must have control over those through whom he operates. This unlimitable removal power, however, does not extend to officers who have quasi-legislative or quasi-judicial functions conferred upon them by act of Congress, such as members of the Federal Trade Commission, the Interstate Commerce Commission, or the Federal Communications Commission. The President has no authority to remove these officers except as given to him by Congress.[21]

The President, Vice President and all civil Officers of the United States, shall be removed from Office on Impeachment for, and Conviction of, Treason, Bribery, or other High Crimes and Misdemeanors.

The first person to be impeached was Senator Blount from Tennessee in 1797, but the Senate dismissed the proceedings against him after deciding that congress members are not civil officers of the United States subject to impeachment. The Senate did, however, expel Senator Blount.

What are impeachable offenses? Throughout our history there have been three constructions:

1. A *loose construction* that incompetent or politically objectionable officers, especially if they be judicial officers, are liable to impeachment and removal from office. This view appears to have been the position of Thomas Jefferson. If it had been adopted by Congress it could have made our governmental system similar to the British system, where government officials are often turned out of office because of lack of confidence in them without any suggestion of wrongdoing on their part.

2. A *strict construction* that the only impeachable offenses are those that break criminal laws. This position was the view of President Nixon and the lawyers who defended him. It appears to have been the view of many of those who voted not to sustain the impeachment charges against Justice Chase and President Andrew Johnson.

3. The prevailing *moderate construction* that impeachable offenses need not be criminal in character but must reflect a serious dereliction of duty, a substantial violation of constitutional and legal responsibilities, and a sustained failure to meet one's obligations. This construction was the view of those on the House Judiciary Committee who voted to impeach President Nixon. It was also the view of those who voted to impeach and then convict Judge Robert W. Archbald (1912–1913) and Judge Halsted L. Ritter (1933–1936), each of whom was convicted on charges of misconduct in office and judicial improprieties, although in neither instance were the offenses criminal in nature.

May a person be impeached and removed from office for misconduct performed before assuming office? We have no precedents. Vice-President Agnew's resignation after pleading no contest to certain offenses, some of which took place while he was governor of Maryland, made it unnecessary for Congress to face that issue.

The interpretation of the impeachment provisions are primarily the responsibility of the House and Senate. Fortunately, only a few precedents are available to give us guidance as to their meaning.

ARTICLE III: THE JUDICIAL ARTICLE

Section 1

The judicial Power of the United States shall be vested in one Supreme Court, and in such inferior Courts as the Congress may from time to time ordain and establish.

The Supreme Court is the only federal court required by the Constitution. The Founding Fathers were purposely vague about the nature of the federal court system because they were unable to agree on the need for inferior (the term refers to the jurisdiction of these courts, not their quality) federal courts. Some thought that since the supremacy clause (see page 130) imposes on state courts a responsibility whenever appropriate to apply the Constitution and federal laws there would be no need for lower federal courts. But the First Congress created such courts and they have always been part of our federal court system.

Under present legislation, there are ninety-four district courts, including territorial courts; twelve courts of appeals with general jurisdiction; one court of appeals with special jurisdiction to hear appeals from all federal courts relating to patents, as well as to review decisions of the Patent Office and of the Court of International Trade; a Court of Claims; a Court of International Trade; a Foreign Intelligence Surveillance Court, consisting of seven district judges who serve part time reviewing applications for electronic surveillance by the government of foreign agents; and a Temporary Emergency Court of Appeals, consisting of eight district and circuit judges, designated by the Chief Justice, who sit in panels of three to hear appeals from the district courts in cases arising under economic stabilization laws. All these courts are inferior to the Supreme Court; all exercise the judicial power of the United States.

In recent years there has been continuing discussion about the possibility of creating some kind of national court of appeals to take from the Supreme Court some of its work. Despite the endorsement by several blue ribbon commissions, the Chief Justice, and some members of the Court, there has been no consensus about what kind of jurisdiction should be given to such a national court of appeals, and Congress has not yet acted.[1]

In addition to those courts created under Article III to exercise the judicial power of the United States, Congress has created other courts under its Article I authority to establish whatever is necessary and proper in order to carry into execution powers granted to the national government. These include district courts in Puerto Rico and the territories (Guam, Northern Mariannas, Virgin Islands), courts for the District of Columbia (in addition to the regular federal courts there), the Court of Military Appeals, the U.S. Claims Court, and the Tax Court. Judges of these so-called legislative or Article I courts may be given nonjudicial duties and may be selected by other procedures and serve for other terms than those prescribed by the Constitution for judges of Article III courts which exercise the judicial power of the United States.

Occasionally it is difficult to know whether a court has been created to exercise the judicial power of the United States under Article III or the legislative power of Congress under Article I. In practice, Congress indicates whether it considers a court to be an Article I or Article III court by specifying whether the judges are to have lifetime or term appointments, although there is nothing to prevent Congress from giving Article I judges lifetime tenure if it wishes, and as it has done in the past. Article I courts can be given nonjudicial duties which would be inappropriate to vest in an Article III court.

The distinction between the conditions making it appropriate for Congress to create an Article I Court and making it inappropriate "has been characterized as one of the most confusing and controversial areas of constitutional laws."[2] In 1982 the Supreme Court declared unconstitutional the system of bankruptcy courts established in 1978 by the Bankruptcy Reform Act of 1978 (BRA). That act created bankruptcy courts, whose judges were appointed for fourteen-year terms, removable for nonimpeachable offenses and unlike Article III judges not given constitutional guarantees that their salaries would not be reduced. These courts were given jurisdiction over all civil proceedings relating to bankruptcy matters, with appeals to be taken from their decisions to the court of appeals. Justice Brennan, speaking for a plurality, ruled that Article III allows legislative courts to be used in only three situations: (1) to establish territorial courts; (2) to establish courts-martial for the military; and (3) to enforce public rights—matters that arise between the government and one of its citizens. The plurality argued that only Article III courts could decide disputes between two individuals. Justice White in dissent contended the plurality's holdings called into question the establishment by Congress of a whole series of administrative tribunals.[3]

For two years Congress debated how to respond to the Court's decision. The House of Representatives wanted to make bankruptcy courts Article III courts, but the Senate opposed this as did the Chief Justice and the Judicial Conference, the policy-making body for the federal judiciary. In the meantime, the Judicial Conference adopted rules dividing jurisdiction between bankruptcy judges and the district courts.

In 1984 Congress finally acted; not, however, as we have noted, without creating additional confusion (see page 102). The new law gives district courts original jurisdiction over bankruptcy matters. It creates bankruptcy judges with fourteen-year terms, eventually to be appointed by the courts of appeals to serve as adjuncts to the district courts and to whom district judges may refer matters arising under the federal bankruptcy laws. The decisions of bankruptcy judges may be appealed to the district judge or to a special appellate panel of bankruptcy judges established by the judicial councils of each federal court of appeals.

As part of the transition, Congress declared that the bankruptcy judges operating under the prior law should continue in office for a period that could last up to four years. The act also "expresses the sense of Congress" that when the courts of appeals appoint persons to full fourteen-year terms they should appoint those who are serving as bankruptcy judges at the time of the enactment. As we have noted, these transitional provisions will either be amended by Congress, perhaps to authorize the courts of appeals to make emergency appointments of bankruptcy judges, or there is likely to be extensive litigation challenging the authority of the judges operating during the transitional period.

The Constitution merely prescribes the boundaries to the judicial power of the United States. Except for the original jurisdiction of the Supreme Court, no federal court has any power to hear any case unless Congress has conferred it. Whether this means that Congress can take away from federal courts jurisdiction to hear particular kinds of cases is presently a hotly debated issue (see page 111).

Judicial power, the only kind of power that constitutional, that is Article III, courts may exercise, is the power to pronounce a judgment and carry it into effect between parties who are engaged in a real and substantial controversy over a legal question.

Unlike the International Court of Justice and some state courts, federal courts have no authority to give advisory opinions. Nevertheless, as a result of legislation defining their jurisdiction, they may render "declaratory judgment," on the respective legal rights of parties before adverse governmental action has been taken against anyone in order to free one or both parties from uncertainty regarding their rights, say, under an ambiguous contract; such judgments are binding on both parties.

Section 1

[continued] The Judges, both of the supreme and inferior Courts, shall hold their Offices during good Behavior,

---

The Constitution provides for the appointment of judges by the President with the consent of the Senate, but it is silent about the size of the courts and the qualification of the judges. Today there are nine members of the Supreme Court; at various times the number has been six, seven, and ten. The number of judges serving on a district court or a court of appeals varies with the number and nature of the cases to be handled. Usually one judge hears a case in a district court, and three circuit judges hear cases in a court of appeals.

Although the Constitution here refers to members of both the Supreme Court and the inferior federal courts as judges, in Article I, Section 3, paragraph 6, it refers to the "Chief Justice." Since the Judiciary Act of 1789, members of the Supreme Court have always been referred to as "Justice," and until November of 1980, more formally as "Mr. Justice." In November 1980, anticipating the arrival of the first woman justice, the "Mr. Justice" was dropped. The Chief Justice is properly designated as the Chief Justice of the United States, not of the Supreme Court; but he is called informally by what we used to refer to as his "Brethren" and is known to fellow justices as "the Chief."

The phrase "during good behavior," which means virtually for life, has been interpreted by some to mean that Congress has the constitutional power to create procedures to terminate judges for "bad behavior," even if the behavior in question falls short of impeachable offenses. Congress has refused to go that far. However, in 1980, following the example of the states, Congress authorized the judicial council of each circuit—which consists of most of the circuit judges and some of the district judges of the circuit—to investigate complaints that judges within the circuit are unable to discharge their duties because of physical or mental disabilities and to look into charges that judges have engaged in conduct inconsistent with their judicial role. If the judicial council finds that a complaint is justified, it may request judges to retire, or censure or reprimand them, or order that no cases be assigned to them, or take "other appropriate actions" short of removal. Appeals from the decision of a council may be taken to the Judicial Conference, which consists of the Chief Justice, the chief judges of the twelve courts of appeals, as well as a number of district judges elected by their peers. This new disciplinary machinery is as yet untried, although in the past judicial councils have disciplined judges.[4]

It is also argued that the good behavior language means that impeachable offenses for federal judges differ in character from those for other officers, such as the President, who is elected for a fixed term. In other words, in addition to "Treason, Bribery, or other High Crimes and Misdemeanors," for which the President, Vice-President, and other civil officers may be impeached, it is argued that federal judges may be impeached on the charges of "lack of good behavior," such as "willful misconduct in office, willful and persistent failure to perform duties of the office, habitual intemperance, or other conduct prejudicial to the administration of justice that brings the judicial office into disrepute."[5] Whatever the merits of this contention, the fact is the House has been more inclined to vote (nine times) and the Senate to sustain (four times, one resigned) impeachment charges against federal judges than against other civil officers, and some of those impeached were charged with misbehavior that fell short of treason, bribery, or other crimes and misdemeanors.

Federal district judges have authority to appoint federal magistrates. Those appointed to full-time positions have eight-year terms; those serving only part-time, in less populated areas, serve four-year terms. Full-time magistrates have authority over a wider range of matters. Among magistrates' duties are disposition of initial motions, including making recommendations to the district judge whether or not evidence should be suppressed (see Fourth Amendment). The magistrate's authority to take these initial actions, subject to final approval by the district judge, has been upheld against claims that it violates the Article III requirement for the appointment and tenure of judges, and the Fifth Amendment requirement that persons have their cases heard from the beginning to end by judges appointed by the procedures and for the terms set forth in Article III.[6] In 1980 magistrates were given additional jurisdiction to preside over civil trials with the consent of both parties, and over nonjury trials for petty offenses with the consent of the defendant.

As we have noted (see page 107), bankruptcy judges, appointed by the courts of appeals for fourteen-year terms, also operate under the supervision of district judges and dispose of matters rising under federal bankruptcy laws.

[continued] and shall, at stated Times, receive for their services, a Compensation, which shall not be diminished during their Continuance in Office

In order to ensure judicial independence, Congress is prohibited from decreasing judicial salaries during the term of any particular judge, although unlike the President's salary, judicial salaries may be increased. The Supreme Court formerly held that income taxes could not be levied against the salaries of federal judges, but this decision was reversed in 1939.[7]

Recently the Supreme Court had occasion to review the compensation clause again. Congress has established a complex scheme calling for adjustments in the salaries of federal employees, including federal judges, to keep up with the cost of living. However, almost every year Congress either sets aside the proposed adjustments or modifies the formulas as applied to members of Congress, cabinet officers, federal judges, and top-level civil servants. A group of district judges sued, claiming that by such actions Congress violated the compensation clause. The Supreme Court said the issue is "when, if ever, does the Compensation Clause prohibit the Congress from repealing salary increases that otherwise take effect automatically pursuant to a formula previously enacted? . . . Is the protection of the Clause first invoked when the formula is enacted or when increases take effect?" The answer is, When they take effect. Thus in the two years when Congress had repealed the proposed raises prior to the effective date, the judges were not entitled to the increases. But in the two years when Congress had not gotten around to repealing or postponing the previously authorized increases until after the date the raises were due to go into effect, as far as the salaries of federal judges were concerned, Congress could not "diminish them," even though in one of the years the President signed the repealing statute on October 1, the very day the salary increases became effective.[8]

2. The judicial Power shall extend to all Cases, in Law and Equity, arising under this Constitution, the Laws of the United States, and Treaties made, or which shall be made, under their Authority;—

This clause and those that immediately follow outline the scope of federal judicial power. The distinction between cases in law and cases in equity is inherited from England. In the former, the party bringing the case usually asks for damages, in the latter, he or she usually asks for an injunction. The common law compensates for injury already done, while equity prevents the injury from occurring. Nowadays the same judges can hear both types of cases and can hear both types of matters in a single case.

Except for the original jurisdiction of the Supreme Court, (see page 114), no federal court has jurisdiction over any case unless Congress exercises its power under this clause. Federal courts, however, have generously interpreted

Congress's authority to confer jurisdiction on them: It extends to giving federal courts the power to construe "every law that the Legislature may constitutionally make."[9] For example, Congress by reason of its authority over foreign commerce and foreign relations may even give federal courts jurisdiction to hear civil suits brought by a foreign plaintiff against a foreign state.[10]

What Congress gives to federal courts under this clause, may it take away? Could Congress, if it wishes, deprive federal judges of the authority to hear certain kinds of cases? Could Congress go so far as to strip federal courts of all jurisdiction to hear all cases? Periodically, members of Congress, disgruntled with how federal judges, especially those on the Supreme Court, have decided a matter, have introduced bills that, if adopted, would take certain kinds of cases from the federal courts. Most recently bills have been introduced either to take from all federal courts their jurisdiction to deal with cases relating to abortion, school prayer, and school busing, or to eliminate the appellate jurisdiction of the Supreme Court over such matters. Adoption of these bills would raise difficult constitutional issues (see page 115) and profoundly affect the nature of our constitutional system.

It is the judges themselves, ultimately those on the Supreme Court, who interpret jurisdictional statutes. In 1980, for example, the Supreme Court substantially expanded the jurisdiction of federal courts by construing the Civil Rights Act of 1871 to permit persons to bring suits in federal courts against state and local officials for violating any rights secured to them by any federal laws—not just those relating to civil rights.[11]

A case may start out in state courts, but if a federal question is involved it may be taken to the Supreme Court from the highest state court to which an appeal can be made. For example, if *X* is tried and convicted of murder under state law in a state court, and he has exhausted his state appeals, he could then ask the United States Supreme Court to pass on his contention that his trial was not a fair one under the due process clause of the Fourteenth Amendment.

Section 2

1. [continued] to all Cases affecting Ambassadors, other public Ministers and Consuls;—

Since the national government is responsible for good relations between the United States and foreign governments, it was reasoned that cases affecting *foreign* public ministers should be within the judicial power of the United States. For the federal courts to assume jurisdiction, these officials must be materially affected by the case without necessarily being parties to it.

Section 2

1. [continued] to all Cases of admiralty and maritime Jurisdiction:—

This jurisdiction is concerned with ships and shipping. Under the English rule, it extended only to the high seas and those rivers in which the tide ebbed and flowed. Under the Constitution, however, such jurisdiction reaches all "navigable waters of the United States, whether or not subject to the ebb and flow of the tide," and "to all causes of damage or injury, to person or property, caused by a vessel on navigable water, notwithstanding that such damage or injury be done or consummated on land."[12] A collision between two boats, whether small pleasure craft or large commercial ones on the navigable waters of the United States, including in a very small river inside a state, is within the admiralty jurisdiction of the United States.[13]

This grant of jurisdiction to federal courts is exclusive. States may not extend their laws, such as workers' compensation, to those areas covered by maritime law. The Supreme Court has twice rejected congressional efforts to permit states to apply such laws to shipboard injuries. The rough dividing line between the state and maritime regimes is the gangplank, with some confusion and legal difficulties still being presented as to which law applies on the seaward side of the pier.[14]

Airplanes are not ships for purposes of admiralty jurisdiction. Congress can exercise its power to regulate foreign and interstate commerce to provide rules for airplane crashes and bring them under federal jurisdiction, as it has done by providing for wrongful death and tort suits caused by airplane accidents on the high seas. But in the absence of such federal regulation, it makes no difference whether an airplane crash takes place over a navigable waterway or in one. Within the United States the law of the state where the accident takes place prevails.[15]

Section 2

1. [continued] to Controversies to which the United States shall be a Party;— to Controversies between two or more States;—*between a State and Citizens of another State* [emphasis added];—

The Eleventh Amendment modified the emphasized portion of the section.

Section 2

1. [continued] between Citizens of different States;—

Article III authorizes Congress to extend federal jurisdiction to any case involving conflicts between citizens of different states. Corporations are considered citizens of the state of their incorporation. Congress has legislated that diversity cases—those found on conflicts between citizens of different states—involving amounts of less than $10,000 shall not be entertained by federal courts. Thus if the only ground for federal jurisdiction is that the case is between citizens of different states and the amount in controversy is less than $10,000, the case is not to be heard in a federal court; it would have to be resolved in a state court, most probably a court in a state in which the incident took place, or that has jurisdiction over the person being sued or over the "thing" being sued about.

1. [continued] between Citizens of the same State claiming Lands under Grants of different States, and

At the time of the adoption of the Constitution, many states had conflicting claims to western lands. Today this clause is unimportant.

1. [continued] between a State, or the Citizens thereof, and foreign States, Citizens or Subjects.

This clause also was modified by the Eleventh Amendment.

In summary, the judicial power of the United States extends to the following cases in law and equity:

1. To those cases because of the *nature of the dispute:*
   a. Cases arising under the Constitution, under a federal law, or under a federal treaty.
   b. Cases arising under admiralty and maritime jurisdiction.
   c. Cases involving title to land that is claimed because of grants of two or more states.
2. To those cases because of the *parties to the dispute:*
   a. Cases in which the United States is a party.
   b. Cases in which a state is a party.
   c. Cases in which the parties are citizens of different states.
   d. Cases that affect foreign ambassadors, ministers, and consuls.

The mere fact that the Constitution grants power to the federal courts over certain types of cases does not, of itself, exclude state courts from exercising concurrent jurisdiction. But Congress is free to make the federal jurisdiction exclusive and has done so, for example, in the following cases: crimes against the United States; suits for penalties and forfeiture authorized by the laws of the United States; civil cases of admiralty and maritime jurisdiction; prize cases (cases arising out of the capture of enemy or abandoned property on the high seas); cases involving patent and copyright laws of the United States; cases arising under bankruptcy laws of the United States; cases to which a state is party (except between a state and its citizens or a state and citizens of another state or foreign country); and cases involving foreign ambassadors and other public ministers.

Within any state, there are two court systems—the state court system and the federal court system—neither of which is superior or inferior to the other. Over some matters both systems have jurisdiction, over others only the state courts, and over still others only the federal courts have jurisdiction. A dispute between two citizens of New York over the terms of a contract signed in New York would be within the exclusive jurisdiction of the New York courts. A suit involving more than $10,000 between citizens of different states would be within the jurisdiction of either the federal courts or the courts of the state in which the defendant is located. A suit arising under the Sherman Antitrust Act would be within the exclusive jurisdiction of the federal courts.

---

2. In all Cases affecting Ambassadors, other public Ministers and Consuls, and those in which a State shall be Party, the supreme Court shall have original Jurisdiction.

"The original jurisdiction of the Supreme Court is conferred by the Constitution, is self-executing and needs no legislative implementation."[16] However, the original jurisdiction of the Supreme Court is not constitutionally exclusive. Congress can give concurrent jurisdiction to other courts as it has done except for suits between states. Suits between a state and the United States, and between a state and a political subdivision of another state or a corporation or a private citizen, are within the Supreme Court's original, but not its exclusive, jurisdiction. The Supreme Court ordinarily refers such suits to lower federal courts for first hearing.

The Supreme Court is reluctant to take cases involving its original jurisdiction since as an appellate tribunal it is "ill-equipped for the task of fact finding."[17] It will not accept original jurisdiction where a "state is only nominally a party and in reality is standing in to vindicate grievances of individuals."[18] But like so many judicial generalizations, there is a contrary one. Although a state may not invoke the original jurisdiction of the Supreme Court to forward the claims of individual citizens, it may act as a representative of its citizens where the injury alleged affects the general population of a state in a substantial way. Thus the Supreme Court ruled that Maryland and a number of other states could challenge a Louisiana tax on natural gas taken from the continental shelf and brought into the state for processing prior to being shipped out of state. The tax fell not on just a few of the other states' citizens, but upon a great many of them. In addition, the states as purchasers of natural gas for governmental purposes had a substantial interest in the matter.[19]

The Supreme Court's role in resolving disputes between states is limited to judicial power—to deciding a legal dispute—and it will not allow itself to become an arbitrator between conflicting states about nonlegal matters.[20] For that purpose, the states must resort to an interstate compact to resolve their differences or go to Congress to seek a settlement.

---

2. [continued] In all the other Cases before mentioned, the Supreme Court shall have appellate Jurisdiction, both as to Law and Fact, with such Exceptions, and under such Regulations as the Congress shall make.

Appellate jurisdiction is the power to hear and decide appeals from decisions of lower courts. In all cases, except those mentioned above, the Supreme

Court has only appellate jurisdiction and, furthermore, only such appellate jurisdiction as is specifically granted it by Congress. The completeness of congressional control of the Supreme Court's appellate jurisdiction is illustrated by the 1869 decision in *Ex parte McCardle,* a case now being cited by those members of Congress proposing to restrict the Supreme Court's appellate jurisdiction as well as the original jurisdiction of the lower federal courts (see page 111).[21] In 1868, the Supreme Court announced that it would hear the appeal of a certain newspaper editor who had challenged the constitutionality of one of the Reconstruction acts. After the Court had already heard arguments on the merits of the case and was still considering the decision, Congress, anticipating that the Supreme Court might declare the act unconstitutional, repealed the habeas corpus provision that had allowed the issue to be appealed to the Supreme Court. The Court thereupon held that it had no power to decide the case. Some scholars have pointed out that McCardle had another route to the Supreme Court. They argue that all the McCardle case stands for is the principle that Congress may abolish the habeas corpus way to the Supreme Court, but not that it may cut off all appeals to the Court on constitutional matters.

Despite the great and increasing volume of federal litigation, the Supreme Court has been able, more or less, to keep up with its work because Congress has given it the authority to select for review only the most important cases within its appellate jurisdiction. There are certain types of cases, however, that the Supreme Court is under statutory obligation to review when asked to do so by the proper party. The Court is the one, however, which decides whether or not the cases fall within its obligatory review requirement. Under the terms of the law, it is to review:

1. Final judgments rendered by the highest state court to which the case could be carried in which a decision was made where there is drawn in question the validity of a treaty or statute of the United States, and the decision is against validity.

2. Final judgments rendered by the highest state court to which the case could be carried in which a decision was made where there is drawn in question the validity of a state statute on the ground of its being repugnant to the Constitution, treaties, or laws of the United States except those applicable only in the District of Columbia,[22] and the decision is in favor of its validity.

3. Decisions of a United States court of appeals in which a state statute is held to be invalid as repugnant to the Constitution, treaties, or laws of the United States.

4. Decisions of federal district courts holding an act of Congress unconstitutional in any civil action to which the United States or one of its agencies or officers is a party.

5. Certain other decisions of district courts that require a three-judge district court.

With the exception of these kinds of cases, which are said to go to the Supreme Court "on appeal," the Supreme Court has discretion whether or not it will accept a case. It accepts, "on writ of certiorari," only those cases that it considers to be of sufficient public importance to merit its attention. The formal distinction between the discretionary "certiorari" and the mandatory "on appeal" procedures should not be given too much weight. The Supreme Court also dismisses many appeals "for want of a substantial federal question." In short, the Supreme Court has wide discretion in determining which cases it will accept, whether the cases are presented to it by certiorari or by appeal.

A distinction needs to be made, however, between the consequence of the Supreme Court dismissing a case for "want of a substantial federal question" and its denial of a writ of certiorari. When the Court denies a writ of certiorari, this action has no value as a precedent. All it means is that for whatever reason four or more justices could not agree that the Supreme Court should accept the case for review. But when the Supreme Court accepts a case under an appeals writ and then dismisses it "for want of a substantial federal question," the Supreme Court has performed its reviewing function even though it has rendered no formal opinion. And the dismissal does have precedential value. For example, if a case comes to the Supreme Court on an appeal in which a state law is challenged as violating the Constitution, but the Supreme Court dismisses "for want of a substantial federal question," lower-court judges should take note that the Supreme Court has reviewed the law and concluded that it does not violate the Constitution. "Votes to affirm summarily and to dismiss for want of substantial federal questions . . . are votes on the merits of the case."[23]

---

3. The Trial of all Crimes, except in Cases of Impeachment, shall be by Jury; and such Trial shall be held in the State where the said Crimes shall have been committed; but when not committed within any State, the Trial shall be at such Place or Places as the Congress may by Law have directed.

This section guarantees the right to a trial by jury to persons accused by the national government of a crime. (See also the Sixth Amendment.)

---

1. Treason against the United States, shall consist only in levying War against them, or in adhering to their Enemies, giving them Aid and Comfort. No person shall be convicted of Treason unless on the Testimony of two Witnesses to the same overt Act, or on Confession in open Court.

This section does not prevent Congress from making it a federal crime to use force and violence against the government or conspiring to do so. It may be possible for aliens to commit treason against the United States because while within the boundaries of the United States they owe our government temporary allegiance.

There are two separate grounds for treason: (1) levying war against the United States and (2) giving aid and comfort to the enemy. Levying war is being part of a group of armed persons actually moving against the government. Giving aid and comfort requires evidence of "adhering to the enemies" of the United States by deliberately promoting the cause of a declared enemy. There is no precise court holding on the matter, but since Congress never formally declared war against North Vietnam, it is doubtful if any person could have been convicted of treason for adhering to its cause and giving it aid and comfort. Those who might have taken up arms and levied war against the United States as part of hostile forces, however, would be more exposed to risk of prosecution for treason even without a congressional declaration of war.

No person may be convicted of treason on the basis of circumstantial evidence alone. The accused must make a confession in open court, or there must be two witnesses to the overt act, which act, either by itself or along with other evidence, convinces the jury of the defendant's guilt.

Section 3

2. The Congress shall have Power to declare the Punishment of Treason, but no Attainder of Treason shall work Corruption of Blood, or Forfeiture except during the Life of the Person attainted.

In sixteenth and seventeenth-century England "attainders of treason" worked "corruption of blood," thereby making it impossible for the traitor's family to inherit from him. Having been traitors themselves in rebelling against King George, the framers may have felt a certain tenderness for such unfortunates.

ARTICLE IV: STATES' RELATIONS

Section 1

Full Faith and Credit shall be given in each State to the public Acts, Records, and judicial Proceedings of every other State. And the Congress may by general Laws prescribe the Manner in which such Acts, Records and Proceedings shall be proved, and the Effect thereof.

Congress has supplemented the full faith and credit clause by providing that "acts, records, and judicial proceedings or copies thereof, so authenticated, shall have the same full faith and credit in every court within the United States and its territories and possessions as they have by law or usage in the courts of such State, Territory, or Possession from which they are taken."

This clause applies especially to judicial decisions. Suppose that a Pennsylvania court awards X a $50,000 judgment against Y, also a Pennsylvanian; after moving to New York, Y refused to pay up. Thanks to the full faith and credit clause, X does not have to prove her case all over again and secure a new judgment against Y from the New York courts. The New York courts will give full faith and credit to the Pennsylvania judgment and in appropriate proceedings will enforce the judgment even if it is not one that the New York courts would have granted originally.

Or suppose that X, a New Yorker, while driving his car in New Jersey, injures Y or his property, and then returns to New York without doing anything about it. Following a certain procedure, Y may sue X in the New Jersey courts; if they decide in his favor, the New York courts will be obliged to aid Y in collecting the judgment in his favor—whether X appeared in the case or not.

How much faith and credit must a state give to a divorce decree granted by another state? The material question raised is that of "domicile." Each state has the power to regulate the marriage and divorce of its own residents. Clearly, a divorce granted by a state to two bona fide residents must be given full faith and credit by all the other states, although they might not themselves have granted the divorce for the grounds alleged. However, if a North Carolinian, for example, should go to Nevada and obtain a divorce after the six weeks necessary under Nevada law, that divorce, although valid in Nevada, is not necessarily one that the Constitution requires the North Carolina courts to recognize. The Supreme Court has ruled that under such circumstances the North Carolina courts could refuse to recognize the Nevada decree on the ground that Nevada courts "lacked jurisdiction" to grant the divorce because the plaintiff, in the eyes of North Carolina, had not acquired a bona fide "domicile" in Nevada.[1] If both parties to the divorce, however, make their appearance in the divorce-granting state and the issue of domicile is raised and decided, neither they nor their heirs can in any other court challenge the validity of the divorce on the ground that the state lacked jurisdiction. It is a rule of American jurisprudence, *res judicata*, that a person is entitled to the "day in court" and may not raise the issue again in an independent proceeding ("a collateral proceeding," as the lawyers call it).[2]

There are some interesting legal problems that stem from the "divisible divorce concept," namely, that although a state may have to recognize a divorce decree of another state when domicile has been acquired in that state, decisions with respect to alimony, property, and custody of children may involve other considerations, and the "forum state" may have greater discretion with respect to these matters. This is not the place to get involved in these highly technical matters—other than to note that situations have occurred where the wife was not the legal widow and the legal widow was not the wife. Obviously the dissolution of a marriage can create all kinds of legal tangles.

The full faith and credit clause is involved in "conflict of laws" questions that arise so frequently in a federal system. Which laws should be applied to decide particular disputes? In a fascinating decision, having all kinds of implications for interstate relations, in 1979, for the first time, the Supreme Court got to the issue of whether a state could be sued against its wishes in the courts of another state. It ruled that it could, and that the full faith and credit clause did not require California courts, in which Nevada was being sued because of an accident that had occurred in California involving a Nevada vehicle and employee, to enforce a Nevada law requiring that such suits take place only in Nevada courts and that limited the amount of money that could be recovered.[3]

Or take, for another example, an accident in which Ralph Hauge was killed. Hauge lived in Wisconsin but commuted to work in Minnesota. He was killed in Wisconsin when the motorcycle on which he was riding as a passenger (but not going to or from work) was struck from behind by an automobile driven by a Wisconsin resident. Although the drivers of both vehicles were Wisconsin residents, as was Hauge, and the accident took place in Wisconsin, his wife brought suit in Minnesota courts against the insurance company to recover for his death—she had moved to Minnesota after her husband's death.

Which law should the Minnesota courts apply, that of Wisconsin or that of Minnesota? It made a difference since the law of Minnesota allowed for three times the amount of damages allowed by the law of Wisconsin. The Minnesota courts chose to apply their own laws. The Supreme Court upheld Minnesota's action against both a challenge that it violated the full faith and credit clause and the due process clause. (The test under both clauses are in effect the same; but, as Justice Stevens in concurrence pointed out, the question was whether the full faith and credit clause required Minnesota to apply Wisconsin laws, or whether the due process clause prevented Minnesota from applying its own laws.) Minnesota, the Supreme Court ruled, had significant enough contact with the accident victim—Hauge had worked in Minnesota, the insurance company did business in Minnesota, and Hauge's wife had become a citizen of Minnesota prior to instituting the litigation—that if it chose to do so it could apply its own rather than the Wisconsin law.[4] Clearly, the trend in recent years is to read the full faith and credit clause to give forum states more latitude in deciding whether to use their own laws rather than those of a sister state in dealing with issues brought before them.

Section 2

1. The Citizens of each State shall be entitled to all Privileges and Immunities of Citizens in the several States.

"That Clause is not one of the contours of which have been precisely shaped by the process and wear of constant litigation and judicial interpretation . . . Historically, it has been overshadowed by the appearance in 1868 of similar language in Paragraph 1 of the Fourteenth Amendment, and by the continuing controversy and consequent litigation that attended the Amendment's enactment and its meaning and application."[5]

Since an American citizen becomes a citizen of a state by residing therein—moving there with an intent to remain, to making it one's permanent domicile—a citizen of a state and a resident of it are for all practical purposes interchangeable terms (see the Fourteenth Amendment.)[6]

The clause does not wipe out all differences between citizens and noncitizens. "It is discrimination against out-of-state residents on matters of fundamental concern which triggers [this clause.]"[7] If the discrimination affects fundamental rights, the state must show there is a "substantial reason" for the difference in treatment. A state may exclude noncitizens from voting in its elections or serving as elective officers. It does not have to permit out-of-state citizens to attend its tax supported institutions, such as schools, or to hunt its game or fish, for the same fee as charged its own citizens. But it does have to allow in-state aliens to attend its public schools on the same terms as its own citizens (see page 232). However, it may not ordinarily tax citizens of other states at discriminatory rates, deprive them of the means of livelihood, or deny them access of livelihood, or deny them access to any part of the state to which they may seek to travel. New Hampshire fell afoul of this clause when it imposed a tax on the income of citizens of other states, but not on its own citizens, even though the nonresidents were exempt from the New Hampshire tax if they paid such a tax to their own state.[8] And South Carolina was told it could not require nonresident commercial shrimp boats to pay a substantially higher fee than its own residents paid.[9] Nor could Alaska attempt to alleviate its unemployment problem by requiring private employers in the oil and gas exploration and transportation business to give preference to Alaska residents[10] (But see page 65, where the Court has sustained similar laws giving employment preference to citizens of a particular city.) On the other hand, Montana was permitted to charge a higher fee to nonresident elk hunters than to its own residents. This higher fee did not interfere with out-of-state hunters livelihood, only their sport and amusement. "Whatever right or activities may be fundamental under the Privileges and Immunities Clause," wrote the Court, "we are persuaded, and hold, that elk hunting by nonresidents in Montana is not one of them."[11]

In short, the clause "does not preclude disparity of treatment in the many situations where there are perfectly valid independent reasons for it"; it does preclude a state from discriminating against nonresidents "seeking to ply their trade, practice their occupation, or pursue a common calling within the State."[12]

American citizens become citizens of a state the moment they move to a state with the intent to remain. May states establish residency requirements that distinguish between its residents for certain purposes in terms of how long they have been residents? Yes, with reservations. Recently the Supreme Court has started to set aside "durational residency" requirements. In reviewing these requirements, the Court sometimes uses this clause, sometimes the equal protection clause, and sometimes bases its decisions on the right to travel.

A state must show a compelling interest before it will be permitted to deny to newly arrived residents the same rights accorded those who have lived there for some time. To illustrate: A state may not make newly arrived citizens wait for a year before becoming eligible for welfare payments, medical care, or voting rights. A day seems to be about as long as the Court will tolerate for welfare payments or medical care,[13] fifty days or so in order to be allowed to vote.[14] On the other hand, states may impose one-year durational residency requirements on those seeking divorces; this is not considered to be such a burden on the right to travel as those requirements declared unconstitutional.[15]

What about a durational requirement to attend public colleges and universities without paying out of state fees? A one year requirement is constitutionally permissible. A state may not, however, create an irrefutable presumption that any person who comes into the state to attend a college is not a resident of the state and cannot disqualify such a person from acquiring residency while attending school.[16] But those who move into the state just prior to enrolling in a state-supported university or college may be required to demonstrate they intend to remain after they finish their schooling, and to give evidence of their intentions by such things as driving licenses, car registration, voting registration, and continuous, year-round residence.

Section 2

2. A Person charged in any State with Treason, Felony, or other Crime, who shall flee from Justice, and be found in another State, shall on Demand of the executive Authority of the State from which he fled, be delivered up to be removed to the State having jurisdiction of the Crime.

This paragraph provides for what is known as "interstate rendition" or, more commonly, "extradition." Despite the positive language of this provision, the Supreme Court has refused to permit federal courts to order governors to extradite fugitives from justice if they chose not to do so. In most instances, under an act of Congress, escaped prisoners are returned to the state from which they have fled by the governor of the state to which they have fled. Governors, however, have complete discretion whether or not to extradite and occasionally have refused to do so. For example, in 1976 Governor Jerry Brown refused to extradite Dennis Banks, an American Indian activist, to South Dakota, from which he had fled after being convicted of "felony-riot." In 1984, Governor Scott M. Matheson of Utah refused to return to Illinois a business official wanted in that state for trial for murder because of an industrial accident in one of his company's plants.[17]

In 1980, a convocation of legal experts proposed that extradition be taken from governors and given to the courts. No state has adopted the draft proposal. Interstate extradition remains an executive matter. Once the governor of the asylum state has issued the warrant of arrest and rendition, the courts of that state have no authority to inquire into the matter either to determine whether the demanding state had probable cause for an arrest or whether the prison conditions of the demanding state violate the Eighth Amendment prohibition against cruel and unusual punishment. These charges are to be heard in the courts of the demanding state, not that of the asylum state.[18]

It should also be noted that Congress has made it a federal crime to travel in interstate or foreign commerce with the intent to avoid prosecution or confinement by a state for certain felonies. Those who violate this law are to be brought back to the federal judicial district in which the original crime is alleged to have been committed, making it possible for federal officers to turn the fleeing felon over to state officials for prosecution or confinement.

Section 2

3. No Person held to Service or Labour in one State, under the Laws thereof, escaping into another, shall, in Consequence of any Law or Regulation therein, be discharged from such Service or Labour, but shall be delivered up on Claim of the Party to whom such Service or Labour may be due.

The Thirteenth Amendment, abolishing slavery, nullified this "fugitive slave" clause.

Section 3

1. New States may be admitted by the Congress into this Union;

The normal procedure is as follows: (1) a petition is filed by the inhabitants of a territory for admission to the Union; (2) a congressional resolution is approved by the President authorizing the inhabitants of the territory to draw up a constitution; (3) the proposed constitution is approved by a majority of both houses of Congress and by the President; and (4) the territory is admitted into the Union.

Although Congress and the President may withhold their approval of admission until the "state" complies with or agrees to certain conditions, once a state is admitted, it possesses the same political powers as the other states. For example, in 1910 President Taft vetoed legislation admitting Arizona to the Union because its proposed constitution permitted the voters to recall state judges. After deleting this clause, Arizona was admitted (in 1912) and promptly proceeded to restore the objectionable provision. Since the right to determine the method of selection, tenure, and removal of its own judges is a political power enjoyed by all states, Arizona's power in this respect could not be less than that of other states; the condition was unenforceable.

In other cases, such as the conditions relating to the public lands in the state, they may be enforced as contracts that do not detract from a state's political power. When admitted to the Union, Minnesota agreed, in return for certain public lands it received from the national government, not to tax land still owned in the state by the national government. This agreement the Court enforced.[19]

The Civil War conclusively settled the question of whether or not a state can constitutionally withdraw from the Union. In the words of the Supreme Court ours is "an indestructible Union composed of indestructible States."[20]

Section 3

1. [continued] but no new State shall be formed or erected within the Jurisdiction of any other State; nor any State be formed by the Junction of two or more States, or Parts of States, without the Consent of the Legislatures of the States concerned as well as of the Congress.

Five states have been formed within the jurisdiction of other states with the consent of the legislatures concerned and of Congress: Vermont from New York in 1791, Kentucky from Virginia in 1792, Tennessee from North Carolina in 1796, Maine from Massachusetts in 1820, and West Virginia from Virginia (by a rump legislature during the Civil War) in 1863. At the time Texas was admitted to the Union, Congress consented to the division of the state into five states if the Texas legislature should ever so wish.

Section 3

2. The Congress shall have Power to dispose of and make all needful Rules and Regulations respecting the Territory or other Property belonging to the United States; and nothing in this Constitution shall be so construed as to Prejudice any Claims of the United States, or of any particular State.

When Puerto Rico, the Philippines, and Hawaii were annexed, the question arose whether or not "the Constitution followed the flag." The chief difficulty sprang from the fact that the new territories had not been molded in the political and legal traditions of the Constitution. To apply all the provisions of the Constitution, for example, would have necessitated in some areas the trial of offenses by juries composed of illiterates. Yet, if the Constitution did not apply, would not the inhabitants be without any safeguards against arbitrary rule?

The Constitution did not offer a clear solution, but the Supreme Court met the problem by distinguishing between "fundamental" and "formal" parts of the Constitution. The fundamental provisions are those that provide for fair trials, freedom of speech, and those rights necessary to an ordered scheme of liberty. The formal provisions are those, such as trial by jury, which at that time were considered to be forms appropriate for Anglo-Saxon justice but not essential for freedom or justice.[21] The Court then went on to rule in the *Insular Cases* that unless Congress provides otherwise, in unincorporated territories—those which Congress has neither explicitly nor implicitly made an integral part of the Union—only the fundamental provisions apply.

Today all territories—Puerto Rico, Guam, Northern Marianas, American Samoa, and the Virgin Islands—are unincorporated. (Puerto Rico, however, has a special commonwealth status in terms of its relationship to the national government and more freedom over its internal matters than do the other territories.) The *Insular Cases* have never been specifically overruled, but their continuing validity is questionable. It was assumed that as far as the constitutional protections for individuals were concerned, all provisions of the Constitution were applicable. Then in 1982, the Court in upholding the Commonwealth of Puerto Rico's authority to vest the right to fill vacancies in its legislature in the voters of the party in which the former legislator was a member seemed to give those cases renewed vitality. Citing the *Insular Cases,* the Court wrote, "It is not disputed that the fundamental protections of the United States Constitution extend to the inhabitants of Puerto Rico. . . . In particular, we have held that Puerto Rico is subject to the constitutional guarantees of due process and equal protection of the laws."[22] In other words, the Fourteenth Amendment applies to Puerto Rico and so presumably does the incorporation into that Amendment of the several provisions of the Bill of Rights as they apply to the states (see page 135). But what does the Court's use of the words "fundamental protections" mean? Does this suggest that the nonfundamental parts of the Constitution do not apply? And in a modern context what are the nonfundamental parts?

Congress clearly may treat territories differently from states "so long as there is a rational basis for its action."[23] Thus Congress was allowed to make lower payments to dependent children under social security in Puerto Rico than in the states. First of all, the right to receive financial aid from the federal government is not a constitutionally protected right. Moreover, the distinction between the payments is rational, said the Court, because (1) Puerto Rican residents (they are, by the way, American citizens, see page 226) do not pay federal taxes; (2) the cost of treating Puerto Rico as a state would be very high; and (3) the payment of the greater benefits might disrupt the Puerto Rican economy.

Section 4

The United States shall guarantee to every State in this Union a Republican Form of Government,

---

The Constitution does not define "a republican form of government." John Adams observed, "The word *republic* as it is used, may signify anything, everything, or nothing." The framers undoubtedly meant a form that, as distinguished from aristocracy, monarchy, or direct democracy, rests on the consent of the people and operates through representative institutions. Whatever it means is a responsibility of the Congress, not of the Supreme Court, to determine. What it means is a political question to be answered by Congress, not by the courts. Whenever Congress permits the senators and representatives of a particular state to take their seats in Congress, that state must be deemed to have "a republican form of government" within the meaning of the Constitution.

Because of the Court's firmness in holding to the view that interpretation of the guarantee clause is a political and not a justiciable question, the clause is seldom raised in litigation. But in 1902, after Oregon adopted the "initiative," whereby its citizens are able to legislate* directly without the intervention of the legislature, a company that had been taxed under a law passed by the initiative procedure argued that such action transgressed the clause requiring states to have republican forms of government. The Court again refused to intervene, holding that "violation of the . . . guaranty of a republican form of government . . . cannot be challenged in the courts."[24]

Long ago Charles Sumner pointed out that the guarantee clause is "a sleeping giant." No other part of the Constitution gives "Congress such supreme power over the states." And there are those who today argue that the clause imposes on Congress the responsibility to supervise state activities directly to ensure that they meet the test of a "republican form of government."[25] But the primary restraint on congressional intervention into "state matters" remains, as it has always been, more political in nature than constitutional. Whenever Congress, responding to national majorities, feels the need to intervene in "state matters," this clause is not the only one available to justify its intervention.

Section 4

[continued] and shall protect each of them against Invasion;

Invasion of a state by a foreign power would also be an invasion of the United States.

Section 4

[continued] and on application of the Legislature, or of the Executive (when the Legislature cannot be convened) against domestic Violence.

---

* Simply stated, the initiative procedure calls for two steps: (1) securing signatures of a required number of voters to a petition calling for submission of the proposed law to the electorate; (2) submission of the proposal to the voters in a general election. If approved by a majority of those voting on the proposition, the proposal becomes a law.

Congress has delegated to the President the authority to send troops into a state to protect it from "domestic violence," on the request of the appropriate state authority. In 1842 there were two governments in Rhode Island, each of which claimed to be the legitimate one. When President Tyler indicated that he was prepared to send troops to defend one of these against the "domestic violence" of the other, he was at the same time determining which government was the legitimate one. The Supreme Court, in refusing to intervene, identified the question as "political" in nature.[26]

When the President finds it necessary, in order to enforce federal laws or federal judicial decrees or to preserve the property or "the peace of the United States," he may send federal law-enforcement agents or even troops to the scene of resistance. Under such circumstances, the President acts neither at the request of state officials nor by their leave. He does not need their consent and may act even against their wishes. Under such circumstances, he is not "ordering troops into a state" but enforcing the laws of the United States that cover the length and breadth of the land.[27]

ARTICLE V: THE AMENDING POWER

The Congress, whenever two thirds of both Houses shall deem it necessary, shall propose Amendments to this Constitution, or, on the Application of the Legislatures of two thirds of the several States, shall call a Convention for proposing Amendments, which, in either Case, shall be valid to all Intents and Purposes, as Part of this Constitution, when ratified by the Legislatures of three fourths of the several States, or by Conventions in three fourths thereof, as the one or the other Mode of Ratification may be proposed by the Congress;

Amendments to the Constitution must be both proposed and ratified. The Constitution provides for two ways to propose and two ways to ratify. So far all amendments have been proposed by Congress, and all but one, the Twenty-first, have been ratified by the state legislatures.

The formal amendatory procedures have been criticized as "undemocratic." One-fourth of the states plus one, which could reflect the wish of much less than one-fourth of the people, could block amendments desired by a large majority. It is also possible for amendments to be adopted without a direct expression of popular opinion. The latter criticism would be largely met were Congress to require ratification by state conventions called for that purpose, rather than by state legislatures chosen to deal with other issues.

Of the many attempts to get Congress to call a constitutional convention, so far the closest to success came in the spring of 1967 when thirty-three state legislatures, only one short, petitioned Congress to call a convention to propose an amendment to reverse Supreme Court rulings requiring both chambers of state legislatures to be apportioned on the basis of population. Suddenly the many unanswered questions about how such a convention might operate ceased to be only of "academic interest." But the thirty-fourth state legislature never acted, pressures for a reapportionment amendment abated, and interest in a constitutional convention temporarily died down.

Concerns about a new constitutional convention have revived because there are two active campaigns for the calling of such a convention. A number of state legislatures have petitioned Congress to call a convention to propose an amendment to permit states to ban abortions. But the most active campaign is by the National Taxpayers Union. By the end of 1984, thirty-two of the required thirty-four legislatures had passed resolutions calling for a national convention to write an amendment requiring the federal budget to be balanced on an annual basis, except during times of war or other emergencies declared by an extraordinary majority of Congress. Although the President has no formal ~ole to play in the amendatory process, President Reagan has endorsed such an amendment. The National Taxpayers Union is mounting a major campaign in the hope of adding the two more convention calls it needs for success. At the same time opponents of such an amendment, including Common Cause, organized labor, and many constitutional scholars, are trying to get states (such as Maryland and Iowa) that had previously adopted a resolution calling for a convention to repeal their call.[1]

There are many questions relating to a constitutional convention for which there are no clear answers. How would a convention be run; how would delegates be apportioned; how would they be chosen? Could members of Congress become delegates? Are the petitions from the several states sufficiently identical to reflect support for a particular amendment; have they been presented within a time period to indicate there is a "contemporaneous national wish" for such an amendment? Congress, not the courts, decides such questions along with choosing which method of ratification would be used.

Of greatest concern is the issue of whether Congress could call for a limited convention and restrict what it could consider. Scholars are divided on whether Congress may tell a convention in advance that the convention's only authority is to propose or reject a specific amendment or deal with limited topics. Moreover, there is no guarantee that once in session a convention would follow congressional directions. It might, as did the Convention of 1787, "run away" and propose an entirely new constitution. It is because of such concerns that many observers believe that if thirty-four legislatures ever petition Congress to call a convention, do so in language that makes it clear they all want a particular amendment, and do it within the proper time period, Congress is more likely to propose the amendment itself than to run the risks of calling a national convention into existence in order to do so.

Proposed amendments must be ratified. Congress decides which of the two methods of ratification shall be used, either by the legislatures of three-fourths of the states (all amendments except the Twenty-first were ratified by this method), or by special state conventions in three-fourths of the states. Governors have no role in the ratification process. When Congress proposed the Twenty-first Amendment repealing the Eighteenth Amendment (prohibition), it left to each state the determination of the manner in which delegates to its ratifying convention should be chosen.

Many questions arising out of Article V, especially those that relate to ratification, are political questions; indeed, it is probable that the Court would, if occasion arose, accept Justice Black's statement made in 1939, "Congress, possessing exclusive power over the amending process, cannot be bound by and is under no duty to accept the pronouncements upon that exclusive power by this Court."[2]

Under present arrangements, Congress decides after the states have acted upon a proposed amendment whether the proper number have acted and have done so within a reasonable time. Can a state legislature after once rejecting an amendment, change its mind and ratify? After it has ratified, may it change its mind and rescind its ratification? If the state constitution calls for ratification to be by a two-thirds vote of each chamber of the state legislature, may a majority of that legislature subsequently rescind that action? When are ratifications untimely? The fact that there is no absolutely clear and agreed-upon answer to these questions points to a danger spot of our Constitution. For the one thing that we should be clear about is what is and what is not part of the Constitution.[3]

The predominant opinion, based on post–Civil-War congressional practices is that after voting against an amendment a state legislature may reconsider and ratify, but that once a legislature has ratified an amendment, its ratification cannot be rescinded and will be counted. On July 20, 1868, Secretary of State Seward certified to Congress that the twenty-eight states (there then being thirty-seven states) had approved the Fourteenth Amendment; however, Ohio and New Jersey had prior to that date "withdrawn their earlier assent." The next day Congress declared the amendment a part of the Constitution and directed the Secretary to promulgate it. On July 28 the Secretary so certified. In the interim two other states added their ratification. (Authority to make the *initial* certification of amendments subject to ultimate congressional approval has since been transferred to the Administrator of General Services.)

This Fourteenth Amendment precedent was frequently cited during the battles over the ratification of the Equal Rights Amendment. Also in the fall of 1978, when Congress extended the period for ratification of ERA, some members argued that since the time was being extended it was only fair that rescissions should be counted (four states had already voted to rescind), but Congress refused to authorize rescissions (see page 272).

Ratification of an amendment must take place within a "reasonable time." Congress determines what constitutes a reasonable time. Beginning with the Eighteenth Amendment, submitted in 1917, Congress placed a seven-year limit right in the body of the proposed amendment. Then, beginning with the Twenty-third Amendment, proposed in 1960, Congress adopted the practice of setting a seven-year limit in the submission resolution rather than making it a formal part of the amendment. Thus, when it appeared that the Equal Rights Amendment would not be ratified within the seven-year limit, advocates of extending the time limit successfully argued that since the time limit was not part of the body of the proposed amendment but was contained only in the resolution submitting it to the states, the time for ratification could be extended by a majority vote in both houses, not by the two-thirds required to propose an amendment. When, in August of 1978, Congress proposed an amendment to give a greater voice in national affairs to the people of the District of Columbia, it pointedly reverted to previous practice and put the seven-year limit right in the body of the proposed amendment (see page 271).

Between 1789 and 1982 over five thousand amendments have been introduced in Congress, but only thirty-three have been proposed. Twenty-six of these have been ratified; one presently is before the state legislatures. Two of the rejected amendments were proposed along with the ten that were finally ratified as the Bill of Rights. Another that was not ratified (1810) would have withdrawn citizenship from any person who accepted a title of nobility or who received without the consent of Congress an office or emolument from a foreign power. On the eve of the Civil War, Congress proposed an amendment that would have prohibited any amendment to the Constitution interfering with slavery in any of the states. In 1924 Congress proposed an amendment that would have given it power to regulate child labor; only twenty-eight states have ratified, no state having done so since 1937. Although when it proposed the amendment, Congress stipulated no time limit for ratification, the proposed amendment is both no longer needed (because the Constitution is now interpreted to give Congress power to regulate child labor) and no longer alive.

The rejection of the Equal Rights Amendment (see page 271) and the probable rejection of the proposed D.C. Amendment are somewhat unusual. During most of our history, if a coalition of political forces was strong enough to get two-thirds of both houses of Congress to propose an amendment, it ordinarily reflected a consensus strong enough to make ratification probable.

Other Methods of Constitutional Development

The Constitution, written before the Industrial and Democratic Revolutions had made their impress on the nation, continues to be a living, fundamental law for our powerful industrial democracy. Obviously, the Constitution has had to change as the nation changed. Although the framework is the same, fundamental alterations have been made in the operation of the government within that framework. The formal amending process has been relatively unimportant in this development; less formal, more subtle methods have been employed.

Congressional Elaboration

The framers were wise and humble men who doubted that they had either the moral right or the necessary wisdom to prescribe the details of how the nation should be governed for future generations. They knew that a rigid, detailed, and restrictive constitution would have little chance to endure. They painted in broad strokes, made their grants of power general, and left to Congress the development of the structure of government by ordinary legislation. Examples of congressional elaboration appear in such legislation as the Judiciary Act of 1789, which laid the foundations of our national judicial system; in the laws establishing the organization and functions of all federal executive officials subordinate to the President; and by its application and interpretation of its powers under the impeachment clauses; and in the rules of procedure, internal organization, and practices of Congress itself.

Presidential Practices

The President has the use of great discretion in developing the nature and role of the office. There has been no change in the formal constitutional position of the President, but nowadays the President participates in the making of legislative policy to an extent not anticipated by the Founding Fathers and if they had anticipated it, they would probably have disapproved. With the growth of political parties, the President became a national party leader and an active participant in party battles. In response to crises, the presidency has grown into the pivotal office of our national government and the President has become a key legislator as well as the nation's Chief Executive.

Judicial Interpretation

As we have already seen, the courts are the authoritative interpreters of the Constitution. The words of the Constitution are sufficiently broad to accommodate divergent interpretations. As conditions have changed, so have judicial interpretations of the Constitution. In the words of Woodrow Wilson, "The Supreme Court is a constitutional convention in continuous session." At one time the Supreme Court ruled that the national government could not regulate child labor.[4] Today the national government does so with the approval of the Supreme Court. The Supreme Court's response to a persistent public demand made formal amendment unnecessary.[5] But perhaps the best illustration of how judicial interpretation has altered our constitutional system is that the power of the courts to interpret the Constitution is itself the result of judicial interpretation (see pages 25–27). It should be noted that although the Supreme Court has the final judicial say about the meaning of our Constitution, it is also interpreted daily by the hundreds of federal judges and thousands of state judges.

Customs and Usages

The President's Cabinet and the local residence requirement for Congress members are examples of constitutional customs. A more significant example is the custom of presidential electors pledging themselves to support the candidates of their party, a practice that has transformed the electoral college into an automatic transmitter of the electorate's choice.

The "Unwritten Constitution": Summary

We can see that surrounding the formal document are customs and usages, congressional statutes, judicial decisions, and presidential practices that supplement the written Constitution. These rules are sometimes called the "Unwritten Constitution." It has been primarily through the use of informal methods of development and alteration in the Unwritten Constitution itself that our governmental system has grown. The Constitution was democratized by the extension of the suffrage within the states and by the extraconstitutional development of national political parties. The national government has been strengthened to meet the emergencies of a national economy and an interdependent world without fundamentally changing the written Constitution. In short, our Constitution provides for a living, organic, and growing governmental system.

[continued] Provided that no Amendment which may be made prior to the Year One thousand eight hundred and eight shall in any Manner affect the first and fourth Clauses in the Ninth Section of the first Article;

This provision referred to the importation of slaves and possesses only historical interest today.

[continued] and [provided] that no State, without its Consent, shall be deprived of its equal Suffrage in the Senate.

Some consider this provision unamendable, and others contend that there are ways in which even it can be changed. It could be repealed, they say, by amendment and then another amendment adopted by the regular procedure that would permit unequal representation in the Senate.

ARTICLE VI: THE SUPREMACY ARTICLE

---

1. All Debts contracted and Engagements entered into, before the Adoption of this Constitution, shall be as valid against the United States under this Constitution, as under the Confederation.

At the time of the Constitutional Convention, the securities and currency issued by the Confederation and the several states had depreciated in value. Later, Alexander Hamilton, Washington's brilliant Secretary of the Treasury, proposed that the national government assume the debts of the several states and pay in full the debts of the Confederation. Adoption of this proposal did much to strengthen the new Union—at a handsome profit to speculators in Confederation securities.

---

2. This Constitution, and the Laws of the United States which shall be made in Pursuance thereof; and all Treaties made, or which shall be made, under the authority of the United States, shall be the supreme Law of the Land; and the judges in every State shall be bound thereby, any Thing in the Constitution or Laws of Any State to the Contrary notwithstanding.

This clause lays down one of the key principles of the Constitution. It makes federalism work. *The powers of the national government are limited, but within the field of its powers it is supreme, and the state courts are bound to uphold this supremacy.* Any provision of a state constitution or any state law is null and void if it conflicts with the Constitution, with a federal law passed in pursuance of the Constitution, or with a treaty made under the authority of the United States. To take a single example, a Pennsylvania law punishing advocacy of sedition against the United States is unenforceable because it conflicts with a similar federal law. (However, a state can pass a law directed at supervision of the state itself.)[1]

A considerable portion of our judges' time is taken trying to determine whether or not the federal government has pre-empted a state from acting. "Pre-emption may be either express or implied. . . . Absent explicit pre-emptive language, Congress's intent to supersede a state law may be inferred because the scheme of federal regulation may be so pervasive as to make reasonable the inference that Congress left no room for the States to supplement it, because the Act of Congress may touch a field in which the federal interest is so dominant that the federal system will be assumed to preclude enforcement of state laws on the same subject, or because the object sought to be obtained by federal law and the character of the obligations imposed by it may reveal the same purpose."[2]

Discerning the will of Congress with respect to pre-emption is no more precise than discerning the meaning of the Constitution. Take the problems of deciding whether Congress has pre-empted the regulation of nuclear energy. There is perhaps no field in which the federal government has exercised more pervasive authority than in regulating nuclear plants in order to insure their safety. Yet a unanimous Court decided California could impose a moratorium on any new nuclear plants until the state energy commission is satisfied that there is a feasible way to dispose of nuclear waste. California acted, so its legislature declared, not for reasons of safety but to prevent excessive costs to its citizens. "The legal reality remains," concluded the Supreme Court," that Congress has left sufficient authority in the states to allow the development of nuclear power to be slowed or even stopped for economic reasons. Given this statutory scheme, it is for Congress to rethink the division of regulatory authority in light of its possible exercise by the states to undercut a federal objective. The courts should not assume the role which our system assigns to Congress."[3]

Federal regulations issued by executive agencies when authorized by Congress have no less pre-emptive effect than federal statutes.[4]

United States Treaty Power

Treaties are of two types, self-executing and nonself-executing. The former require no implementation by Congress to have internal application as supreme law of the land. If the President, with the consent of two-thirds of the Senate, ratifies a self-executing treaty giving foreign nationals certain rights in return for reciprocal concessions for American nationals, such a treaty is valid as internal law. It takes precedence over any conflicting state constitutions or laws. Nonself-executing treaties, while bringing into existence a binding international obligation, require action by Congress in the form of implementing legislation; this legislation becomes supreme law of the land, enforceable in the courts.

Note, whereas the supremacy clause only makes those "laws of the United States . . . made in pursuance" of the Constitution the supreme law of the land, it makes "all treaties made, or which shall be made, under the authority of the United States supreme law." Does this difference in constitutional language have any significance?

Treaties, like national laws, must conform to the national Constitution. A treaty or a law implementing a treaty that abridged First Amendment freedoms would be just as unconstitutional as a law that did the same thing. As Justice Black phrased it in *Reid* v. *Covert,* "This Court has regularly and uniformly recognized the supremacy of the Constitution over a treaty."[5] Nonetheless, the limitations of federalism, such as they are, do not apply to limit the scope of the national government's treaty-making power as they do to its law-making powers.

These questions came to the Supreme Court in the famous case of *Missouri*

v. *Holland* (1920). After Congress, in 1913, passed a law regulating the hunting of migratory birds, several district judges ruled that the law was unconstitutional because regulation of wild game is not among the powers delegated to the national government. Three years later, the United States became party to a treaty with Canada (via Great Britain) in which the national government promised to protect the birds migrating between Canada and this country in return for a promise by Canada to do the same. To fulfill our obligations under this treaty, Congress passed a law even more stringent than its 1913 enactment. This time the case went to the Supreme Court. Justice Holmes, speaking for a unanimous Court, said:

> Acts of Congress are the supreme law of the land only when made in pursuance of the Constitution, while treaties are declared to be so when made under the authority of the United States. . . . We do not mean to imply that there are no qualifications to the treaty-making power; but they must be ascertained in a different way. . . . The only question is whether it is forbidden by some invisible radiation from the general terms of the Tenth Amendment. . . . We see nothing in the Constitution that compels the Government to sit by while a food supply is cut off and the protectors of our forest and our crops are destroyed.[6]

Today, discussions of whether or not the treaty power is broader than the national lawmaking power have lost much of their significance. With the liberal construction of the national government's legislative powers, there are few subjects of national importance that Congress cannot directly regulate. Fears that the President and the Senate will use the treaty power to interfere with states' rights are hard to understand, for if there is ever such a desire, there are other and easier procedures to use to accomplish this goal.

The Existence of the States and the Supremacy Clause

Although the powers of Congress are determined by what has been granted to it by the Constitution without any reference to the states, Congress is not to exercise its powers in a fashion that impairs the states' integrity or ability to function effectively. Yet it is easier to make this generalization than to cite examples of how the existence of the states constrains the exercise of congressional powers. The only case in modern times is *National League of Cities* v. *Usery,* when the Supreme Court held that federal wage and hours regulations could not be applied to the employees of state governments. Here Congress, said the Court, had interfered with the states' "freedom to structure integral operations in areas of traditional governmental functions . . . functions essential to separate and independent existence."[7]

Since the decision in *National League of Cities* the Court has gone out of its way to make it clear that the reach of that decision is exceedingly limited. Commerce clause legislation is invalid only if the challenged legislation regulates the "States as States," addresses matters that are "indisputably attributes of state sovereignty," and "directly impairs" the ability of states "to structure integral operations in areas of traditional functions." "Moreover, even showing that these three requirements are met does not guarantee that a . . . challenge to congressional commerce power will succeed. There are situations in which the nature of the federal interest advanced may be such that it justifies State submission."[8]

Despite *National League of Cities* the Court has upheld the application to the states of federal statutes forbidding the retirement of most state employees prior to age seventy. (Thus Congress can compel states to keep employees they do not want, but Congress may not regulate what the states must pay them.) The Court has also distinguished between "traditional state activities that are integral parts of state governments"—generally immune from federal regulation—and all other state activities, such as a state-owned railroad, that are not immune from federal regulation.[9] The Court also allowed Congress to force state utility commissions to adopt certain procedures and consider certain standards in order to encourage conservation of energy, the efficient use of facilities, and equitable rates to consumers.[10]

The decisions following *National League* are hard to reconcile with it. Justice Stevens is of the view, "that *National League of Cities* not only was incorrectly decided, but also is inconsistent with the central purpose of the Constitution itself, that it is not entitled to the deference that the doctrine of stare decisis ordinarily commands for this Court's precedents. . . . I believe that the law would be well served by a prompt rejection of National League of Cities' modern embodiment of the spirit of the Articles of Confederation."[11] The Chief Justice and Justices O'Connor and Rehnquist, however still champion *National League of Cities.* Justice O'Connor in *FERC* v. *Mississippi* (1983) has accused the majority of permitting "Congress to kidnap state utility commissions into the national regulatory family."[12] Justice Blackmun responded by attacking her dissenting opinion as "demonstrably incorrect, and absurd." Clearly, federalism issues still generate strong emotions, at least among Supreme Court justices.[13]

If *National League of Cities* is not much of a barrier to congressional exercise of the commerce power, it is even less of one when Congress acts to enforce the Fourteenth and Fifteenth Amendments (see page 253). The fact that congressional actions to enforce these amendments may interfere with essential state functions is of no constitutional consequence.[14] Clearly, *National tional League of Cities* does not mark a reversal in the direction of modern constitutional interpretation, which has been generous in its construction of the scope and reach of congressional powers. Still, it does give Congress a mild warning that the existence of the states does set some limits as to how it may exercise the powers granted to it.

---

3. The Senators and Representatives before mentioned, and the Members of the several State Legislatures, and all executive and judicial Officers, both of the United States and of the several States, shall be bound by Oath or Affirmation, to support this Constitution;

This clause makes it clear that the first allegiance of all Americans, including state officials, is to the national Constitution. If a state governor, for example, is ordered by his or her state constitution or legislature to perform an act that is contrary to the Constitution, his or her duty is nonetheless to comply with the national Constitution.

3. [continued] but no religious Test shall ever be required as a Qualification to any Office of public Trust under the United States.

This provision applies only to the national government, but as a result of the adoption of the First and Fourteenth Amendments the same prohibition applies to state and local governments.[15]

Note, Article I, Section 3, paragraph 6, and Article II, Section 1, paragraph 8, on pages 44 to 96 are additional evidence of the framer's concern for religious freedom. Whenever the Constitution calls for an oath to God to tell the truth or to perform responsibilities, an alternative is provided for those who may have religious convictions against the swearing of such oaths. They, or anyone, may choose merely to affirm that they will tell the truth or carry out their duties.

ARTICLE VII. RATIFICATION OF THE CONSTITUTION

The Ratification of the Conventions of nine States, shall be sufficient for the Establishment of this Constitution between the States so ratifying the Same.

The Constitutional Convention was a revolutionary body. The delegates were representatives of the states acting in response to a call by the Congress of the Confederation. Since the Articles of Confederation could be amended only with the consent of all thirteen state legislatures, and since they created a "perpetual Union," Congress, when it called the Convention, had explicitly stated that no recommendations should be effective until approved by Congress and ratified in accordance with the terms of the Articles—that is, by all thirteen state legislatures. Nevertheless, the delegates to the Convention boldly assumed power to exceed their mandate and to propose an entirely new government that was to go into effect upon the ratification by specially chosen conventions of only nine of the thirteen states.

Done in Convention by the Unanimous Consent of the States present the Seventeenth Day of September in the Year of our Lord one thousand seven hundred and Eighty seven and of the Independence of the United States of America the Twelfth. In Witness whereof We have hereunto subscribed our Names,

(For a discussion of the signing of the Constitution, see page 14).

Amendments to the Constitution

THE BILL OF RIGHTS

Much of the opposition to ratification of the Constitution stemmed from its lack of specific guarantees of certain fundamental rights. The Constitutional Convention failed to adopt such guarantees because they were thought to be unnecessary and dangerous—unnecessary because the Constitution itself prohibits bills of attainder, ex post facto laws, and suspension of the writ of habeas corpus except in times of public danger, and requires trial by jury in federal criminal cases; dangerous because prohibitions might furnish an argument for claiming powers not granted the new government. Thus to forbid the national government to *abridge* freedom of the press might be thought to imply that it had the power to *regulate* the press if it could do so without abridging it. It was also urged that the protection of fundamental rights ultimately rested not on paper guarantees but in the hearts and minds of the nation's citizens.[1]

Despite these arguments, there was a general demand for a bill of rights; the Constitution was adopted with the understanding that the first business of the first Congress would be the consideration of amendments suitable for the purpose. Congress proposed twelve such amendments on September 25, 1789, ten of which were ratified and became part of the Constitution on December 15, 1791. The two that were not ratified prescribed the ratio of representation to population in the House of Representatives and prohibited any increase in Congress members compensation until an election for representatives had intervened.

THE BILL OF RIGHTS AND THE STATES

By 1789, most state constitutions contained a bill of rights. In general, people were confident that they had sufficient political power to prevent abuse of authority by state and local officials. But the national government was new, distant, and threatening; the Bill of Rights was added to the Constitution to restrict its powers. In *Barron* v. *Baltimore,* John Marshall confirmed the obvious: The Bill of Rights applies only to the national government, and it imposes no restraints on state and local authorities.[2]

The national government, however, responsive to a broadly based political community, did not prove to be as much a threat to civil liberties and civil rights as did state and local governments. Furthermore, the primary responsibility for the administration of justice vests in the states; the failure of the national Constitution to restrain state and local authorities left large segments of governmental activity without federal constitutional limitation. True, state constitutions contain most of the same guarantees as are found in the Bill of Rights; however, state judges, who alone have jurisdiction to construe their respective state constitutions, until very recently have seldom applied their state bill of rights so as to restrain state or local officials (see page 138).

After the adoption of the Fourteenth Amendment, which does apply to state (and local) governments, the Supreme Court was urged to construe the amendment, especially its due process clause, as applying to the states the same limitations that the Bill of Rights applies to the national government. Although the Supreme Court brought within the scope of the due process clause a provision of the Bill of Rights forbidding the taking of private property without just compensation, for decades it refused to go further.

Then, in 1925, in *Gitlow* v. *New York,* the Supreme Court took the momentous step of holding that the word *liberty* in the due process clause of the Fourteenth Amendment includes liberty of speech.[3] By the early 1940s, the Supreme Court had incorporated within the due process clause all the provisions of the First Amendment. In short, by construction of the Fourteenth Amendment, the major substantive restrictions that the Bill of Rights places on the national government in order to protect freedom of religion, speech, press, petition, and assembly were given national constitutional protection against abridgment by state and local authorities.

What of the other parts of the Bill of Rights? If the due process clause of the Fourteenth Amendment imposes on state governments the same limitations that the First Amendment places on the national government, why does not the rest of the Bill of Rights also come within the scope of the Fourteenth? For some time a persistent minority of the Supreme Court justices so argued; that is, they would have construed the due process clause of the Fourteenth Amendment to mean that the states should follow precisely the same procedures that the Bill of Rights requires of the national government. What national authorities cannot do because of the Bill of Rights, these justices contended, state authorities could not do because of the due process clause of the Fourteenth Amendment. The Supreme Court still has not gone quite so far as to incorporate totally into the Fourteenth Amendment all the applicable provisions of the Bill of Rights, but it has come very close to doing so.

The Court applies the Doctrine of Selective Incorporation, or Selective Absorption, or, because it was explained by Justice Cardozo in *Palko* v. *Connecticut,* it is also known as the Palko Test.[4] According to this view the Fourteenth Amendment's due process clause does not prescribe any specific procedures for the administration of justice or the execution of governmental affairs. Rather, it forbids states to adopt a procedure that "offends some principle of justice so rooted in the traditions and conscience of our people as to be ranked as fundamental," or to deprive people of rights "implicit in the concept of ordered liberty." The application of this general standard of fundamental fairness resulted in the selective incorporation or absorption into the due process clause of some but not all the provisions of the Bill of Rights. The distinction between those incorporated and those not incorporated within due process was that the former provisions protect rights such as freedom of speech and the press, which are so fundamental as to be "implicit in the concept of ordered justice," whereas provisions in the latter category, such as that requiring indictment by grand jury (which the Fifth Amendment prescribes for the national government), merely provide certain procedures that will secure justice, but these are not the only procedures that will do so. States could indict persons other than by grand jury and still do justice.

Beginning in the 1930s and accelerating after 1964, the Supreme Court selectively incorporated provision after provision of the Bill of Rights into the requirements of the due process clause of the Fourteenth Amendment. Moreover, in 1968 the Court majority revised the Palko Test to permit the easier incorporation of additional provisions: The Supreme Court now asks if a particular procedure is considered fundamental for an American regime of ordered liberty. Using this standard, the Supreme Court ruled that trial by jury for serious offenses is essential for due process. The Court conceded that in some societies justice is secured without using juries (in England most criminal trials take place before judges without juries), but "in the American states, as in the federal judicial system . . . a general grant of jury trial for serious offenses is a fundamental right, essential for preventing miscarriages of justice and for assuring that fair trials are provided for all defendants."[5]

By 1970, for all practical purposes, the Bill of Rights had been incorporated into the Fourteenth Amendment. Today, except for the Second, Third, and Tenth Amendments, which are not applicable, the Fourteenth Amendment imposes on states all the requirements that the Bill of Rights imposes on the national government *except* those calling for indictment for serious crimes by a grand jury and the Seventh Amendment requirement of trial by jury in all civil cases involving more than $20.

What does it mean to say that the Bill of Rights, or at least most of it, has been absorbed into the Fourteenth Amendment? It has three major consequences: The Supreme Court has jurisdiction to review cases involving the application of these provisions and to establish standards to guide the behavior of state and local as well as national authorities; the federal district judges, through habeas corpus petitions, have enlarged jurisdiction to hear complaints by persons alleging that they are being held contrary to the commands of the Constitution; Congress has the power to pass whatever laws are necessary and proper to implement constitutional guarantees.

The "nationalization" of the Bill of Rights has not, however, ended constitutional debate or resulted in each provision of the Bill of Rights being treated in the same fashion. The old battles are emerging in new forms. For example, the Supreme Court is now distinguishing between some "constitutional rights so basic to a fair trial that their infraction can never be treated as a harmless error" and "some constitutional errors which in the setting of a particular case are so unimportant and insignificant that they may, consistent with the Federal Constitution, be deemed harmless, not requiring the automatic reversal of the conviction." Examples of the former are use of coerced confessions, denial of the right to counsel, lack of an impartial judge. An example of the latter might be a passing comment by a prosecutor about a defendant's failure to take the stand. Such comment violates the right against self-incrimination, but if the state reviewing courts find that it was "harmless beyond a reasonable doubt," the Supreme Court might not insist on reversal.[6] In the same fashion, to admit into evidence a codefendant's confession when the codefendant refused to take the stand, and was thereby not subject to confrontation, violated the confrontation clause of the Sixth Amendment, but in view of the defendant's own minutely detailed and consistent confession the Court has ruled such a violation to be a harmless error.[7]

The Supreme Court has also distinguished among provisions in terms of whether its decisions incorporating them are to be applied prospectively or retroactively. For example, on May 20, 1968, the Supreme Court held for the first time that the Fourteenth Amendment requires states to try persons for serious crimes before juries, but it subsequently ruled that persons tried without benefit of juries before May 20, 1968, need not be retried. At the time of their original trials, states were following the then authoritative construction of the Constitution, and it cannot be said that all convictions made in the absence of jury are so inherently unfair that they should be upset years after they were imposed. The court has ruled otherwise, however, with respect to other "incorporations"; for example, after bringing the Sixth Amendment guarantee of the right to the assistance of counsel into the Fourteenth Amendment, the Supreme Court held that any person presently under sentence imposed without the assistance of counsel is entitled to a retrial even though at the time of the original trial the state was following the then authoritative construction of the Constitution. No trial held without the assistance of counsel can be considered fair.[8]

Whereas one of the major constitutional debates of the 1960s was whether all the provisions of the Bill of Rights should be incorporated into the due process clause of the Fourteenth Amendment, one of the constitutional debates of the 1970s was whether the due process clause of the Fourteenth Amendment is confined to the specific provisions of the Bill of Rights. The late Justice Black, representing only a minority point of view, contended that unless the Bill of Rights specifically forbids authorities from doing something, they are free to do it. He was suspicious of a general standard of due process and of tests such as those of "fundamental fairness" that allow justices to roam at will "in their own notions of what policies outside the Bill of Rights are desirable and what are not."[9] The majority view, however, is that there are no superfluous words in the Constitution. The due process requirements of the Fifth and Fourteenth Amendments are additional limitations on national and state governments beyond those enumerated in the other provisions of the Bill of Rights; and in addition to the specific rights listed in the Bill of Rights, the due process clauses protect other fundamental rights, such as the right of privacy.

Ever since the Supreme Court incorporated most of the provisions of the Bill of Rights into the Fourteenth Amendment, little attention has been paid by state judges—or anybody else—to the bills of rights in their respective state constitutions. "The Supreme Court took such complete control of the field that state judges could sit back in the conviction that their part was simply to await the next landmark decisions."[10]

After the United States Supreme Court began to retreat from an expansive interpretation of some provisions of the Bill of Rights in the mid-1970s, especially those relating to the rights of persons accused of crimes, some observers, including Justice Brennan, urged state supreme courts to step into the breach. State judges, they have argued, should do for civil liberties what some of them have long done for business liberties, that is, find in their own state constitutions protections beyond those provided by Supreme Court interpretations of the national Constitution. Justice Stanley Mosk of the California Supreme Court pointed out that using their state constitutions, "state supreme courts—once thought to be mere bus stops en route to the U.S. Supreme Court—can have the final word."[11] A few state supreme courts have taken up the challenge, particularly in the arena of rights of criminal defendants and protection of the press.

The trend toward a greater state court role in protecting civil liberties has become stronger in recent years, especially in Oregon, California, New Jersey, Wisconsin, Massachusetts, and Washington. Examples are the decision of the Minnesota Supreme court barring searches of newsrooms allowed by the U.S. Supreme Court in *Zurcher* v. *Stanford* (see page 159); decisions in California and other states requiring an equalization of funding among school districts not required by the Supreme Court's interpretation of the U.S. Constitution in *San Antonio School District* v. *Rodriguez,* (see page 231); and decisions of some state courts requiring exclusion of unconstitutionally seized evidence which will keep such evidence out of those state courts despite the Supreme Court's limited good faith exception announced in *United States* v. *Leon* (see page 180).

Although the trend toward state courts staking out a different line of interpretation than the U.S. Supreme Court could become strong if the Supreme Court moves more toward the views of its most conservative justices, for the moment, few lawyers are familiar with state constitutional law. Despite many law review articles calling for an independent state court role, most "state courts . . . go no further than the United States Supreme Court in protecting constitutional rights."[12] The United States Supreme Court and the United States Constitution remain the dominant protections for civil liberties and civil rights.

AMENDMENT I: RELIGION, SPEECH, ASSEMBLY, AND PETITION

Congress shall make no law respecting an establishment of religion,

---

The First Amendment is directed specifically to Congress. The Fourteenth Amendment, as now interpreted, imposes the same restrictions on the states.

God is not mentioned in the Constitution, and the word *religion* occurs in only one other place—in the prohibition of any religious test as a qualification for office. The framers of the Constitution were not irreligious. Several of them came from states with established religions, but all probably agreed that religious matters should not fall to the jurisdiction of the national government.

Establishment clause cases are not easy. They stir deep feelings, and the justices, reflecting differences in the nation, are often divided among themselves. Jefferson's "wall of separation between church and state" has become "as winding as the famous serpentine wall" he designed for the University of Virginia.[13] "The Establishment Clause . . . erects a blurred, indistinct, and variable barrier depending on all the circumstances of a particular relationship."[14]

Especially troublesome questions arise when a dispute breaks out between factions within a congregation or between a congregation and its own external church authorities. Obviously civil judges should not decide in such a dispute which side is orthodox and which heretical. But if the dispute involves questions about who owns church property, the Supreme Court has given judges permission to decide such issues by using rules previously established by the Court. Four dissenting members of the Court argue judges should inquire no further than to find out who the highest church authorities may be and to defer to the conclusion of those authorities.[15]

Some have argued that the establishment clause does not forbid governmental support for religion but merely governmental favoritism toward a particular religion. The Supreme Court has rejected this construction.[16] All levels of government must be completely neutral, aiding neither a particular religion nor all religions. "A given law might not *establish* a state religion but nevertheless be one "respecting" that end in the sense of being a step that could lead to such establishment and hence offend the First Amendment."[17] Indeed, in *Lemon* v. *Kurtzman,* the Court established a three-part test for a statute to survive an establishment challenge, especially if it sends out a warning signal by engendering political divisiveness along religious lines: (a) the statute must have a secular purpose; (b) its primary effect must neither advance nor inhibit religion; and (c) "excessive entanglement" with religion must be avoided by the government.

In recent years, however, the Court has given an "accommodationist" interpretation to the establishment clause. It has emphasized, in *Lynch* v. *Donnelly* (see page 43), the Constitution [does not] "require complete separation of church and state; it affirmatively mandates accommodation, not merely tolerance of all religions, and forbids hostility toward any."[18] The Court's new accommodationist view does not reject the test announced in *Lemon* v. *Kurtzman,* but has given a new twist to it. For a statute to survive a challenge that it violates the establishment clause, the statute's "secular legislative purpose" need not be an exclusively secular one; the statute must still have a "primary effect that neither advances nor inhibits religion" but it is okay if the benefit to religion is only slight or incidental or happens to coincide or harmonize with the tenets of some religions, and, although the statute and its administration must still avoid "excessive government entanglement with religion," divisiveness along religious lines by itself is not sufficient to invalidate government conduct.[19] (This "accommodationist" interpretation of the Lemon test, or what the dissenting justices describe as a "relaxed application" of it,[20] splits the Court five to four so future appointments to the Court will especially affect future interpretations of the establishment clause.)

Applying these generalities we find the establishment clause forbids states to introduce devotional exercises of any variety into the public school curriculum, including denominationally neutral prayers, devotional reading of the Bible, recitation of the Lord's Prayer, or the posting of the Ten Commandments on the walls of public classrooms.[21]

The Court has not, as is often said, made it unconstitutional for students to say prayers in the public schools. Any student can pray any time he or she wishes to do so. What the Constitution forbids is the sponsorship or encouragement, directly or indirectly, of prayer by public school authorities. On its way to the Supreme Court is the question of the constitutionality of the laws of twenty-three states authorizing an official moment of silence at the opening of each school day during which time students may engage in voluntary prayer or meditation: the lower federal courts have declared some of these laws unconstitutional and in 1984 the Senate voted down a silent-prayer proposed constitutional amendment.

However, in 1984 Congress did make it unlawful for any public high school receiving federal funds (almost all of them do), to keep student groups from using school facilities for religious worship if the school otherwise opens its facilities for other student meetings. (What Congress did was to make it unlawful for such high schools "to deny equal access to, or discriminate against, any student who wishes to conduct a meeting within that limited open forum on the basis of the religious, political, philosophical, or other content of the speech at such meetings." Although adopted to provide equal access for worship, this law also provides federal protection for unpopular and unfashionable student groups to hold meetings in high schools during noninstructional times.) Congress made it clear that it was not authorizing any public official to influence the form or content of any prayer or religious activity, to require any person to participate in religious activities, or to authorize any school to expend public funds beyond the incidental cost of providing the space for student-initiated meetings.

The Supreme Court has already decided that a university that makes its facilities generally available to student activities does not violate the establishment clause if it allows some student groups to use its facilities for religious worship. On the contrary, if the university were to ban religious activities while allowing other kinds of programs, it would violate the constitutional provision "prohibiting the free exercise" of religion (see page 144). However, in sustaining this practice, the Court pointedly noted, "University students are, of course young adults. They are less impressionable than younger students and should be able to appreciate that the University's policy is one of neutrality toward religion."[22] Moreover, the Court has refused to set aside lower court rulings forbidding the use of public school facilities by religious groups and by students who wish to conduct prayer meetings before the start of classes. These actions suggest that what the establishment clause permits at the college level it may forbid in precollegiate public schools. Now that Congress has acted to provide equal access for religious worship in public high schools that question is likely to come back to the Supreme Court for full dress review.

A state may not proscribe from its school curriculum the teaching of Darwin's theory of evolution because of "its supposed conflict with the biblical account, literally read."[23] School authorities may not permit religious instructors to come into the public school building during the school day to provide religious instruction, even on a voluntary basis.[24] On the other hand, the Constitution does not prevent the study of the Bible or religion in public schools when presented as part of a secular program of education. School may release students from part of the compulsory school day in order to secure religious instruction, provided it takes place outside of the school buildings.[25]

An especially troublesome and controversial area relates to governmental aid to church-operated schools. The principles are easy to formulate, the application difficult. A state may provide aid to promote the well-being and education of students; it may not give aid to religion. At the college level the problems are relatively simple. Tax funds may be used to build buildings and operate programs at church-operated schools, provided tax funds are not used to support sectarian education. These grants to colleges require no elaborate intervention of governmental authority to ensure that they will be used only for secular purposes.[26]

At the elementary and secondary level the problems are greater. The secular and religious parts of the institution are more closely interwoven. The students are younger, more susceptible to indoctrination, and the chances are that aid given to church-operated schools will seep over to aid for religion.[27] Therefore, the Supreme Court has looked at tax assistance to church-operated elementary and secondary schools with much greater skepticism than such aid at the college level.

Tax funds may be used to provide school children, including those in church-operated schools (except those that deny admission to pupils because of race or religion),[28] with textbooks,[29] lunches, and transportation to and from schools.[30] Also approved have been the use of public funds to provide and score standardized tests, diagnostic services for speech and hearing provided in the schools, and guidance and remedial services provided outside church-operated schools.[31] A state may reimburse sectarian schools for the costs to administer state required and prepared tests and for costs to comply with state attendance and data-collection requirements.[32] These uses of tax dollars are viewed as promoting the health, safety, and secular education, not as aiding religion.

The Court, in *Mueller* v. *Allen,* has also approved a tax deduction for public and private school expenses, including tuition payments, even though the bulk of the deductions are claimed by parents sending children to sectarian schools.[33] These uses of tax dollars are viewed as promoting the health, safety, and secular education of students, not for aiding religion.

On the other side, tax funds may not be used to maintain facilities, provide instructional equipment such as maps, charts, records, or laboratory equipment,[34] provide auxiliary services such as counseling to students inside church-operated schools, produce teacher-prepared tests, or transport students to and from field trips.[35] A state may not directly reimburse parents for tuition paid to send children to parochial schools. (It may do so indirectly, as we have noted, if it provides a tax exemption to cover expenses to send children to either public or private schools.[36])

If taxes can be used for textbooks, why not for teachers; if for standardized tests, why not for teacher-prepared tests; if for transportation to schools, why not for transportation to field trips; if for books, why not for maps; if for counseling outside of a parochial school, why not for inside it? "A textbook is ascertainable," but a teacher's handling of a subject is not.[37] A standardized test is not prepared by church schools, but teacher-prepared tests are an "integral part of the teaching process."[38] Transportation to and from schools is a routine round trip every student makes every day and is unrelated to any aspect of the curriculum; field trips are controlled by teachers and are an aid to instructional programs. Counseling outside a school is less likely to get involved with religious matters than that within the "pervasively sectarian atmosphere of the school."[39] As for its approval of tax-purchased books but disapproval of tax purchased records, maps, and other kinds of instructional materials, the Court has recognized there is a "tension" between its holdings. Nonetheless, the judges argue, when a standardized textbook is used both in public and church-operated schools it provides assurances that the books will not be sectarian or used for sectarian purposes, whereas there is much greater danger that other kinds of teaching materials may be diverted to religious purposes.[40]

Laws requiring business establishments to close on Sunday and tax exemptions for church property, along with that of other nonprofit institutions, have passed the Supreme Court's tests. As to the former, whatever their original purpose, they now have the secular purpose and effect of promoting family living by providing a common day of rest and recreation.[41] As to the tax exemption, it neither advances nor inhibits religion, is neither sponsorship nor hostility, and unlike a direct subsidy does not involve excessive entanglement, perhaps even less entanglement than there would be if churches were not included within the nonprofit exemption and were subject to taxation.[42]

Lynch v. *Donnelly* (1984) most clearly establishes a new accommodationist orientation by at least five members of the Court. The Court held that the City of Pawtucket, Rhode Island, could pay for and display the Nativity scene in the heart of its shopping district, along with Santa's house, sleigh, Christmas trees, lights, and other symbols of the Christmas season. The Court concluded that the city fathers had commercial, not religious purposes in mind, that the effect provided little or no benefit to religion in general or to the Christian faith in particular, and there was no excessive entanglement between religion and government. The City, said the Court, "has principally taken note of a significant historical religious event long celebrated in the Western World. . . . The creche in the display depicts the historical origins of this traditional event long recognized as a National Holiday."[43] Justice Brennan, in dissenting argued, "the creche is far from a mere representation of a 'particular historic religious event.' . . . It is, instead, best understood as a mystical re-creation of an event that lies at the heart of Christian faith. To suggest, as the Court does, that such a symbol is merely 'traditional' and therefore no different from Santa's house . . . is not only offensive to those for whom the creche has profound significance, but insulting to those who insist for religious or personal reasons that the story of Christ is in no sense a part of 'history' nor an unavoidable element of our national heritage."

Despite signs of a more relaxed interpretation of the establishment clause, the Court (*Larkin* v. *Grendel's Den*, 1982) set aside a Massachusetts law giving churches the right to veto liquor licenses for taverns located within a 500-foot radius of the church. "The mere appearance of a joint exercise of legislative authority by Church and State," said the Court, "provides a significant symbolic benefit to religion."[44] And the Court had little difficulty deciding that Minnesota had violated the establishment clause when it exempted all religious organizations receiving more than half of their total contributions from their own members from certain registration and reporting requirements of its charitable contributions act. Said the Court, "The clearest command of the Establishment Clause is that one religious denomination cannot be officially preferred over another. . . . It is plain that the principal effect of the fifty per cent rule . . . is to impose the registration and reporting requirements of the Act on some religious organizations but not on others."[45]

Yet the next year (*Marsh* v. *Chambers,* 1983) the Court simply ignored the three-part test to sustain the centuries old practice of paying chaplains to open sessions of state legislatures and Congress. It merely noted that the nation from its very beginning had opened its legislative sessions in this fashion and that legislators, unlike school children, are adults "presumably not readily susceptible to . . . peer pressure."[46] The dissenting justices contended, "if any group of law students were asked to apply [the three part test of the Lemon decision] to the question of legislative prayer, they would nearly unanimously find the practice to be unconstitutional," suggesting that the dissenters, if professors, would flunk their colleagues in a constitutional law test.

---

or prohibiting the free exercise thereof;

"The Court has struggled to find a neutral course between the two Religion Clauses, both of which are cast in absolute terms, and either of which, if expanded to a logical extreme, would tend to clash with the other."[47] To illustrate, if Congress drafts those who have religious scruples against participation in war, it might violate the free exercise clause, but if it exempts them, it might violate the establishment clause. So far Congress and the Court have avoided this particular issue. Congress could draft conscientious objectors. Its modern practice, however, is to exempt from military conscription persons who by reason of religious belief are conscientiously opposed to participation in war, but not those who opposed on "political, sociological, or philosophical grounds." In part to avoid a clash between the two clauses, the Supreme Court has construed the word *religious* so broadly that any deeply held humanistic opposition to participation in any and all wars in any form was included within the congressional granted exemption.[48]

Because there can be no compulsion by law of any form of worship and because the government recognizes neither orthodoxy nor heresy, everyone has an absolute right to believe whatever he or she wishes. A state may not compel a religious belief nor deny any person any right or privilege because of beliefs or lack of them. Such things as religious oaths—for example, an oath that one believes in the existence of God—as a condition of public employment are unconstitutional. So also are disqualifications of clergy from serving in public offices. "However widely that view [that clergy would promote the interests of one sect] may have been in the 18th century by many, including enlightened statesmen of that day, the American experience provides no persuasive support for the fear that clergymen in public office will be less careful of antiestablishment interests or less faithful to their oaths of civil office than their unordained counterparts."[49]

Although carefully protected, the right to act in accordance with one's belief is not, and cannot be, absolute. Religion may not be used to justify action or refusal to act that is contrary to a nondiscriminatory law properly enacted to promote the public safety, morals, health, or general welfare of the community. No one has a right to refuse "to bear arms," to refuse to pay taxes, including social security taxes, to practice polygamy, or to invade the rights of others because of religious convictions. Persons may be required to comply with Sunday closing laws in the interest of providing a common day of rest and recreation even if Sunday is not their sabbath.[50] Parents may be compelled to have their children vaccinated as a condition of attending public schools, despite the fact that vaccination violates their religious beliefs.[51] The Society of Krishna Consciousness could be confined to selling and distributing their literature at a state fairgrounds to a fixed location, even though the distribution and selling of religious literature is a ritual for them. (The Krishna were free to wander the fairgrounds and talk with patrons.)[52] Amish can be required to collect and pay social security taxes for their employees even though both payment and receipt of social security benefits is forbidden by their faith. (Congress exempts from such payments self-employed persons who have religious scruples but not employers or employees.)[53] A church affiliated *school* can be denied benefits of a tax deductible status for the contributions it receives if it engages in racially discriminatory practices.[54] Whether a church could be denied such benefits because of its discriminatory practices has not been decided; but the answer is probably not.)

The Supreme Court, however, will closely scrutinize laws infringing on religious practices and insist upon some compelling public purposes. "Only those interests of the highest order and those not otherwise served can overbalance legitimate claims to the free exercise of religion."[55] In *Bob Jones University* v. *United States* (1983), the Court concluded that the government's "fundamental, overriding interest in eradicating racial discrimination in education," justifies denying tax deductible status to contributions to Bob Jones University, because that University, in accord with the religious convictions of those who charted and operated it, prohibits interracial dating between students. (The Court noted, "We deal here only with religious *schools*—not with churches or other purely religious institutions; here, the governmental interest is in denying public support to racial discrimination in education.")[56]

On the other side, a state's interest in promoting patriotism does not justify its compelling Jehovah's Witnesses (or anyone else) to salute the flag, which to them is a symbol of the Evil One, as a condition of attending public schools, or to force people to display on license plates a state motto, in this instance New Hampshire's motto, "Live free or die."[57] Along the same lines, in face of three centuries of established religious practices, a state may not compel the Amish to send their children to schools beyond the eighth grade.[58] States may not require parents to send children to public schools if parents wish to educate them in religious ones.[59] Nor would the Supreme Court permit states to deny unemployment compensation to Sabbatarians who refused to accept positions requiring them to work on Saturday or Jehovah's Witnesses who quit jobs for religious reasons. In neither case did the state show a substantial countervailing interest to justify this burden on the free exercise of religion. But what of the state's contention that it would violate the ban on establishing a religion to provide unemployment benefits to those who quit jobs for religious reasons, while denying such benefits to those who quit for personal but nonreligious reasons? Chief Justice Burger, for the Court, responded that the payment of unemployment benefits to those unemployed for religious reasons "reflects nothing more than a governmental neutrality in the face of religious differences," a conclusion prompting Justice Rehnquist in dissent to charge that the Court's opinion added "Mud to the already muddied waters of First Amendment jurisprudence."[60]

What criteria define belief or practices as religious? The Constitution provides no definition, and the Supreme Court has been reluctant, understandably, to get into this question. Clearly, "far-out" religions are entitled to the same constitutional protections as are the more traditional ones. However, as Chief Justice Burger has written, "Only beliefs rooted in religion are protected by the Free Exercise Clause. . . . One can, of course, imagine an asserted claim so bizarre, so clearly nonreligious in motivation, as not to be entitled to protection under the Free Exercise Clause. . . ."[61] But, as he has also written, "religious beliefs need not be acceptable, logical, consistent, or comprehensible to others in order to merit First Amendment protection."[62] As difficult as the cases involving the two religion clauses have been, they promise to become even more complicated as the pervasiveness of governmental actions continue and as the number of less orthodox religious groups expands.

---

or abridging the freedom of speech

The right of freedom of speech is essential to the preservation and operation of democracy. "Nevertheless, there are categories of communication and certain special utterances to which the majestic protection of the First Amendment does not extend because 'they are no essential part of any exposition of ideas, and are of such slight social value as a step to the truth that any benefit that may be derived from them is clearly outweighted by the social interest in order and morality. . . .'[63] Libelous speech is such a category." Anyone (except, under most circumstances, a member of Congress, a judge, or the President) who slanders or libels another may be penalized. "Obscene" speech is not entitled to constitutional protection, nor is child pornography." "Fighting words" that by their very utterance injure and provoke others to imminent attack are outside of the pale of protection. So are incitements of others to immediate acts of violence. (Also apparently outside the scope of constitutional protection are words that "create an immediate panic," see below.) Constitutional problems are involved, however, in the definition and determination of what speech is libelous, obscene, child pornography, seditious incitement, or "fighting words." The Supreme Court is very suspicious of definitions that cast their nets too wide.

Fighting words must be limited to those that "have a direct tendency to cause acts of violence by the person to whom, individually, the remarks are addressed"; the mere fact that the words are abusive, harsh, or insulting is not sufficient.[64] In fact, one close student of the subject, David O'Brien, has concluded that the Burger Court has so narrowly applied the category as to virtually eliminate it. O'Brien quoted John Hart Ely, "Fighting words are no longer to be understood as a euphemism for either controversial or dirty talk but requires instead an unambiguous invitation to a brawl."[65] Nonetheless, the Supreme Court as recently as 1982 reaffirmed that "fighting words"—those that provoke immediate violence—are not protected by the First Amendment. In fact, the Court reached back to the old "clear and present danger test" to add what may become a new category of words not entitled to constitutional protection, namely, "words that create an immediate panic."[66] We shall have to await subsequent decisions to determine whether this is really a new category of speech outside the scope of the First Amendment or perhaps just another way to talk about fighting words.

Libel prosecutions used to be a favorite means of suppressing criticism of government officials and preventing discussion of public issues. In seventeenth century England, seditious libel was defined to include criticism of the King or his ministers, whether true or false, and the stirring-up of public discontent. Under the Constitution, however, no one can be convicted of defaming *public officials* or *public figures,* either in a civil suit or a criminal trial, merely because of issuing false statements. There also must be proof that the false comment was made "with knowledge that it was false or with reckless disregard of whether it was false or not."[67] (In establishing the fact that a publication was made with knowledge of its falsity or with reckless regard for its truth, public officials and figures may inquire into the state of mind of editors and publishers: The First Amendment does not protect conversations among newspeople from judicial scrutiny.)[68]

A different libel rule prevails for comments made about private individuals. Moreover, persons do not lose their status as private individuals merely because their names get into the papers because they have been robbed, or because they have gotten a divorce that received a great deal of publicity, or because of being a scientist supported by a federal grant whose work a United States senator thinks to be a waste of public funds. A state has the authority to adopt less stringent standards to prove libel of private individuals than of public officials or public figures. A state may permit a private individual to recover actual damages upon a showing of fault on the part of those responsible for the defamatory falsehood—for example, issuing a false statement without taking responsible precautions to check it. Damages to be awarded under this less stringent test, however, are only to recompense the defamed individuals to the extent that they can show actual damages.[69] (Punitive damages, those imposed as punishment, may only be awarded to private individuals by meeting the same stringent standards as those imposed on public figures and officials.) The reasons to permit easier libel actions by private persons than public ones is that the former have less effective opportunities to respond to defaming statements; they have not voluntarily exposed themselves to the risk of injury from defamatory falsehoods; the public's interest in knowing about them is less compelling; and they are entitled to some protection of their right to privacy.

First Amendment and due process concerns (see page 191) do not keep a person who has been libeled from bringing an action in any state in which the magazine or newspaper regularly circulates.[70] On the other hand, First Amendment considerations do require appellate courts to set aside the normal rule that the findings of trial courts are to be reversed only when they are clearly erroneous. In reviewing libel judgments, appellate courts are to make an independent judgment to "determine whether the record establishes actual malice with convincing clarity."[71]

What of obscenity? The producing, selling, mailing, or transporting of obscene matter is not entitled to constitutional protection, although its mere possession for private use cannot be made a crime.[72] The Supreme Court, however, has had the same difficulty as has everybody else who has tried to define obscenity. As Justice Brennan has written, "No other aspect of the First Amendment has, in recent years, commanded so substantial a commitment of our time, generated such disharmony of views, and remained so resistant to the formulation of stable and manageable standards."[73] Since the Supreme Court entered the field in 1957, there have been over eighty-five separate opinions written by the justices.

In *Miller* v. *California* (1973), Chief Justice Burger, speaking for five members of the Court, once again tried to clarify the constitutional standards. A work—a book, a film, a play—may be considered obscene provided (1) the average person, applying contemporary standards of the community in which the court sits, finds that the work, taken as a whole, appeals to a prurient interest in sex; (2) the work depicts in a patently offensive way sexual conduct specifically defined by the law or by decisions of the courts;[74] and (3) the work taken as a whole, lacks serious literary, artistic, political, or scientific value.[75] The Chief Justice explicitly rejected part of the previous test, the so-called *Memoirs* v. *Massachusetts* formula, namely, that no work should be judged obscene unless it was "utterly without redeeming social value." He argued that such a test made it impossible for a state to outlaw hard-core pornography. He also stipulated, and the Court has since reaffirmed, that the standard of offensiveness is to be that of the community from which the jury comes, rather than what the jury might believe to be the standards of the nation.[76] The jury is to use its common sense and general knowledge about local community standards. Because of the variability of community standards, it is possible for a book or a movie to be legally obscene in one state or city but not in another. A jury may not, however, take into account the effect of the materials on children in determining community standards, otherwise it would reduce the adult population to reading or seeing only that which is fit for children.[77]

In determining whether materials are obscene, a jury may consider the motives of sellers to see if they are engaging in commercial exploitation of sexually offensive materials: The circumstances of distribution are relevant to deciding whether the materials are being forced on people and the motives of sellers are relevant in determining whether social importance claimed for materials is a pretense or a reality.[78]

When persons are being criminally prosecuted for selling obscene materials, the state must prove its case beyond a reasonable doubt, including not merely the fact of the sale but that the materials are obscene. There is a less burdensome standard of proof required for civil actions; for example, when governments try to close theaters as a public nuisance by proving they routinely show only obscene movies. The Supreme Court has not been clear, however, whether the less stringent standard of "preponderance of the evidence" will do or whether in judging matters to be obscene in a civil proceeding states have to use the more demanding "clear and convincing" standard or one of its variants.[79]

There were many who read the *Miller* decision, and its companion cases, to mean that the Supreme Court would no longer have to review each book or movie in order to second-guess the local judge or jury; rather the Court would merely look to see if the proper standard had been applied and leave the determination of its application to the trial courts. But in *Jenkins* v. *Georgia* (1974), the Court announced, "it would be a serious misreading of *Miller* to conclude that juries have unbridled discretion in determining what is patently offensive." And after a review of the movie *Carnal Knowledge,* the Court held that it was not patently offensive and that, contrary to the conclusion of the jury in Albany, Georgia, it was not constitutionally obscene.[80]

Some members of the Supreme Court would go even further. Justices Brennan and Marshall, after struggling for years to develop a constitutional definition, have come to the conclusion that it is impossible to do so without endangering protected speech and miring the Court in "case-by-case determination of obscenity." These justices would let adults see or read whatever they wish, and would permit only narrowly drawn statutes designed to prevent pornography from being forced on persons or made available to minors.[81] Justice Stevens also finds criminal prosecutions for obscenity constitutionally unacceptable because of the impossibility of giving any precision to the standards, especially "offensiveness to the community." He would permit, however, some latitude for civil regulations that treat panderers of obscenity as public nuisances, and he finds acceptable time, place, and manner civil regulations for the sale and distribution of pornography.[82]

Non-obscene but erotic literature and movies, although constitutionally protected, nonetheless are entitled to less protection than political speech. Cities may regulate by zoning ordinance where "adult motion pictures" may be commercially shown. "The state may legitimately use the content of these materials as a basis for placing them in a different classification from other motion pictures."[83]

There are limits, however. "When a zoning ordinance infringes upon a protected liberty, it must be narrowly drawn and must further a sufficiently substantial governmental interest." So said the Court when it struck down a zoning ordinance of the Borough of Mount Ephraim in New Jersey that had excluded from a small shopping district all live entertainment, and by doing so prevented "non-obscene nude dancing" in an adult book store. Chief Justice Burger in dissent chided his colleagues for trivializing and demeaning the First, "that great Amendment."[84]

When it comes to children, all the rules are different. Sexually explicit materials either about minors or aimed at minors are not protected by the First Amendment. State and local governments—provided they act under narrowly drawn statutes—can, for example, ban the knowing sale of "girly" magazines to minors, even if such materials would not be considered legally obscene if sold to adults. States may make it a crime to depict visually sexual conduct by children, even if the depicted behavior would not be considered obscene if done by adults. Even those members of the Court who would allow adults to read and see anything about adults, agree that when it comes to children the states may step in to make criminal the production or sale of pornographic materials about children or aimed at them.[85]

Commercial speech is now entitled to constitutional protection, but there are "common sense" differences between it and other kinds of speech so that it is subject to more regulation than are other varieties. Decisions of the Supreme Court dealing with "more traditional First Amendment problems do not extend automatically to this as yet uncharted area."[86] For example, overbreadth analysis is not applicable, perhaps not the prohibitions against prior restraint. See page 151. Commercial speech is subject to a four-part analysis. "At the outset we must determine whether the expression is protected by the First Amendment. (1) For commercial speech to come within that provision, it at least must concern lawful activity and not be misleading. (2) Next, we ask whether the asserted governmental interest is substantial. If both inquiries yield positive answers, we must determine (3) whether the regulation directly advances the governmental interest asserted, and (4) whether it is more extensive than is necessary to serve that interest."[87]

A law forbidding "false and misleading" political speech would be clearly unconstitutional. Who is to say in the realm of political matters what is false and misleading? But a law forbidding false and misleading advertising is not unconstitutional. What is false and misleading advertising can be established. Moreover, advertiser access to the truth about their products and prices "substantially eliminates any danger that governmental regulation of false or misleading . . . advertising will chill accurate and nondeceptive commercial expression."[88] Advertising via radio and television also merits special consideration and is subject to greater restraint than print media.

When it comes to advertising by professionals,—doctors, lawyers, pharmacists—truthful advertising cannot be forbidden. Misleading advertising can be prohibited entirely. That which *may* be misleading can be regulated by narrowly drawn restrictions if the state demonstrates a particular regulation furthers it's substantial interest.[89]

Applying these guidelines about state regulation of commercial speech, here are some specific examples. Without constitutional objection Congress and the federal regulatory agencies can ban advertising of cigarettes over radio and television. A state may forbid the practice of optometry under a trade name.[90] Since it is illegal to discriminate in employment on the basis of sex, a city may make it illegal for newspapers to publish want ads under the headings, "Male Help Wanted" or "Female Help Wanted," just as it could forbid advertisements for prostitution or for illegal drugs. The Court warned, however, that governments may not forbid newspapers to publish advertisements advocating "sexism or other controversial subjects."[91] A state may not forbid pharmacists from advertising the prices of prescription drugs or lawyers from advertising their charges, or listing their fields of specialization, or the states in which they are licensed, or from mailing their business cards.[92] A city may not ban "For Sale" signs in front of homes, even though the purpose is to prevent panic selling by whites in neighborhoods becoming racially integrated.[93] Nor may governments ban advertising of contraceptives.[94]

Not only has the commercial speech exception been withdrawn, but the Court has specifically ruled that corporations, including utilities, are entitled to freedom of speech. A state may not prohibit corporations from spending money to influence votes on referendum proposals, nor ban promotional advertising by an electric utility, nor prohibit a utility from including pronuclear statements in its bills.[95] Justices Brennan and Marshall, two stalwart champions of freedom of expression, dissented from these decisions, contending that corporations, as artificial persons spending stockholders' funds, could be reasonably subject to limitations not permissible to natural persons.

What of seditious speech—that is, advocating the use of force as a political tactic or as a means to overthrow the government? Since World War I, the Supreme Court has considered issues relating to seditious speech a number of times in a variety of contexts. In 1951, in *Dennis* v. *United States*, the Court sustained the application of the Smith Act, a federal statute making it illegal to advocate the violent overthrow of government, to the leaders of the Communist Party of the United States, even though there was no evidence that they actually urged people to commit specific actions of violence.[96] However, that decision, although never specifically overruled, has subsequently been undermined by later rulings. The Supreme Court has made it clear that the Smith Act cannot be applied except to those who incite *imminent* lawless action.

The net result of these several decisions is that seditious incitement, if narrowly defined by statute and narrowly applied by the courts, is another exception to the protection of the First Amendment. Or perhaps it is better to state it positively: The First Amendment protects the abstract advocacy of violence and forbids a government to make it a crime or to punish persons for what they advocate except "where such advocacy is directed to inciting or producing imminent lawless action and is likely to incite or produce such action. . . . The mere abstract teaching . . . of the moral propriety or even moral necessity for a resort to force and violence is not the same as preparing a group for violent action and steeling it to such action. . . . A statute which fails to draw this distinction impermissibly intrudes upon the freedoms guaranteed by the First and Fourteenth Amendments."[97] Only speech that is a concrete and direct incitement to violent acts is not constitutionally protected. Narrowly drawn and interpreted statutes that proscribe such speech are constitutional.

Outside the areas of fighting words, libel, obscenity, and seditious incitement, the Supreme Court has elaborated a whole series of doctrines to measure the constitutionality of laws that appear to restrict freedom of expression. It is especially suspicious of laws that impose restraints prior to publication, including licensing schemes that require permission before a speech can be made, a motion picture shown, a newspaper published, or that in any way try to interpose the authority of government between someone trying to communicate something and the audience. The Supreme Court has not gone so far as to declare all forms of prior censorship unconstitutional, but "a prior restraint on expression comes to this Court with a 'heavy presumption' against its constitutionality."[98] In the celebrated case of *New York Times Company* v. *United States* (1971) the Supreme Court held that the government had not met this burden when the Attorney General tried to secure a court injunction against the publication by *The New York Times, The Washington Post,* and other newspapers of the so-called Pentagon Papers, a classified study of some of the decisions leading to our involvement in the Vietnam War. Three concurring justices—Black, Douglas, and Brennan—made it clear that in their view the First Amendment forbids a court to impose, however briefly and for whatever reasons, any prior restraint on a newspaper. (Justice Brennan might make an exception during time of war to permit prior restraint on the publications of troop movements.) The dominant view, however, was more limited: In this particular instance the government had failed to show that the publication of these particular documents would cause immediate and specific damage to the nation's security.[99]

In the Pentagon Papers case, the government attempted to assert its right to act without any specific congressional authorization. But in 1979, when the government learned that *The Progressive* was about to publish an article entitled, "The H-Bomb Secret: How We Got It, Why We're Telling It," federal prosecutors went before a federal district judge and sought an injunction pursuant to the Atomic Energy Act. This act authorizes the government to enjoin the dissemination of restricted data concerning the design, manufacture, or utilization of atomic weapons. The district judge concluded that he could "find no plausible reason why the public needs to know the technical details about hydrogen bomb construction" and issued a preliminary restraining order. The courts refused to expedite the case and it never reached the Supreme Court's docket because the government abandoned the effort to enjoin publication after the information in the article was published in other places.[100]

Today, other than for motion pictures and then only for obscenity, the only prior censorship that has passed judicial muster have been requirements that literature not be distributed on a military base without prior approval of post headquarters. The Supreme Court acknowledged special military interests in keeping military activities free of partisan political entanglements and noted that military bases are not ordinary forums of public discussion.[101] And the Court held that the First Amendment does not preclude the CIA from enforcing employment agreements requiring agents to submit all their writings about the CIA for prepublication review, even though they contain no classified materials.[102] The Court has also permitted judges to restrain newspapers from publishing information the newspapers obtained by using pretrial discovery procedures to compel their legal adversaries to produce materials. Said the Court, "An order prohibiting dissemination of discovered information before trial is not the kind of classic prior restraint that requires exacting First Amendment scrutiny."

Governments may adopt reasonable regulations relating to *time, place,* and *manner* of the exercise of First Amendment freedoms. "The First Amendment does not guarantee the right to communicate one's views at all times and places or in any manner that may be desired."[103] No one has the right to take over a church ceremony to show a movie, to hold a political rally on a military base, or to sell and distribute literature in places not designed for that function— such as a fairgrounds during the time of a state fair (a regulation prohibiting such distribution on public streets and parks presents entirely different questions.)

Regulations designed to regulate the time, place, and manner are subject to a three-part test. (The Supreme Court seems partial to three-part tests.) The regulation must be "neutral" with respect to the content of the expression and be applied even-handedly; must leave open ample alternative channels for communication of the information, and must be "narrowly tailored" to serve a significant governmental interest. (Justice Stevens is of the view that this generalization is of little help. He quipped, "Any student of history who has been reprimanded for talking about the World Series during a class discussion of the

First Amendment knows that it is incorrect to state that a time, place, or manner restriction may not be based upon either the content or subject matter of the speech."[104]

Laws that have an impact on freedom of expression, even if the impact is indirect, must be justified by a compelling public interest. The government must adopt measures to accomplish its legitimate goals that are narrowly drawn to avoid more restraint than is necessary. Overly broad or vaguely worded statutes that have a "chilling effect upon First Amendment rights" are especially suspect. "Because First Amendment freedoms need breathing space to survive, government may regulate in the area only with narrow specificity."[105] In fact, an overly broad statute affecting freedom of speech may be declared "facially invalid," that is, the Court may hold not merely that the law as applied to a particular person is unconstitutional, but that the law on its face is unconstitutional. In such instances, even if the defendant's language might have been punished under a more narrowly drawn statute, the defendant has standing to challenge the law.

To illustrate the application of these several generalizations, here are a few examples taken from a substantial number of Supreme Court decisions adverse to state action: Schaumburg, Illinois, was not allowed to forbid direct solicitation of funds by organizations that did not use at least 75 percent of the money they collected for direct charitable purposes. Such an ordinance was unconstitutional, overbroad, and facially unconstitutional. It effectively prevented solicitation by "advocacy organizations," organizations that use funds to advocate causes—clean the air, ban the bomb, stop production of nuclear energy, ban abortions, and so on.[106] A Maryland statute that prohibited a charitable organization from paying expenses of more than 25 percent of the amount raised, but authorized a waiver of this limitation where it would prevent the organization from raising contributions met the same constitutional fate.[107] A Jacksonville, Florida, ordinance was declared unconstitutional that forbade drive-in theaters to show pictures of female nudes that might be visible from any public street or public place (the Court strongly hinted that a more narrowly drawn, nondiscriminatory traffic regulation requiring screening of drive-in movie theaters from the view of motorists might be permissible.[108] New York's attempt to ban "sacrilegious movies" and publications of "criminal deeds of bloodshed or lust . . . so massed as to become vehicles for inciting violent and depraved crimes" was declared unconstitutional because the definitions used were so vague that no one could know what was or was not allowed.[109] A Louisiana statute was held overbroad that declared it unlawful "for any person wantonly to curse or revile or to use obscene or opprobrious language toward or with reference to any member of the city police while in the actual performance of his duties."[110] A similar fate befell an Ohio ordinance making it a crime for a person "to abuse another by using menacing, insulting, slanderous, or profane language."[111] The University of Missouri was told that it lacked constitutional authority to expel a student for distributing an underground campus publication containing indecent materials, the materials falling short of the constitutional definition of obscenity.[112] The Georgia legislature violated the Constitution when it denied a seat to a duly elected member because of critical comments he had made about American participation in the

Vietnam War.[113] Virginia could not punish a newspaper for publishing confidential proceedings of a judicial review commission even though the legislature thought such publications presented a clear and present danger to the orderly administration of justice.[114]

In summary, the Supreme Court has come very close to the view that except for the narrowly defined categories of libel, obscenity, and seditious incitement to violence, "pure speech," including that of corporations, unconnected with action is constitutionally protected from any except reasonable "time, place, and manner" regulations.

When speech becomes bracketed with action, it may lose its constitutional immunity. "We cannot accept the view," wrote Chief Justice Warren, "that an apparently limitless variety of conduct can be labeled speech whenever the person engaged in the conduct intends thereby to express an idea."[115] Or as Chief Justice Burger has written, "Conduct that the State police power can prohibit on a public street does not become automatically protected by the Constitution merely because the conduct is moved to a bar or a 'live theatre' stage, any more than 'live' performance of a man and woman locked in a sexual embrace at high noon in Times Square is protected by the Constitution because they simultaneously engage in a . . . political dialogue."[116]

For decades the Department of State contended that Congress had given to the President and the Secretary of State the power to withhold passports from persons whose activities abroad are causing or likely to cause serious damage to the national security or foreign policy of the United States. Others argued that Congress had not delegated any such powers and could not do so because it would abridge the rights to travel and to speak. The Supreme Court avoided the issue. Then in 1981 the Court agreed with the Secretary of State: The particular facts in the case involved a former employee of the Central Intelligence Agency traveling abroad for the express purpose of exposing CIA agents and taking measures to drive them out of the countries where they were operating. The ex-agent conceded that his activities were causing or were intended to cause serious damage to national security. "Here," said the Court, "beliefs and speech are only part of the respondent's campaign," which involved "conduct that presented a danger to American officials abroad."[117]

Although when speech becomes enmeshed with conduct it loses its character as "pure speech," even so the "Court has repeatedly warned States and government units that they cannot regulate conduct connected with [First Amendment freedoms] through the use of sweeping, dragnet statutes that may, because of vagueness, jeopardize these freedoms . . . [However the Court has been] careful to point out that the Constitution does not bar enactment of laws regulating conduct, even though connected with speech, press, assembly, and petition, if such laws specifically bar only the conduct deemed obnoxious and are carefully and narrowly aimed at that forbidden conduct."[118]

The line between speech and conduct is, of course, not easy to draw. A majority of the justices held that school authorities had violated the Constitution when they suspended two students who had defied their principal by quietly and passively wearing black armbands to school to protest the Vietnam War. Justice Black, long a champion of free speech, wrote a vigorous dissent: "I think . . . that the armbands did exactly what the elected school officials and principal foresaw they would, that is, took the students' minds off their class work."[119] The Supreme Court had less difficulty in unanimously sustaining the constitutionality of the 1965 amendment to the Selective Service Act that made it a crime knowingly to destroy or mutilate draft cards.[120]

State laws or state-sanctioned bar regulations that forbid lawyers to solicit business—"ambulance chasing"—involve speech-conduct and are permissible as applied to lawyers soliciting clients for profit, but are not permissible as applied to lawyers working for nonprofit associations such as the American Civil Liberties Union or the National Association for the Advancement of Colored People. In the case of the former: "In-person solicitation by a lawyer of remunerative employment is a business transaction in which speech is an essential but subordinate component. While this does not remove the speech from the protection of the First Amendment . . . it lowers the level of appropriate judicial scrutiny." "A lawyers's procurement of remunerative employment is a subject only marginally affected with First Amendment concerns. It falls within the State's proper sphere of economic and professional regulation."[121] In the case of the latter, however, "collective activity undertaken to obtain meaningful access to the courts is a fundamental right within the protection of the First Amendment. . . . The ACLU engages in litigation as a vehicle for effective political expression and association, as well as a means of communicating useful information to the public . . . In the context of political expression and association . . . a state must regulate with significantly greater precision. . . . A very distant possibility of harm" flowing from soliciting clients by nonprofit associations does not justify the same kind of restraints as are appropriate for lawyers soliciting clients for pecuniary gains.[122]

In the 1974 amendments to the Federal Election Campaign Act of 1971, Congress regulated the amount that could be spent on behalf of, or contributed to, candidates or political parties for the election of candidates. Whether considered as speech or as speech-conduct, or as the right to associate for political purposes, "these regulations were directly aimed at political communications." Nonetheless, the Supreme Court in *Buckley* v. *Valeo* sustained limitations on *contributions* people, including candidates, could make from their own funds to assist in the election of candidates. Reasoned the Court, limitations on contributions only marginally restricts a contributor's ability to express political views. The Court took a different view, however, on congressional limitations on the amount people could directly spend and declared those restrictions unconstitutional. "Restriction on the amount of money a person or group can spend on political communication during a campaign necessarily reduces the quantity of expression by restricting the number of issues discussed, the depth of their exploration, and the size of the audience reached."[123] However, if candidates or a political party accept funds that the national government now makes available to qualified presidential candidates and political parties involved in such elections, they can be required—as a condition of accepting these federal funds—to limit the amount they spend, regardless of source. Left open for future litigation is whether the expenditures of independent committees organized without any apparent connection to a candidate but working in his or her behalf are subject to the limits imposed on the candidate by the acceptance of federal funds.

The Court's holding sustaining the constitutionality of limitations on contributions to candidates has not been extended to limitations on contributions to groups working for or against ballot measures. The interest in preventing corruption of officials, which provided the basis for the finding that restrictions could be placed on contributions to candidates and their committees, does not justify such restrictions when it comes to groups working for or against ballot measures.[124]

The Court has upheld, however, the right of Congress to forbid trade unions and corporations from making contributions or expenditures from company or union funds to elections in which candidates are chosen (in contrast to elections in which issues are being voted on). Congress has allowed these associations to form PACs (Political Action Committees), to solicit funds from their own stockholders, officers, and members to be used to make political contributions to candidates. Trade union and corporate PACs are not allowed to solicit from any persons except those that belong to the union or corporation. Trade association PACs are subject to another set of restraints and reporting requirements. The Supreme Court has supported Congress's justifications for imposing these limitations on the right to associate both to prevent actual corruption in these elections and the appearance of corruption.[125]

Does the First Amendment restrict the ability of a school board to decide which books may be kept in the school library? The Supreme Court had a hard time with this question. The justices wrote seven different opinions and seventy-four pages, but they were unable to get a majority behind any of the opinions. Apparently what it comes down to is that the First Amendment does apply, actions of school boards are subject to federal court review, school boards have wide discretion in managing which books are suitable for the library, but they may not remove books from library shelves simply because they dislike the ideas contained in those books. The dissenting justices felt that the choice of which books belong in a school library should be left to school boards.[126]

A fascinating cluster of issues was raised by a 1980 decision of the California Supreme Court. The United States Supreme Court had previously established that the federal Constitution does not give one a right to go into a privately owned shopping center against the wishes of the owner to distribute handbills or engage in picketing on matters unrelated to the shopping center's own operations.[127] The Supreme Court of California, however, ruled that whatever the United States Constitution provides, the California Constitution protects "speech and petitioning, reasonably exercised, even when the centers are privately owned." But what of the rights of the owners of the shopping centers? Can a state compel them to allow their property to be used by persons to express views that the owners might find distasteful? The United States Supreme Court ruled that what California had done in this particular case was all right—allow a group of high school students to set up a card table in the corner of a large shopping center to gather signatures on a petition even though the owners of the shopping center had ordered them off the property. But the justices carefully limited the holding to the facts of the case before them and emphasized that the decision was not "blanket approval for state efforts to transform privately owned commercial property into public forums."[128]

or of the press;

Until recently there has been little attention paid to the question of whether the press has freedoms beyond those of other persons. It was assumed that freedom of speech was used as a synonym for freedom of the press. One explanation of the fact that the Constitution speaks to the two freedoms separately is that freedom of speech was thought to protect oral communications, and freedom of the press, written ones. Another explanation is that the framers added the phrase "of the press" because "dissemination" had more often been the object of official restraint than had mere personal expression. Although Justice Stewart wrote, "That the First Amendment speaks separately of freedom of speech and freedom of the press is no constitutional accident, but an acknowledgment of the critical role played by the press in American society,"[129] the prevailing view is that of the Chief Justice: "The First Amendment does not 'belong' to any definable category of persons or entities; it belongs to all who exercise its freedoms."[130] If Justice Stewart's view ever prevails, then the Court will have to face the issue of who qualifies for the special benefits of "the press."

Although the Court has never defined the press, it has been especially solicitous of protecting publications from any kind of taxation that could possibly have an intimidating effect on them. General taxes, along with such economic regulations as fair labor standards acts, anti-trust laws, and so on, can be applied to the press. But when Huey Long as governor of Louisiana persuaded the legislature to impose a tax on some newspapers that had been critical of him, the Supreme Court (*Grosjean* v. *American Press Co.*, 1936) declared this taxation unconstitutional. The Court perceived that the tax had been imposed to punish a select group of newspapers.[131]

So careful is the Court to protect the press from possible governmental threats that in *Minneapolis Star* v. *Minnesota Comm. of Revenue*, 1983, it declared a Minnesota tax unconstitutional, even though it had been adopted with no evil intent and in amount less than the sales taxes on other enterprises. Rather than collect a sales tax on every newspaper or magazine sold, Minnesota imposed a tax on ink and paper used by publications, exempting the first $100,000 worth of ink and paper consumed in each calendar year so that the tax fell most heavily on the largest newspaper in the state. "Whatever the motive of the legislature in this case," said Justice O'Connor for the Court, "we think that recognizing a power in the State not only to single out the press but also to tailor the tax so that it singles out a few members of the press presents such a potential for abuse that no interest suggested by Minnesota can justify the scheme."[132]

The only limitation the Supreme Court has ever permitted on a newspaper's right to the truthful publication of materials, whether they have obtained such materials lawfully or unlawfully, is when newspapers are parties to a suit and use the discovery process of a court. (Prior to trial parties may use the power of the court to secure and discover information from their opponents that may be relevant to the pending lawsuit.) Under such circumstances, newspapers are not entitled to any exemption from protective orders of a judge not to publish the materials, and they can be kept from using the information obtained through the use of such processes. A newspaper may disseminate identical information covered by the protective order of a court as long as it is gained through means independent of the court's process.[133]

Some newspeople claim not only the right to be free from governmental interference to publish what they wish, but also the right of access to all news sources. However, there is no general constitutional "right of access" that gives newspeople, or anybody else, a right to go wherever they wish to interview whomever they desire or to see whatever documents they claim are of general public interest. Neither the First nor the Fourteenth Amendment guarantees to the news media the right of access to governmental information beyond that available to the public generally. Laws have been sustained that deny to reporters the right to interview prisoners or to take television cameras or recording instruments into prisons.[134]

Although there is no general constitutional right of access, in *Richmond Newspapers, Inc.* v. *Virginia* (1980), in what Justice Stevens called a "watershed case," the Supreme Court did rule "that the acquisition of newsworthy matter is entitled to some constitutional protection." The Court held that a trial judge could not, even with the consent of the prosecutor and defendant, close a trial to the press and public without a specific finding by the judge that there is some "overriding interest" that would justify such a closure. Said Chief Justice Burger, "It is not crucial whether we describe this right to attend criminal trials to hear, see, and communicate observations as a right to access, or a right to gather information." Whatever it is called, the Court did find that the right of access to trials is protected by a combination of the First, Ninth, and Fourteenth Amendments. Moreover, Chief Justice Burger even seemed to concede some special role for the press. Although pointedly saying that media representatives enjoy only the same right of access as the public, he did recognize that the media often function as "surrogates for the public," and are "accorded special seating and priority of entry so that they may report what people in attendance have seen and heard."[135] Clearly, if this right of public access is extended to other governmental proceedings beyond trials, the decision will deserve Justice Stevens's accolade.

Since *Richmond,* in which at least some of the justices grudgingly conceded that the public and press have a First Amendment right to attend trials, the Court has talked more enthusiastically about the values of open trials. Five members have specifically stated that "the press and general public have a constitutional right of access to criminal trials."[136] This right of access to courtrooms is now firmly established within the First Amendment.

Recently, the Court has declared unconstitutional a Massachusetts statute requiring the exclusion of the press and public during the testimony of a minor victim in a sex-offense trial.[137] It also refused to allow a trial judge in a rape and murder case to close the jury selection process. The trial judge stated that he was taking this action to protect the privacy of potential jurors who were subject to questioning about their past sexual experiences and attitudes. But the Supreme Court, speaking through Chief Justice Burger, was unpersuaded. The presumption that trials must be kept open, including questioning of jurors, could be overcome "only by an overriding interest based on findings that closure is essential to preserve higher values and is narrowly tailored to serve that interest. The interest is to be articulated along with findings specific enough that a reviewing court can determine whether the closure order was properly entered."[138] In other words, a trial judge who closes any portion of a trial better have very persuasive reasons, and must put those reasons in writing so that they can be reviewed by appellate judges.

Congress has taken significant steps to provide access to government files. The Freedom of Information Act of 1965, as amended in 1974, provides that federal agencies are to make information available on request, with certain exceptions, such as defense secrets, criminal investigation files, and interoffice memorandums relating to pending decisions. If they fail to do so, the act provides for prompt judicial action to implement the requirements of the law.

Freedom of access to the public can also be inhibited by the news media themselves. In some cities there may be only a single newspaper and it may also own the local television station. The Court has been hostile to attempts by government to impose access regulations on the printed media or give persons a "right to reply" to media attacks on them. A unanimous Court ruled that Florida acted unconstitutionally when it adopted a law giving to political candidates a right to reply in a newspaper's columns to critical editorial comments by that newspaper. The government lacks the power to make newspapers publish what they do not wish to publish. As Chief Justice Burger wrote, "A responsible press is an undoubtedly desirable goal, but press responsibility is not mandated by the Constitution and like many other virtues, it cannot be legislated."[139] The Court has been more lenient with respect to attempts to provide access to the broadcast media: Congress does have the power to confer upon "legally qualified candidates for Federal office" a right to demand from broadcasters that they sell them time on behalf of their candicacy. The Federal Communications Commission, in order to implement this requirement, may define when a campaign has started and may impose sanctions upon licensees who fail to provide this access.[140]

Does the First Amendment confer on newspeople an immunity from being compelled by a grand jury or other governmental agencies to divulge the sources of their information? Although some states have conferred a qualified privilege on newspeople in order that they may more readily gather the news, the First Amendment provides no such immunity. A reporter has no less an obligation than any other citizen to respond to a grand jury subpoena and answer relevant questions.[141] Nor does the First Amendment protect the files of newspeople from being searched by the police with a valid search warrant. It does not make any constitutional difference that the newspeople may themselves be innocent of any suspected wrongdoing.[142] Congress has, however, by law provided special protection for newspeople from such searches. Congress has prohibited courts from issuing warrants to federal, state, and local police officers that would authorize these officers to search "the products of news organizations and others engaged in First Amendment activities," except when the newspeople are themselves suspected of a crime related to the materials they are holding or when there is reason to believe that the immediate seizure of the materials is necessary to prevent death or serious bodily injury. (Materials in newspeople's files are still vulnerable to subpoenas.)

The Constitution protects communications via the mails, radio, television, motion pictures, billboards, handbills, and picketing. For each of these media there are special problems that result in different degress of protection. "Each method of communicating ideas is 'a law unto itself' and that law must reflect the 'differing natures, values, abuses, and dangers of each method.' "[143]

Fifty years ago Justice Holmes wrote: "The United States may give up the Post Office when it sees fit, but while it carries it on the use of the mails is almost as much a part of free speech as the right to use our tongues."[144] Justice

Holmes, however, wrote in dissent, and the prevailing doctrine was that the use of the mails was a privilege that the federal government could freely condition. Then, in 1965, the Supreme Court, in *Lamont* v. *Postmaster General,* adopted Justice Holmes's position and ruled unconstitutional a 1962 congressional act that directed the Postmaster General to detain unsealed foreign mailings of "communist political propaganda" and to deliver them only upon the addressees' request. In striking down the first act of Congress ever to be held in conflict with the First Amendment, Justice Douglas said for the Court, "The Act sets administrative officials astride the flow of mail to inspect it, appraise it, write the addressee about it, and await a response before dispatching the mail. . . . The regimen of this Act is at war with the 'uninhibited, robust, and wide-open' debate and discussion that are contemplated by the First Amendment."[145] Six years later the Court unanimously extended the *Lamont* decision to void laws authorizing postal authorities to make administrative determinations of obscenity, exclude it from the mails, and cut off all mail to persons sending it.[146]

Customs officials, in contrast to postal authorities, may seize obscene materials, even if they are not for sale but for private use. But this type of administrative action must be reviewed promptly by the courts. Judicial proceedings must be commenced within fourteen days of the seizure and concluded within sixty days.[147]

Whereas administrative censorship of the mails is unconstitutional, householder censorship is not. "The mailer's right to communicate must stop at the mailbox of an unreceptive addressee."[148] The Supreme Court upheld a law giving any householder the absolute right to ask the postmaster to order mailers to delete their names from all mailing lists and to refrain from sending any advertising materials that householders in their sole discretion believe to be "erotically arousing or sexually provocative." It makes no constitutional difference if the householder includes in such a category a "dry-goods catalogue." This is not governmental censorship.[149] Moreover, Congress may forbid the deposit into any "authorized" mailbox of any materials on which no postage has been paid. Mailboxes are part of the national postal system and do not have a public forum status such as a street.[150]

To be distinguished from administrative interference with the mails and the customs, Congress has the authority to make it a crime knowingly to send obscene material through the mails, even if it is sent to adults who have requested it.[151] Congress may even make it a crime, as it has done, to transport such material in commerce, even if it is carried in a briefcase and is designed only for private use.[152]

What of broadcasting? "Of all forms of communications, it is broadcasting that has received the most limited First Amendment protection."[153] "The broadcast media pose unique and special problems not present in traditional free speech cases." "There is no 'unabridgeable' First Amendment right to broadcast comparable to the right of every individual to speak, write, or publish." "This is not to say that the First Amendment is irrelevant . . . to broadcasting. . . . But it is the right of viewers and listeners, not the right of the broadcasters, which is paramount."[154]

However, after having said all these things the Supreme Court in *FCC* v. *League of Women Voters of California* (1984), in a five to four watershed decision, for the first time declared unconstitutional a federal statute regulating broadcasters. That statute stated, "No noncommercial educational broadcasting station which receives a grant from the Corporation for Public Broadcasting [all public television stations and most public radio stations] . . . may engage in editorializing." Justice Brennan, writing for the majority, distinguished this ban from the previously sustained "fairness doctrine"—a requirement that all licensees must provide for balanced presentation of all points of view—on the grounds that the ban on editorializing strikes at "the heart" of the First Amendment. It "singles out noncommercial broadcasters and denies them the right to address their chosen audience on matters of public importance." The restriction was not "narrowly tailored to further a substantial government interest."[155] The dissenting justices felt that those who took government dollars could be subject to what they considered to be reasonable limitations designed to protect the stations from being unduly influenced by federal authorities, to keep the stations from becoming privileged outlets, and to prevent government subsidies of editorials to which many taxpayers might object.

Perhaps the most important consequences of *FCC* v. *League of Women Voters of California,* may be the footnotes in the majority opinion noting that the "prevailing rationale for broadcast regulation has come under increasing criticism in recent years" because technological changes such as cable, direct beam broadcast, and video tapes might be undermining the theory that the scarcity of channels justifies substantial government regulation of television. "We are not prepared, however," said Justice Brennan, "to reconsider our long-standing approach without some signal from Congress or the FCC that technological developments have advanced so far that some revision of the system of broadcast regulation may be required." In another footnote, the Court said that if the FCC demonstrates that the "fairness doctrine" reduces, rather than enhances free speech, "we would then be forced to reconsider the constitutional basis" of its earlier rulings upholding the doctrine. In short, the Court has invited Congress to reconsider the matter and hinted that it might be hospitable to a regime of less government regulation of broadcasting.[156]

Still standing, however, is the authority of the FCC in order to promote diversity to forbid, under certain conditions, jointly owned newspaper-broadcast-state combinations located in the same community.[157] Moreover, although the FCC may not censor in advance what is broadcast, it has authority to forbid the use of indecent language, even though such language may not be obscene; to rebuke a station for broadcasting such language; and to take into account the fact that a station has done so in subsequent determinations of license renewals. Justice Stevens, speaking for the plurality, in justifying this greater restraint on broadcasting than on other forms of communication, emphasized that broadcasting, unlike the printed media, "confronts the citizen, not only in public, but in the privacy of the home," and "is uniquely accessible to children, even those too young to read."[158]

The Constitution tolerates more regulation of motion pictures than of printed media. A state or city may require motion pictures to be licensed prior to being shown to the public, whereas such prior censorship is not permitted in the case of printed media.[159] However, even with respect to motion pictures the Supreme Court is suspicious of prior restraint; it insists that procedures must be established to ensure prompt judicial determination that a particular picture is unfit to be shown.[160] And the only permissible grounds on which a license may be withheld is obscenity, as constitutionally defined.[161]

Live performances such as plays and reviews are, along with motion pictures, entitled to constitutional protection.[162] Yet live theater is subject to greater regulation than either the printed page or the motion picture. One could not escape prosecution for a murder or an assault just because it was part of the plot of a play. And the First Amendment does not protect those who operate places licensed to sell alcoholic beverages from state regulations forbidding live performances that portray sexual conduct or display certain parts of the body in establishments that also sell liquor.[163]

The right to picket, when picketing is unaccompanied by threats or violence, is protected by the Constitution, but since picketing involves "elements of both speech and conduct . . . picketing can be subjected to controls that would not be constitutionally permissible in case of pure speech."[164] Even peaceful picketing can be restricted by a state if it is conducted for an illegal purpose, that is, designed to pressure someone to do something that the law forbids them to do.[165]

However, the Constitution forbids statutes aimed at picketing that are too sweeping in what they condemn and that are not narrowly and clearly drawn. At the same time the Constitution, via the equal protection clause of the Fourteenth Amendment as well as the First Amendment, forbids a state to choose among the kinds of peaceful picketing that it will allow based upon the subject matter of the expression of the pickets. Illinois, for example, found itself in constitutional difficulty when in order to draw its ban on picketing of residences as narrowly as possible, exempted peaceful picketing of places of employment involved in labor disputes.[166] The Court declared the statute unconstitutional because it made an impermissible distinction between labor picketing and other peaceful picketing contrary to the requirements of the equal protection clause. Justice Rehnquist in dissent wrote in his usual picturesque language, "Time after time, the States have been assured that they may properly promote residential privacy. . . . Here, where Illinois has drafted such a statute, avoiding an outright ban on all residential picketing, avoiding reliance on any vague or discriminating standards, and permitting categories of permissible picketing activity at residences . . . the Court in response confronts the State with the Catch-22 of the less restrictive categories are constitutionally infirm under principles of equal protection. . . . The State is damned if it does and damned if it doesn't."[167]

It should also be noted that the Constitution is not the only restraint on a state's ability to regulate picketing. A state may not interfere with picketing that federal legislation protects under the Taft-Hartley Act or other laws.

As to handbills, sound trucks, and billboards, the Court has ruled: Reasonable content-neutral restraints can be imposed on the time, place, and manner where handbills may be sold or distributed (see page 145). It can be made an offense to throw paper on the streets, but passing out leaflets on public streets cannot be restrained by a desire to keep the streets clean. A state may not ban handbills that do not carry the name and address of the author.[168] The Federal government may forbid the use of mailboxes for distribution of leaflets.[169] A government may ban sound trucks that give out loud and raucous noises.[170] A city may ban the posting of signs on public property.[171]

As to billboards on private property, the answer is not clear: They are entitled to constitutional protection and a San Diego ordinance banning off-site billboards was declared unconstitutional in a decision that was "a virtual Tower of Babel from which no definitive principles can be clearly drawn." A plurality of the justices found that San Diego had erred in allowing on-site commercial billboards but not on-site noncommercial messages. Two other justices felt the vice of San Diego's action was its failure to prove that such action was necessary for traffic safety or to improve the beauty of the city.[172]

---

or the right of the people peaceably to assemble, and to petition the government for a redress of grievances.

People who wish to protest or otherwise express their views have no constitutional right to do so "whenever and however and wherever they please."[173] No one has a right to take over a school, to seize and hold the office of a mayor or most especially to take over a university. State and local governments have the power to make reasonable regulations to preserve order.

However, the Constitution does protect the right to assemble peaceably in *public places* (see below). Regulations designed to preserve the public peace and time, place, and manner regulations as applied to public meetings must be precisely drawn and fairly administered. The courts will look carefully at regulations or police actions that trench on this right, especially in circumstances that raise the suspicion that the law is not being applied evenhandedly. It is unwilling to approve regulations that permit authorities to determine at their own discretion which groups will be allowed to hold public meetings or that give police wide discretion to determine whom to arrest and courts latitude to determine whom to convict. For example, the Court has sustained a Louisiana statute forbidding parading near a courthouse with the intent to influence a judge, juror, or witness (that precedent may be in danger; see *United States* v. *Grace* below),[174] but it struck down the application of another Louisiana law defining disturbing the peace so broadly that it would permit arrest merely for holding a meeting on a public street or public highway.[175]

In *United States* v. *Grace* (1983), the Court, while not ruling on regulations forbidding the display in the Supreme Court building or on its grounds "of any flag, banner, or device designed or adapted to bring into public notice any party, organization, or movement" held the law unconstitutional as applied to sidewalks surrounding the Supreme Court building. The Solicitor General had argued that since judges, unlike legislators and executives, are supposed to decide cases on the basis only of the record before them, Congress is constitutionally justified in preventing conduct that gives even the appearance that judges are subject to outside influences. Whereas Congress could not keep persons from parading outside a legislative chamber or an executive office, the government contended, it could prevent persons from doing so around a courthouse. The Supreme Court refused to buy this contention.[176]

"Streets and parks have immemorially been held in trust for the use of the public, and time out of mind, have been used for purpose of assembly, communicating thoughts between citizens and discussing public questions."[177] In these areas the state may enforce content-neutral time, place, and manner regulations but they must be "narrowly tailored to serve a significant government interest, and leave open ample alternative channels of communication."[178] Thus the Supreme Court, assuming for purposes of the case but not deciding that "overnight sleeping in connection with a demonstration is expressive conduct protected to some extent by the First Amendment," upheld a Park Service regulation that allows persons to hold rallies, even to pitch tents and stay in them, but not to sleep in them on the Mall in downtown Washington and in Lafayette Park, across the street from the White House.[179]

When the state opens up public property beyond streets and parks and designates it as a public area, it is "bound by the same standards as apply in a traditional public forum. Reasonable time, place, and manner regulations are permissible, and a content-based prohibition must be narrowly drawn to effectuate a compelling state interest."

"Public property which is not by tradition or designation a forum for public communication is governed by different standards. . . . In addition to time, place, and manner regulations, the state may reserve the forum for its intended purposes, communicative or otherwise, as long as the regulation on speech is reasonable and not an effort to suppress expression merely because public officials oppose the speaker's view."[180] Thus, as we have noted, a city may ban the posting of handbills on telephone polls and lampposts. School mail facilities are not a public forum and a school board may keep all unions or associations other than the one that won collective bargaining rights from using the interschool mail system and teacher mailboxes.[181]

Does the Constitution require police officers to protect unpopular groups whose public meetings and demonstrations in public forums arouse others to violence? If the answer were no, then the right of unpopular minorities to hold meetings would be seriously curtailed. It is almost always easier for the police to maintain order by curbing the peaceful meetings of the unpopular minority than to move against those threatening the violence. But if police were never to have the right to order a group to disperse, public order would be at the mercy of those who might resort to street demonstrations just to create public tensions and provoke street battles.

The Supreme Court has refused to give a categorical answer to this question; the answer depends on the circumstances. In 1951 (*Feiner* v. *New York*) the Court upheld the conviction for "unlawful assembly" of a sidewalk speaker who continued to talk after being ordered to stop by the only two policemen present. There was no evidence that the police interfered because of objection to what was being said. But in view of the hostile response of the audience, the police were fearful a riot might ensue that they could not contain or prevent.[182] The *Feiner* case has never been overruled, but since then the Supreme Court has tended to emphasize the need for governments to move under more precisely drawn statutes.

In *Edwards* v. *South Carolina* (1963) the Court reversed the conviction of 187 black students for breach of the peace because of their holding a protest meeting in front of the South Carolina State House. The police had been afraid that their gathering would provoke a clash with a crowd of onlookers. After trying to keep the groups apart for forty-five minutes, the police told the students to disperse and when they failed to do so arrested them. "The Fourteenth Amendment," said the Court, "does not permit a State to make criminal the peaceful expression of unpopular views."[183]

The Supreme Court followed the *Edwards* rather than the *Feiner* precedent when it reversed the conviction under a disorderly conduct statute of Dick Gregory and other demonstrators for failing to obey a police command to stop marching in front of the mayor of Chicago's house at a time when a large number of onlookers became unruly toward the demonstrators. Although the Supreme Court reversed the decision, the Court made it clear that the situation would have been different if Chicago had acted under ordinances specifically forbidding demonstrations after certain hours in residential areas, or making it an offense to disobey a police officer when there is an imminent threat of violence and the police have made all reasonable efforts to protect the demonstrators from hostile bystanders. The Court's objection was to the fact that Gregory and his followers had been convicted of disorderly conduct when there was no evidence they had been acting disorderly.[184]

Again in *Coates* v. *Cincinnati* (1971) the Court held as void for its vagueness and overbreadth an ordinance that forbade three or more persons to assemble on sidewalks and there conduct themselves in a manner annoying to persons passing by. "A city is free to prevent people from blocking sidewalks, committing assaults, obstructing traffic, littering streets, but it must do so by ordinances directed with reasonable specificity toward the conduct to be prohibited. . . . It cannot constitutionally do so through the enactment and enforcement of an ordinance whose violations may entirely depend upon whether or not a policeman is annoyed."[185]

What of public facilities, such as libraries, courthouses, schools, or swimming pools, that are designated to serve purposes other than public assembly? As long as persons use such facilities within the normal bounds of conduct, they may not be constitutionally restrained from doing so. But if they attempt by sit-ins or other kinds of demonstrations to interfere with programs or try to appropriate facilities for their own use, a state has constitutional authority to punish, provided it does so under laws that are not applied in a discriminatory fashion and that properly limit the discretion of those enforcing the laws. "The crucial question is whether the manner of expression is basically incompatible with the normal activity of a particular place at a particular time."[186] To illustrate the application of these general rules: A small group of protestors who quietly remained in a library for ten to fifteen minutes to protest racial discrimination, but who did not interfere with the operations of the library, could not constitutionally be charged with violating a general breach of the peace ordinance;[187] a group of protestors could be punished for deliberately making a noise that disturbed the peace and good order of a school under an ordinance directly aimed at preventing demonstrations in and around school buildings;[188] a group of students could be convicted for trespass when they marched in a jailhouse to protest the arrest of fellow students and to protest segregation and refused to leave the jail upon the order of the sheriff.[189]

"While the freedom of association is not explicitly set out in the Amendment, it has long been held to be implicit in the freedoms of speech, assembly, and petition."[190] (There is another aspect of the freedom of association, a "fundamental element of personal liberty" protected by the due process clauses that relates to intimate human relationships such as the family and close friends.)[191] Examples of laws declared unconstitutional for interfering with the right to associate are as follows: Although a state college may refuse to grant a student organization the right to use facilities unless it agrees to abide by reasonable campus rules, it may not deny such privileges to an organization because of disapproval of its aims or generalized apprehensions that its activities could lead to disruptions.[192] Government may not demand that an organization make public the names of members unless it can demonstrate some compelling and legitimate need to know.[193]

What about the 1974 amendments to the Federal Election Campaign Act of 1971 that compel political parties to maintain records and disclose contributions of more than $10 and disbursements of more than $100? The Supreme Court, conceding that these compelled disclosures could seriously infringe on the rights of association and could have a chilling effect on peoples, right to associate, somewhat reluctantly upheld these requirements, including their application to minor parties, as necessary and proper ways for the government to enhance voters' knowledge about a candidate's possible allegiances and interests, to deter corruption, and to help enforce contribution limitations.[194] The Court, indicated, however, that if a minor party could show that disclosure of its contributors' names might subject such contributors to threats or reprisals or impair the party's ability to receive funds, the disclosure and reporting requirement as applied to that party might well be declared unconstitutional.

True to this promise, in 1982 the Court held that the Ohio campaign law could not be applied to the Socialist Workers Party and that that Party could not be required to report the names and address of campaign contributors, or even the names and address of those with whom it does business. "The First Amendment prohibits a state from compelling disclosures by a minor party that will subject those persons identified to the reasonable probability of threats, harassment, or reprisals. Such disclosures would infringe the First Amendment rights of the party and its members and supporters."[195] Democrats and Republicans, however, can still be required to disclose publicly their contributions to their political party and hope that their boss is of the same political persuasion.

The Supreme Court has rejected the contention of a lawpartnership that it need not comply with Title VII forbidding sex discrimination in employment because of its constitutional right of association.[196] The Court has also (Robert v. United States Jaycees) sustained the application of the Minnesota Human Rights Act to compel the Jaycees to admit women. The Act makes it an "unfair discriminatory practice . . . to deny any person the full and equal enjoyment of goods, services, facilities, privileges, advantages . . . of a place of public accommodation because of race, color, creed, religion, disability, national origin, or sex." The Jaycees argued, among other things, that the law interfered with their constitutionally protected right to associate with persons of their own choice for the purpose of expressing their views. Justice Brennan, speaking for the majority, conceded, "There can be no clearer example of an intrusion into the internal structure or affairs of an association than a regulation that forces the group to accept members it does not desire. Such a regulation may impair the ability of the original members to express only those views that brought them together."[197] However, the Court decided the Jaycees (and the law partnership) had failed to demonstrate that allowing women to become members and to vote would change the content or impact of the organization's speech.

The Court's opinion was carefully crafted to try to make it clear that the right to associate is constitutionally protected and will take priority over a state public accommodation regulation for many kinds of associations. At one extreme are families and churches, at the other extreme such things as buyer cooperatives or large associations with only nominal membership requirements. The Court indicated that its decision would have been different for organizations such as the Kiwanis, which it mentioned by name, and other private groups organized for political, religious, cultural, or social purposes. Factors to be considered in determining whether an organization is to be covered by anti-discrimination laws are "size, purpose, policies, selectivity, congeniality." (Justice O'Connor in her concurring opinion would have drawn the line between an association that chooses to be expressive, which would not be covered, and one that enters the marketplace of commerce in any substantial degree which "loses the complete control over its membership that it would otherwise enjoy if it confined its affairs to the marketplace of ideas.") As the Jaycees are concerned, their local chapters are neither small nor selective, and to compel them to admit women interfered only incidentally and insignificantly with their rights to associate for the purpose of expressing views (see also page 250). Pending before the Court is the issue of whether the Boy Scouts fall on the side of the Jaycees or on the side of associations constitutionally protected in their rights to exclude members because of sex.

Recent Supreme Court decisions have applied the right to associate in such a fashion as to strengthen the autonomy of national political parties. In *Cousins* v. *Wigoda,* the Court held that the Democratic National Convention, rather than the state from which they came, had the final say as to which of two competing delegations should be seated.[198] This holding was reinforced in 1981 when the Court decided the Democratic Party could exclude from its National Convention delegates chosen in the Wisconsin open primary: The Wisconsin law allowed persons who had not publicly declared their affiliation with the Democratic Party to participate in the process that effectively decided for which candidate the Wisconsin delegates would vote at the National Convention. The rules of the Democratic Party forbade the seating of delegates so chosen and these rules prevailed.[199]

Today when we speak of "petitioning the government for the redress of grievances," we call it lobbying. And lobbying is done primarily through people forming associations. Lobbying is a protected right, but like other protected rights is not immune from regulation. Congress and most states require associations that spend considerable sums of money to influence legislation to register and make public their records. These laws have been upheld, provided "lobbying" is narrowly defined. While lobbying is a constitutional right, "Congress is not required to subsidize lobbying," and non-profit groups may lose their tax exempt status and contributions to them may no longer be deductible if "a substantial part of the activities" is "carrying on propaganda, otherwise attempting to influence legislation."[200]

"The right of access to the courts is an aspect of the First Amendment right to petition the Government for redress of grievances, and although governments may regulate to prevent "baseless litigation," they may not halt the prosecution of lawsuits unless these suits lack any reasonable basis in fact or law.[201] Litigation has become an increasingly important means whereby interest groups pursue their public policy objectives.

Persons may associate together and engage in boycotts for political purposes. Although violence is not entitled to constitutional protection, even if motivated for political purposes, the mere fact that some violence may flow from a political boycott is not sufficient to permit the imposition of liability on all participants where there is no evidence that they agreed to the use of unlawful means. Thus the Supreme Court reversed the imposition of damages by Mississippi courts on the NAACP for promoting a boycott of white merchants in Claiborne County as a means to bring about political, social, and economic change. The First Amendment did not, however, bar recovery of damages from those who engaged in violence or threatened it for losses directly caused by their unlawful conduct.[202]

The First Amendment offers less protection to secondary political boycotts by trade unions. Secondary boycotts "in commerce"—those against someone other than workers' own employers—are forbidden by the National Labor Relations Act. After the Soviet Union invaded Afghanistan, the longshoremen's union refused to unload cargoes shipped from the Soviet Union, but the Supreme Court held this to be illegal and unprotected. Justice Powell, speaking for a unanimous Court, wrote, "We have consistently rejected the claim that secondary picketing by labor unions in violation of [the National Labor Relations Act] is protected activity under the First Amendment. . . . It would seem even clear[er] that conduct designed not to communicate but to coerce merits still less consideration under the First Amendment.)"[203]

What of the freedom not to associate? May a state compel lawyers to join bar associations or may it pass laws allowing employers to make agreements with unions that require workers either to join the union or make payments to it as a condition of securing or retaining employment? To oversimplify a complex problem, laws permitting or compelling such arrangements are constitutional provided individuals are not compelled to make contributions for political or ideological purposes. Compelled contributions may be used to support the professional purposes of a bar association and the collective-bargaining, contract-administration, grievance-adjustment purposes of a union, including costs of running conventions, social activities related to union programs, and general publication expenses.[204] Unions may not take dues from unwilling members under a union shop situation and then later rebate to them the funds used for political purposes. They must make it possible for such unwilling members to pay the lower amounts initially.[205]

Minnesota raised the troublesome tension between rights to associate and not to do so when it gave unions of state employees, including faculty unions (in addition to the regular right to be the collective bargaining agent) a special exclusive right "to meet and confer" with administrators and talk with them about matters of common concern beyond issues directly relating to employment. Twenty community college instructors who were not members of the union charged that giving this special privilege to unions deprived faculty members who chose not to join the union of their free speech rights. The Court did not agree: "[The instructors]," wrote Justice O'Connor for the Court, "have no constitutional right to force the government to listen to their views. They have no such right as members of the public, as government employees, or as instructors in an institution of higher education." It is of special interest, at least to faculty members, that Justice O'Connor went out of her way to write, "[T]his Court has never recognized a constitutional right of faculty to participate in policymaking in academic institutions . . . Faculty involvement in academic governance has much to recommend it as a matter of academic policy, but it finds no basis in the Constitution."[206]

A troublesome question grows out of the conflict between the constitutional right to engage in political activity, to join political organizations, and to speak freely and the right of the government to regulate the conditions of public employment. Persons may be disqualified from public employment who are actively attempting to overthrow the government by force and who are unwilling to take an oath to support the Constitution. But neither the national government nor the state governments may make it a condition of employment that employees abandon their constitutional rights of freedom of speech or of association. The Court has struck down all except the most narrowly drawn oath requirements, including those that bring within their net persons who are members of organizations that may have unlawful purposes but who themselves do not participate in these unlawful activities or share the unlawful purposes.[207]

Many years ago public employees had no rights to object to the conditions placed upon the terms of their employment, including those that restricted the exercise of constitutional rights. Justice Holmes, while sitting on the Supreme Judicial Court of Massachusetts, quipped, "A policeman may have a constitutional right to talk politics, but he has no constitutional right to be a policeman."[208] That famous epigram no longer expresses current interpretation of the Constitution. "A public employee does not relinquish First Amendment rights to comment on matters of public interest by virtue of government employment."[209] However, when public employees write or speak about matters of only personal interest that relate to their jobs, they may be fired for insubordination or for disrupting their offices, and except under the most unusual circumstances, the federal courts will not get involved to review the wisdom of a personnel decision taken by a public agency.

The application of these constitutional guidelines, like all such guidelines to specific cases, is not always easy: The Court ruled that the private communication of a teacher protesting racial discrimination to a school board was constitutionally protected, but circulation of a questionnaire by an assistant district attorney to her fellow staff members right after refusing to accept a transfer was not.[210]

The First Amendment rights of speech and association do not protect government employees from federal and state regulations forbidding civil servants from taking "an active part in the political management of political campaigns." The Hatch Act, as the federal law is known, has been twice sustained, despite the contention that it is overbroad, vague, and interferes with the right of association. The Court concluded that it is a reasonable measure to free employees from political pressures and to ensure that they are not coerced into political action in behalf of the part in power.[211] A state may also require certain officeholders to resign if they wish to run for other offices or make certain officeholders ineligible for certain posts until after the term for which they were elected or appointed has expired.[212]

Among the more amazing decisions of recent years are those in which the Supreme Court has struck down the political patronage system, a system older than the nation. The Court has ruled that those governmental employees who occupy positions where party membership is "not relevant" may not be discharged because of their failure to belong to the winning political party. Justice Stevens, providing examples of those public employees constitutionally protected from discharge for party reasons and those who are not, cited a coach of a state university football team. Such a coach, he pointed out, formulates policy, but nonetheless, he argued, "no one could seriously claim that Republicans make better coaches than Democrats, or vice versa." (Justice Stevens apparently doesn't know too many political partisans.) On the other side, Justice Stevens mentioned election judges, and assistants who help governors write speeches, as examples of officials who could be discharged for political reasons. The immediate cases before the Court involved deputy sheriffs and assistant public defenders. Although the sheriff and the public defender had been elected in partisan elections, the Court ruled that once elected they could not fire their deputy sheriffs and assistant public defenders for belonging to the political party that lost the election. Justice Powell, in dissent, wondered why the voters, who could also have elected deputy sheriffs and assistant public defenders on party tickets if they had wished, could not delegate authority to those whom they had elected, to hire only those of the winning party faith.[213] So far no Supreme Court decision has dealt with the power of a President to replace top policymaking officials of the federal executive branch, but the logic of its decisions and the litigious nature of our times suggest that it may not be too long before some discharged federal official brings the question to the Court.

AMENDMENT II: MILITIA AND THE RIGHT TO BEAR ARMS

A well regulated Militia, being necessary to the security of a free state,* the right of the people to keep and bear Arms, shall not be infringed.

This amendment was designed to prevent Congress from disarming the state militias, not to prevent it from regulating private ownersip of firearms. In upholding a federal law making criminal the shipment in interstate commerce of sawed-off shotguns, the Court found no evidence that such weapons had any reasonable relationship "to the preservation or efficiency of a well regulated militia." The Second Amendment, it held, "must be interpreted and applied" with a view to maintaining a militia. "The Militia which the States were expected to maintain and train is set in contrast with Troops which they were forbidden to keep without the consent of Congress. The sentiment of the time strongly disfavored standing armies; the common view was that adequate defense of country and laws could be secured through the Militia—civilians pri-

---

* This refers to "state" in the generic sense rather than to states of the Union.

marily, soldiers on occasion."[1] As recently as 1980 the Court reemphasized, "The Second Amendment guarantees no right to keep and bear a firearm that does not have 'some reasonable relationship to the preservation or efficiency of a well-regulated militia.' "[2]

The Second Amendment applies even to this limited extent only to the national government. It in no way limits the power of the state and local governments to regulate firearms. As Justice Douglas wrote in an opinion dissenting on another point: "A powerful lobby dins into the ears of our citizenry that . . . gun purchases are constitutional rights protected by the Second Amendment. . . . There is under our decisions no reason why stiff state laws governing the purchase and possession of pistols may not be enacted. There is no reason why pistols may not be barred from anyone with a police record. There is no reason why a State may not require a purchaser of a pistol to pass a psychiatric test. There is no reason why all pistols should not be barred to everyone except the police."[3]

AMENDMENT III: QUARTERING OF SOLDIERS

No Soldier shall, in time of peace be quartered in any house, without the consent of the Owner, nor in time of war, but in a manner to be prescribed by law.

Certain remarks of Justice Miller are appropriate here: "This amendment seems to have been thought necessary. It does not appear to have been the subject of judicial exposition; and it is so thoroughly in accord with all our ideas, that further comment is unnecessary."[1]

AMENDMENT IV: SEARCHES AND SEIZURES

The right of the people to be secure in their persons, houses, papers, and effects, against unreasonable searches and seizures, shall not be violated,

Since the Fourth Amendment has been incorporated into the due process clause, the limitation against unreasonable searches and seizures applies to state and local as well as to federal officers. It does not apply to private individuals unless they are operating under instructions from law enforcement officers.

The Constitution does not forbid searches and seizures but only "unreasonable ones by agents of the government." What distinguishes a reasonable from an unreasonable search and seizure, as Justice Powell has written, "is an opaque area of the law."[1] It is also an area in which the justices are divided. The Warren Court took the view that with few limited exceptions any search or seizure without a warrant is unreasonable.[2] The Burger Court has tended more to the view that "it is not whether it was reasonable to procure a search [or arrest] warrant, but whether the search itself was reasonable."[3] In the application of the Fourth Amendment, each decision often depends on refinements in the facts; the justices are not often of one mind, and the Court has had difficulty in developing generalizable doctrines.

The Fourth Amendment protects against unreasonable searches and seizures both of people and their property. People have somewhat less protection from searches and seizures than does their property. Police have no general right to stop people, but not all stops of persons by police are subject to the Fourth Amendment; in other words, the Fourth Amendment does not require police to have a justification to approach persons to ask them questions.

If, however, by means of physical force or a show of authority police restrain the movement of people, even though there is no arrest, the Fourth Amendment comes into play. Police may stop, detain, and question people, but only if they have "some objective manifestation that the person stopped, is or is about to be, engaged in criminal activity, or that there is reasonable grounds to believe the person is wanted for past criminal conduct."[4] (The Supreme Court in an opinion with Fourth Amendment overtones declared unconstitutional for vagueness (see page 194) an ordinance giving police authority to ask persons who loiter or wander the streets for "credible and reliable" identification and to account for their presence.)[5]

It is difficult to draw the line between police questioning someone who consents to respond, which does not raise Fourth Amendment issues, and when police constraint is imposed and the Fourth Amendment comes into play. If all that happens is that the police ask questions in a noncoercive atmosphere, there is no detention. But if the persons refuse to answer and the police take additional steps to obtain an answer, then the Fourth Amendment applies.

The Fourth Amendment clearly covers arrests where police take people into custody and "book" them for a crime. Here the police must have either probable cause to believe that the person has committed a crime or an arrest warrant. Sometimes, the police lack probable cause to make an arrest but have the objective justification to detain a person for questioning, and as a result of the interrogation (but see page 189 for ground rules that apply to such interrogations) get the evidence they need to justify a probable cause arrest.

Probable cause justifies police arrests without warrants only in *public places*. Without some exigent circumstance—such as when somebody's life is in danger, evidence is about to be destroyed, or when the police are in hot pursuit of a person seen committing a *serious* crime—police may arrest on probable cause only in public places, not in a person's home.[6] (Even with a warrant, police may not track down a suspect and break into somebody else's home in order to make an arrest.)[7] "Police bear a heavy burden when attempting to demonstrate an urgent need that might justify warrantless searches or arrests in a private home. [Moreover] . . . application of the exigent-circumstances exception in the context of a home entry should rarely be sanctioned when there is probable cause to believe that only a minor offense . . . has been committed."[8]

An arrest may sometimes be justified on the basis of a *search* warrant: A warrant to search for contraband carries with it authority to detain the occupants of the premises while the search is conducted, and if the search uncovers evidence that establishes probable cause to arrest the persons found on the premises, their initial detention does not violate the Fourth Amendment.[9] (A search warrant for particular items in a particular place permits this detention of the persons found there; it does not permit their personal search except to ensure they do not have dangerous weapons. However, if the search uncovers evidence justifying their arrest on probable cause, then they can be searched to the same extent as if they had been arrested with a warrant.)

Here are a few examples of the application of these generalizations from recent cases. There was no constitutional violation when officers approached a person in an airport and requested identification and the person responded. This was not considered a detention. But when police asked another person if he would consent to a search of his suitcases, and took him to a small room for the search, the Court concluded that this was an "in custody" detention requiring police to have some objective justification beyond their mere suspicion.[10]

In one of the more controversial decisions of recent terms, the Court in *INS* v. *Delgado,* gave a green light to the Immigration and Naturalization Service's use of "factory sweeps" to catch illegal aliens. The INS, either with the employer's consent or with a broadly worded search warrant, sends its agents into factories where it thinks illegal aliens may be working in order to question everyone about their citizenship. The fact that INS agents were posted at the exits, said Justice Rehnquist for the majority, did not turn the encounter into a detention. It was merely a classic case of a consensual encounter between individuals and officials.[11] Justice Brennan in his dissent wrote, "It is simply fantastic to conclude that a reasonable person could ignore all that was occurring throughout the factory and . . . have the temerity to believe that he was at liberty to refuse to answer the questions and walk away.[12]

What about police searches of persons and their property? "It is a cardinal principle that searches conducted outside the judicial process, without prior approval by a judge or a magistrate, are per se unreasonable under the Fourth Amendment—subject only to a few specifically established and well-delineated exceptions."[13]

The exceptions where searches may be undertaken without warrants are as follows:

1. The automobile exception: "The law of search and seizure with respect to automobiles is intolerably confusing. The Court apparently cannot agree even on what it has held previously, let alone on how these cases should be decided."[14] The exception is justified in part because of the mobility of automobiles and in part because persons are not entitled to the same expectations of privacy in their automobiles as in their homes or other places. Police have no general right to stop automobiles or to search the occupants of an automobile. But if officers have probable cause to believe that an automobile is being used to commit a crime, including traffic offenses, or if it contains persons who have committed crimes, or contains evidence of crimes or contraband, they may stop the automobile, detain the persons found therein, search them, and any containers or packages found inside the car. "When police officers have probable cause to believe there is contraband inside an automobile that has been stopped on the road, the officers may conduct a warrantless search of the vehicle, even after it has been impounded and is in police custody."[15] This does not mean that police are free to roam at will and search things and persons found inside automobiles, but if they have probable cause that would justify the issuing of a warrant, police may engage in such an automobile search without first securing such a warrant from a magistrate. For example, if police have probable cause to think that an automobile might contain contraband, it would justify a warrantless search of the car and its trunk for that contraband. It would not justify their searching the trunk of the car for undocumented aliens. "The scope of a warrantless search of an automobile thus is defined . . . by the object of the

search and the places in which there is probable cause to believe that it may be found."[16]

2. Officers may stop and search suspects if they have reason to believe they are dealing with armed and dangerous persons, regardless of whether or not they have probable cause to make an arrest. Such "Terry" searches (named after the case in which this exception was announced, *Terry* v. *Ohio*,) must be limited to a quick "pat down" for weapons that might be used to assault the arresting officer.[17]

3. When making a lawful arrest, either with an arrest warrant or because of probable cause, police may make a warrantless, full search of the person involved, the areas under their immediate control, and all the possessions they take with them to the place of detention.[18]

4. If an officer, under exception 2, stops and frisks a suspect to look for weapons, but instead finds criminal evidence that justifies an arrest, then under exception 3, the officer can make a full search. To illustrate: An officer, acting on an informer's tip, approached a man sitting in a car. The officer ordered the suspect to get out of the car, but the suspect merely rolled down the window. The officer saw a bulge on the suspect's waistband. He reached over and into the car and removed a gun from the suspect's waistband. The officer arrested the suspect, although the mere possession of a weapon was not a crime, made a search and found heroin. Justice Rehnquist, speaking for the Court, said: "The Fourth Amendment does not require a policeman who lacks the precise level of information necessary for probable cause to arrest to simply shrug his shoulders and allow a crime to occur or a criminal to escape." The dissenting justices argued that the majority had ignored the fact that the stop-and-frisk exception to the warrant requirement had been "begrudgingly" granted only to protect the safety of officers of the law.[19]

5. When there is probable cause to make an arrest, even if one is not made, limited searches are permitted if necessary to preserve easily disposed of evidence such as scrapings under fingernails.[20]

6. Searches based on voluntarily given consent, even if the persons who give the consent are not told they have a right to refuse to grant permission, are allowed.[21]

7. Searches are permissible at border crossings of persons and the goods they bring with them.[22] The border search exception also permits officials to open mail entering the country if they have "reasonable cause" to suspect it contains merchandise imported contrary to the law.[23] (The border search exception does not extend to searches by Puerto Rican authorities of persons coming from the continental United States—this is not an international crossing.)[24]

8. The plain view exception permits officers to seize and search evidence if (1) they are lawfully in a position from which the evidence can be viewed; (2) it is immediately apparent to the police that the items they observe are evidence of a crime, or contraband; (3) the officers must discover the evidence "inadvertently," that is they may not rely on the plain view exception as a pretext.[25]

9. Seizures are permissible under "exigent circumstances," that is, when officers do not have time to secure a warrant before evidence is destroyed, a criminal escapes capture, or there is need "to protect or preserve life or avoid serious injury."[26] Here are some examples of exigent circumstances: Firefighters and police may enter a burning building without a warrant and remain

there for a reasonable time to investigate the cause of the blaze after the fire has been extinguished. However, after the fire is put out, the emergency is not to be used as an excuse to make an exhaustive, warrantless search for evidence not in plain sight. Police may enter a building in hot pursuit of a fleeing felon or because immediate aid is needed to save life or to avoid injury: Officers may seize any evidence that is in plain view during the course of their legitimate emergency activities. But as we have noted, the circumstances justifying a warrantless search into a home must really be urgent and the crime involved must be serious (see page 172).

The premises protected against warrantless searches include any place where a person has a legitimate expectation of privacy, including hotel rooms, rented homes, apartments of friends, first-class mails, or even a telephone booth.[27] "The Fourth Amendment protects people, not places; more particularly, it protects people from unreasonable government intrusions into their legitimate expectations of privacy."[28] The Amendment does not, however, cover all places where one has a legitimate right to be—only those where one has a legitimate expectation of privacy, "those expectations that society is prepared to recognize as reasonable."[29] Nor does the mere fact that one's property has been seized establish by itself that one's Fourth Amendment rights have been violated.[30] Thus, since no one has a legitimate expectation of privacy in the glove compartment of a car in which one is merely a passenger or in the numbers one dials into a telephone system, evidence taken from such places can be used even if taken without a warrant.[31] Prisoners have no reasonable expectation of privacy in their cells entitling them to the protection of the amendment against unreasonable searches or seizures of their property.[32]

The Fourth Amendment does not protect "open fields," and even if one owns a field and does post no-trespassing signs or otherwise tries to exclude others from entering the property, it may be searched by police officers without warrants or probable cause. "In the case of open fields, the general rights of property protected by the common law of trespass have little or no relevance to the applicability of the Fourth Amendment.[33] The Amendment does apply, however, to "the curtilage," the common-law term for the land immediately surrounding and associated with a home.

[continued], and no Warrants shall issue, but upon probable cause, supported by Oath or affirmation, and particularly describing the place to be searched, and the persons or things to be seized.

"Our constitutional fathers were not concerned about warrantless searches, but about overreaching warrants. It is perhaps too much to say that they feared the warrant more than the search, but it is plain enough that the warrant was the prime object of their concern."[34] "Since the general warrant, not the warrantless search, was the immediate evil at which the Fourth Amendment was directed, it is not surprising that the Framers placed precise limits on its issuance. The requirement that a warrant only issue on showing of a particular probable cause was the means adopted to circumscribe the warrant power."[35]

When a search warrant is required, a magistrate, a judicial officer, or a clerk of a court, must grant it. Police must appear before such a magistrate and under oath indicate they have "probable cause" to believe the search will produce criminal evidence. If it subsequently appears that the police knowingly or recklessly made a false statement to the magistrate, the evidence so obtained cannot be used (see exclusionary rule).[36] The magistrate need not be a legally trained judge, but a prosecutor or a state's attorney will not do, nor will justices of the peace who receive a fee if they issue a warrant but no fee if they refuse to do so.[37]

The magistrate must "perform his 'neutral and detached' function and not serve merely as a rubber stamp for the police."[38] Thus it was impermissible for a town justice to issue an open-ended search warrant and then go along with the police on a raid of an adult book store in which the justice made an on-the-spot decision about which items should be included in the warrant and which excluded. The fact that the judge visited the scene was not the problem, but he did not act as a judicial officer, but as an adjunct law enforcement officer. "He did not manifest that neutrality and detachment demanded of a judicial officer."[39]

The "probable cause" that justifies the issuance of a warrant is hard to define; it is a "fluid concept." It requires, however, that a magistrate can reasonably conclude, based on the totality of the circumstances, that there is a substantial basis for believing that a search would uncover evidence of wrongdoing.[40] The warrant the magistrate issues must specify what places are to be searched and what things are to be seized. A blanket authorization to search indiscriminately is a general search warrant and violates the Constitution. (The standards for administrative, in contrast to police, searches are much less stringent.) A warrant to search a public place, like a tavern, does not authorize a warrantless search of customers in the tavern.[41]

A magistrate may issue a valid warrant to enter any place where police have demonstrated to the magistrate's satisfaction particular property may be located that is evidence of crime. The fact that the place is owned by an innocent party or that the person in possession of the things to be searched is not suspected of any law violations makes no constitutional difference.[42] However, as we have noted, Congress has by law prohibited the issuance under most circumstances of warrants to allow the search of the work products of persons "engaged in First Amendment activities."

Once a valid search warrant has been obtained, the Fourth Amendment does not prohibit police from using force or stealth to execute the search warrant where such is the only way that a warrant may be effectively executed. Thus under some circumstances, with a warrant, police may break down a door and enter a premise.

The Fourth Amendment protects commercial buildings as well as private homes, covers civil as well as criminal investigations, and includes searches by government officers other than the police, such as internal revenue agents, health inspectors, and occupational and safety inspectors. But judges are less likely to impose stringent conditions on nonpolice searches and searches of business firms than they are on police searches of homes.

Health and building code inspectors must secure a warrant before they may enter a home or commercial warehouse if the occupants refuse to give them entry. Congress may not give inspectors enforcing the Occupational Safety and Health Act (OSHA) authority to make warrantless and unannounced spot checks of the numerous and varied businesses regulated by the statutes if the owners do not wish them to do so.[43] However, in these instances an "administrative search warrant" rather than a criminal search warrant is all that is required. Inspectors do not have to prove to a magistrate that they have probable cause to believe that violations are taking place, but merely that an inspection is authorized by law, is based on a general administrative plan for the enforcement of the law, and that they are acting reasonably to enforce it.

Warrantless searches are permitted for certain kinds of business. First are industries "that have such a history of governmental oversight that no reasonable expectation of privacy . . . could exist for a proprietor over the stock of such an enterprise. Liquor and firearms are industries of this type; when an entrepreneur embarks upon such a business, he has voluntarily chosen to subject himself to a full arsenal of governmental regulation."[44] Secondly, although Congress cannot authorize warrantless inspections of all businesses, it may do so for specific businesses when it "reasonably" determines that warrantless searches are necessary to further a regulatory scheme, and the federal regulatory presence is sufficiently comprehensive and defined that the owner of the commercial property cannot help but be aware that the property will be subject to periodic inspections undertaken for specific purposes. Thus Congress could constitutionally authorize warrantless inspections of the nation's underground and surface mines, an industry "among the most hazardous in the country."[45] Nor do field inspectors working for environment protection agencies need warrants to make open field inspections of smoke sighted coming from a stack.[46] And welfare aid may be cut off if the recipients of the aid refuse permission for caseworkers to make home visits.[47]

"Administrative warrants," which government inspectors must get from a judicial magistrate in order to conduct searches of nonpublic work areas or to make inspections of private homes, are not to be confused with administrative subpoenas, which administrators may issue in order to compel persons to produce records that under the law they are required to keep. For example, the Secretary of Labor is authorized to determine whether employers are complying with the Fair Labor Standards Act and to issue subpoenas directing employers to appear at certain offices and bring with them specified records. While subpoenaed employers might go to a federal court to question the reasonableness of such a subpoena, they have no right to insist upon a judicial rather than an administrative warrant.[48]

The inventions of science have confronted judges with novel problems in applying the prohibitions against unreasonable searches and seizures. Obviously, the framers of the Fourth Amendment had in mind physical objects such as books, papers, letters, and other kinds of documents they felt should not be seized by police except on the basis of limited search warrants issued by magistrates. But what of tapping phone wires or using electronic devices to eavesdrop? In *Olmstead* v. *United States,* decided in 1928, a bare majority of the Supreme Court held that there was no unconstitutional search unless there was seizure of physical objects or an actual physical entry into a premise. Justices Holmes and Brandeis, in dissent, argued that the Constitution should be kept up with the times; the "dirty business" of wiretapping produced the same evil invasions of privacy that the framers had in mind when they wrote the Fourteenth Amendment.[49]

Forty years later, in *Katz* v. *United States* (1967), the Supreme Court adopted the Holmes-Brandeis position: "The Fourth Amendment protects people—and not simply 'areas'—against unreasonable searches and seizures." The use by police officers of electronic devices to overhear a conversation in a public telephone booth is a search and seizure within the meaning of the Constitution. "Wherever a man may be [since modified to where a person has a legitimate expectation of privacy], he is entitled to know that he will remain free from unreasonable searches and seizures."[50]

Since conversations are now constitutionally protected against unreasonable searches and seizures, legislatures and judges have had to develop rules to determine the conditions under which conversations may be intercepted. The basic federal legislation is contained in the Crime Control and Safe Streets Act of 1968, which Congress adopted over President Johnson's objection. He felt that it would lead to a "nation of snoopers bending through the keyholes of the homes and offices of America, spying on our neighbors." The 1968 act makes it a crime for any unauthorized person to tap telephone wires or use or sell electronic bugging devices in interstate commerce. But it authorizes the Attorney General to secure permission for federal agents to engage in bugging by applying for a warrant from a federal judge for a whole range of specified federal offenses. The Attorney General must authorize the wiretapping personally or through an assistant specifically designated by him for that purpose. This authority may not be further delegated.[51]

At the state level, the act also authorizes the principal prosecuting attorney of any state or its political subdivision to apply to a state judge for a warrant approving wiretapping or oral intercepts for felonies. Judges are to issue warrants only if they decide that probable cause exists that a crime is being, has been, or is about to be committed and that information relating to that crime may be obtained only by the intercept. In addition to these intercepts under warrant, the act permits police officers to act without a warrant for forty-eight hours in "an emergency situation relating to conspiratorial activities threatening the national security" or involving organized crime.

The Crime Control Act of 1968 specifically left undisturbed whatever constitutional authority the President might have to authorize, without securing a warrant, bugging and tapping to protect our national security. But a unanimous Supreme Court, including three Nixon appointees (Rehnquist did not participate), held that the President's authority to act to protect the nation against foreign attack and violent overthrow does not include the right, without judicial warrant, to authorize electronic surveillance of persons suspected of *domestic* subversion. Justice Powell, speaking for the Court, said, "The danger to political dissent is acute where the government attempts to act under so vague a concept as the power to protect domestic security."[52] The Court pointedly did not rule on the scope of the President's authority to authorize surveillance of foreign agents inside or outside the country.

In 1978 by the Foreign Intelligence Surveillance Act, Congress stated that except for officials of the National Security Agency—the agency in charge of making and breaking codes—no officials may "bug" foreign agents except with a warrant first secured from the United States Foreign Intelligence Surveillance

Court created by the Act. This Court, consisting of seven designated federal district judges, grants secret warrants permitting the "bugging" of foreign agents. But in 1981 this Court announced that it would no longer issue warrants for "black-bag jobs"—that is the surreptitious entry for the purpose of a physical search—on the grounds that Congress had only authorized warrants for the purpose of electronic surveillance. Justice Department officials made it clear that in their view the President could authorize such searches of foreign agents as part of his inherent constitutional authority as commander in chief and director of our foreign affairs.[53] The Supreme Court has not yet ruled on this specific question.

"Bugging devices" are covered by the Crime Control and Safe Streets Act, and the Fourth Amendment protects one from unreasonable searches by the government via such devices. However, as long as police make no illegal entries or do not violate the laws, neither the Constitution nor any federal law requires police officers to secure warrants before they resort to undercover tactics, including the use of secret cameras or recording devices on their persons or on that of undercover agents (but see below). Police may use the devices of science to extend their range of their "eavesdropping" of what they can hear, see, film, record, or smell. These modern devices include dogs trained to sniff luggage and detect the presence of drugs inside them.[54]

One must choose one's friends with care, for there is no violation of the Constitution if one tells a friend a secret and the friend in turn informs the police. Except inside your own home, and not even always then (see below), if your "friend" is wired for sound so that what one says is transmitted back to police officers, there is no constitutional violation. Similarly, police may listen in on a telephone conversation over an extension phone with the consent of one of the parties to the conversation but without the knowledge of the other.[55]

The Court has upheld the warrantless installation of an electronic tracking device, a beeper, inside a container of chemicals being transported in an automobile when it revealed no information that could not have been obtained through visual surveillance.[56] However, the Court is beginning to show some concern about the warrantless use of these electronic devices, smuggled inside a person's home where there is the greatest expectation of privacy. The monitoring of a beeper in a private residence violates the Fourth Amendment rights of those who have a justifiable interest in the privacy of the residence, even if the beeper were placed there without any trespass.[57]

How to enforce the Fourth Amendment? Officers who engage in unreasonable searches and seizures are, under most circumstances, guilty of violating the criminal laws.[58] They can also be sued for civil damages by those whose rights have been violated, and since 1978 the governments that employ them can also be sued. But victims of unreasonable searches are seldom in a position to sue the police. And police and prosecutors are seldom likely to move against fellow officers for engaging in unlawful searches.

To enforce the Fourth Amendment we rely on the exclusionary rule. (It is also used to enforce the Fifth and Sixth Amendments; see page 190.) The Supreme Court first adopted the rule for use in federal courts in 1914 in *Weeks* v. *United States* and applied it to the states in 1961 in *Mapp* v. *Ohio*.[59] Under this rule evidence obtained in an improper fashion, that is, in violation of the Constitution or statute, cannot be introduced against those whose Fourth

Amendment rights have been violated. By excluding such evidence judges hope to deter officers from violating the Fourth (or Fifth or Sixth) Amendment. Now that the Fourth Amendment "affords protection against the uninvited ear, oral statements, if illegally overheard, and their fruits are also subject to suppression."[60] Thus, the exclusionary rule applies to statements obtained following an illegal arrest "just as it does to tangible evidence seized in a similar manner or obtained pursuant to an otherwise illegal search and seizure."[61]

There have always been critics of the exclusionary rule. "Why," they quote Justice Cardoza, should the criminal "go free because the constable has blundered"?[62] They argue that the rule is ineffective, there are more desirable ways to prevent police misconduct, it keeps relevant and reliable evidence from the trier of the facts, and it deflects the search for the truth. Defenders of the rule respond that not only does the exclusionary rule have a deterrent effect on police misconduct, but that judges, who are also agents of the government, should have no part in violating the Fourth Amendment. As Justice Brennan has written, "because the evidence-gathering role of the police is directly linked to the evidence-admitting function of the courts, an individual's Fourth Amendment rights may be undermined as completely as by one as by the other."[63]

Starting in 1971 the Court began to back away from the full sweep of the exclusionary ruling. In *New York* v. *Harris* it allowed unconstitutionally obtained evidence to be used to contradict a defendant's testimony and to challenge credibility.[64] And as we have noted, in *Stone* v. *Powell,* the Supreme Court told federal district judges that if the issue of the constitutionality of how evidence had been secured had been reviewed by state courts, petitioners should not be allowed to use *habeas corpus* petitions to get another review of these same questions by federal judges.[65]

In 1984 the Court made two other exceptions to the exclusionary rule, one relatively minor, one major. The minor one, *Nix* v. *Williams,* is the "inevitable discovery exception" permitting the use of physical evidence that would inevitably have been discovered even if the police first learned about it in an unconstitutional fashion. For example, although police first learned the whereabouts of the body of a child by unconstitutionally questioning the suspect (see page 211), evidence of the body's discovery could be used at the trial because it was clear that the two hundred volunteers who were combing the area would have found the victim's body anyway.[66] The Court has also reaffirmed an older exception where the connection between the illegal police conduct is so attenuated as to dissipate the taint, and where the police have had an independent source for the discovery of the same evidence.[67]

The major exception to the exclusionary rule is the "objective good faith" one. For years some members of the Court, as well as many outside, have urged it to make a good faith exception that would "not require the exclusion of evidence obtained by the police in a reasonable belief that they have obtained it in a constitutional manner."[68] The Court has not gone that far, yet. It did rule, however, that where a police officer has obtained a search warrant from a magistrate who acted in the proper neutral and detached way, evidence so obtained should not be excluded even if it subsequently is established that the magistrate lacked probable cause to issue the warrant (*United States* v. *Leon*)[69] or if it turned out that the warrant was defective (*Massachusetts* v. *Sheppard*).[70] This does not mean that if the police obtained the warrant by knowingly or recklessly submitting false information or acted on a warrant which they should have known to be defective, the good faith exception would apply. The police officers' belief in the validity of the warrant must be "objectively reasonable. An officer's subjective belief, based on ignorance of constitutional requirements, will not protect an invalid warrant."

The Court left open for another day the question of whether the good faith exception will apply to good faith warrantless searches. Cases raising those issues are working their way to the Supreme Court.

Justice Stevens, who along with Brennan and Marshall, continues to champion the exclusionary rule, vigorously opposed the Court's good faith exception for searches where police have obtained warrants. He wrote a long and especially bitter dissent. Charging that the Court in effect had converted the "*Bill of Rights* into an unenforced honor code that the police may follow in their discretion. The Constitution requires more; it requires a *remedy*. If the Court's new rule is to be followed, the Bill of Rights should be renamed."[71] He accused his colleagues of having "acquired a voracious appetite for judicial activism in [their] Fourth Amendment jurisprudence, at least when it comes to restricting the constitutional rights of the citizen . . . ."[72]

The exclusionary rule protects only those whose rights have been violated, not other persons, as one Jack Payner discovered to his unhappiness. Payner was brought to trial because Internal Revenue agents had found incriminating evidence against him in his banker's briefcase. The agents had used a female private investigator to lure Payner's banker out to dinner, during which time the agents swiped the briefcase, copied documents found in it, and then returned it to the department. Federal courts found the agents had knowingly and willfully violated the Fourth Amendment rights of the banker, but Payner had no expectations of privacy in the banker's briefcase and since Payner's rights had not been violated, evidence taken in the "briefcase caper" could be used against him.[73]

The exclusionary rule does not apply to a grand jury. Such a jury cannot instruct its agents to violate the Fourth Amendment or issue subpoenas that do; but if illegally procured evidence becomes available to a grand jury, the jury may consider it, even though the evidence may not be used in a subsequent criminal trial.[74]

Nor does the exclusionary rule apply to civil proceedings, not even to deportation proceedings to determine eligibility to remain in this country that could result in someone's being forced to leave.[75] (The exclusionary rule applies, however, to criminal prosecutions for the crime of entering or remaining unlawfully in this country. In most instances the government prefers to resort to civil proceedings to deport than to criminal prosecutions to imprison.)

AMENDMENT V: GRAND JURIES, DOUBLE JEOPARDY, SELF-INCRIMINATION, DUE PROCESS, AND EMINENT DOMAIN

No person shall be held to answer for a capital, or otherwise infamous crime, unless on a presentment or indictment of a Grand Jury,

---

The Fifth Amendment introduces us to the oldest institution known to the Constitution, the grand jury. It hails from the days of William the Conqueror;

the trial, or petty (also spelled *petit*) jury, is an offshoot from it (see the Sixth Amendment). Like its English forerunner, the federal grand jury is composed of not more than twenty-three members, of whom twelve are sufficient to make a "presentment" or return an "indictment"—that is, to accuse some person or persons of an offense against the laws of the United States, on the basis either of evidence gathered by itself or of evidence laid before it by a prosecuting officer. Since the "accused" is not being tried, the grand jury's proceedings are secret and one-sided (*ex parte*), only the government being represented. Although persons brought before grand juries have no right to have attorneys with them in the grand jury room, the federal government permits such persons to consult with their lawyers any time they wish in adjacent quarters.

Grand juries, like all other juries, must be selected without respect to race, sex, or ethnic origin. To discriminate violates the constitutional rights of those who are indicted as well as the rights of any person who might be denied the opportunity to serve on a grand jury. Systematic discrimination in selection of grand jurors requires reversal of a conviction based on an indictment brought by such a jury.

The Supreme Court, however, although reconfirming that "purposeful discrimination against Negroes or women in the selection of grand jury foremen is forbidden by the Fifth Amendment," concluded that it would be an inappropriate remedy to reverse the conviction and to dismiss the indictment brought in by a grand jury presided over by a foreman alleged to have been selected in a discriminatory fashion. The office of grand jury foreman, unlike the grand jury, is not established by the Constitution and "the ministerial role . . . is not such a vital one that discrimination in the appointment of an individual to that post significantly invades the distinctive interests of the defendant protected by the Due Process Clause."[1]

Indictment by grand jury is the one provision of the Bill of Rights relating to criminal prosecutions that the Supreme Court has not construed to be within the scope of the due process clause of the Fourteenth Amendment. States are, therefore, free to indict by other means, and they have been using the grand jury less and less. At the moment only twenty-two states require grand jury indictments; three require it only when the crime is punishable by death or life imprisonment. In the others the prosecuting attorney simply files an information affidavit that there is evidence available to justify a trial.[2] (To hold a person in custody, however, the prosecutor's information must be followed by a hearing before a magistrate for presentation of evidence showing probable cause.)[3]

---

except in cases arising in the land or naval forces or in the Militia, when in actual service in time of War or public danger;

The exception is much more significant than merely dispensing with grand jury indictments for persons in the armed forces. For this clause, along with Article I, Section 8, giving Congress the power to make "rules for the government and regulations of the land and naval forces," means that persons subject to trial before military courts are not entitled to the same procedural rights as are civilians. The Supreme Court has progressively narrowed the exception by limiting the jurisdiction of military tribunals. Neither civilian employees of the armed forces overseas nor civilian dependents of military personnel accompanying them overseas may be tried by court-martial.[4] Ex-soldiers may not be tried by the military for crimes committed while they were in service.[5] At least during peacetime and while serving in the United States, military personnel may not be tried by a court-martial for nonservice-connected crimes committed off base and off duty.[6]

Which rights are constitutionally required in military courts has not been the subject of much Supreme Court litigation. Congress, however, has created a Uniform Code of Military Justice and created a Court of Military Appeals, the so-called GI Supreme Court. That court has extended to armed forces personnel the right to a speedy trial, the right to confront witnesses, the right to protection against unreasonable searches and seizures, the privilege against self-incrimination, the right to public trial, the right to compulsory service of process, and the right to *Miranda*-type warnings (see page 189). Persons within the armed forces ordinarily must exhaust their military appeals from court martial through the Court of Military Appeals before federal courts will interfere.[7]

---

nor shall any person be subject for the same offense to be twice put in jeopardy of life or limb;

Although the constitutional language "jeopardy of life or limb" suggests proceedings in which only the most serious penalties can be imposed, the Clause has long been construed to mean something far broader than its literal language."[8] The guarantee consists of three separate constitutional protections. "It protects against a second prosecution for the same offense after acquittal. It protects against a second prosecution for the same offense after conviction. And it protects against multiple punishments for the same offense."[9] The problem with this often-quoted statement, as Justice Rehnquist has pointed out, is that the words "same offense" is "a phrase deceptively simple in appearance but virtually kaleidoscopic in application."[10]

"Historians have traced the origins of our constitutional guarantee against double jeopardy back to the days of Demosthenes . . . Despite its roots in antiquity, however, this guarantee seems both one of the least understood and, in recent years, one of the most frequently litigated provisions of the Bill of Rights, [the] Court has done little to alleviate the confusion. . . ."[11] Since 1971, when Congress authorized government appeals in all criminal prosecutions except when banned by the double jeopardy clause, the Supreme Court in a series of confusing decisions has tried, without too much success, to "create order and understanding" about the meaning of double jeopardy. Here is what the Court seems to be saying:

Jeopardy attaches in both national and state jury trials as soon as the jury has been sworn and in case of nonjury trials as soon as the judge begins to hear the evidence (in contrast to the original common law and current English interpretation where the limitations against double jeopardy are restricted to cases in which there has been a complete trial culminating in acquittal or conviction).[12]

If a trial ends in acquittal, the double jeopardy clause unequivocably bars reprosecution.[13]

If a trial ends with a guilty verdict, "The general rule is that the Clause does not bar reprosecution of a defendant whose conviction is overturned on appeal," or set aside by the judge.[14] However, if the verdict is set aside because it is based on insufficient evidence, it has the same effect as a judgment of acquittal, "because it means that no rational factfinder could have voted to convict the defendant."[15] However, if the verdict of guilty is set aside because of "the weight of the evidence," the state may reprosecute. Such a reversal does not mean that acquittal was the only proper verdict, but merely that the reviewing court sits as a "thirteenth juror" and disagrees with the jury's resolution of conflicting testimony. "This difference of opinion no more signifies acquittal than does a disagreement among the jurors themselves."[16]

If a trial terminates before a final verdict, the double jeopardy clause may or may not prevent retrial. It prevents retrial if an indictment is dismissed or the case terminated because the evidence is insufficient to justify conviction. This is tantamount to an acquittal.[17] But, except for dismissals because of insufficient evidence, most midtrial terminations are not likely to prevent reprosecution, despite the Court's generalization that once jeopardy attaches and a trial starts a defendant is ordinarily entitled to have it run its course and not again be placed in the agony of having to be retried. For the Court has a counter-generalization: "The Double Jeopardy Clause . . . does not offer a guaranty to the defendant that the State will vindicate its societal interest in the enforcement of the criminal laws in one proceeding."[18] Persons may be retried if the jury is unable to agree on a verdict (a hung jury); if, at the defendant's request, the judge terminates the proceedings because of failure of the government to properly frame the indictment; or even because of a prosecutor's action that causes the judge to declare a mistrial, unless the "prosecutor's actions . . . were done in order to goad the defendant into requesting a mistrial."[19]

The double jeopardy clause does not apply to sentencing decisions with the same force that it applies to redeterminations of guilt or innocence. On retrial if the responsibility for setting a sentence is vested in a jury, a defendant may receive a more severe sentence than was received at the first trial. However, if a judge is responsible for the sentence, as is true in most jurisdictions, a judge may not ordinarily impose a harsher punishment than was given in the first trial, and if the judge does so, he or she must justify such action in writing.[20] Moreover, a state cannot impose the death penalty on retrial if at the first trial, the first jury declined to do so, nor may a judge impose the death penalty on a person after the life sentence he had initially received was set aside on appeal.[21]

The Supreme Court sustained an act of Congress (an act of Congress has never been held to violate the double jeopardy clause) that permits the federal government to ask the court of appeals to review a sentence imposed by a district judge. Under such circumstances the defendant is not placed in jeopardy again, but merely has to defend against an increase in the severity of the sentence imposed.[22]

A single act may violate several statutory provisions, but the double jeopardy clause prevents prosecution (but not punishment, see below) for a single act separately under several laws or provisions of a law unless "each provision requires proof of a fact that the other does not."[23] This means that prosecution for a greater, or more serious, offense may be precluded after prosecution for a "lesser included offense" and vice versa. To illustrate: After Nathaniel Brown's conviction by Ohio for joyriding—taking an automobile without the owner's consent—he could not be tried again for that same act under a different provision against auto theft—joyriding with intent to deprive permanently the owner of possession.[24] The double jeopardy clause also prevented the reprosecution of a man by the name of Ashe after he had been tried and acquitted of participating with others in the armed robbery of one of six men while they were playing poker. He was acquitted, chiefly on the matter of identification. Six weeks later he was convicted of robbing another of the poker players. The Supreme Court set his conviction aside because he had already been tried for the offense of being one of the robbers of the poker players. Chief Justice Burger argued in dissent, "What the Court is holding, is, in effect, that the second and third and fourth criminal acts are 'free' unless the accused is tried for the multiple crimes in a single trial."[25]

While conviction of a lesser offense probably precludes prosecution for the greater offense, the same is not true of a guilty plea to the lesser offense. After Thomas Hill was shot to death in his apartment, Kenneth Johnson was indicted for murder, involuntary manslaughter, aggravated robbery, and grand theft. His guilty pleas to the charges of manslaughter and grand theft were accepted by the court over the state's objection: Johnson then argued that it would be double jeopardy if the state were to prosecute him for murder. But the Supreme Court rejected his contention, "The acceptance of a guilty plea to a lesser included offense while charges on the greater offense remain pending . . . has none of the implications of an 'implied acquittal' which results from a verdict convicting a defendant on lesser included offenses rendered by a jury charged to consider both greater and lesser included offenses."[26]

The double jeopardy clause does not prohibit multiple punishments after a single trial for an act that is contrary to several statutes; "It does no more than prevent the sentencing court from prescribing greater punishment [under each statute] than the legislature intended."[27]

There is no double jeopardy in trying persons both for a substantive offense and for conspiring to commit that same offense.[28] And since "acquittal on criminal charges does not prove that the defendant is innocent; it merely proves the existence of a reasonable doubt as to his guilt," a civil action which requires less proof is permissible, providing the purpose of the civil action is remedial and not punitive.[29] Here are two examples: after a person was acquitted of smuggling, the government was allowed to seek forfeiture of the goods alleged to have been illegally brought into the country;[30] and after a person was acquitted of knowingly engaging in selling firearms without a license, the government was allowed to institute civil proceedings to force him to give up the weapons.[31]

The double jeopardy clause does prevent a government from trying delinquents for the same offense in the regular courts after trying them in juvenile courts. (A mere preliminary hearing on whether or not to try a person as a juvenile with a decision to transfer to adult court would not be double jeopardy.[32])

The double jeopardy clause prevents only trial by the *same government* for the same offense. It does not keep the national and state governments from trying a person for the same act if it violates the law of each government, even if the defendant is acquitted of the charge in the courts of the first government to bring him or her to trial.[33] It should be noted that although prosecution for the same act by the national and state governments is not forbidden by the Constitution, in most instances federal policy precludes federal prosecution if there has been a previous state prosecution for the same act.[34] (Whenever civil rights violations are involved, however, the presumption against federal prosecution can be readily overcome.)

The double jeopardy clause does not bar prosecution of Indians both in tribal courts and in federal courts, since tribal courts, although their jurisdiction is subject to supervision by Congress, receive their jurisdiction from the tribes—an independent sovereign, at least for this purpose—and they are not arms of the federal government.[35] In contrast, trial by both a state and one of its municipalities for the same act is double jeopardy.[36] Municipal corporations are creatures of the state, and constitutionally speaking a city and its state are the same government. The same is true of the national government and a territorial government, and probably true of the national government and the District of Columbia.

---

nor shall be compelled in any criminal case to be a witness against himself;

Originally construed to mean only that persons might not be forced to testify against themselves, this provision has been broadened in a variety of highly significant ways. It is now included within the Fourteenth Amendment as a limitation on the states,[37] thereby permitting a person to claim the right in order to avoid the risk of prosecution by either national or state authorities.[38] Until these constructions, a witness before a federal agency could not invoke the Fifth Amendment to avoid prosecution by a state agency, and a witness before a state agency could not claim the Fourteenth Amendment to refuse to answer questions that might lead to prosecution by the national (or state) government.

The privilege protects persons from being compelled to answer incriminating questions put by any government agency, for example, the Federal Trade Commission. Furthermore, it provides some protection from complying with certain laws—specifically aimed tax laws, for example, when compliance would expose a person to "real and appreciable risk" of self-incrimination because it would furnish evidence of illegal activities. For example, professional gamblers cannot be made to pay a special excise tax on receipts from professional gambling under circumstances where it would provide evidence of their illegal activity.[39] On the other hand, the self-incrimination clause does not prevent a state from requiring drivers involved in accidents to stop and notify the owner or person in charge of the property damaged of their name and address since this is a more general statute not directly aimed at uncovering illegal action.[40] And the self-incrimination clause does not protect in the matter of future transgressions of the law; hence Congress may require that when persons sell or give certain kinds of firearms, they must file with federal authorities the name and address and fingerprints of the transferee. The information provided cannot be used as evidence in a criminal proceeding respecting a prior or concurrent violation, but failure to file the information is a crime, as is the possession of an unregistered weapon.[41] Nor does this clause—which is limited to criminal prosecutions—preclude Congress from requiring persons in charge of offshore facilities to report any discharge of oil into navigable waters and to pay a penalty for doing so. Such action may also be a criminal offense, but since the penalty imposed is civil, it does not trigger the protections afforded by the Constitution to a criminal defendant. (The statute provides some limited immunity in that the notification itself of oil discharge cannot be used against the reporting person.)[42]

The Supreme Court also quickly disposed of the claim that the "Solomon Amendment" requiring men who wished to apply for federal student financial assistance to furnish proof that they had registered with the Selective Service System compelled persons to incriminate themselves. Chief Justice Burger wrote for the Court, "a person who has not registered clearly is under no compulsion to seek financial aid."[43] Justices Marshall and Brennan, who dissented, felt that the problem was not that simple since those who had failed to register were in violation of the law. Wrote Justice Marshall,"If appellees assert their Fifth Amendment privilege by their silence, they are penalized for exercising a constitutional right by the withholding of education aid. If they succumb to the economic coercion either by registering, or by registering but claiming the privilege as to particular disclosures, they have incriminated themselves."[44]

Although persons are not entitled to refuse to answer questions merely because the answers might be embarrassing, lead to public ridicule, or incriminate others, they are entitled to refuse to answer questions that may furnish the police with links to evidence that could result in their being prosecuted even if the ultimate outcome would be acquittal.

The protection against self-incrimination extends only to testimonial evidence. One cannot claim the right in order to refuse to submit handwriting samples, to give voice samples, to be fingerprinted, to appear in a police lineup, to submit to a breathalyzer test, or even to give a blood sample. Moreover, the mere fact that one refused to give fingerprints, or submit to a breathalyzer, or give blood samples could be used as incriminating evidence in a court.[45]

The self-incrimination clause, at least for the moment, also protects against subpoenas for one's *personal* books and papers in one's *own* possession. The important condition is that the material be personal and in one's possession. Tax records in the hands of one's accountant are not protected, for example, nor are books or papers that one might have as a union officer, or that belong to a corporation of which one is an officer, or that belong to a partnership, or even the papers of a one-person business firm.[46] However, in this latter example the act of producing incriminating documents may be protected, since the mere act of producing them may amount to testifying against oneself. But even this minimal protection for business records should not be read too generously, for the Supreme Court, although not there yet, appears to be moving toward Justice O'Connor's position "that the Fifth Amendment provides absolutely no protection for the contents of private papers of any kind."[47]

If a government grants immunity from prosecution as broad as the protection provided by the self-incrimination clause, then a witness may be compelled to respond under pain of fine or imprisonment. Often the government would rather have the evidence than prosecute, and for many decades Congress authorized the granting of "transactional immunity," meaning that a person denied the right to claim self-incrimination and compelled to testify could not be prosecuted for any transactions mentioned as a part of the compelled testimony.

Then, in 1970, Congress restricted the immunity. No longer does it grant immunity for any crimes mentioned. The immunity conferred only denies the government the right to use any information derived directly or indirectly from the compelled testimony. The Court has said this "use and derivate use immunity" is coextensive with the Fifth Amendment requirement, so that persons given "use and derivate use immunity" may not claim the privilege to refuse to answer incriminating questions. However, if they are subsequently prosecuted, the government has to prove the evidence it proposes to use was derived from legitimate sources wholly independent of the compelled testimony.

All immunized testimony, however, may be used in prosecutions for perjury. It may also be used in most civil suits.[48] A person, therefore, previously granted immunity for criminal prosecution may claim the Fifth Amendment right not to respond to incriminating questions in a civil deposition lest that testimony be used against him or her in a criminal prosecution.[49]

The self-incriminating clause provides some protection for public employees who cannot be fired merely for invoking the self-incriminating clause when questioned by their superiors. However, they may be dismissed if they refuse to answer questions directly relating to the performance of their official duties, provided they are not required to relinquish their constitutional immunity nor to have such compelled evidence used against them in subsequent criminal prosecutions. Similarly, unless they are given immunity, contractors may not be denied the right to do future business with a state merely because they have refused to testify before a grand jury about past contracts.[50]

It is in the areas of protection for those accused of a crime that the self-incrimination clause has had its most important and controversial extensions. The clause gives to defendants the right to refuse to take the stand at their trials in order to refrain from answering any question, incriminating or not. The burden is upon the government to prove guilt; the defendant has no responsibility to help. If defendants choose not to take the stand, there is nothing that can prevent jurors from speculating about why they stand mute in the face of a criminal accusation. But a judge may and must, if requested to do so, use the unique power of the jury instruction to reduce the speculation to a minimum by instructing the jurors that a defendant has a constitutional right not to testify; the fact that he or she does not do so should not be used as an inference of guilt, and should not prejudice the jury against the defendant in any way.[51] If defendants do take the stand, the prosecution may cross-examine them on all of their testimony, even including the fact that prior to their arrest they remained silent and did not respond to police accusations.

Traditionally, the right to refuse to incriminate oneself applied only at the time of one's formal trial. But what good was this constitutional protection, or the guarantee of the right to assistance of counsel, or the presumption of innocence, if long before the accused were brought before a judge he or she was detained and, without help of an attorney, forced to prove innocence to the police? Do not such procedures reduce the courtroom proceedings to a mere formality?

In the 1930s, the Supreme Court began to move against these tactics. At first it used the more general due process standards, to reverse convictions obtained by using evidence secured by torture, by prolonged psychological coercion, or by involuntary confession. It acted not so much because these practices amount to self-incrimination but because such brutal procedures and, "The use of coerced confessions, whether true or false, is forbidden because the method used to extract them offends constitutional principles."[52] And "*any* criminal trial use against a defendant of his *involuntary* statement is a denial of due process of law, 'even though there is ample evidence aside from the confession to support the conviction.' "[53]

In 1966, in *Miranda* v. *Arizona,* the Supreme Court abandoned case-by-case determination of where police interrogation has gone too far: It brought the self-incrimination clause into play.[54] It announced that henceforth no conviction could stand if evidence introduced at the trial, even though voluntarily given, had been obtained by the police as a result of "custodial interrogation" unless suspects had been: (1) notified that they are free to remain silent; (2) warned that what they say may be used against them in court; (3) told they have a right to have their attorney present during the questioning; (4) informed that if they cannot afford to hire their own lawyers, attorneys will be provided for them; (5) permitted at any stage of the police interrogation to terminate it. If suspects answer questions in the absence of attorneys, the prosecution must be prepared to demonstrate that the suspects knowingly and intelligently waived their rights to remain silent and to have their own lawyer present. Failure to comply with these requirements will lead to reversal of convictions even if other independent evidence would be sufficient to establish guilt.

"Custodial interrogations" cover all questioning by police, including by Internal Revenue agents in circumstances where investigators have fixed on an individual for possible criminal prosecution, "regardless of the nature or severity of the offense of which he is suspected or for which he was arrested" under circumstances where people have lost their freedom to leave.[55] Custodial interrogations do not depend on whether persons are in custody in a police station or have been placed under formal arrest. They cover all investigations where persons are deprived of freedom of action "to a degree associated with a formal arrest."[56]

Miranda warnings are not required, however, merely for police to talk with suspects, even in police stations, if suspects have voluntarily gone to the station and are free to go whenever they wish and are under no legal restraint.[57] Nor are Miranda warnings required at routine traffic stops.[58] Nor are such warnings required when a probation officer questions a probationer about an earlier crime or when persons have been called to appear before a grand jury.[59]

The Supreme Court has also created a "public safety" exception to the Miranda requirement. In *New York* v. *Quarles* the Court was faced with the following fact situation: On September 11, 1980, officers were patrolling in Queens when a young woman approached the car. She told them she had just been raped by a man who had then gone into an A & P market and that he was carrying a gun. The officers drove the woman to the store, saw the suspect, frisked him and discovered he was wearing a shoulder holster which was empty. After handcuffing him the officer asked him where the gun was and the suspect said, "The gun is over there," and pointed to some empty cartons. The officer retrieved a loaded .38-caliber revolver, formally placed the defendant under arrest and then read him his Miranda rights. The lower courts held that neither the gun nor the defendant's statement, "The gun is over there" could be introduced at his trial since this evidence had been obtained before the Miranda warning had been given. The Supreme Court agreed that prior decisions would have required that result, but concluded: "There is a 'public safety exception' to the requirement. . . . We do not believe that the doctrinal underpinnings of Miranda require that it be applied in all its rigor to a situation in which police officers ask questions reasonably prompted by a concern for the public safety."[60] The Court, speaking through Justice Rehnquist acknowledged: "In recognizing a narrow exception to the Miranda rule, to some degree we lessen the desirable clarity of that rule."

After a *Miranda* warning has been given and a suspect requests that an attorney be present, police are in danger of violating the suspect's rights "even if what they say to a suspect is not punctuated by a question mark." In *Edwards* v. *Arizona,* the Court established a *per se* rule that once a suspect asks to have an attorney present, no waiver of that right, however voluntary, can be valid if made in response to further police questioning.[61] Of course, not all conversation between the police and the accused must cease. But if from these conversations the suspect makes incriminating statements away from counsel, such statements cannot be introduced in a court against the suspect unless they clearly were not provoked by the police, directly, or indirectly.

The *Miranda* doctrine also applies in a modified form to psychiatric examinations initiated by the state. A state may order such examinations to determine whether or not an accused is mentally competent to stand trial, and an accused is not entitled to have an attorney present during the examination. However, the state may not use any evidence from such an examination to determine guilt or severity of the sentence unless it has first given a *Miranda* hearing to the suspect, an opportunity to consult with an attorney prior to the examination, and made it clear that the suspect does not have to answer incriminating questions.[62]

The *Miranda* prohibitions apply primarily to evidence relating to issues of guilt or innocence. Thus a prosecution, in order to challenge a defendant's credibility, may introduce evidence obtained in violation of the *Miranda* ruling to contradict statements a defendant legally volunteers from the witness stand. Otherwise a defendant might give perjured testimony free from the risk of confrontation with prior inconsistent utterances. However, the exception does put pressure on defendants to refrain from taking the stand in their own defense since their own testimony may open the way for the prosecution to use evidence that could not otherwise be introduced.[63]

In short, as a result of the Supreme Court's liberal construction of the self-incrimination clause, it now applies to all governments, serves to protect persons in all settings in which their freedom of action is curtailed, and has become an essential mainstay of our adversary system. A government seeking to punish persons must produce the evidence against them by its own independent labors and cannot force suspects to contribute to their own conviction.

Needless to say, many police officers are highly critical of these Supreme Court decisions, since they restrict the police's ability to question suspects, an ability they believe to be essential for the solution of many crimes.

Although governments cannot compel persons to incriminate themselves, most cases are disposed of by guilty pleas. Increasingly such pleas result from bargaining in which prosecutors agree to drop more serious charges in return for defendants' guilty pleas to lesser ones. It was not until 1971 that the Supreme Court in *Santobella v. New York* dispelled any "lingering doubts about the legitimacy of the practice . . . and . . . plea bargaining was no longer shrouded in secrecy and deliberately concealed."[64]

A year earlier, however, in *Brady* v. *United States,* the Court had listed the advantages of the practice: "For a defendant who sees slight possibility of acquittal, the advantages of pleading guilty and limiting the probable penalty are obvious. . . . For the State there are also advantages—the more promptly imposed punishment after an admission of guilty may more effectively attain the objectives of punishment; and with the avoidance of trial, scarce judicial and prosecutorial resources are conserved for those cases in which there is a substantial issue of the defendant's guilt or in which there is substantial doubt that the State can sustain its burden of proof. It is this mutuality of advantage that perhaps explains the fact that at present well over three-fourths of the criminal convictions in this country rest on pleas of guilty. . . ."[65]

Since *Santobello* the Court has established ground rules for the implementation of plea bargaining which ensure that the guilty plea is knowingly made and the prosecutor's promise is upheld. (A prosecutor may withdraw an offer and then the defendant has a right to withdraw a guilty plea.[66]) Counsel must be present during plea negotiations and a record must be made to show that the plea was knowingly and voluntarily made with a full understanding of its consequences.

---

nor be deprived of his life, liberty, or property, without due process of law.

A parallel clause is found in the Fourteenth Amendment as a limitation on the states. The due process clauses of the Fifth and Fourteenth Amendment have resulted in more cases and controversies than any other in the Constitution, although the equal protection clause of the Fourteenth Amendment is quickly catching up. Despite the number of cases, it is impossible to give these due process clauses any exact, final, and completely satisfactory explanation. Indeed, the Supreme Court itself has refused to give due process precise definition, stating that it prefers to rely on "the gradual process of judicial inclusion and exclusion."[67]

The due process clause only restricts the actions of governments. In recent years a question that for decades was only significant with respect to the application of the equal protection clause (see page 248) has now become an issue with respect to the application of the due process clauses; namely, when is an action an action of the state or done under the color of law and when is it merely private action? In part, the question has become more important because of the Supreme Court's more liberal construction of 42 U.S.C 1983 (see page 249) permitting persons to bring suits against those who act under the color of law "to deprive them of any right secured by law or the Constitution." In part, the issue of what is and what is not "state action" comes about because of the more expansive application of the protections of the due process clauses to more and more arenas.

When we get to the equal protection clause we will discuss at greater length the factors which cause the Court to decide when the Fifth or Fourteenth Amendments come into play because state action is involved. (The Fifth Amendment contains no equal protection clause, but the Supreme Court has interpreted the due process clause of the Fifth Amendment (*Bolling* v. *Sharpe,* 1954) to limit the national government in precisely the same way that the equal protection clause of the Fourteenth Amendment limits state's.)[68] Here are a couple of examples of cases turning on the question of whether the action was that of the state or of private agencies or persons, and thus whether the due process clause applied. A private nursing home transferred Medicaid patients whose expenses are paid by federal and state funds to a facility that provided lower levels of care after a utilization review committee, required by federal regulations, concluded that this was the appropiate level for the patients. The patients subject to this transfer argued they had been denied due process because they had not been given a proper hearing. The Supreme Court said that the due process clause did not apply. True, the nursing home was extensively regulated by the state—the state paid the expenses—but the decision about appropriate level of care turned on medical judgments made by private parties according to professional standards and the nursing home was not performing a function that has traditionally been the exclusive prerogative of the state.[69] On the other hand, when a creditor using procedures established by Virginia law went into a Virginia court to attach property of one of his debtors, the debtor was allowed to sue the creditor under Section 1983 on the grounds that the creditor acting under the color of state law had violated the debtor's due process rights.[70]

The Court has expanded the meaning of the "property" and the "liberty," especially the latter, that are protected by the due process clause. Originally, "liberty" meant freedom from physical restraint; it has been expanded to denote "not merely freedom from bodily restraint but also right of the individual to contract, to engage in any of the common occupations of life, to acquire useful knowledge, to marry, to establish a home and to bring up children, to worship God according to the dictates of his own conscience, and generally to enjoy those common law privileges long recognized as essential to the orderly pursuit of happiness by free men."[71] Also brought under the liberty protected by due process is the right of privacy, a largely undefined right. The part of it which has received the most protection is "marital privacy."

In fact in recent years the Court has so expanded the term "liberty" as to blur the distinction between a privilege—something given by the government as a matter of grace—and a right—something to which you are entitled. Public welfare, housing, education, employment, professional licenses, access to courts to press criminal appeals, and so on are now more and more matters of entitlement, and to deprive someone of them calls into play some form of due process protection.[72]

Prior to 1937 the most important phrase of this "new liberty" protected by the Supreme Court was "liberty of contract,"[73] that is, business liberty. Since

1937 the Supreme Court has abandoned the doctrine of "liberty" of contract, "but this action did not foreshadow a return to the old narrow conception of liberty. On the contrary, the "liberty" of the Fifth and Fourteenth Amendments has been expanded to include the basic civil liberties.

Property, too, has been expanded. At one time thought to be primarily physical "things," property now includes a whole bundle of rights. Unlike the "liberty" which the due process clause protects because it comes from the Constitution itself, the due process clause does not by itself create property interests. Rather, it extends various procedural safeguards to property interests created by other parts of the Constitution or, more commonly, by state law.[74]

Despite the expansive interpretations of liberty and property and the extension of the due process clause to a whole range of proceedings, "the range of interests protected by procedural due process is not infinite. . . . Not every grievous . . . loss invokes[s] procedural protections of the Due Process Clause."[75] A state, for example, does not have to give nontenured faculty members procedural rights before it decides not to renew their appointments. They have no property right in their jobs that flow from the Constitution. (The state by its own laws and procedures can confer property rights in teaching jobs, and if it does so then it cannot take such rights away without due process.) True, teachers are entitled to freedom of speech, along with everybody else, and they cannot be denied that freedom without due process, but "the interest in holding a job at a state university, simpliciter, is not itself a free speech interest" "nor one that cannot be denied without procedural due process."[76]

"Prisons are not beyond the reach of the Constitution."[77] Prisoners must be provided a reasonable opportunity to exercise their religious freedoms, to petition the government, and not be subject to cruel and unusual punishments. A prisoner, however, has no liberty right to be transferred from one prison to another whether in state or across states[78] (but see page 198). Nor do prisoners, even those being held in pretrial detention, have a liberty right to have contact with members of their families or friends who come to visit them.[79]

One has neither a property right nor a liberty right to a government job and can be dismissed from such employment without due process protection. (However, if the reasons for the dismissal of most government employees are because of membership in a different party from the one that won the last election, or merely because the employees have exercised First Amendment rights, such action might be a denial of the right to association and therefore bring First Amendment rights into play.[80] Moreover, if the reasons for dismissal are publicized, it could amount to governmental imposition of stigma upon a person, which would infringe on one's liberty and thus require some kind of due process.[81] Foster parents are not entitled to due process before their foster children can be taken from them for, unlike natural parents, they have no property rights to or liberty rights in their foster children.[82]

Out-of-state lawyers have no property rights to practice in the courts of the state in which they may be present.[83] Automobile manufacturers have no rights to establish new franchises in a state wherever and whenever they wish.[84] Patients in a nursing home supported by government funds have no property right to continued residence in the home of their choice, nor liberty right not to be subject to the emotional trauma of having to move as the result of governmental action taking away support from the nursing home in which they are living.[85] Nor do prisoners have any rights to due process before being denied a parole or a reduction in the length of their sentences. (They do have a right to due process prior to having a parole, once granted, taken away. "There is a difference between losing what one has and not getting what one wants.")[86]

"Once it is determined that due process applies, the question remains what process is due."[87] There are two kinds of due process—*procedural* and *substantive*. Procedural due process refers to the methods by which the law is enforced. It requires, to paraphrase Daniel Webster's famous definition, a procedure that "hears before it condemns, proceeds upon inquiry, and renders judgment only after [a] trial in which the essentials of justice have been preserved."

There are several ways in which a law itself may violate procedural due process. First, "a statute which either forbids or requires the doing of an act in terms so vague that men of common intelligence must necessarily guess at its meaning and differ as to its application violates the first essential of due process of law."[88] Not only does a vague statute run the risk of entrapping the innocent, it "impermissibly delegates basic policy matters to policemen, judges, and juries . . . on an *ad hoc* and subjective basis, with the attendant dangers of arbitrary and discriminatory application."[89] A vague statute "furnishes a convenient tool for harsh and discriminatory enforcement by local prosecuting officials . . . confers on police a virtually unrestrained power to arrest and charge persons with a violation, and "entrusts lawmaking to the moment-to-moment judgment of the policeman on the beat."[90]

Examples of statutes struck down for vagueness are "a suspicious person ordinance" providing that any person found on a street at late or unusual hours at night without any visible or lawful business and who did not give a satisfactory account of him/herself might be fined or imprisoned,[91] and a statute requiring persons who loiter or wander on the streets under circumstances that make police suspicious to provide a "credible and reliable" identification to account for their presence when asked by a police officer to do so.[92] A similar fate befell a vagrancy ordinance declaring to be vagrants a wide variety of ill-defined classes such as "rogues and vagabonds," "dissolute persons who go about begging," "common night walkers," and so on.[93] Yet another example: A Pennsylvania statute was held void for vagueness made doctors criminally liable who, after determining that a fetus "is viable or . . . may be viable," failed to exercise "that degree of professional skill, care, and diligence necessary to preserve the life and health of the fetus," and to adopt the particular abortion technique "which would provide the best opportunity for the fetus to be aborted alive so long as a different technique would not be necessary in order to preserve the life or health of the mother . . ."[94]

On the other side, an ordinance requiring a business to obtain a license if it sells any items "designed or marketed for use with illegal cannabis or drugs," i.e., a so-called "head-shop," was ruled not to be unconstitutionally vague on its face.[95] The Court also upheld an ordinance directing the chief of police to consider whether an applicant for a license to run a coin-operated amusement center has any "connection with criminal elements." The Court pointed out that although the ordinance would be too vague to convict a person of the offense of having such a connection, or might even be too vague to support the denial of a license, the Constitution does not preclude a city from giving vague directions to officials who are authorized to make investigations and recommendations.[96]

A second way in which a law itself may violate procedural due process is by creating an improper presumption of guilt. Persons are presumed innocent. Due process places the burden on the government in criminal prosecutions to prove guilt beyond a reasonable doubt.[97] This burden cannot be shifted nor the standard of proof diminished by a law that creates a presumption of criminal guilt *unless* the fact the law infers "is more likely than not—based upon history, common sense, and experience—to flow from the fact proved."[98] For example, a law presuming that any person who committed a crime of violence and possessed a firearm had received that firearm in violation of the law was declared unconstitutional. This presumption shifted the burden of proof from the government to such persons; they had to prove they had not obtained the firearm illegally. But to prove that a person has committed a crime of violence does not establish that such a person "more likely than not" had obtained the firearm in his or her possession illegally.[99] Similarly, the Court has declared unconstitutional laws creating the presumption that possessors of marijuana or cocaine obtained the drugs through illegal importation.[100] The constitutionality of such a presumption in the case of heroin has been sustained, since little if any heroin is made in this country, virtually all of it is illegally imported, and any one convicted of its possession has more likely than not obtained it illegally.[101] The Court has also sustained a law that created a presumption that persons in possession of stolen property knew the property had been stolen.[102]

A third way a law can violate procedural due process is to take away a liberty or property interest without a proper hearing. What makes a hearing proper is discussed below. Here are just a few examples of laws declared unconstitutional on such grounds: a law providing for automatic revocation of a driver's license after an accident[103] (but revocation is permissible after three convictions for moving violations);[104] a law permitting the listing in liquor stores of the names of persons who have engaged in "excessive drinking" and forbidding sales of liquor to such persons where there were no provisions for those whose names were listed to be first notified and given a hearing;[105] and a law disqualifying unwed fathers as fit parents without giving such fathers a hearing to determine their fitness.[106]

Traditionally, procedural due process is applied when the government is trying to deprive someone of liberty or property by securing a conviction in a court of law. As applied in a courtroom, due process requires as a minimum the careful observance of the provisions of the Bill of Rights as outlined in Amendments Four through Eight. But courtroom due process goes beyond the provisions of the Bill of Rights. A court could follow each particular provision of the Bill of Rights and still deny due process if, for example, the judge in a manner or mood showed bias toward the defendant or if the judge had a financial interest in the outcome of the trial. In other words, due process requires fundamental fairness, a fair and impartial trial.[107] Thus it is impossible to provide a fair trial for a person not mentally competent to understand the nature of the proceedings, or not able to consult with counsel or to assist in the preparation of the defense.[108]

Due process also protects persons arrested as a consequence of a prosecutor's information. They may not be detained in jail unless there is first a hearing before a magistrate to establish probable cause, but again the hearing need not be accompanied by the full range of adversary safeguards—counsel, confrontation, cross-examination, and compulsory process for witnesses.[109]

To give more examples of what kind of process is due: A juvenile cannot be declared delinquent without a hearing in which the juvenile is given the right to confront hostile witnesses and to cross-examine them, to present oral evidence, and to be represented by counsel; the level of proof must demonstrate delinquency by what is required in a criminal trial, namely beyond any reasonable doubt, but the juvenile is not entitled to have the decision made by a jury. Furthermore, after a hearing and a finding of a "serious risk" that a juvenile "may before the return date commit an act which if committed by an adult would constitute a crime," a juvenile may be kept in preventive detention for a limited time.[110]

A person who has been convicted in a criminal case still retains due process rights. A person on parole or probation may be returned to prison only after notice and hearing. At such a hearing the probationer or parolee is entitled to a written statement of the charges, disclosure of evidence, the opportunity to be heard and to present evidence and witnesses, the right to confront and cross-examine witnesses (unless the hearing officer finds good cause to the contrary, such as danger to life if witnesses are present), a neutral and detached hearing body (but not necessarily one composed of lawyers), and a written statement as to evidence and reason for revocation of parole or probation.[111]

The probationer or parolee is entitled to be represented by counsel, but the state need supply counsel for indigents only if in the particular hearing such representation is necessary for the hearing to be fair; for example, because of the complexity of the issues or the special inability of the parolee or probationer to speak effectively for him or herself.[112] In any hearing in which a request for the assignment of counsel is refused, the hearing officer must state in the record the reasons for the refusal.

Nor does due process stop at the jailhouse door. Prisoners may not be punished for misconduct without due process. Prison disciplinary proceedings need not provide the "full panoply of rights due to a defendant in a criminal prosecution, but inmates are entitled to advanced written notice of a claimed violation, a written statement of the factual findings, and reasons for the disciplinary action taken. At the hearing prisoners are entitled to call witnesses and present documentary evidence unless permitting them to do so would be "unduly hazardous." Due process does not, however, require that prisoners be allowed the rights of confrontation and cross-examination and the right to counsel, except for illiterates who may need assistance in providing their defense, but the help need not be a lawyer. If by statute a state gives a liberty interest to a prisoner to remain in the general prison population, such prisoners are entitled to due process before being placed in segregation. (Pennsylvania satisfied this requirement when after a prison riot an inmate was confined to administrative segregation pending an investigation into his role in the riot, received notice of the disciplinary charges the day after his alleged misconduct took place, a hearing committee reviewed the evidence against him five days later, and he was given an opportunity to present a statement to the committee.)[113]

The Supreme Court has stated that these requirements for procedures to be used in prison disciplinary hearings are not "carved in stone,"[114] and future circumstances might suggest different procedures. Furthermore, in recent years the Burger Court has warned federal judges not to use the Fourth Amendment (which does not protect prisoners, see page 175), the cruel and unusual punishment clause of the Eighth Amendment (see page 213), or the due process clause to substitute their own judgments as to how best to run a prison for the judgments of the prison officials. The Supreme Court has also ruled that the due process clause does not require that prisoners be allowed to watch as their cells are searched nor does it protect them from random "shakedowns of their cells."[115]

Outside of criminal prosecutions, due process does not necessarily require that criminal procedures be followed. The question in each instance is what must be done to ensure fundamental fairness. It is hard to generalize because of the wide variety of governmental proceedings involved. Among the many forums where procedural due process is required are disbarment proceedings, determinations of eligibility for welfare payments, parole and probation revocations, legislative contempt proceedings, congressional committees and administrative tribunals, disciplinary proceedings in state universities, colleges, and public schools, and confinements in mental institutions.[116]

The Court debates the issue of what due process requires in these noncourtroom proceedings in terms of three questions outlined in its decisions in *Mathews* v. *Eldridge*: (1) What are the private interests at stake? (2) What is the government's interest? (3) What are the risks the procedures used will lead to an erroneous decision?[117]

In emergency situations where protection of public health and safety is paramount, summary administrative actions may be taken. For example, an unsafe mine can be closed or a passport revoked merely with a statement of reasons and an opportunity for a prompt postrevocation hearing.[118] The national government may seize property being brought illegally into the country and follow with a hearing later (see page 198). However, these are unusual situations. In all but these few emergency situations, due process requires at a minimum adequate notice and an opportunity to be heard prior to the deprivation of the protected liberty or property interest.

A hearing does not necessarily have to be formal or adversary in nature. To illustrate: A student is entitled to notice and to an informal hearing (unless the student's presence poses a continuing danger to persons or property) before being suspended from a public school for disciplinary reasons, but the hearing may be informal, perhaps only a brief talk with the principal.[119] For long-term expulsion the procedures must be a little more formal, but dismissal for academic reasons calls for even less rigorous procedures, no hearing whatsoever being required.[120] A municipally owned utility, before terminating service for failure to pay bills, must notify customers of procedures that permit them to protest the proposed termination.[121] Apparently the federal government must provide some kind of hearing procedure for persons whose claims under the Medicare program have been turned down, but a review by a hearing officer, who does not necessarily have to be a lawyer, appointed by insurance carriers under contract from the government without further judicial review, is sufficient.[122]

To give more examples of what kind of process is due: Natural parents are entitled to due process before their children may be taken from them. They must be given an opportunity to be heard in a rather formal proceeding, and the state is required to support its allegations to meet the "clear and convincing standard" of proof, a more demanding standard that "preponderance of evidence" used for civil proceedings but less demanding than the "beyond a reasonable doubt" standard used in criminal prosecutions.[123] Parents do not, however, have an automatic right to court-appointed counsel: The trial judge must make a decision in each instance whether or not due process requires the assistance of counsel. In fact, the Court has suggested due process probably requires the automatic appointment of counsel for indigents only in situations where they "may be deprived of . . . physical liberty."[124]

Admissions into mental institutions have caused considerable litigation. Children are entitled to due process before they can be placed by their parents in mental institutions, but due process does not require a formal adversarial hearing, merely a neutral medical determination by a doctor or other professional.[125] Prisoners, however, even though not entitled to due process before being transferred from one prison to another, are entitled to such protection before they can be taken from prison and placed in a mental hospital, even if the placement is within the time period of their sentence. Moreover, prisoners must be given written notice before being transferred to a mental hospital, a hearing before an independent decision-maker, an opportunity to present evidence and cross examine witnesses, and a written statement as to the decision. Four justices think such prisoners are entitled to legal counsel; the fifth would not require such assistance be provided by a lawyer. He agrees, however, that there must be qualified and independent assistance, perhaps by a psychiatrist or psychologist.[126]

An issue that has caused considerable division within the Court, and some heat, is the due process requirements for state proceedings that afford relief for creditors against delinquent debtors. Prior to the garnishment of wages there must be a hearing.[127] (Garnishment is a process by which an employer is ordered by a court to pay directly to an employee's creditors amounts deducted from the wages due to the employee.) A hearing is necessary before goods sold on the installment plan can be repossessed.[128] A prepossession hearing is *not* necessary if a judge orders a sheriff to take possession of property in which title is still vested in the seller.[129] A hearing is necessary before a creditor can place a hold on and garnish a bank account.[130] If a creditor uses a state law and state courts to seize property in the hands of his debtor, but does so in a fashion that a court subsequently decides violates the due process clause, that creditor may be sued by his debtor for acting under the color of state law and acting jointly with the state to violate his constitutional rights under the due process clause (see page 192).

The national government may seize property being brought into the country illegally, but it cannot keep noncontraband property without holding a hearing held within a reasonable time. What time is reasonable involves the weighing of the four factors involved in the Sixth Amendment requirement for speedy criminal trials (see page 204); the length of delay, reason for the delay, the defendant's assertion of a right to an early hearing, and whether in fact the delay has prejudiced the defendant. Applying these standards the Court recently held that an eighteen-month delay in filing civil proceedings for forfeiture of currency seized by custom officials because it had not been properly listed on the form was not a denial of due process.[131]

Whereas procedural due process places limits on the manner in which governmental power may be exercised, substantive due process withdraws certain subjects from the full reach of governmental power regardless of the procedures used. Substantive due process, which began to be important in the Supreme Court about 1890, requires that the Court be convinced that the law—not merely the procedures by which the law would be enforced, but its very purpose—is fair, reasonable, and just.

Prior to 1937 the Supreme Court used substantive due process and the expanded definitions of liberty to strike down many laws that the justices thought to be unreasonable regulations of business liberty. Indeed the Supreme Court, for a time, became the final arbiter of our economic and industrial life. During this period, the Court struck down laws regulating hours of labor, establishing minimum wages, regulating prices, forbidding employers to discharge workers for union membership, and so on, on the ground that they were unreasonable interferences with the liberty of employers and employees to contract with one another.[132]

Since 1937 the Supreme Court has refused to apply substantive due process to laws regulating the economy.[133] This rejection does not mean that the Court has abandoned the doctrine of substantive due process. Quite the contrary, it has been given new life as a judicially imposed limitation on both state and federal governments' power to regulate civil liberties and civil rights.

Closely related to the revival of the doctrine of substantive due process, and often merging with it, has been the Supreme Court's development of new tests to determine whether or not a state or federal law deprives a person of the equal protection of the law. A specific clause in the Fourteenth Amendment forbids states to deprive any person of the equal protection of the law. There is no such clause applying to the national government, but the Supreme Court has construed the due process clause of the Fifth Amendment to incorporate an equal protection requirement for the national government. And when we discuss the equal protection clause, we shall see that as presently interpreted it has many similarities with substantive due process.

Indeed, it is sometimes difficult to determine whether the Supreme Court is striking down a law because it violates the due process clause or because it is a denial of equal protection. This merging of the two provisions is especially pronounced when the Court invokes its relatively new doctrine against "irrebuttable presumptions." Take several examples: The Supreme Court declared unconstitutional a law of Congress aimed at preventing middle-class college students from getting food stamps. The law makes ineligible for food stamps any household that contained any person over the age of eighteen who had been claimed as a tax dependent the prior year by somebody not living in that house. The Supreme Court ruled that the law created an unreasonable irrebuttable presumption because there is often no relation between the need of a household and the fact that it contains a person claimed the year before as a tax dependent by someone not living in the household.[134] Along the same lines, when Congress in order to deny food stamps to "hippy communes" declared ineligible for such stamps any household containing an individual not related to any other member of the household, the Supreme Court declared the "classification to be wholly without any rational basis."[135] And then there was the regulation of the Cleveland Board of Education that created the irrebuttable presumption that no pregnant teacher should be allowed to teach beyond the fifth month of her pregnancy or to return to work until her child was three months old. Justice Stewart announced in *Cleveland Board of Education* v. *LaFleur* that the "maternity leave rules directly affect 'one of the basic civil rights of man [sic],' " that they are "wholly arbitrary and irrational," and that hence they violate the due process clause of the Fourteenth Amendment.[136]

A similar but this time unsuccessful challenge was made to the constitutionality of a provision of the social security law limiting widows' eligibility to collect their husbands' benefits. The provision makes eligible for benefits only a widow who had been married to the covered person for at least nine months prior to his death. Congress adopted such a provision to prevent persons from getting married just before the death of a covered person so that the widow could collect his benefits. Although the law created an irrebuttable presumption denying benefits to women who married with an anticipation of shortly becoming widows, this time a Supreme Court majority upheld the law, saying the question is not whether justices think such a law is wise, but whether Congress can rationally choose to adopt such a provision.[137]

In *Jones* v. *United States* (1983) the Court decided that Congress had acted reasonably when it determined that those acquitted of criminal charges by reasons of insanity should be confined to a mental hospital until such time as the government authorites decided they are no longer ill or dangerous.[138] Moreover, to justify the continuation of the confinement, even if longer than the person could have been kept in prison, the goverament merely has to prove the need to retain the person in a mental hospital by a "preponderance of evidence" rather than to meet the more stringent standard of "beyond a reasonable doubt" necessary to imprison someone for commission of a crime. Although there are procedural due process and equal protection overtones to this decision, in essence the justices were agreeing with Congress that it is reasonable to put persons acquitted of crimes by reason of insanity into confinement until they are clearly no longer dangerous.

Cleveland Board of Education v. *LaFleur* and other cases involving the doctrine of irrebuttable presumptions are classic examples of substantive due process. The Supreme Court justices in *LaFleur* essentially decided that in their opinion the Cleveland Board of Education's regulation was "unreasonable." They stated that the ordinance was "wholly arbitrary and irrational," despite the fact that a good many school boards throughout the nation had adopted similar regulations in the belief that they were reasonable. Another example of substantive due process is the Court's decision striking down as an unreasonable restraint on liberty a state regulation permitting confinement of nondangerous mentally ill persons when no treatment was provided for them; the Court left to another day the determination of constitutionality if confinement were accompanied by medical treatment.[139]

For some time, the Court applied substantive due process but was reluctant to admit that it had been doing so. However, in recent years, it has openly begun to inspect laws in terms of their "reasonableness." For example, the

Court had before it an ordinance limiting occupancy in homes to single families and defining single families in such a fashion as to exclude a grandmother from living with two grandchildren who were cousins rather than brothers. Justice Powell, speaking for a plurality of four with the concurrence of other justices, declared this zoning ordinance unconstitutional. Justice Powell conceded:

> substantive due process has at times been a treacherous field for this Court. There *are* risks when the judicial branch gives enhanced protection to certain substantive liberties without the guidance of the more specific provisions of the Bill of Rights. As the history of the Lochner era demonstrates, there is reason for concern lest the only limits to such judicial intervention became the predilections of those who happen at the time to be members of this Court. That history counsels caution and restraint. But it does not counsel abandonment. . . .

Justice White in dissent pointed to

> Justice Black's constant reminder . . . that the Court has no license to invalidate legislation which it thinks merely arbitrary or unreasonable. . . . The Judiciary . . . is the most vulnerable and comes nearest to illegitimacy when it deals with judge made constitutional law having little or no cognizable roots in the language or even the design of the Constitution. . . . The Court should be extremely reluctant to breathe still further substantive content into the Due Process Clause so as to strike down legislation adopted by a state or a city to promote its welfare. Whenever the Judiciary does so, it unavoidably preempts for itself another part of the governance of the country without express constitutional authority.[140]

Perhaps the most celebrated—certainly the most controversial—illustration of the modern Supreme Court's use of substantive due process is its ruling in *Roe* v. *Wade*[141] that the constitutionality of a state's regulation of abortions varies during each trimester of a woman's pregnancy. During the first trimester (about the first three months), it is unreasonable and unconstitutional for a state to interfere with a woman's right to choose an abortion or to interfere with her doctor's medical judgments about how to carry it out. The woman's right to decide may not be conditioned on the wishes of a husband, or a minor's decision be made subject to the approval of her parents or a judge, although a state may require that her parents be notified if she is still living at home.[142] During the second trimester the state's interest in protecting the health of women who undergo abortions becomes compelling, and a state may make reasonable regulations about how, where, and when abortions may be performed. During the third trimester the state's interest in protecting the unborn child is so important that the state can proscribe abortions altogether, except when necessary to preserve the life or health of the mother.

Four years later, in *Maher* v. *Roe,* the Court concluded that although a woman has the constitutional right to an abortion during the early months of pregnancy, she has no right to have the state pay for it. A state may refuse to pay the medical expenses for poor women for a nontherapeutic abortions, even though it does cover such expenses related to child birth.[143] Several years later, in *Akron* v. *Akron Center for Reproductive Health,* the Court held the state of medical science had so progressed that most abortions during the early part of the second trimester could now be performed safely in a doctor's office. Thus, a state regulation requiring all such abortions to be performed in a hospital, along with some other state regulations, unduly burden a woman's constitutional right to an abortion.[144]

All these conclusions about what is and what is not a reasonable state regulation stem from the words, "no state shall deprive any persons of his life, liberty, or property without due process of law." In fact, as the Court has written somewhat apologetically, "While our decisions . . . do not form checkerboard bright lines between black squares and red squares . . ." today substantive due process is likely to be bound by "the individual's freedom of choice with respect to certain basic matters of procreation, marriage, and family life."[145]

---

nor shall private property be taken for public use, [without just compensation, *discussed below*]

These limits on the power of eminent domain were the first provisions of the Bill of Rights to be incorporated within the Fourteenth Amendment and thus to be made applicable to the states.[146]

This clause places a restriction on the government's power of eminent domain—that is, the power to take private property for public use—a power existing in all governments. Even in those governments organized on the principle of private ownership, the rights of society are paramount to those of any one owner.

Private property may be taken under the eminent domain power, even if the owner is fairly compensated, only for *public* use. In *Hawaii Housing Authority* v. *Midkiff* (1984) the Supreme Court put to rest the notion that the words "public use" should be read literally to mean that the taken property must be owned and operated by a government and open to use by "the public." The Hawaii legislature in 1967 adopted a Land Reform Act authorizing authorities to condemn the land of large landowners, transfer ownership of the condemned land to tenants or others and to lend funds or arrange for the financing of the land so purchased. The landowners who lost their property argued that although they were paid, it nonetheless violated the Constitution in that the Act took property from one person and made it available to others for their own private use. The Court of Appeals for the Ninth Circuit agreed. In its judgment, the Act was simply "a naked attempt on the part of the state of Hawaii to take the private property of A and transfer it to B solely for B's private use and benefit." But the Supreme Court said that although "one person's property may not be taken for the benefit of another private person without a justifying public purpose, even though compensation be paid,"[147] it can be taken if it serves a public purpose. It is the legislature who determine what constitutes a public use. "The Court . . . will not substitute its judgment for a legislature's judgment as to what constitutes a public use unless the use be palpably without reasonable foundation. . . . The Hawaii Legislature's judgment to break up land oligopolies and correct the evils associated with such concentrated landownership was a classic exercise of a State's police powers and clearly serves a public use."[148]

The question of what constitutes a "taking" for purposes of the Fifth Amendment has proved to be a problem of considerable difficulty. "While [the] Court has recognized that the 'Fifth Amendments guarantee [is] designed to bar Government from forcing some people alone to bear public burdens which, in all fairness and justice, should be borne by the public as a whole,' [the] Court, quite simply has been unable to develop any 'set formula' for determining when 'justice and fairness' require that economic injuries caused by public action be compensated by the government, rather than remain disproportionately concentrated on a few persons."[149] Ordinarily, but not always, the taking must be direct. The clause does not require compensation merely because government action may result in a property loss, for example, the imposition of a tax, even if the tax is so stiff as to drive a person out of business. It does not make any constitutional difference if the state imposes a tax on a business with which the state is competing.[150] The clause does not require compensation for losses incidental to the exercise of government power, for example, the passage of a price-control measure. Such a law deprives persons of the right to raise their prices and so decreases, presumably, the value of their property and clearly reduces their profits. But the government is not required to award compensation for such regulations. Nor does the government have to pay damages when it temporarily occupies a building in the course of restoring order in a riot situation.[151] Nor is it required to reimburse people for the losses they may suffer because Congress lowers the tariff or raises it or declares war. California's interest in maintaining open spaces justified it in zoning five acres of "the best suburban property in California" in such a way as to permit at most the construction of only five houses on that land.[152] A government may designate a building as a "historic landmark" and impose on owners of such buildings requirements for their maintenance and restrictions on their developments without having to pay "just compensation," as the owners of the Grand Central Terminal in New York discovered. They were denied the right to make changes in that structure which would have increased their rental returns. Justice Rehnquist, the Chief Justice, and Justice Stevens in dissent argued that "Penn Central is prevented from further developing its property basically because it did too good of a job in designing and building it. The city of New York, because of its unadorned admiration for the design, has decided that the owners of the building must preserve it unchanged for the benefit of sight-seeing New Yorkers and tourists."[153]

On the other side, even when title is left in the hands of the owners, sometimes the courts will find that the government has "taken" property and owes compensation to its owners. To illustrate: If airplanes take off and land over land adjacent to airports at such levels that the land is no longer suitable for its prior use, say, raising chickens, this is a compensable taking.[154] Similarly, the Supreme Court indicated that if in fact a congressional scheme to keep the bankrupt northeastern railroads operating results in such significant losses to them that it amounts to an "erosion taking," the government is liable for just compensation for having taken railroad property by forcing them to continue to operate at huge losses.[155] Along these same lines, the government must provide compensation if it wants to provide public access to a private lagoon adjacent to the ocean which the owners have dredged out at their own expense in order to make it accessible to the ocean.[156]

---

without just compensation.

In cases of disagreement between the government and the individual about what price is just, decision is referred to a disinterested body; ultimately a court of law makes the final decision. What is "just compensation" is not always an easy question to answer. By and large, "the owner is entitled to receive what a willing buyer would pay in cash to a willing seller at the time of the taking."[157] An owner is not entitled to compensation for the special value of the property to the owner—an old broken-down house which she loves dearly will still bring her only the compensation for an old broken-down house.

An interesting taking and compensation case involved Indian lands. In 1980 the Supreme Court ruled that the national government had exceeded its powers to abrogate Indian treaties and to manage tribal lands, and in 1877 the government had acted in bad faith by "taking" the Black Hills from the Sioux Indians. These Indians, ruled the Court, are now entitled to the $17 million that the Black Hills had been worth in 1877, plus 5 percent annual interest compounded since then, for a total of almost $100 million. Justice Rehnquist dissented. Among other things he accused Congress, which had provided for a special appeal by the Sioux Indians, of interfering with the independence of the courts by, in effect, reversing a 1942 holding of the Court of Claims. That court had concluded that when the national government gave the Sioux $43 million of rations and 900,000 acres of grazing lands in return for the Black Hills, it had adequately paid for the Hills and had rendered the transaction not a "taking."[158]

AMENDMENT VI: CRIMINAL COURT PROCEDURES

In all criminal prosecutions, the accused shall enjoy the right to a speedy [trial]

"This guarantee is an important safeguard to prevent undue and oppressive incarceration prior to trial, to minimize anxiety and concern accompanying public accusation, and to limit the possibilities that long delay will impair the ability of an accused to defend himself."[1] This right differs from other constitutional rights in that "there is a societal interest in providing a speedy trial which exists separate from, and at times in opposition to, the interests of the accused," who often finds delay to his or her advantage. It also differs in that if it is determined that a defendant has been denied a speedy trial, the only remedy is the drastic one of dismissal of the charges without the possibility of their reinstatement, for the fault is not correctable, as are other violations of the Sixth Amendment, by a retrial.[2]

The speedy trial requirement applies to states, via the Fourteenth Amendment, but an arrest or indictment by the national government does not bring the clause into play with respect to prosecutions by a state or vice versa.[3]

The right to a speedy trial starts from the time a person has been indicted, not from the time arrest or from the time police discover evidence of a crime (there is no right to "speedy arrest.") Nor does the speedy trial guarantee apply after the government, acting in good faith, formally drops charges, although undue and prejudicial delay by the prosecution prior to arrest or indictment, or after first dropping charges and then reinstating them, could create a due process claim.[4]

The Supreme Court has refused to give this rather vague concept any precise time frame.[5] Rather, the Court has listed four factors that must be taken into account in determining whether the right to a speedy trial has been violated: length of the delay, reasons for the delay, a defendant's demand for waiver of the right to an immediate trial, and whether the delay has worked to a defendant's disadvantage.[6]

A trial clearly may be "speedy" in a legal sense even though it admits of considerable delay, especially delays caused by the counsel for the accused. "The many procedural safeguards provided an accused mean that the ordinary procedures for criminal prosecution are designed to move at a deliberate pace."[7] But when Texas failed for six years to try a prisoner in a federal penitentiary who had requested that the state proceed with its charges against him, Texas failed to meet the constitutional requirement and the state had to dismiss its charges against him.[8]

After a study found that, in some of the busier courts, a defendant had to wait on the average for as long as a year between arrest and trial, Congress adopted a complicated law designed to expedite criminal trials in federal courts. The 1974 Speedy Trial Act provides for a maximum time span of one hundred days between arrest and trial. If the deadline is not met, the judge is to decide whether to dismiss the charges with prejudice, which will bar reprosecution, or with prejudice, which will allow for reprosecution. Although it is not clear that defendants' causes have been advanced if charges against them are dropped without prejudice, the law has set forth a congressionally defined goal that justice should move more swiftly in the future than it has in the past. This defined goal has been effective in moving criminal prosecutions more quickly through the federal system.

---

and public trial,

A public trial is essential to due process and therefore is a right secured to defendants in state as well as in federal courts.[9] The right to a public trial belongs to defendants and not to television camera operators, photographers, or newspaper reporters. The requirement of a public trial is satisfied if the members of the public and press have an opportunity to attend the trial and to report what they observe. The press do not have a right to be allowed to broadcast or tape the trial. Nor does the First Amendment grant to the press any rights to information about the trial superior to that of the general public.[10]

In 1979 in *Gannett Co.* v. *DePasquale* the Supreme Court went so far as to declare that because the Sixth Amendment confers rights on defendants—not the press and the public—that a judge could, with the consent of the defendant, close a *preliminary* hearing to the public. But the decision created such adverse criticism, especially from the press, that three justices felt compelled to find an occasion to emphasize that the *Gannett* decision applied only to preliminary hearings.[11] Then a year later in *Richmond Newspapers, Inc.* v. *Virginia* (as we have noted on page 158), the Court interpreted the First Amendment so as to limit severely the scope of the *Gannett* decision. Since then *Gannett* has been ever further restricted. An accused has a Sixth Amendment right to insist on a public trial, including a pretrial suppression hearing, and judges' authority to close trials or preliminary hearings is limited to those few instances when they can show an overriding need to do so and articulate the reason so that it may be reviewed by an appellate court.[12]

More constitutional questions have been raised by too much rather than too little public involvement in trials. Too intense or lurid publicity about a trial may lead to conditions in which calm deliberation by a jury considering only the evidence presented in open court becomes difficult if not impossible. Televising trials may create such distractions that it could deny the defendant due process. In 1965 four justices even went so far as to conclude that there could be no due process if trials were televised at all,[13] but more recently the Court concluded that a state could, if it wished, permit the telecast of trials notwithstanding the objection of the defendants.[14] However, with or without cameras, if a judge allows newspeople to hound witnesses or permits the prosecutor to make damaging statements to the press in a way that deprives the defendant of a right to trial by an impartial jury free from outside influences, such actions create due process problems. As the Supreme Court said, "Trial courts must take strong measures to ensure that the balance is never weighted against the accused."[15]

---

by an impartial jury

Despite the fact that Article III requires a trial by jury of all federal crimes in the state in which the crime was committed, the right was considered so important that it was further guaranteed by the Sixth Amendment. The Fourteenth Amendment "guarantees a right of jury trial in all [state] criminal cases which, were they tried in a federal court, would come within the Sixth Amendment's guarantee of trial by jury."[16]

Trial by jury is a constitutional requirement for serious but not petty crimes. Petty offenses are those punishable by no more than six months in prison and a $500 fine.[17]

The jury trial requirement applies to convictions for criminal contempt if the penalty imposed exceeds imprisonment for six months.[18] It does not apply to civil contempts or to other noncriminal proceedings, such as deportation or loyalty and security hearings.

Trial by jury used to be thought to include all the elements recognized by common law at the time the Constitution was adopted, the most important being a jury consisting of no more and no less than twelve members, and the requirement of a unanimous verdict for conviction. Recently, however, the Supreme Court has decided that a twelve-person requirement is not an "indispensable component of the Sixth Amendment."[19] A jury composed of at least six people will do. Less than six, the Court decided, promotes inaccurate and biased verdicts, causes lack of consistency in verdicts, and prevents juries from adequately representing a cross section of the community. Reduction in jury number below six provides no particular saving in court time or financial costs.[20] (Although the Sixth Amendment no longer requires a twelve-member jury, most states and the federal government continue to use such juries.)

As to unanimity, it is constitutionally required for conviction by federal but not by state juries. This anomalous result comes about because Justice Powell, who had the swing vote on the issue, takes the view that the Sixth Amendment, which applies to the federal government, calls for unanimous verdicts, but the Fourteenth Amendment, which applies to the states, while requiring them to use juries for serious crimes, does not require that juries be unanimous for convictions. How much less than unanimous is not clear. The Court has approved convictions by nine out of twelve,[21] but reversed those by five out of six, and has said that if a state wants to use the minimum number of jurors permitted under the Constitution, that is, six, then the decisions must be unanimous.[22]

Defendants may waive the right to a jury trial, but a judge may insist on such a trial even against the wishes of the defendant, for there is no constitutional right *not* to be tried by a jury.[23] Defendants can in fact by a plea of guilty waive the right to any kind of trial. The record, however, must clearly show that defendants knew what they were doing and were fully aware of the consequences of their actions.

A person is entitled to trial by an impartial jury, which means a jury that represents a "fair cross section" of the community and from which no person has been excluded because of race, sex, national origin, or religion. A defendant does not have to be a member of an excluded class to object to a trial by a jury from which persons have been excluded because of race, sex, national origin, or religion.[24] And practices or statutes that bias the selection of particular categories of persons are likely to run afoul of this "fair cross section requirement." Thus a Missouri statute was declared unconstitutional that allowed women, but not men, to be excused from jury duty merely by so requesting.[25] There is no violation of the Constitution, however, if a judge exempts women from service who request it because of the need to stay home with small children, even if the granting of such requests results in an all-male jury. For no one has a right to be tried by a jury made up of any particular ratio of persons of a sex, race, religion, or national origin, merely to be tried by a jury selected in a constitutional manner.

In order to ensure that the jury is impartial, both the prosecution and the defense have a right to question prospective jurors about their possible biases. There is no per se—that is, automatic—constitutional rule that permits a defendant to question jurors about racial prejudice except when "there are substantial indications of the likelihood of racial or ethnic prejudice affecting the jurors in a particular case." Apart from such circumstances, the Constitution leaves it to the trial court to determine the need for such questions. The Supreme Court has, however, in exercising its general supervisory power over federal courts, adopted a rule requiring federal judges to permit such questioning when requested by a defendant accused of a violent crime, and where the defendant and the victim are members of different racial or ethnic groups.[26]

The Supreme Court has refused to make it a matter of constitutional right for defendants with beards to interrogate potential jurors about their possible prejudice against bearded persons; the Court left this matter to the discretion of the trial judge.[27] Of a more serious nature, at least to persons without beards, the Court ruled that a jury from which persons had been excluded because of their general objections to the death penalty could not be impartial with respect to choosing between a sentence of life or death and that such a jury would not represent a fair cross section of the community.[28]

---

of the State and district wherein the crime shall have been committed, which district shall have been previously ascertained by law,

---

Early English juries were always from the neighborhood of the accused, which was sometimes an advantage for the accused, sometimes the contrary. One of the grievances against George III was that his government had forced American colonists to stand trial in England for offenses alleged to have been committed in America. To prevent the national government from using such procedures, both Article III and the Sixth Amendment require trials to be held in the state in which the crime was committed (the Sixth Amendment adds district). Defendants may, however, petition for removal of the trial from the district on the grounds that the community has been so inflamed and prejudiced against them that it would be impossible to select a fair and impartial jury in the district in which the crime was committed.

---

and to be informed of the nature and cause of the accusation;

There are no common-law judge-written offenses against the United States; the only federal criminal acts are those the Congress has forbidden. A statute must state precisely the acts that are forbidden and must include all the ingredients essential to a proper judgment of guilt of the crime. A law violates this requirement if it is so vague as to provide no clear standard by which to alert persons of what actions have been made criminal, and by which judge and jury may be guided in determining guilt.

---

to be confronted with the witnesses against him;

Under most circumstances a witness's evidence cannot be introduced at a trial unless the witness is present to be subject to cross-examination.[29] In conformity with the "Framers' preference for face-to-face accusation, the Sixth Amendment establishes a rule of necessity. In the usual case . . . the prosecution must either produce or demonstrate the unavailability of the declarant whose statement it wishes to use against the defendant. . . . Once a witness is shown to be unavailable . . ." the clause countenances only hearsay marked with such trustworthiness that "there is no material departure from the reason for such a rule." . . . There must be ample "indicia of reliability."[30] Among the exceptions to face-to-face accusation are certain deathbed statements, evidence given at a prior trial by a witness who had since moved to a foreign country, and evidence given at a preliminary hearing by a witness no longer available to testify.[31] Defendants may lose their right to confront adverse witnesses if they engage in such disruptive behavior that their trials cannot proceed as long as they remain in the courtroom, or if they voluntarily absent themselves from the proceedings.[32] On the other side of the ledger, in most circumstances states may not use the confession of one defendant against another if the first defendant exercises the right not to take the stand and thus not be available for cross examination about the confession;[33] a state may not introduce the accusatory statements of juveniles whose anonymity it wishes to preserve.[34]

---

to have compulsory process for obtaining witnesses in his favor,

---

In the eighteenth century under the English common law, persons accused of felonies or treason were not allowed to introduce any witnesses in their own defense. England abolished this general disqualification in 1787, but retained a number of restrictions on the kind of witnesses who could be called. For awhile we followed English practices, but in 1918 the Supreme Court declared that all persons of competence who may have knowledge of the facts involved in a case should be allowed to be called with a few exceptions (see below).[35]

The clause which has been incorporated into the due process requirement of the Fourteenth Amendment,[36] does not by its terms grant to criminal defendants the right to secure the attendance and testimony of any and all witnesses; it guarantees them "compulsory process for obtaining *witnesses in his favor.*" Defendants cannot establish a violation of their constitutional right to compulsory process merely by showing that the government has not helped to produce a witness; they must make some "plausible showing of how" the witness' testimony would have been both material and favorable to their defense.[37]

The husband-wife privilege has been limited. A husband may no longer deny his wife, or vice versa, the right to testify if she wishes to do so.[38] However, the common-law testimonial privileges protecting communications between lawyer and client, priest and penitent, doctor and patient still give to those involved in such communications the privilege of refusing to testify if they wish to claim it. The disqualification of witnesses because of mental infirmity or infancy remains undisturbed.

A state has no authority to compel the attendance in its court proceedings of witnesses outside its jurisdiction. Nonetheless, it must make a good faith effort to secure witnesses for the defense wherever they are located.[39]

---

and to have the Assistance of Counsel for his defence.

What was once a right of defendants to be represented by an attorney during trial, provided they could afford to obtain such assistance, has now become a positive obligation, for federal authorities since *Johnson* v. *Zerbst* (1938) and for state authorities since *Gideon* v. *Wainwright* (1975), to secure lawyers for those who are unable to pay for their own: "Where assistance of counsel is a constitutional requirement, the right to be furnished counsel does not depend on request."[40] (However, whenever indigent defendants become financially solvent, a state may require them to repay the state for the legal services previously rendered to them.)[41]

Unless the record clearly shows that defendants, in full awareness of what they were doing, waived their right to counsel, the absence of such counsel will render criminal proceedings unconstitutional. And to complicate the issue, the right to assistance of counsel includes the right *not* to be assisted by counsel, provided the record clearly shows defendants—again with full awareness of what they were doing—asked the judge for the right to defend themselves.[42] Although judges must grant such a request, the appointment of standby counsel by the judge does not violate defendants' right to conduct their own defense, provided the standby counsel's participation does not interfere with the defendants' actual control over the presentation of their defense and cannot reasonably be thought to have undermined the defendants' appearance before the jury in the status of representing themselves.[43]

Once official action focuses upon a person, the right to the assistance of counsel attaches.[44] (Under the Fifth Amendment persons, even though not formally accused of a crime but subject to custodial interrogation, have the right to refuse to answer questions until furnished with an attorney.) After criminal charges have been initiated, whether by formal charge, preliminary hearing, indictment, information, or arraignment, defendants are entitled to have a lawyer at their side whenever and wherever they appear, and substantial rights may be affected. Included are occasions when defendants are subject to identification by victims, such as lineups (but not when arrays of photographs are used); preliminary hearings; the trial itself, of course; the time the judge sums up the evidence; and the time of sentencing.[45]

When a right of appeal has been established (and all jurisdictions now provide at least one appeal for all criminal convictions), defendants are entitled to the help of an attorney in order to make that appeal. For appeals other than the one provided as a matter of right, a state need not furnish attorneys at public expense.[46]

If placed on probation, persons are entitled to legal help at any time when there may be a hearing to revoke probation.

A defendant unable to afford counsel is not entitled to the attorney of his or her choice and is not guaranteed a "meaningful attorney-client relationship," only that counsel will be competent.[47] How competent? The Sixth Amendment right to counsel is the right to the *effective* assistance of counsel. However, the burden is upon the defendant to prove that counsel assigned to him or her was not effective, and the defendant must show, first, that counsel's performance was deficient because of serious errors, and second, that this deficient performance did in fact prejudice the defense to such an extent that the defendant was deprived of a fair trial.[48]

Confessions or other evidence secured in violation of the right to the assistance of counsel are subject to essentially the same exclusionary rules as are applied to enforce the Fourth Amendment. And what police and prosecutors cannot do directly—namely, cross-examine defendants without counsel when it has been requested—they cannot do indirectly. For example, although there is no constitutional prohibition against the use of undercover agents, prosecutors violated the Sixth Amendment when they instructed a paid informer located in the same jail with the accused to listen and report any damaging statements made by the accused. The government agents had intentionally created a situation likely to induce the accused to make incriminating statements without the assistance of counsel.[49]

Perhaps the decision that went to the limit of the application of this principle was a five-to-four holding in *Brewer* v. *Williams* (1977). That decision reversed Williams' conviction for murdering a child because it had been based on a confession made to the police while they were transporting him to jail and after his attorney had requested that he not be questioned that evening. The police induced Williams' confession by telling him that because it was snowing so hard, the child might not be able to have "a Christian burial" unless he would tell them where the child's body could be found.[50] (On retrial, under the "inevitable discovery rule," the evidence about the location and condition of the victim's body were admitted at the trial and he was convicted again. This time his conviction was sustained, see page 180).[51]

Does the right to the assistance of counsel—or, stated in terms of its more significant corollary: Does the right to have the government furnish and pay for counsel if one cannot afford it—extend only to trials for serious offenses or to all trials? In 1972, in *Argersinger* v. *Hamlin,* the Supreme Court answered the question: "No accused may be deprived of his liberty as the result of any criminal prosecution, . . . whether or not a jury trial is required . . . in which he was denied the assistance of counsel.[52] The only trials exempt from the assistance of counsel requirement are those in which fines are the sole penalty actually imposed.[52] (This requirement differs from that for jury trials. There must be a jury offered for any trial in which imprisonment for more than six months *may* be imposed, even though in fact only a fine is levied.)[53]

The *Argersinger* decision has had a substantial effect on the administration of justice. Jurisdictions are now attending to the procedures used to make legal assistance available. At the present time, in some jurisdictions judges assign counsel, but the growing practice in the larger states and cities is to create and support from tax funds an office of public defender. At the federal level, Congress now requires each district court to have an organized plan to ensure that indigents are adequately represented.

AMENDMENT VII: TRIAL BY JURY IN COMMON-LAW CASES

In Suits at common law, where the value in controversy shall exceed twenty dollars, the right of trial by jury shall be preserved, and no fact tried by a jury, shall be otherwise re-examined in any Court of the United States, than according to the rules of the common law.

This provision refers to litigation in federal courts and has *not* been incorporated into the due process requirement of the Fourteenth Amendment. It concerns suits at common law and does not prevent the two parties from dispensing with a jury with the consent of the court. It does not apply to equity proceedings, which are seldom before a jury.

For many years it was generally thought that the constitutional right to jury trial extended only to actions arising under the common law, not to those arising out of statutes enacted by Congress. But in 1974 the Supreme Court declared the contrary: "The Seventh Amendment does apply to actions enforcing statutory rights, and requires a jury trial upon demand, if the statutes create legal rights and remedies, enforceable in an action for damages in the ordinary courts of law."[1] Perhaps even more startling, the Court has also stipulated that the jury need not be of the size and character known to the common law. The Court has ruled that a jury of six members is satisfactory[2]—most federal district courts are presently employing some form of jury for civil cases with fewer than twelve members.[3] There is no holding on the question of whether unanimity is required, but in view of rulings with respect to criminal juries required by the Sixth Amendment, it would seem that federal civil juries that proceed by less than unanimity would not meet the constitutional requirement. There are no directly applicable Supreme Court precedents, however, and decisions in such cases are likely to divide the Court.

AMENDMENT VIII: BAIL AND CRUEL AND UNUSUAL PUNISHMENTS

Excessive bail shall not be required,

It is a basic principle of American justices that no person is guilty until pronounced so after a fair trial; thus the mere fact that one has been arrested or accused of a crime by a grand jury or a prosecutor's information affidavit does not justify depriving a person of his or her liberty. Moreover, persons accused of crimes are to be given the opportunity to prepare their defense. If accused persons are thrown in jail prior to conviction and excessive bail is imposed on them, they may be denied the full opportunity to prepare for trial and may be deprived of their freedom prior to a determination of any guilt. For these reasons, bail set at a figure higher than might reasonably be calculated to assure the presence of a defendant at a trial is "excessive."[1] Much depends upon the nature of the offense, the reputation of the offender, and ability to pay. Bail of a larger amount than is usually set for a particular crime must be justified.

May a judge keep somebody in preventive detention if the judge is persuaded that the person is dangerous and likely to commit another crime? Thirty-two states provide for preventive detention. In 1984 Congress authorized federal judges to do so after a hearing in which they determine and give their reasons in writing that the person before them is dangerous to witnesses or to the community. The Supreme Court has never ruled directly whether preventive detention is constitutional. As we have noted, it has sustained the constitutionality under the due process clause of the Fourteenth Amendment of preventive detention for juveniles. However, Justice Rehnquist in speaking for the Court went out of his way to make it clear that what is constitutionally permissible for juveniles may not be so for adults. He pointed out that juveniles "countervailing interest in freedom from institutional restraints, even for the brief time involved here, is undoubtedly substantial. But that interest must be qualified by the recognition that juveniles, unlike adults, are always in some form of custody."[2]

Congress provided a substantial implementation of the Eighth Amendment by the adoption of the Bail Reform Act of 1966, the first significant federal bail legislation since the Judiciary Act of 1789. Until Congress acted, impoverished defendants often stayed in jail for days: In a case cited by President Johnson when he signed the bill into law, a man spent 101 days in jail because he could not raise bail on a false complaint. Another man who was unable to raise bail waited 54 days for trial on a traffic offense in the District of Columbia for which he could have been sentenced to no more than 5 days.

The Bail Reform Act of 1966, applying only to federal courts, allows magistrates to release persons without bail if after taking into account such factors as past record, family and community ties, seriousness of offense charged, weight of evidence, and character of the accused, bail seems unnecessary to assure appearance at time of the trial.

---

nor cruel and unusual punishments inflicted.

This ban limits government in three ways:

1. It limits barbaric punishments such as burning at the stake, crucifixion, breaking on the wheel, use of rack and thumbscrew, service in chains at hard labor.

The Eighth Amendment limits the conditions in which a state may operate its prisons and treat those convicted of crimes. "The Constitution does not mandate comfortable prisons" and to the mere extent that conditions "are restrictive and even harsh they are part of the penalty that criminals pay for their offenses."[3] "Double-celling" is not a violation. But when governments confine persons without proper diet, in excessively crowded and unsanitary conditions, and knowingly deny prisoners needed medical care, they violate the Constitution.[4] Federal judges have declared the manner in which at least twenty-four states have operated their prisons, in some cases their entire prison systems unconstitutional.

2. It prohibits excessive punishments "grossly out of proportion to the severity of the crime or that make no measurable contribution to acceptable goals of punishment and hence are nothing more than the purposeless and needless imposition of pain and suffering." For example, the Court set aside the sentence of death for the crime of rape of an adult woman in the absence of additional physical attack or abuse.[5]

Outside the context of capital punishment, successful challenges to the proportionality of particular sentences have been exceedingly rare, but not unknown. William James Rummel found out how rare such challenges are. The Supreme Court, although saying the proportionality principle would come into play in, say, the extreme case of a legislature making overtime parking a felony punishable by life imprisonment, held that the Eighth Amendment did not prevent Texas from applying its recidivist statute to Rummel. The Texas statute calls for the mandatory life imprisonment of any person convicted for a third time for a felony. In Rummel's particular case his convictions were for relatively minor offenses: fraudulent use of a credit card to obtain $80 worth of merchandise, passing a forged check in the amount of $28.36, and accepting $120.75 to repair an air conditioner that he never intended to repair. Justice Powell in dissent along with three other justices, wrote somewhat bitterly, "In my view . . . a mandatory life sentence for defrauding persons of about $230 crosses any rationally drawn line separating punishment that lawfully may be imposed from that which is prescribed by the Eighth Amendment."[6] Two years later the Court reaffirmed its unwillingness to get involved in the review of the proportionality of sentences and refused to set aside a forty-year sentence and a $20,000 fine for the crime of intending to distribute nine ounces of marijuana. The Court reaffirmed that for crimes classifiable as felonies, the length of the sentence imposed is purely a matter of legislative prerogative.[7]

Then just a year later Justice Powell and the dissenting justices in the Rummel case, along with Justice Blackmun from the Rummel majority, while insisting that their decision "is entirely consistent with" the Rummel ruling, rejected the view that the prohibition against disproportionate sentences does not apply to anything but cases involving capital punishment. They set aside South Dakota's sentencing of Jerry Helm to life in prison without possibility of parole after his conviction for his seventh nonviolent felony. In determining whether or not punishments are disproportionate, the Court majority set forth three guidelines: (1) the gravity of the offenses and the harshness of the penalty; (2) the sentences imposed on other criminals in the same jurisdiction; and (3) the sentences imposed for the commission of the same crime in other jurisdictions.[8] Chief Justice Burger, with whom Justices White, Rehnquist and O'Connor joined in dissent, accused the majority of ignoring the Rummel decision. He wrote: "The controlling law governing this case is crystal clear, but today the Court blithely discards any concept of stare decisis, trespasses gravely on the authority of the States, and distorts the conception of proportionality of punishment by tearing it from its moorings in capital cases. . . ." He accused the majority of adopting a view that amounts to nothing more than a determination "that a sentence is unconstitutional if it is more severe than five justices think appropriate."

3. It limits what can be considered a criminal offense: for example, the mere act of being addicted to drugs or being a chronic alcoholic cannot be made a crime, for this would inflict punishment simply for being ill.[9] However, being drunk in public, or buying drugs or possessing them can be made criminal, for such statutes do not punish persons for being ill but for their behavior.[10]

The Eighth Amendment prohibition against cruel and unusual punishments applies only to criminal sanctions; it does not protect public school children from corporal punishment by their teachers (the due process clause does apply).[11]

What of capital punishment? After much soul-searching and many decisions, the Supreme Court ruled that the death penalty is not per se cruel and unusual punishment for the crime of murder. But it must properly be imposed. Death is a different kind of punishment from any other, both in terms of its severity and finality. The sentencing process as well as the trial itself must satisfy both due process and Eighth Amendment requirements.[12]

The state must ensure that whoever imposes the penalty—judge or jury—does so only after careful consideration of the character and record of the person and the circumstances of a particular crime. The automatic use of the death sentence for every person convicted of a specified capital offense, for example murdering a police officer, will not do.[13] It is essential that the capital-sentencing decision allow for consideration of whatever mitigating circumstances may be relevant to either the particular offender or the particular offense, and "any of the circumstances of the offense that the defendant prefers as a basis for a sentence less than death."[14] A state may not leave the decision whether to impose capital punishment upon a particular defendant solely to the untrammeled discretion of a jury."[15] Nor may a state adopt a vague standard to guide judges and juries in distinguishing between those persons convicted of murder who will be subject to the death penalty and those who will not.[16]

In all states that have capital punishment, whenever a defendant requests a jury trial, of course, only the jury can determine guilt. And most states leave to the jury the responsibility after guilt has been established to decide whether the sentence should be life or death. Three states, Florida, Alabama, and Indiana, allow a judge to override a jury's recommendation of life, and the Court has concluded that "placing the responsibility on a trial judge to impose the sentence in a capital case is [not] so fundamentally at odds with contemporary standards of fairness and decency" that this practice violates either the Eighth Amendment or the due process clause of the Fourteenth.[17]

The Court, although four justices do not agree, has made it clear that "the death penalty may be properly imposed only as to crimes resulting in the death of the victim."[18] The Eighth Amendment forbids, for example, the imposition of the death penalty for the rape of an adult in the absence of additional physical attack or abuse, or the death penalty for participating in an armed robbery where persons are killed but where the accused does not kill, attempt to kill, or intend to kill. In fact there is some suggestion in the language of the Court that the death penalty may properly be imposed only on those who have committed an "outrageously wanton and vile murder."[19] The Court has, however, rejected the contention that "the Fourteenth Amendment requires a state appellate court, before it affirms a death sentence, to compare the sentence in the case before it with the penalties imposed in similar cases."[20]

AMENDMENT IX: RIGHTS RETAINED BY THE PEOPLE

The enumeration in the Constitution, of certain rights, shall not be construed to deny or disparage others retained by the people.

This amendment embodies the dominant political thought of eighteenth-century America, which taught that before the establishment of government, people existed in a state of nature and lived under the natural law, which endowed them with certain natural rights. When, by mutual consent, people created government, they granted to it their natural right of judging and executing the natural law but retained the rest of their natural rights. In accordance with this theory, the Bill of Rights did not *confer* rights but merely *protected* those already granted by the natural law. The Ninth Amendment made it clear that the enumeration of rights to be protected did not imply that the other natural rights not mentioned were abandoned.

Although the Supreme Court recognized that this amendment protects the right to engage in political activity against unreasonable national regulation,[1] until 1965 no law had been declared unconstitutional because of disparagement of any of these unenumerated rights, nor had there been any suggestion that this amendment limited the powers of the states. Then, the Court ruled that a Connecticut law forbidding the use of contraceptives violated the right of marital privacy and stated that this right is "within the penumbra of specific guarantees of the Bill of Rights" and is one of the fundamental rights reserved by the Ninth Amendment to the people against disparagement by a state or the national government.[2] More recent decisions tend to peg the right of privacy within the protections of the due process clauses of the Fifth and Fourteenth Amendments.

Among the other rights found in the Ninth Amendment, but always in connection with other constitutional provisions, are the right to be presumed innocent, the right to be judged by a standard of proof beyond a reasonable doubt in a criminal trial, the right to travel interstate, and the right to attend a criminal trial. "These important rights (which appear nowhere in the Constitution or Bill of Rights), have nonetheless been found to share constitutional protection in common with explicit guarantees . . ."[3]

After the incorporation of most of the specific provisions of the Bill of Rights into the Fourteenth Amendment, some anticipated that the "glittering generalities" of the Ninth Amendment would become a new constitutional battle ground. But those justices who want to protect from governmental intrusion what they consider to be basic rights not otherwise specifically secured in the Constitution have found the language of due process and equal protection clauses sufficiently commodious to suit their needs.

AMENDMENT X: RESERVED POWERS OF THE STATES

The powers not delegated to the United States by the Constitution, nor prohibited by it to the States, are reserved to the States respectively, or the people.

This amendment was adopted to assuage fears. It does not alter the distribution of powers between the national and state governments. It adds nothing to the Constitution; in the words of Justice Stone, "It is merely a truism."[1] Or as we have noted in the words of Justice Rehnquist, "One of the greatest 'fictions' of our federal system is that Congress exercises only those powers delegated to it, while the remainder are reserved to the States or to the people."[2] Nonetheless, for a hundred years after John Marshall's death, the Supreme Court from time to time held that some of the reserved powers of the states were sovereign powers and hence set a limit to the delegated powers of the national government. When the national government used its specifically granted taxing and spending powers in such a way that agricultural production was regulated, its action was held by the Supreme Court, in 1937, to be repugnant to this amendment, since the regulation of agriculture is a power reserved to the states.[3]

Earlier, the Supreme Court ruled that, since the power to regulate the conditions of employment is reserved to the states, Congress could not use its powers to regulate interstate commerce or to tax for the purpose of driving employers of children out of the interstate market.[4] In short, under what was known as the doctrine of dual federalism, the Supreme Court used the Tenth Amendment to limit some of the enumerated powers of the national government.

Subsequently, however, the Court has returned to Marshall's view that the Tenth Amendment and the reserved powers of the states do not limit the national government to exercising the powers given it by the Constitution. Today it makes no constitutional difference whether or not an act of Congress touches or governs matters otherwise subject to state regulation. Congressional regulations supersede any conflicting state regulation.

When it comes to the application of national laws directly to the states, that is, as to how the states and local governments exercise their powers, "the Tenth Amendment . . . is not without significance." It declares "the constitutional policy that Congress may not exercise power in a fashion that impairs the States' integrity or their ability to function effectively in a federal system."[5] And as we have noted, the Court even declared that the federal minimum wage and hours law could not be applied to the states.[6] But this is not a typical holding, and as we also noted has since been even further limited. The Court is more likely to sustain the application of nondiscriminatory federal legislation to state and local governments along with everybody else.

The relationships between the national and the state governments are not asymmetrical. The national government represents all the people, each state only a part of them. Although national regulations may be applied to the states, except with the consent of Congress no state can tax or otherwise regulate a federal agency. To give one of many examples: No state may levy any tax on liquor sold for use in military installations.[7] But Congress can collect from the states aircraft registration fees for helicopters, including state-owned helicopters used for police work.[8]

Note that the Tenth Amendment does not say that powers not *expressly* delegated to the United States are reserved to the states. The framers of the Tenth Amendment specifically rejected such a statement, for its adoption would have seriously curtailed the scope of natural powers. Moreover, it should be emphasized that the states must exercise their reserved powers subject to the national government's supremacy and national constitutional limitations. For example, states have the reserved power to establish public schools, but they may not exercise this power contrary to the Fourteenth Amendment or to any other constitutional limit. Nor can they exercise it in such a way as to conflict with national regulations—for example, by compelling eighteen-year-olds who might be subject to a national draft to attend schools. The national power to raise and support armies and navies takes precedence over a state's power to educate.

PRE-CIVIL WAR AMENDMENTS
AMENDMENT XI: SUITS AGAINST STATES

The Judicial power of the United States shall not be construed to extend to any suit in law or equity, commenced or prosecuted against one of the United States by Citizens of another State, or by Citizens or Subjects of any Foreign State.

This amendment was proposed March 4, 1794, and proclaimed January 8, 1798.

Article III, Section 2, paragraph 1, among other things, extends the judicial power of the United States to "cases and controversies between a state and citizens of another state." During the struggle over ratification of the Constitution, many persons objected to this clause on the ground it would permit a private individual to hail a state before a federal court; they were assured by Hamilton and others that because of the doctrine of "sovereign immunity," no state could ever be sued without its own consent. In 1792, however, the Supreme Court applied the literal terms of the Constitution and upheld the right of the federal courts to take jurisdiction in a case commenced by a citizen of South Carolina against Georgia.[1] Since many states were in default on their debts, there was a great alarm lest a series of similar suits should result. Immediately after the Supreme Court's decision, the Eleventh Amendment was proposed, and its ratification in effect "recalled" the decision.

The amendment in its literal terms only immunizes a nonconsenting state from federal court suits brought by citizens of another state or by citizens of a foreign state. It has always been construed, however, to incorporate the doctrine of sovereign immunity and thus to extend immunity to states against suits brought in federal courts by foreign nations and, more importantly, by a state's own citizens.[2] Justice Brennan persists in contending that the amendment does not apply to suits brought against a state by its own citizens, but he is the only justice who argues so. The amendment does not, however, immunize counties, cities, school boards, or regional authorities created by interstate compact from such suits.[3]

The immunity of the states does not depend upon the state's being actually named as a party, but includes suits where private individuals seek to impose a liability that must be paid from public funds. Thus the amendment barred a federal district court from ordering Illinois officials to award retroactive welfare benefits they had wrongfully withheld.[4] The amendment, however, does not prevent a federal admiralty court from ordering state officials to turn over to private individuals property they have salvaged but which these officials believe the state owns.[5]

If a state commences a prosecution against an individual in a state court, the Eleventh Amendment does not prevent that individual from appealing to the Supreme Court the decision of the highest state court to which the case may be carried, if the case involves a question arising under the Constitution, federal laws, or a treaty of the United States. The taking of the case from state courts to the Supreme Court is not considered to be the initiation of a new case by the individual against a state, merely the continuation of the one originally commenced or prosecuted by a state.

Although the Eleventh Amendment protects a state against suit in federal courts without its own consent, a state can be sued without its consent in the courts of another state—so the Supreme Court decided in 1979.[6]

Congress may make state participation in federal programs conditional on the willingness of a state to waive its immunity—as it has done, for example, in the Federal Employers Liability Act (FELA) that makes railroads financially responsible for personal injuries sustained by their employees. When a state operates a railroad after passage of FELA, it tacitly consents to all the provisions of the act, including those opening it to suit in a federal court.[7] On the other hand, Congress did not condition state consent to suit when it extended the Fair Labor Standards Act to state employees. Running a railroad is of a different order, said the Court, from operating schools and hospitals, and unless Congress makes clear its intent to impose waiver of immunity for suits on states as a condition for participating in the latter type of activities, the Court would not do so.[8]

The Eleventh Amendment must be read in connection with other constitutional provisions, most especially the Fourteenth, which to some extent has modified the Eleventh. When Congress exercises authority granted to it by Section 5 of the Fourteenth Amendment (see page 253) and authorizes suits against persons acting under the color of law, it opens federal courts to suits against those officials "which are constitutionally impermissible in other contexts."[9] Moreover, when enforcing the Fourteenth Amendment federal judges are not kept by the Eleventh Amendment from requiring a state to provide funds for remedial programs to implement school desegregation plans.[10]

In the landmark case of *Ex parte Young*, the Supreme Court declared that the Eleventh Amendment does not prevent federal courts, on the application of private individuals in appropriate proceedings, from restraining state officers who are acting unconstitutionally.[11] By the principle of the "rule of law," a state officer who acts beyond the law ceases to be an officer and thus ceases to be a representative of the state. However, inconsistently, but fortunately for the protection of constitutional rights, when state officers act beyond the law, their action is state action for the purpose of bringing the Fourteenth Amendment into play, but not state action for the purpose of preventing suits for injunctions under the Eleventh Amendment. Moreover, Congress has authorized civil suits against officials who willfully deprive persons of their constitutional rights even if they acted "under the color of law." (The phrase "under the color of law" means authorized to act on behalf of the government. The phrase, which comes from the post-Civil War Civil Rights Acts, applies to anybody acting in an official role, whether or not the specific actions are authorized.) In order to collect damages from officials, it is necessary to prove they acted knowingly or with malicious intent to deprive persons of their constitutional rights.[12] The states and municipalities may be required to pay compensatory damages for wrongs done by their officials, even if done in good faith, but punitive damages may not be collected from states and municipalities.[13]

Congress has even authorized federal courts to levy the cost of attorneys' fees against state officials in favor of a winning party in a civil rights action.[14] (Unlike other officials, judges have absolute immunity and cannot be sued for their judicial acts, even when such actions are in excess of their jurisdiction and are done maliciously or corruptly.[15] Nonetheless, judges may be liable for the payment of attorneys' fees resulting from prospective injunctive actions, actions designed not to collect damages but to prevent them from interfering with rights in the future.[16] Prosecutors, who have almost as much immunity from federal suits in the performance of their responsibilities as do judges, are also subject to liability for payment of attorneys' fees resulting from actions designed to enjoin them from acting improperly in the future.[17])

Debates over the meaning of the Eleventh Amendment continue to stir deep passions. In 1984, the Supreme Court split five-to-four over the question of whether *Ex parte Young* should be liberally construed to prevent citizens from seeking injunctive relief in federal courts from the actions of their own state officials for acting contrary to *state* law. (*Ex parte Young* clearly allows such suits to prevent state officials from violating *federal* law or the *federal* Constitution in the future.) Justice Powell, speaking for the majority, refused to extend the Young doctrine to permit suits in federal courts by private persons against state officials for violating state law. Such an action, he argued, "would emasculate the Eleventh Amendment." Justice Stevens, dissenting for the minority of four, accused the majority of repudiating "at least 28 cases" and said rather bitterly, "No sound reasons justifies . . . this Court's voyage into the sea of undisciplined lawmaking."[18]

AMENDMENT XII: ELECTION OF THE PRESIDENT

The Electors shall meet in their respective states and vote by ballot for President and Vice-President, one of whom, at least, shall not be an inhabitant of the same state with themselves; they shall name in their ballots the person voted for as President, and in distinct ballots the person voted for as Vice-President, and they shall make distinct lists of all persons voted for as President, and of all persons voted for as Vice-President, and of the number of votes for each, which lists they shall sign and certify, and transmit sealed to the seat of the government of the United States, directed to the President of the Senate;—The President of the Senate shall, in the presence of the Senate and House of Representatives, open all certificates and the votes shall then be counted;—The person having the greatest number of Votes for President, shall be the President, if such number be a majority of the whole number of Electors appointed; and if no person have such majority, then from the persons having the highest numbers not exceeding three on the list of those voted for as President, the House of Representatives shall choose immediately, by ballot, the President. But in choosing the President, the votes shall be taken by states, the representation from each state having one vote; a quorum for this purpose shall consist of a member or members from two-thirds of the states, and a majority of all the states shall be necessary to a choice. *And if the House of Representatives shall not choose a President whenever the right of choice shall devolve upon them, before the fourth day of March next following, then the Vice-President shall act as President, as in the case of the death or other constitutional disability of the President.*—The person having the greatest number of votes as Vice-President, shall be the Vice-President, if such number be a majority of the whole number of Electors appointed, and if no person have a majority, then from the two highest numbers on the list, the Senate shall choose the Vice-President; a quorum for the purpose shall consist of two-thirds of the whole number of Senators, and a majority of the whole number shall be necessary to a choice. But no person constitutionally ineligible to the office of President shall be eligible to that of Vice-President of the United States [emphasis added].

This amendment was proposed December 8, 1803, and declared in force by the Secretary of State September 25, 1804.

The emphasized portion of this amendment has been superseded by the Twentieth Amendment and modified by the Twenty-fifth.

The presidential electoral system is the classic example of how custom and usage have amended and democratized the Constitution. As previously mentioned, the authors of the Constitution expected electors to be distinguished citizens who would in fact, as well as in form, choose the President and the Vice-President. Their expectations were not fulfilled because of the rise of national political parties. By the election of 1800, electors had come to be party puppets, pledged in advance to vote for the candidates nominated by their respective parties. In this election, the Republican-Democratic electors were in a majority. Since under the original provisions for selecting the President and the Vice-President each elector voted for two individuals without indicating which was his choice for President and which for Vice-President, Aaron Burr, the Republican-Democratic candidate for Vice-President, secured the same number of electoral votes as Thomas Jefferson, the Republican-Democratic candidate for President. This circumstance transferred the election to the House of Representatives, where the Federalists were in control. Although many Federalists favored Burr as the lesser of two evils, Hamilton threw his great influence on the side of Jefferson, who was finally elected on the thirty-sixth ballot. The Twelfth Amendment was designed to prevent such a situation from occurring again.

The two major differences between the Twelfth Amendment and the original provisions of the Constitution, which were repealed by it, are as follows: Today electors are required to cast separate votes for President and Vice-President, clearly designating which is their choice for President and which for Vice-President. In the event no person receives a majority of the electoral votes for President, the House of Representatives chooses from the three persons with the most electoral votes (the original provision was from the five highest). Each state has one vote in the House. If no person receives a majority of the electoral votes for Vice-President, the Senate chooses between the two persons with the most electoral votes, each senator having one vote.

Today presidential and vice-presidential candidates are chosen by political parties in national nominating conventions. On the first Tuesday after the first Monday in November, the voters select the electors, who are morally pledged to cast their electoral votes for the candidates chosen by their particular national convention. In most states, the electors' names do not even appear on the ballot; only the names of the candidates to whom they are pledged appear. Thus the electors have been reduced to automata and "the Electoral College," as the electors are known collectively, to an automatic registering device.

The development of the two-party system had another consequence for the Electoral College that the framers did not anticipate. It greatly lessened the probability that the House of Representatives would be called on to make the final selection. Only once since 1801 has the House exercised this duty. In the election of 1824, before the full development of our party system, Andrew Jackson, John Quincy Adams, and William Crawford received the most electoral votes, but not one of them had a majority. The House, voting by states, chose John Quincy Adams. The only time the Senate has been called upon to make the final selection for the Vice-Presidency was in 1837, when it favored Richard M. Johnson over Francis Granger. With only two major political parties there is no dispersion of the vote, and one party is assured of a majority of the electoral votes. Whenever a strong third party develops, as was the case in the 1968 election with George Wallace's American Independence Party (and in 1980 with the Anderson candidacy), the probability of final selection by the House and Senate is greatly increased.

All the state legislatures except Maine now provide for the selection of electors on a general statewide straight-ticket basis. Each voter casts one vote for the Democratic, Republican, American Independent, or other party electors. This statewide straight-ticket voting means that the party that receives the most popular votes in a state receives *all* that state's electoral votes. For example, in 1984 Reagan (that is, the Republican electors) received 59 percent of the popular vote in New York; Mondale received 41 percent. Ronald Reagan, nevertheless, received all thirty-six of New York's electoral votes. It is even possible for a person to obtain a majority of the popular vote without receiving a majority of the electoral vote. Let us take a hypothetical case involving two states to illustrate this point:

State X—15 electoral votes:	Republican popular votes 255,000
	Democratic popular votes 250,000
State Y—5 electoral votes:	Republican popular votes 20,000
	Democratic popular votes 50,000

Results:

Republican popular votes 275,000—Republican electoral votes	15
Democratic popular votes 300,000—Democratic electoral votes	5

This very thing happened in 1876, when Tilden received more popular votes but lost the electoral vote to Hayes, and again in 1888, when Cleveland, despite his larger popular vote, was defeated by Harrison.

The present system helps to preserve one-party domination in that anything less than a plurality of a state's popular vote does not count. A party that believes that it has little chance of winning a plurality of the popular vote is not likely to spend much time or effort campaigning in that state. However, were the President elected by a direct vote of the people or were electoral votes distributed in proportion to the popular vote, there would be more incentive for both parties to campaign throughout the United States instead of concentrating on the pivotal states.

Despite the widely supported view that the Electoral College needs to be reformed, it has been difficult to secure agreement about what reforms should be made. The 1980 elections temporarily revived and intensified the concerns about the risks inherent in our present arrangements: If John Anderson had secured enough electoral votes to keep both major party candidates from obtaining a majority, electors might have been tempted to exercise some discretion, or, more probably, the election would have been thrown into the House of Representatives, where the Anderson supporters might have had the votes necessary to determine the presidential choice between the two major party candidates. The chaos that could result from the installation of a President selected through such procedures is hard to exaggerate.

For many years, amendments have been introduced in Congress to change the procedures for electing the President and the Vice-President. Representatives of the less populous states have opposed substituting direct popular election. Since states have as many electoral votes as they have senators and representatives, the smaller states carry greater weight in the Electoral College than they would in a nationwide direct election. Some people have proposed that we do away with the individual electors but retain the system of electoral votes and distribute a state's electoral vote in the same ratio as its popular vote. Such a change would obviate any danger of an elector's disregarding the wishes of the voters (as happened in 1956, 1960, 1968, and 1972), lessen the influence of strategically located minorities, weaken the one-party system where it now exists, and ensure the election of the candidate with the largest popular vote. This change has been opposed by those who fear it would weaken the influence of people living in large cities, who often have the balance of power in presidential elections. The objections hold even more strongly against proposals to have electors chosen by congressional districts rather than on statewide tickets.

Reform of the Electoral College remains a lively issue in Congress. Currently the most prominently mentioned proposal is to give the presidency to the person who receives the most popular votes. If no candidate receives 40 percent of the votes cast there would be a run-off election. Opponents are fearful that such a procedure would cause a proliferation of candidates, undermine political parties, and weaken federalism. A group of political scientists and politicians meeting under the auspices of the 20th Century Fund has proposed that we keep the present Electoral College formula (without the human electors to cast the ballots) for distribution of state votes, but give the candidate with the most popular votes a bonus of 102 electoral votes—two for each state and the District of Columbia. The National Bonus Plan would guarantee that the popular vote winner would become President, would encourage greater voter participation, and would discourage minor parties. Its advocates argue that it is "a creative new idea that might successfully mold the best features of the Electoral College and direct elections."[1]

The operation of the Electoral College could also be altered if more states, especially those with a large number of electoral votes, should follow the lead of Maine, which in 1969 adopted a provision that one presidential elector is to be chosen from each of its two congressional districts with the state's remaining two electors chosen at large.

CIVIL WAR AMENDMENTS

The Thirteenth, Fourteenth, and Fifteenth Amendments were adopted after and as a result of the Civil War. They were, so to speak, the terms of surrender dictated by the North to the South. Congress, for example, insisted that the southern states ratify the Fourteenth Amendment before federal troops were withdrawn and the states restored to full participation in Congress.

The purpose of these three amendments was to free the black slaves, grant them citizenship, and protect their rights, especially the right to vote, against infringement by the states. As Justice Miller wrote, "No one can fail to be impressed with the one pervading purpose of them all, lying at the foundation of each . . . we mean the freedom of the slave race, the security and firm establishment of that freedom, and the protection of the newly-made freeman and citizen from the oppressions of those who formerly exercised unlimited dominion over him."[1] Clearly the purpose of these amendments was to deprive the states of the "right" to impose disabilities on blacks because of their race, color, or previous condition of servitude. It was to take almost three-quarters of a century, however, before the Civil War amendments were to be used for this purpose.

AMENDMENT XIII: SLAVERY

Section 1

Neither slavery nor involuntary servitude, except as a punishment for crime whereof the party shall have been duly convicted, shall exist within the United States, or any place subject to their jurisdiction.

This amendment was proposed on January 31, 1865, and declared in force by the Secretary of State on December 18, 1865.

Before the adoption of this amendment, each state could determine for itself whether or not slavery should be permitted within its borders. The Thirteenth Amendment deprived both the states and the national government of that power. The amendment was aimed at black slavery. Without violating the amendment, persons may still be compelled to help build public roads (under the common law, men could be drafted for a certain number of days every year for this purpose, although in some cases, payment of taxes exempted them from such duties); to pay alimony; or to serve on a jury, in the militia, or in the armed forces.

Several state laws that made failure to work after receiving money *prima facie* evidence of intent to defraud have been held to be contrary to the Thirteenth Amendment. In effect, these laws made it a crime punishable by imprisonment to fail to work after securing money on the promise to do so.[2] Such laws established a condition of "peonage," involuntary servitude forced upon a person in order to work off a debt.

Section 1 of the Thirteenth Amendment is one of the two provisions of the Constitution that an individual can violate directly, for it is self-executing (the other is the Twenty-first Amendment). By its "own unaided force and effect" the Thirteenth Amendment abolished slavery and established universal freedom.

After all these years the Supreme Court has not decided "whether the Thirteenth Amendment itself reaches practices with a disproportionate effect as well as those motivated by discriminatory purpose, or indeed whether it accomplished anything more than the abolition of slavery."[3]

Section 2

Congress shall have the power to enforce this article by appropriate legislation.

"Whether or not Section 1 by its own force did anything more than abolish slavery is still an open question. But it is no longer open that under Section 2 Congress has the power to determine what are the badges and incidents of slavery, and the authority to translate that determination into effective legislation."[4] This more expansive interpretation of congressional power is of recent origin. Prior to 1968 the prevailing view was that all Section 2 did was to give Congress power to prevent the imposition of slavery and peonage, narrowly defined. Hence, it was ruled that Congress had no power under Section 2 to legislate against racial discrimination.[5]

Then in 1968, in *Jones* v. *Mayer,* the Supreme Court construed Section 2 in a significantly new way, or some would say the Court finally got around to interpreting the section as its framers intended. The case grew out of a suit filed by Mr. and Mrs. Joseph Lee Jones against a developer in St. Louis County [Missouri] who refused to sell them a home because Mr. Jones was black. The Joneses cited an almost unused section of the Civil Rights Act of 1866 that reads, "All citizens of the United States shall have the same right, in every State and Territory, as is enjoyed by white citizens thereof to inherit, purchase, lease, sell, hold, and convey real and personal property." Few thought that the Joneses had a good case; almost 90 years earlier the Court had ruled that Congress lacks power under the Fourteenth Amendment (see page 253) to legislate against discrimination unless it is imposed or supported by governmental action. The Thirteenth Amendment was thought to cover only slavery; the Civil Rights Act of 1866 had always been construed to cover only state-imposed discrimination. Besides, Congress in 1968 had just passed the Civil Rights Act covering discrimination in housing that many thought superseded any impact the 1866 law might have had.

As anticipated, the district court dismissed the complaint, and the court of appeals affirmed, both courts concluding that the Civil Rights Act of 1866 applies only to state action and does not reach private refusals to sell. But the Supreme Court reversed. Significant beyond the immediate facts of this case was the Supreme Court's interpretation of Section 2 of the Thirteenth Amendment. Justice Stewart, speaking for the Court, proclaimed:

> The Thirteenth Amendment authorized Congress to do more than merely dissolve the legal bond by which the Negro slave was held to his master; it gave Congress the power rationally to determine what are the badges and the incidents of slavery and the authority to translate that determination into effective legislation . . .
> When racial discrimination herds men into ghettos and makes their ability to buy property turn on the color of their skin, then it too is a relic of slavery . . .
> At the very least, the freedom that Congress is empowered to secure under the Thirteenth Amendment includes the freedom to buy whatever a white man can buy, the right to live wherever a white man can live. If Congress cannot say

that being a free man means at least this much, then the Thirteenth Amendment made a promise the Nation cannot keep.[6]

Since the *Jones* decision the Supreme Court has several times reaffirmed its validity.[7] In short, Section 2, as now construed, gives Congress the authority to enact whatever legislation is necessary and proper to overcome all incidents and badges of slavery no matter from what source they may be imposed.

AMENDMENT XIV: CITIZENSHIP, PRIVILEGES AND IMMUNITIES OF UNITED STATES CITIZENSHIP, DUE PROCESS, AND EQUAL PROTECTION OF THE LAWS

Section 1

All persons born or naturalized in the United States, and subject to the jurisdiction thereof, are citizens of the United States and of the State wherein they reside.

This amendment was proposed June 13, 1866, and declared in force by the Secretary of State July 28, 1868.

In the *Dred Scott* case (1857), Chief Justice Taney had declared that the framers did not include blacks as part of the sovereign "people of the United States" and he wrote: "[Negroes] were not intended to be included, under the word 'citizen' in the Constitution, and can therefore claim none of the rights and privileges which that instrument provides for and secures to citizens of the United States. On the contrary, they were at that time considered as a subordinate and inferior class of beings, who had been subjugated by the dominant race, and, whether *emancipated or not* [italics added], yet remained subject to their authority, and had no rights or privileges but such as those who held the power and the government might choose to grant them."[1] The opening sentence of the Fourteenth Amendment reversed this decision.

Persons born in the United States but not subject to the jurisdiction thereof are children of foreign diplomats and children born of alien enemies in the event of a hostile occupation of the United States. Although the Indian tribes are subject to the jurisdiction of the United States, they have been considered in a special category, and the Fourteenth Amendment did not directly confer citizenship upon them. However, all Indians are now citizens of the United States by act of Congress. All other children born in the United States become citizens even if their parents are aliens.

The clause confers citizenship on the principle of *jus soli*—by reason of place of birth; it does not prevent Congress from conferring citizenship by *jus sanguinis*—by reason of blood. For example, by law of Congress, children born outside the United States to American citizens are citizens of the United States "from birth." Citizenship may also be acquired by naturalization.

The Constitution confers citizenship on all persons born or naturalized in the United States. Although naturalization secured by fraud may be canceled through proper judicial action and persons may under certain conditions voluntarily renounce their citizenship, what the Constitution confers, Congress cannot constitutionally take away. But at various times Congress has tried to do so. It has declared that persons who do certain things—vote in elections in other nations, join the military forces of another nation, leave the United States during time of war to avoid the draft, be dishonorably discharged for desertion during wartime, become a naturalized citizen and live abroad for a stipulated number of years—shall be construed as having expatriated themselves and by judicial action be subject to having their citizenship taken from them. The Supreme Court, however, has held these provisions unconstitutional. "In the last analysis expatriation depends on the will of the citizen rather than on the will of Congress and its assessment of his conduct."[2]

Congress has the power, nonetheless, to declare that persons who perform certain acts, for example, swearing allegiance to another country, create a presumption that they intend to relinquish citizenship. In such an instance a court may take citizenship away if the government proves by a "predominance of the evidence"—the ordinary burden one must sustain to win a civil suit and not the more stringent standard of "clear and convincing evidence" or the criminal one of "beyond a resonable doubt"—that the person both voluntarily performed the expatriating act, and did so with the "intent to abandon citizenship."[3]

The Fourteenth Amendment confers citizenship only on persons born or naturalized in the United States. Congress can confer citizenship upon others. It has done so for some persons born outside the United States. Since it is Congress (not the Constitution) that confers this citizenship, Congress may set reasonable condition as to how such citizenship may be obtained and retained. Thus the Court sustained a provision expatriating persons born outside the United States to a citizen parent and an alien if such persons do not return to the United States and live here for five continuous years between the ages of fourteen and twenty-eight.[4]

Section 1

[continued] No State shall make or enforce any law which shall abridge the privileges or immunities of citizens of the United States;

After the adoption of the Thirteenth Amendment, several southern states that were restored by President Johnson promptly adopted legislation that, in the words of Justice Miller, "imposed upon the colored race onerous disabilities and burdens, and curtailed their rights in the pursuit of life, liberty, and property to such an extent that their freedom was of little value." These laws convinced Congress, again to quote Miller, "that something more was necessary in the way of constitutional protection to the unfortunate race who had suffered so much."[5] Accordingly, Congress insisted on the ratification of the Fourteenth Amendment as a condition of restoring southern state governments to full participation in the government of the Union.

Despite the obvious purpose of the Fourteenth Amendment to protect blacks from the "oppressions of those who had formerly exercised unlimited dominion" over them, it was not until the 1940s that the amendment was used primarily for this purpose. And it has not been the "privileges or immunities" clause that has been used but rather the due process and equal protection clauses.

The Supreme Court, in the *Slaughter House Cases,* so narrowly construed the privileges or immunities clause in the very first case in which the Fourteenth Amendment came before it that the clause has never had much significance. The Court held that there are two distinct citizenships, state and federal, and that the "fundamental" civil and political rights that we enjoy are privileges or immunities stemming from *state,* not *United States,* citizenship. In other words, this clause conferred no new rights on United States citizens but merely made explicit a federal guarantee against abridgment of already established rights.

The privileges or immunities of United States citizens (which this clause forbids states to abridge) are those that owe their existence to the Constitution and the law and treaties of the United States, such as the right to travel in the United States, the right to engage in interstate and foreign commerce, the right to protection of the national government on the high seas and in foreign countries, and the right to vote in primaries and general elections in which congress members and presidential electors are chosen and to have that vote properly counted. And while the Supreme Court in past decisions has held that some important rights are not privileges or immunities of United States citizens—such as the right to be secure in one's home, the right to refuse to give self-incriminatory evidence in state courts, the right to engage in a legal occupation, the right to attend public schools, the right to vote in state elections—the significance of these decisions has been substantially undermined by more recent rulings.[6] These may not be privileges of United States citizens as such, but today they are protected by the due process and equal protection clauses of the Fourteenth Amendment (see below). Furthermore, with the expansion of federal civil rights laws, there are a large number of such rights that owe their existence to federal laws and thus are protected from state (or private, for that manner) abridgment.

Section 1

[continued] nor shall any State deprive any person of life, liberty, or property, without due process of law;

It should be emphasized that this clause, as well as the privileges and immunities clause and the equal protection laws clause (see below), is directed to the states, their officials, and local governments. Private wrongs—wrongful acts of private individuals—if not sanctioned in some way by a state, do not violate the Fourteenth Amendment. In brief, the Fourteenth Amendment protects individuals against *state,* not *private,* action.

As has been noted, after the Supreme Court's interpretation of the privileges or immunities clause rendered it ineffective as a protector of "fundamental rights," an attempt was made to make the due process clause serve this purpose, an attempt that was not completely successful until the 1960s. The Supreme Court still has not gone so far as to make the due process clause of the Fourteenth Amendment a mirror image of the Bill of Rights, although in fact most provisions of the Bill of Rights have been incorporated into the due process clause.

Section 1

[continued] nor deny to any person within its jurisdiction the equal protection of the laws.

The equal protection clause, often merging into substantive due process, is the Court's major instrument to scrutinize state regulations. When a state law is challenged as a violation of the equal protection clause the Court chooses among three different "tiers or tests."

The lowest, or least stringent, is the traditional rational basis test. Under this test, "it's enough that the State's action be rationally based and free from invidious discrimination."[7] "It does not offend the Constitution merely because the classification is not made with mathematical nicety or because in practice it results in some inequality."[8] When using this test the justices emphasize that the Constitution does not forbid governments from making any distinctions among people, for it could not legislate without doing so. What it forbids is unreasonable classification when there is no relation between the classes the law creates and permissible governmental goals. When the act relates to social and economic legislation and does not employ suspect classifications (see page 229) or impinge on fundamental rights (see page 230), it must be upheld against equal protection attack when the legislative means are rationally related to a legitimate governmental purpose. Moreover, such legislation carries with it a presumption of rationality that can only be overcome by a clear showing of arbitrariness and irrationality.[9] As the rational basis test has traditionally been applied, primarily to measure the constitutionality of legislation impinging on business activities or the distribution of public benefits under general legislation such as social security, it essentially means that any law is constitutional so long as it serves some legitimate governmental purpose, even if not the purpose stated by the legislature.[10]

A minority of the Court—Powell, Brennan, Marshall, and Stevens—have argued that the rational basis test should be firmed up slightly. They argue that when the legislature makes clear the purpose it intends a statute to serve, thus assuring the courts that the legislature has made a conscious policy choice, such action should receive "the most respectful deference." But when no clear legislative purpose appears from a reading of the statute and the only thing before the Court is the purpose as stated by a government lawyer litigating the constitutionality of the statute, then the Court should require that the classification bear a "fair and substantial relation" to the asserted purpose. This marginally more demanding scrutiny indirectly would test the plausibility of the tendered purpose."[11] However, a majority of the Court has rejected this construction of the rational basis test, and it is probably accurate to say, as Justice Stevens has charged, that once the Court decides that the rational basis test should be applied and "if any 'conceivable basis' for a discriminatory classification will repel a constitutional attack . . . judicial review . . . constitute[s] a mere tautological recognition of the fact that Congress [or a state legislature] did what it intended to do."[12]

The top tier or most stringent scrutiny under the equal protection clause reverses the normal presumption of constitutionality: A state must demonstrate a "compelling governmental interest," and that it has "adopted those means to accomplish the intended ends that put the least possible restraint on the fundamental right in question."[13] This compelling governmental test is used whenever the law impinges on "fundamental rights" or deals with a "suspect classification"; in a moment we will get back to discussion of what makes a right fundamental and a class suspect.

Recently the Court has adopted a "middle tier" where the test is not as rigid as the upper tier, or compelling state interest test, or as relaxed as the rational basis test. This intermediate tier requires that the law be more than a rational means to legitimate governmental end, but not that it be the only means to accomplish a compelling government interest. Rather the law must serve "important governmental objectives and must be substantially related to the achievement of these objectives."[14] This intermediate tier applies when the law embodies neither a suspect class nor a fundamental right, but when it involves an almost suspect or, as it is sometimes called, a "disfavored" classification.

Obviously it makes a substantial difference which kind of equal protection test is applied. If the Court uses the lower tier test it almost never declares a law unconstitutional. If it decides that the upper tier analysis should be used, it almost never declares the law constitutional. If it decides that the middle tier test applies, then it is more difficult to predict the outcome. What then determines which test is to be applied?

The upper tier test applies if the law impinges on *fundamental rights* or deals with *suspect classifications*. The justices have not been too clear on what makes a right fundamental, but they have explained that it is not whether it is considered important. The rights to food, to shelter, and to education are basic, but in a constitutional sense they are not fundamental rights because they are not rights the Constitution "explicitly or implicitly" guarantees, such as the right of free speech, freedom of religion, to associate, personal privacy, to travel in the United States (but not abroad) if one is under no legal restraint or not fleeing from officials, the right of access to the courts, the right to marry, and the right not to have the government interfere with obtaining an abortion during the early stages of pregnancy (a right deriving from the right to privacy—for women to make "intimate decisions" affecting their bodies).[15] Important as are the rights to food, shelter, and education there is nothing in the Constitution guaranteeing to any person that government will provide them with an education, a house, or welfare benefits; and more to the point, there are no specific constitutional provisions protecting these rights from governmental regulations, in contrast to the fundamental rights, which are so protected. Apparently, for example, the right to an abortion is fundamental because it is part of the right of privacy protected by the Constitution; however, the right to education is not fundamental in a constitutional sense; a distinction that some find difficult to draw.

The upper tier test also applies to suspect classifications. The traditional criteria to determine which groups fall into a suspect and therefore especially protected class are "an immutable characteristic determined solely by the accident of birth, or a class saddled with such disabilities, or subjected to such a history of purposeful inequal treatment, or regulated to such a political powerlessness as to command extraordinary protection from the majoritarian political process."[16] Classifications based on race, and its close cousin national origins (or, as it is now called, ethnic groups), are clearly suspect. And as far as states are concerned; so is alienage (the condition of being alien), although because of Congress's power to regulate immigration, national legislation affecting aliens is not subject to the same rigid scrutiny as are state laws.[17] Religion is probably a suspect classification, although there is no specific Supreme Court decision to this effect other than those stemming from the First Amendment.

The intermediate tier test applies to laws that deal with disfavored classifications, in which at the moment are located illegitimacy and sex. "Illegitimacy is analogous in many respects to the personal characteristics that have been held to be suspect," wrote Justice Powell for the Court. "We nevertheless conclude that the analogy is not sufficient to require our most exacting scrutiny."[18] Yet in reviewing laws imposing disabilities on illegitimate children the Court has made it clear that the intermediate test to scrutinize such laws is "not a toothless one."[19] As to classifications based on sex—the Supreme Court keeps referring to these as gender-based classifications, but as one wag has pointed out, nouns have gender, people have sex, the Supreme Court has waffled. At one time it came close to declaring sex classifications to be suspect and to be subject to the most stringent upper tier test. More recently, it has treated such classifications as disfavored and subject to the intermediate tier test.

Let's see how these general tests have been applied. The rational basis test was applied to sustain Illinois's exemption of individuals from paying personal property taxes while at the same time imposing such taxes on corporations. "Where taxation is concerned, and no specific federal right apart from equal protection is imperiled, the states have large leeway in making classifications and drawing lines which in their judgment produce reasonable systems of taxation."[20] Ohio was permitted to deny unemployment benefits to those laid off because of strikes in other companies. The statute did not involve any fundamental rights or "apply to any protected class and the test therefore is whether the statute has a rational relation to legitimate state interests."[21] There was no constitutional violation in the Texas practice of providing educational revenues for local schools largely from local property taxes, even though such practices produced fewer dollars to educate children in some poor districts than children in districts where more valuable property is located.[22] The village of Belle Terre, New York, had authority to adopt zoning regulations that effectively excluded any except single families or no more than two individuals from occupying houses in the village. Six students at the State University of New York at Stony Brook challenged the ordinance as violating their rights, but the Court said, "We deal with economic and social legislation where legislatures have historically drawn lines which we respect against the charge of violation of the Equal Protection Clause if the law be 'reasonable,' not arbitrary and bears 'a rational relationship to a permissible state objective,'" ". . . The police power is not confined to elimination of filth, stench, and unhealthy places. It is ample to lay out zones where family values, youth values, and the blessings of quiet seclusion and clean air make the area a sanctuary for people."[23]

Other examples of the application of the rational basis test: A state may deny unemployment benefits to those who attend day schools while making them available to those who attend night school, it being reasonable to assume that those who go to school during the day are less likely to be available for employment than are those who go to school after the workday.[24] To combat abuses by those who would exploit veterans, Congress may limit educational benefits under the G.I. Bill to courses which do not enroll more than 85 percent of the students whose fees are being paid for by other persons, including federal agencies, or exclude courses offered for less than two years.[25] New York could subject harness-racing trainers to more drastic restrictions than thoroughbred-racing trainers because of a legislative determination that the former kind of activity justifies more stringent regulation.[26] Minnesota could ban the sale of milk in plastic nonreturnable bottles while allowing its sale in paperboard non-returnable cartons.[27] Congress could alter the benefits of those eligible for both railroad retirement and social security payments.[28] Congress could provide death benefits to widows, widowers, and divorced spouses who are responsible for the care of minor children, but deny such aid to unwed mothers. The Court concluded, "The denial of mother's insurance benefits to a woman who never married the wage earner bears a rational relation to the government's desire to ease economic privation brought on by the wage earner's death," since the wage earner never was legally required to support the unmarried mother of his child while he was alive, the possibility of severe economic dislocation upon his death is more remote than in the case of a woman he had wed.[29] Congress could permit veterans organizations, but no others, to engage in lobbying activities without jeopardizing their tax exempt status. "Our country has a long-standing policy of compensating veterans for their past contributions by providing them with numerous advantages."[30]

Until recently in almost every instance when the Court concluded that the rational basis test applied, it was in effect concluding that the law was constitutional. After all, if a majority of a state legislature has voted for a particular law, it is rather presumptuous for judges to declare that the legislators have acted without any rational basis. Nonetheless the Supreme Court ruled that Alaska failed to pass even the minimal test when it proposed to distribute income derived from its oil revenues to its citizens in varying amounts based on the length of each citizen's residency in Alaska. In language reminiscent of Justice Holmes, who at the beginning of the century often reminded the then conservative majority that it had no mandate to impose its views on states, Justice Rehnquist, the Court's most conservative member wrote, "In striking down the Alaskan scheme, the Court seems momentarily to have forgotten 'the principle that the Fourteenth Amendment gives the federal courts no power to impose upon the States their view of what constitutes wise economic or social policy.' "[31]

The Court has also, in the words of the dissenting justices, patched "together bits and pieces of what might be termed quasi-suspect-class and quasi-fundamental-rights analysis"[32] in order to declare unconstitutional a Texas statute denying illegal alien children the right to a free public education. Although conceding that illegal aliens are not a suspect class and that the right to an education is not a fundamental right, the Court nonetheless held that Texas had to "offer something more than a rational basis for its classification."[33] Texas failed to prove to the justices' satisfaction that its action was justified by a substantial state interest in saving money or discouraging illegal aliens from moving to Texas. Chief Justice Burger, dissenting with Justices Rehnquist and O'Connor, argued "The Constitution does not . . . vest judges with a mandate to try to remedy every social problem," and contended, "Today's cases, I regret to say, present yet another example of unwarranted judicial action which in the long run tends to contribute to the weakening of our political processes."

As to laws affecting fundamental rights, the constitutional right to travel ensures new residents who move into a state the same rights to vital governmental benefits and privileges in the state to which they migrate as are enjoyed by long-term residents. As we have noted (page 119), Article IV, Section 2 protects citizens who move from one state to another, and those protections often merge with equal protection clause considerations (the latter also extending to aliens as well as to citizens). As we have noted, requirements that one must be in a state a certain length of time—so-called durational residency requirements—before being entitled to certain benefits are suspect because of their impact on the right to travel. Durational residency requirements beyond fifty days before one may vote are unconstitutional, as are such requirements beyond one day before one is eligible for welfare and health benefits.[34] A state may, however, require one to be a resident for a year to get a divorce, or enroll in state-supported educational institutions at state-resident rates.[35] And the right to travel does not include the right to take with one benefits of the place from which one came; therefore, Congress may limit social security benefits to the residents of the states and the District of Columbia, and exclude those persons who move to Puerto Rico.[36] Nor does it impermissibly infringe upon the right to travel for a state to set harsher criminal penalty for parents who abandon their children and leave the state than for parents who abandon children but remain in the state.[37]

Here are some additional examples of laws that impinged on fundamental rights and therefore were subject to rigorous judicial scrutiny resulting in their being declared unconstitutional: laws denying to persons living on a federal enclave the right to vote;[38] laws making property ownership a requirement in order to serve on a school board;[39] requirements that only persons who had paid some kind of property tax be allowed to vote in city bond elections;[40] similar requirements that only taxpayers be allowed to vote for revenue or general obligation bonds;[41] as well as requirements that only parents or taxpayers be permitted to vote in school board elections;[42] laws making it a crime for a doctor to prescribe a contraceptive device to an unmarried but not to a married person;[43] laws denying to unwed fathers but not to unwed mothers an opportunity to take custody of children on the death of the other parent;[44] the practice of retaining those unable to pay fines in prison (it is permitted to keep in jail those unwilling but able to pay fines);[45] the provision of religious services for Christians and Jews in prisons, but not for Buddhists;[46] laws imposing such high fees on candidates in primaries that it is difficult for those without funds or without backers to run;[47] suffrage requirements making ineligible to vote those persons residing in a state because of military duty;[48] requirements that to get on a statewide ballot petitions must contain signatures of so many persons in so many counties, because they discriminated against city people;[49] laws making it difficult for minor parties to obtain places on a ballot;[50] a law forbidding remarriage to persons under court obligations to provide child support unless a court is satisfied that the children covered by the support order will be taken care of.[51]

This brings us to suspect classifications, of which the most suspect is race.

The Fourteenth Amendment, and most especially its equal protection clause, was adopted precisely for the purpose of protecting blacks against discrimination by state and local governments, so we have had more constitutional experience with classifications based on race than we have had with other suspect classification. As recently as 1984 the Supreme Court had occasion to remind us, "A core purpose of the Fourteenth Amendment was to do away with all governmentally imposed discrimination based on race. Classifying persons according to their race is more likely to reflect racial prejudice than legitimate public concerns; the race, not the person, dictates the category. Such classifications are subject to the most exacting scrutiny; to pass constitutional muster, they must be justified by a compelling governmental interest and must be 'necessary . . . to the accomplishment' of its legitimate purpose."[52] Earlier the Court had spoken against racial classifications in more emphatic terms, calling them "Odious to our systems," and "in most instances irrelevant."[53]

Despite the fact that the Fourteenth Amendment was adopted for the protection of the recently freed slaves, at first it was not applied in that regard. In fact, in *Plessy* v. *Ferguson* (1896) the Supreme Court held that a state could compel racial segregation in the use of public facilities, provided equal facilities were available for all races. Only Justice Harlan dissented, saying: "In view of the Constitution, in the eye of the law, there is in this country no superior, dominant ruling class of citizens. There is no caste here. Our Constitution is color-blind, and neither knows nor tolerates classes among citizens. In respect of civil rights, all citizens are equal before the law.[54]

Under the guise of the "separate but equal formula," Jim Crow laws, as segregation laws came to be known, were passed in southern states to cover all phases of life from birth to death, from hospitals to burial grounds. For decades, the facilities provided for blacks were separate but not equal. Beginning in the 1940s, the Supreme Court began to insist that states must either stop requiring segregation in the use of public facilities or start providing blacks with exactly equal facilities.

Finally, in the spring of 1954 in *Brown* v. *Board of Education,* the Supreme Court reversed its 1896 holding as applied in public schools and ruled that "separate but equal" is a contradiction in terms and that segregation is itself discrimination.[55] A year later the Court ordered school boards to proceed with deliberate speed to desegrate public schools at the earliest practicable date.[56] In 1969, fourteen years after its first ruling that school segregation was unconstitutional, and in the face of massive resistance to compliance in many parts of the South, the Supreme Court withdrew its earlier grant of time to school authorities to work out the problems in bringing about desegregation. The Court stated: "The time for mere 'deliberate speed' has run out. . . . Delays in desegregating schools systems are no longer tolerable. . . . The burden of a school board today is to come forward with a plan that promises realistically to work and promises realistically to work now."[57] In 1964 Congress authorized the Department of Justice to enter the fray by filing school desegregation suits. It also stipulated in Title VI of the Civil Rights Acts, "No person . . . shall on the ground of race, color, or national origin, be excluded from participating in, be denied the benefits of, or be subjected to discrimination under any program or activity receiving federal financial assistance," which meant that federal funds could be cut off from any district that refused to desegregate. By the time schools opened in the fall of 1970 *de jure* segregated school systems had been abolished. No longer was any school legally defined as a school for blacks or for whites.

The Constitution requires authorities not *merely* to *cease* discriminating, but to take action to remedy the consequence of their past discriminatory conduct. School authorities, and judges formulating desegregation decrees, as a means of dismantling a segregated school system may require the assignment of pupils and teachers to schools on a racial basis. "Just as the race of students must be considered in determining whether a constitutional violation has occurred so must race be considered in formulating a remedy. To forbid, at this stage, all assignments made on the basis or race, would deprive school authorities of the one tool absolutely essential to the fulfillment of their constitutional obligation to eliminate existing dual schools systems."[58] Judges formulating desegregation decrees may also require remedial programs[59] and the busing of pupils from one school within the district to another.

Busing has become a highly controversial constitutional and political issue. Busing, of course, is not a new practice. Many children have long been bused to schools. But as a means to overcome previously required segregation many feel that it is evil.

In a unanimous but cautiously worded decision the Supreme Court in *Swann* v. *Charlotte Mecklenburg Board of Education* (1971) held that a federal judge has authority to order, among other things, students to be bused a reasonable distance beyond their own neighborhoods as a means of eliminating all vestiges of state-imposed segregation. No students should be bused so far that the time or distance of travel presents risk to their health or impinges on the educational process. The Court rejected the notion that the constitutional command to desegregate means that every school in every community must always reflect the racial composition of the school system as a whole. Exact racial balance is not required. And "all things being equal with no history of discrimination, it might well be desirable to assign pupils to schools nearest their homes." But in districts that previously operated segregated systems, "desegregation plans cannot be limited to walk-in schools."[60]

What about interdistrict busing? In many cities blacks are crowded into the central cities and there has been a "white flight" to the suburbs. In such situations it is difficult to achieve integration if the central city and suburban schools are considered separately. But unless it is demonstrated that school district lines have been drawn for the purpose of maintaining segregation and that the suburban districts are being operated in a racially discriminatory fashion, a judge may not require cross-district busing.[61]

If Congress accurately reflects public views, busing is not popular. Each year Congress adopts some kind of legislation limiting the ability of the executive departments to impose busing on school districts or to participate in litigation that would have that effect. The Supreme Court, however, continues to support busing as one of the techniques that judges may require of school districts in appropriate situations to bring about integration, despite the fact that Justices Powell, Stewart, and Rehnquist have expressed their skepticism that busing will work.[62]

The Court has continued to maintain a distinction between remedies appropriate for school districts where racial imbalance is the continuing consequence of a prior-segregated school system or the result of purposeful intent to segregate, and on the other hand remedies appropriate for school districts where racial imbalance is not the result of governmental segregative purposes.[63] In the former kind of school districts, judges may impose system wide remedies and force authorities to take affirmative action to disestablish any vestiges of a dual school system. In the latter kind of school district where racial imbalance is not the result of purposeful governmental action, judges lack any such authority. Therefore, a crucial finding is whether or not any racial imbalance that exists is a consequence of prior violations of the equal protection clause.

The Constitution does not require states to take corrective action to overcome *de facto* segregation. However, if they wish to do so, states may act to secure racial balance in their public schools even if the existing imbalance is not the result of purposeful past segregative governmental action. This is precisely what the Seattle School Board did. In March of 1978 it decided that mandatory reassignment of students was necessary if the racial isolation in its schools, caused by segregated housing patterns, was to be eliminated. This action generated so much opposition that a statewide initiative measure forbidding any board to order mandatory reassignment of students for the purpose of achieving racial balance was overwhelmingly approved. The Supreme Court, however, struck down this action, not because Washington had an obligation to provide such busing, but because the initiative petition had a racially discriminatory purpose, and Washington had unconstitutionally distorted its political process so as to place special burdens on the ability of blacks to achieve legislation they felt would benefit them.[64]

On the very same day, however, the Supreme Court, with only Justice Marshall dissenting, refused to overturn a California action, also adopted as the result of an initiative process, that stripped California courts of the power to order mandatory busing unless it were necessary to remedy a violation of the United States Constitution. The consequence of this action was to set aside a busing plan which the California courts had imposed upon Los Angeles on the grounds that the California Constitution required school boards to overcome racial segregation regardless of whether it was *de facto* or *de jure* in origin. The United States Supreme Court held that the mere repeal of legislation not required by the federal Constitution in the first place is not unconstitutional. California, by the action of its courts having gone beyond the requirements of the federal Constitution, was free by the action of its voters to return to "the standard prevailing throughout the United States." Those who initiated the action in California to strip the courts of the power to order boards to impose mandatory busing without constitutional violation were not motivated, said the Supreme Court, by discriminatory purposes. Moreover, even though California courts could no longer order school boards to adopt busing to overcome *de facto* segregation, the boards themselves, unlike those in Washington, retained the power to do so if they wished.[65] In short, it is unconstitutional for a state to take from a school board the power to order mandatory busing to overcome racial imbalance not caused by the state, but it is all right if the state takes from its courts the power to order such busing without a finding of a violation of the United States Constitution. Thus do our justices weave distinctions that others sometimes have difficulty in understanding.

Brown v. *Board of Education* applied only to public schools. Since that decision the Supreme Court has declared unconstitutional laws requiring segregation in recreational facilities, public transportation, places of public accommodation, and court houses. Any use of governmental power to keep people of different races apart is clearly unconstitutional.[66]

Today, any law or governmental practice that invidiously discriminates against any person because of race is unconstitutional. Nowadays governmentally sanctioned discriminatory action is not likely to be overt, although there are still examples. Two decades ago the Court had to set aside state laws making marriage between persons of different races illegal.[67] And as late as 1984 the Court had to reverse a state court's decision to take from a mother the custody of her child because of her remarriage to a person of a different race.[68] The Court did so unanimously and in one of its briefest opinions of recent years. Much more common are more subtle kinds of discrimination.

How is discrimination to be proved? The mere fact that a law or governmental practice has a differential impact on persons of difference races (or sex) by itself does not establish it as unconstitutional. "The invidious quality of a law claimed to be racially discriminatory must ultimately be traced to a racially discriminatory purpose. Disproportionate impact is not irrelevant, but it is not the sole touchstone of an invidious racial discrimination forbidden by the Constitution. Standing alone, it does not trigger the rule that racial classifications are to be subjected to the strictest scrutiny and are justified only by the weightiest of considerations."[69]

The face of disproportionate effect, however, is not unimportant. For if a governmental practice or law adversely affects members of one race, it shifts the burden of proof to the government to demonstrate that it has not engaged in discriminatory conduct.[70] In a series of cases that overlap Fifteenth Amendment considerations, the Court has moved back and forth over the question of what evidence is necessary to prove discrimination in at-large election systems—those in which city council members or county representatives are elected citywide and countrywide rather than by election districts. The effect of these systems in most cities, even if there is a substantial black minority population, is to keep the city council all white. But it is hard to prove that this was the intent of those who established the system, and it is even harder to prove that it is the intent of those who maintain it.

In Mobile, Alabama, the city government long consisted of three commissioners elected at large. Under this system black commissioners were never elected. But since there was no evidence that this form of city government—used in many cities—was adopted and maintained for the purpose of diluting the votes of blacks, there was no violation of the Fourteenth (or Fifteenth) Amendment.[71] Then two years later the Court, another plurality speaking, sustained a decision of a federal judge that the at-large system of elections in Burke County, Georgia, violated the Fourteenth Amendment. The plurality announced that in counties where blacks make up a majority of the population, where no black has ever been elected, where there is evidence of past discrimination against blacks, where the public body in question has been unresponsive in meeting the claims of blacks, a finding that the at-large voting system has been maintained for the purpose of denying blacks equal access to the county political process "is not clearly erroneous."[72]

What is not unconstitutional may be illegal. Most recent civil rights statutes have been interpreted to forbid discriminatory actions that have a discriminatory impact even if there is no intent to discriminate, but not all of them (nor the older civil rights statutes) have been modified to outlaw impact without intent.

Congress, in amending the Voting Rights Act of 1965 in 1982, under its authority of Section 5 of the Fourteenth Amendment and Section 2 of the Fifteenth, stated that, although blacks have no legal right to have members elected in numbers equal to their proportion in the population, where blacks make up a substantial proportion of the population, the fact that few or none of them get elected because of some practice or procedure, such as at-large elections, is part of the "totality of circumstances" judges may take into account to determine if there has been a violation of the act.

Congress has also stipulated that most federal grants are not to be used in any way to discriminate against blacks, women, the aged, or the disabled. For most programs, Congress has made it illegal to use federal funds for practices that have a discriminatory effect even if those practices would fall short of being unconstitutional because there is no proof of discriminatory purposes. For example, the Civil Rights Act of 1964 provides that even though a job standard or a test to determine eligibility for employment may be neutral on its face, if these things have a differential impact on persons by race or sex, even if there is no intent to discriminate, the burden shifts to the employer to demonstrate that the requirement has a manifest relationship to the employment in question.[73] On the other hand, the Civil Rights Act of 1866, (now 42 U.S.C. 1981), although covering private as well as governmental discrimination, reaches only purposeful discrimination.[74] It provides, "All persons within the jurisdiction of the United States shall have the same right in every State and Territory to make and enforce contracts, to sue, be parties, give evidence, and to the full and equal benefit of all laws and proceedings for the security of persons and property as is enjoyed by white citizens." To win a suit under Section 1981, plaintiffs must prove purposeful discrimination.

What if governments adopt programs to remedy disadvantages that minorities suffer because of the lingering effects of past discrimination against them? What if governments adopt programs, or require private employers to adopt, race-conscious remedies, popularly known as affirmative action by those who support them and as reverse discrimination by those who oppose, that provide special protections for minorities? Are these kinds of classifications suspect? Are they unconstitutional? There has been no more hotly debated constitutional issue of our times than this one.

In recent years the Supreme Court has faced this issue four times. *California Regents* v. *Bakke* was twice argued before the Court and the issues were extensively debated within the country—more than sixty groups filed *amicus curiae,* friend of court, briefs. In that decision, handed down in 1978, the Court by five to four, declared unconstitutional the dual admissions program of the Medical School of the Davis Campus of the University of California. That program had set aside certain places for blacks and other minorities. Justice Powell, announcing the judgment of the Court, but in an opinion in which no other justice completely joined, ruled that the white plaintiff, Allan Bakke, had been deprived of his constitutional rights. The vice of the Davis program was that it had created a two-track system that "focused solely on race." However,

Justice Powell concluded, the university did have a legitimate educational purpose in trying to obtain a diverse student body, and that for such a purpose it could, if it wished, take race into account as "one element in a range of factors." If it wanted to do so, a public university could adopt an affirmative action admission program in which each applicant would be treated as an individual, and all applications would be considered within the same pool, and the race of each applicant would be taken into account. Under such circumstances the applicant who loses out on "the last available seat to another candidate receiving a 'plus' on the basis of ethnic background, . . . would have no basis to complain of unequal treatment under the Fourteenth Amendment."[75]

In 1979, in *Steelworkers* v. *Weber,* the Court upheld a training program of a private employer who had been prompted to act by federal requirements, in which certain openings were reserved for blacks. The Weber case was decided in terms of the requirements of Title VII of the Civil Rights Act of 1964 rather than the Constitution, but the issues were similar.[76] Then in 1980 in *Fullilove* v. *Klutznick* the Court sustained the Public Works Act of 1977 requiring that at least ten percent of federal funds granted to local public works projects be used to procure services or supplies from minority business enterprises, defined as those owned by United States citizens "who are Negroes, Spanish-speaking, Orientals, Indians, Eskimos, and Aleuts."[77]

In 1984 the Supreme Court returned to the question of the appropriateness of race-conscious remedies in the much talked-about case of *Firefighters* v. *Stotts.* In 1974 Memphis had adopted via a consent decree a court-approved affirmative action plan, in response to action initiated by the Department of Justice, designed to increase the number of black firefighters. The plan was starting to work and the number of blacks on the force increased from three to ten percent, compared to a thirty-seven percent black citizenry. Then in 1980 as the result of budget problems the city had to layoff employees, including firefighters and it prepared to do so in accord with its established seniority plan—last hired, first fired. This would have resulted in the layoff of twenty-five whites and fifteen black junior firefighters, undercutting much of the progress that had been made. The blacks took the issue to the district court that had approved the original consent order, and the judge told the city not to follow seniority "insofar as it will decrease the percentage of blacks."

Chief Justice White, writing for the Court in an opinion joined by Burger, Powell, Rehnquist and O'Connor, ruled that under the terms of Title VII a court may not order a city to disregard seniority when it lays off employees unless individual employees can demonstrate that they have been the actual victims of discrimination. "Mere membership in the disadvantaged class is insufficient to warrant a seniority award; each individual must prove that the discriminatory practice had an impact on him. Even when an individual shows that the discriminatory practice has had an impact on him, he is not automatically entitled to have a nonminority employee laid off to make room for him. He may have to wait until a vacancy occurs, and if there are nonminority employees on layoff, the Court must balance the equities in determining who is entitled to the job."[78]

The precise ruling in *Firefighters* v. *Stotts* was very narrow, applying only to seniority systems protected by Title VII. The Court went out of its way to say, "Whether the City, a public employer, could have taken this course without violating the law is an issue we need not decide." The case was also limited to consent decrees in which layoffs were not discussed and to which white employees or unions were not parties. The Court left the constitutional issues open, and its language could be interpreted to apply only to terminations and not to initial-hiring affirmative action plans. Nonetheless, some of Justice White's language, noted above, could be interpreted as calling into question race-conscious remedies that advantage persons who belong to discriminated groups. What *Firefighters* v. *Stotts,* like other Supreme Court decisions, means is what the Supreme Court, other courts, members of Congress, Presidents, Attorneys General, and lots of interest groups and active citizens will come in the years ahead to say it means.

As a result of these decisions, we can conclude, at least tentatively, that the Constitution does not forbid all affirmative action programs or exclude all governmentally sanctioned racial classifications. However, such classifications are to be approached with considerable caution.

Chief Justice Burger and Justice Powell, who wrote the leading opinions in *Fullilove* and *Bakke,* the two cases where the constitutional issues were most directly confronted (although in neither case did their opinions command the support of a majority) argue that in a remedial context there is no requirement that governments "act in a wholly color-blind fashion." But although remedial programs that establish racial classifications should be subject to strict judicial scrutiny, they would uphold programs that create race-conscious remedies, provided those remedies are closely tailored to accomplish their goals and provided the remedies do not subject nonminorities not guilty of any discriminatory practice to great disadvantage. They also give more weight to the judgment of Congress that a race-conscious remedy is needed that is similar to a judgment by a judge, a state legislature or a state university: Congress is a co-equal branch of the federal government and by the Fourteenth Amendment is granted the power "by appropriate legislation to enforce the provisions of this article." Justices White, Powell, O'Connor, and, most of the time, Justice Stevens are in general agreement on these same views.

Justices Marshall, Brennan, and Blackmun would go further. They would have upheld the constitutionality of admissions programs by universities and colleges that set aside certain spaces for minorities. They would have upheld the right of a district court to design "race-conscious relief" under Title VII, including protecting blacks from the consequences of seniority systems. These justices contend that although racial classification designed for remedial purposes should be subject to a more rigorous review than the rational-basis standard, such remedial uses of race should *not* be required to meet the strict scrutiny test of a compelling public need. For these justices, the proper inquiry is whether such remedial classifications "serve important government objectives, are substantially related to the achievement of those objectives [the same test the Court uses for sex-based classifications], and do not stigmatize any group or single out those least well represented in the political process to bear the brunt of a beginning program."[79] They also distinguish classifications that create a preference for blacks and other minorities from those that create preferences for whites. The former are permissible some of the time; the latter are forbidden most, if not all, of the time. Whites, unlike blacks and other minorities, do not have the "traditional indicia" of a suspect class. They have not been systematically subjected to discrimination because of race or deliberately put into positions of political powerlessness.

In his *Bakke* opinion Justice Marshall, after stressing the fact that the very purpose of the Fourteenth Amendment was to protect blacks, wrote: "While I applaud the judgment of the Court that a university may consider race in its admissions process, it is more than a little ironic that, after several hundred years of race-based discrimination against Negroes, the Court is unwilling to hold that a race-based remedy for the discrimination is permissible." In *Fullilove*, he wrote: "By upholding this race-conscious remedy [the 10 percent minority set-aside], the Court accords Congress the authority necessary to undertake the task of moving our society toward a state of meaningful equality of opportunity, not an abstract version of equality in which the effects of past discrimination be frozen into our social fabric." Justice Blackmun in his *Bakke* concurrence was somewhat less enthusiastic: "I yield to no one in my earnest hope that the time will come when an affirmative action program is unnecessary and is, in truth, a relic of the past . . . [But] in order to get beyond racism, we must first take account of race. There is no other way."

Justice Rehnquist (Justice Stevens is less clear on this point) has stood by the more traditional view first espoused by the first Justice Harlan dissenting in *Plessy* v. *Ferguson* that the Constitution is color-blind. Justice Rehnquist agrees with Justice Stewart, who wrote, "So far as the Constitution goes, a private person may engage in any racial discrimination he wants, but . . . a sovereign State may never do so. And it is wholly irrelevant whether the State gives a 'plus' or 'minus' value to a person's race . . . or whether the discrimination is called 'affirmative action' or by some less euphemistic term . . . Two wrongs simply make two wrongs."[80]

Where does all this Supreme Court decision-making leave us with respect to race? The Court still firmly adheres "to the traditional view that racial classifications that stigmatize—because they are drawn on the presumption that one race is inferior to another or because they put the weight of government behind racial hatred and separatism"—are not only suspect, but outlawed.[81] A majority still adhere to the view that all practices and all programs that classify people by race or ethnic origin are suspect and should be subject to strict judicial scrutiny. However, where a race-conscious remedy is carefully created to help minorities overcome present effects of past discrimination, it may be constitutionally permissible, especially if the remedy has been adopted by Congress.

This bring us to alienage. The decisions regarding state laws relating to aliens "have not formed an unswerving line."[82] So far as the states are concerned, "restrictions on lawfully resident aliens primarily affecting economic interests are subject to heightened judicial scrutiny," but such "strict scrutiny is out of place when the restriction primarily serves a political function. . . . Some state functions are so bound up with the operation of the State as a governmental entity as to permit the exclusion from those functions of all persons who have not become part of the process of self-government."[83] In other words, some state laws regulating aliens are subject to strict scrutiny, some are not.

The Court has declared unconstitutional laws imposing a blanket prohibition against all public employment of aliens, forbidding them to practice law or civil engineering, denying them financial assistance for higher education, and depriving them of the right to serve as a notary public.[84] Yet despite the fact that it has recently said the political exception is to be narrowly construed, it has been used to uphold state regulations excluding aliens from serving as state police officers, probation officers, and public school teachers, as well as keeping aliens from voting, serving on juries, and for fulfilling "important nonelective executive, legislative, and judicial positions."[85]

In 1982 Justice Brennan, speaking for the Court, ignored the whole question of whether lawfully admitted aliens should be treated as a suspect classification and, resorting to federal supremacy principles, set aside a practice of the University of Maryland charging nonimmigrant aliens (children of diplomats and those who work for international associations) out-of-state tuition. Said the Court, "state regulation not congressionally sanctioned that discriminates against aliens lawfully admitted to the country is impermissible if it imposes additional burdens not contemplated by Congress."[86] In his dissenting opinion, in which the Chief Justice joined, Justice Rehnquist argued there is reason to doubt whether political powerlessness is any longer a legitimate reason for treating aliens as a "suspect classification" deserving of "heightened judicial solicitude."[87]

Then in 1984, (*Beranal v. Fainter*) after appearing to have been wavering on the issue, the Court, in an opinion in which every justice except Rehnquist joined, reaffirmed in rather strong language that so far as state regulations of aliens is concerned, they are to remain a suspect classification other than for the "political function" exception, and that exception is to be narrowly construed: "otherwise the exception will swallow the rule and depreciate the significant that should attach to the designation of a group as a 'discrete and insular' minority for whom heightened judicial solicitude is appropriate."[88]

Illegitimacy, once thought to be subject to upper tier analysis as a suspect classification, is now being reviewed in terms of the intermediate test. Classifications based on illegitimacy are no longer considered suspect and thus subject to the Court's most exacting scrutiny. However, "In view of the history of treating illegitimate children less favorably than legitimate ones," the Court has "subjected statutory classifications based on illegitimacy to its heightened intermediate test." The scrutiny applied to them is not a toothless one." A classification based on illegitimacy is unconstitutional unless it bears an evident and substantial relation to the particular . . . interests [the] statute is designed to serve."[89] Since 1968 the Supreme Court has reviewed more than fourteen laws alleged to discriminate against illegitimate children and has struck down most of them, including laws that prevented illegitimate children from suing to recover for the wrongful death of a parent, from receiving benefits under workers' compensation, from suing a father for child support, from securing benefits under various welfare programs, from inheriting only from their mother but not from their fathers, or from having only two years in which a paternity suit could be filed in their behalf.[90]

As to classifications based on wealth, poverty standing alone is not a suspect classification. Laws that adversely affect the poor are not necessarily subject to any especially heightened scrutiny. For example, Medicaid coverage—governmental assistance for medical care for those unable to pay for it—can be limited to exclude payment for abortions except when necessary to save the life of the woman.[91] A state has no constitutional duty to see to it that those living in school districts where most are poor have the same funds for their schools as are available to persons living in districts where many of the people are well to do.[92]

Poverty, however, is not always without signficance as far as equal protection analysis is concerned. Laws that prevent the absolutely destitute, rather than those who are merely poor, from being able to enjoy some legal benefits because of their poverty—have received close judicial scrutiny and have been declared unconstitutional (see below).[93] And although the right to run for office is not a "fundamental right," the Court has been especially suspicious of filing-fee provisions that may make it difficult for those without funds to run for office since "economic status is not a measure of a prospective candidate's qualifications to hold elective office, and a filing fee alone is an inadequate test of whether a candidacy is serious or spurious."[94]

The equal protection clause, often mixed with due process considerations, also provides some protection for the poor in courtroom situations. In addition to forbidding discrimination in the administration of justice, the clause imposes on states a limited positive obligation to see to it that the poor have equal treatment with those who can afford proper legal counsel, investigators, appeals, and so on. If a state makes a transcript a requirement for an appeal, it must furnish transcripts to those unable to afford them.[95] As mentioned earlier, for the one appeal each state provides as a matter of right, it must provide indigents with attorneys to help them carry their appeal to the next higher court; the state does not, however, have to provide an attorney at public expense for discretionary appeals, including those to the United States Supreme Court.[96]

Although defendants' poverty in no way immunizes them from punishment, "a state cannot force into jail those who cannot pay fines or it cannot revoke probation because of failure to pay a fine or restitution upon which probation had been conditioned." A state may imprison someone for willfully refusing to pay court costs or a fine, or failing to make a genuine effort to get a job or borrow the money to pay the fine; it cannot imprison a person solely because he or she lacks the resources to pay.[97]

In contrast to criminal prosecutions, where the state "hails a defendant into court," states have less of an equal protection and due process obligation to provide the poor with equal access to the civil courts. Yet even here there are some constitutional requirements. A state may not, for example, deny access to its courts to those unable to pay filing fees for a divorce. The right to marry and to get a divorce are basic rights, and the state has a monopoly in regulating the marital relationship: to deny the poor access to the courts means in effect they cannot get a divorce.[98] In contrast, the United States may deny access to its courts to persons unable to pay a small filing fee for a bankruptcy petition. There is no constitutional right to be absolved of one's debts, and there are ways of handling debts other than becoming a legal bankrupt. As Justice Stewart said in dissent, "Some of the poor are too poor even to go bankrupt."[99] A state may also collect a general filing fee from those wishing to appeal decisions of welfare agencies.[100] And although the precise grounds were denial of due process, the equal protection aspect was paramount when the Supreme Court ruled that a state must pay for a blood grouping test for a person involved in a paternity suit who lacked the funds to do so.[101]

The equal protection clause also prohibits states from imposing poll taxes as a condition of eligibility to vote; this is apart from the prohibition contained in the Twenty-fourth Amendment. Even if there is no evidence that a poll tax might discriminate against blacks or the poor, it establishes an unreasonable classification based on wealth. "Wealth, like, race, creed, or color, is not germane to one's ability to participate intelligently in the electoral process."[102]

Age is not a suspect classification. Although Congress has started to make some age classifications illegal, the Court has never struck down a law because of an unconstitutional age classification. On the contrary, it has sustained a law of Massachusetts disqualifying persons from being state police officers after age fifty, and an act of Congress making retirement from the Foreign Service compulsory at age sixty.[103]

Mentally ill persons, according to some of the lower federal courts, should be considered a suspect classification. The mentally ill, they argue, "historically have been subjected to purposeful and unequal treatment; they have been relegated to a position of political powerlessness; and prejudice against them curtails their participation in the pluralist system and strips them of political protection against discriminatory legislation."[104] But so far the Supreme Court has side-stepped the issue.

What of classifications based on sex? The Supreme Court has vacillated. It was as late as 1971 before any classification based on sex was declared to violate the equal protection clause. Prior to that time, state laws excluding or restricting women's participation on juries had been sustained, as well as many laws purporting to provide special protection for women, such as one in Ohio forbidding any woman other than a wife or daughters of a tavern owner to serve as barmaid.[105] (Since the adoption of the Civil Rights Act of 1964, such laws or regulations of companies affecting interstate commerce that discriminate against persons because of sex are illegal, for example, a company regulation denying employment to women with preschool-age children but not to men with such children.)[106]

The first time the Supreme Court ever declared a state law unconstitutional because of discrimination based on sex was in the fall of 1971, when a unanimous Court in *Reed* v. *Reed* stated that the arbitrary preference Idaho gave to fathers over mothers in the administration of their children's estates "cannot stand in the face of the Fourteenth Amendment's command."[107] Then a year later, in *Frontiero* v. *Richardson,* the Court invalidated a federal law that permitted a serviceman to claim as his dependent his wife but allowed a servicewoman to claim her husband as a dependent only if in fact he was dependent on her for over half of his support. Justice Brennan wrote for a plurality that "there can be no doubt that our Nation has had a long and unfortunate history of sex discrimination. Traditionally, such discrimination was rationalized by an attitude of 'romantic paternalism' which, in practical effect, put women not on a pedestal, but in a cage."[108]

Since then the following sex-based distinctions have been declared unconstitutional: a law specifying that males are entitled to child support from their father until they are twenty-one but females only until they are eighteen;[109] laws imposing different rules for jury service for women than for men;[110] social security regulations giving widows more benefits than widowers;[111] a state law prohibiting the sale of beer to males under twenty-one but to females under eighteen;[112] laws giving husbands exclusive rights to dispose of community property owned jointly with wives,[113] laws making women eligible for alimony but not men;[114] laws giving unwed mothers, but not unwed fathers, the right to consent to the adoption of their children;[115] social security provisions providing aid to children with unemployed fathers but not to those with unemployed mothers;[116] workers' compensation laws giving widows death benefits but widowers only if they could prove they were incapacitated or otherwise dependent upon their wives' earnings;[117] the policy of the Mississippi University for Women limiting enrollment to women in its school of Nursing (as well as all its other schools).[118] Nor may the government, including members of Congress discriminate because of sex in the selection of public employees.[119] (Note, a good many of the laws were struck down because they discriminated against men.)

On the other side, the Court has sustained some sex-based distinctions, and it is likely to continue to do so, especially since the failure to ratify the Equal Rights Amendment. Here are some examples. A Florida law granting a $500 exemption from the state property tax to widows but not to widowers. "There can be no dispute that the financial difficulties confronting the lone woman in Florida or in any other State exceed those facing the man." The dissenters pointed out that there are such things as rich widows and poor widowers and argued that the need for the exemption would not appear to be related to one's sex.[120] A regulation was upheld permitting male naval officers only nine years in which either to be promoted or to be discharged while providing thirteen years for women because women have less opportunity within the naval service for promotion.[121] A social security regulation was sustained giving women but not men the right to eliminate some low-earning years from the calculation of their retirement benefits in order to compensate them for past economic discrimination.[122] Congress may give preferential admission to the country to alien mothers but not to alien fathers of illegitimate children.[123] A state may treat fathers of illegitimate children differently than mothers of such children, for example, requiring that mothers must always be notified prior to the adoption proceedings of their children, but only notifying those fathers who have shouldered some responsibility or acknowledged their responsibility for their children.[124] The Court sustained California's disability system for private employers, which excluded from benefit coverage the medical costs growing out of normal pregnancy, the majority arguing there was no sex discrimination in such a scheme since benefits under the program paid to women were as great as, in fact greater than, those paid to men.[125] (Congress changed the law to reverse the impact of this decision.) A narrowly divided Court sustained the conviction by California of a seventeen-year-old male for statutory rape of a sixteen-year-old female under a law that makes it a crime for a male to have intercourse with a female under eighteen, but not for a female to have intercourse with an under-age male. The Court majority argued that such a law was not based on archaic assumptions about the proper role of the sexes, but upon a legitimate state interest in avoiding teen-age pregnancies, and since only women can become pregnant, men and women are not similarly situated with respect to the risks associated with pregnancy. The minority argued that the law discriminated against men and the state could have accomplished its objectives just as well with a gender-neutral law making it a crime for both teenage men and women to engage in sex.[126]

Veterans' preference laws have also been sustained despite the fact that such laws adversely effect women. The Supreme Court upheld a Massachusetts law giving veterans a lifetime preference in public employment because the law reflects no purpose to discriminate against women, but designed to favor those who have served in the armed forces, male and female.[127] And as we have noted, the Court upheld the power of Congress to order the registration of males and not of females for potential military conscription largely on the grounds that only men could be assigned to combat duty. "This is not a case," wrote Justice Rehnquist for the majority, "of Congress arbitrarily choosing to burden one of two similarly situated groups, such as would be the case with an all-black or all-white, or an all-Catholic or all-Lutheran, or an all-Republican or all-Democratic registration. Men and women, because of the combat restrictions on women, are simply not similarly situated for purposes of a draft or registration for a draft." The dissenters did not challenge the exclusion of women from combat posts, but charge the Court with placing its "imprimatur on one of the most potent remaining public expressions of 'ancient canards about the proper role of women' by categorically excluding women from a fundamental civic obligation." The armed forces, they argue, need many people beyond those given combat assignments. Women are presently serving with great glory and honor in the armed forces, and should not be excluded from the obligation to register, which can be divorced from conscription, since the purpose of the registration requirement is "to provide an inventory of what the available strength is within the military qualified pool in this country."[128]

To summarize with respect to classifications based on sex: They are not subject to as severe scrutiny as those based on race, but to sustain a classification based on sex the burden is on the government to show that it serves "important governmental objectives," and is substantially related to the achievement of these objectives. Treatment of women differently than men (or vice versa) is forbidden when supported by no more substantial justification than "archaic and overboard generalizations," "old notions," and "the role-typing society has long imposed upon women."[129]

What may not be forbidden by the Constitution, however, may be illegal. Congress has used its powers to make sex-based distinctions illegal in many areas of employment and education. For example, a state may not under the terms of the Civil Rights Act of 1964, Title VII, require that prison guards be over 5 feet 2 inches tall and weigh more than 120 pounds, because the impact of such a law discriminates against women. (On the other hand, the practice of denying women the right to be prison guards in all-male, maximum-security-type institutions is not illegal.)[130] Similarly, the Civil Rights Act makes illegal the practice of the Los Angeles Department of Water and Power of charging women more than men for pension benefits.[131] Although women live longer than men, the statute makes it unlawful to discriminate against any individual because of such individual's race, color, religion, sex, or national origin and precludes such treatment of an individual woman different from a man even though, "Unless women as a class are assessed on extra charge, they will be subsidized, to some extent, by the class of male employees."[132]

In his *Bakke* opinion Justice Powell suggested that preferential programs designed to assist women offer fewer constitutional obstacles than those "premised on racial or ethnic criteria." With respect to gender he wrote, "there are only two possible classifications. The incidence of the burdens imposed by preferential classification is clear. There are no rival groups who can claim that they, too, are entitled to preferential treatment. Classwide questions as to the group suffering previous injury and groups which fairly can be burdened are relatively manageable for reviewing courts."[133]

Recent judicial constructions of the equal protection clause are instructive in showing how judges move from the simple to the complex. As they are presented with new applications of old rules, they proceed to make more and more refined distinctions until the picture becomes so confused and complicated that the judges try to rationalize past decisions and again provide more simplified guidelines. We started with an interpretation of the equal protection clause based on one test—the rational basis test. Then the judges added the more stringent requirement—the overriding public purpose test. Then they came up with a test to be applied in some instances that is less rigid than the overriding public purpose test, but more demanding than the rational basis test—"substantially related to important governmental objectives." And now there is a tendency to break into two the rational basis test, one when the legislature clearly states the purposes it wants to achieve and another when it does not. Perhaps the next step will be a completely new restructuring and new guidelines.

To summarize, the Supreme Court has been using the equal protection clause, and its multi-tiered analysis, to differentiate among various kinds of state laws and to subject these laws to varying degrees of scrutiny. Critics of these newer, and more rigid, equal protection tests contend that all they amount to is that the judges are substituting their own policy judgments for those of the legislatures. Justice Rehnquist, for example, has written in dissent, "This Court seems to regard the equal protection clause as a cat-of-nine-tails to be kept in the judicial closet as a threat to legislatures which may in view of the judiciary get out of hand in passing arbitrary, illogical or unreasonable laws." "In enforcing the generalities of the Equal Protection Clause," he wrote, "judges are in the position of Adam in the Garden of Eden," and the Court's decisions can be described as "endless tinkering with legislative judgments in a series of conclusions unsupported by any central guiding principles."[134] From the opposite side of the Court, Justice Marshall is also no fan of the "intellectually disingenuous 'two-tier' equal protection analysis."[135] He believes it does not describe the more subtle analysis that the Court should undertake. And from what might be called the middle of the Court, Justice Blackmun has expressed his "unrelieved discomfort with what seems to be a continuing tendency in this Court to use as tests such easy phrases as 'compelling state interest' and 'least drastic means'. . . . I have never been able fully to appreciate just what a compelling state interest is. If it means 'convincingly controlling,' or 'incapable of being overcome upon any balancing process,' then of course, the test merely announces an inevitable result, and the test is no test at all. And, for me, 'least drastic means' is a slippery slope and also the signal of the result the Court has chosen to reach. A judge would be unimaginative indeed if he could not come up with something a little less 'drastic' or less 'restrictive' in almost any situation, and thereby enable himself to vote to strike legislation down. This is reminiscent of the Court's indulgence, a few decades ago, in substantive due process in the economic areas as a means of nullification. I feel, therefore, and have always felt, that these phrases are really not very helpful for constitutional analysis. They are too convenient and result oriented, and I must endeavor to disassociate myself from them."[136]

The equal protection clause also protects access to the ballot and voting power. Except where the Constitution provides otherwise, as it does with respect to apportionment of presidential electors and senators among the states, the equal protection clause prohibits most electoral schemes that give one person's vote more weight than another. Thus Georgia's county unit system for counting votes of governors had to go because it gave rural voters a much greater voice in the selection of statewide executive officers than voters living in cities.[137] An Illinois law suffered the same fate because it gave more weight to rural than to urban signatories on petitions to secure a place on statewide ballots by requiring that of the 25,000 signatures needed at least 200 must come from each of 50 of the state's 102 counties.[138] But certain special purpose units of government, such as water control or irrigation districts, that perform limited functions affecting definable groups have been permitted to distribute votes according to the value of the land owned,[139] and the one person-one vote principle does not apply to the selection of judges.[140]

As previously noted, the Supreme Court has applied the equal protection clause to insist that state legislatures be apportioned on the basis of population.[141] In the forty-nine two-chambered state legislatures (Nebraska has only one chamber), the membership of both chambers must be based on population.[142] The requirement of equal population districts also covers all local government units that exercise legislative functions such as county commissions[143] and junior college districts.[144] Local units do not, however, have to meet such precisely mathematically equal standards as those required for congressional districts, nor do state legislatures have to meet the same rigid standards for their own districts as they are required to meet when laying out congressional districts.[145] A somewhat parenthetical note: Although it is the legislature's duty to reapportion, if it fails to do so the task may fall to a federal judge. If so and if the federal court develops a reapportionment plan, the Supreme Court has instructed the judges to avoid multimember districts and has told them that they are obliged to achieve more population equality among districts than might be required if the legislature had proposed the reapportionment plan.[146]

All of the preceding discussion has related to discrimination imposed by the action of a government. Although discrimination by private individuals may violate a law, such action does not violate the equal protection clause or, as we have seen (page 192), the due process clause unless it is aid-supported or positively encouraged by state action. Thus, one of the more important issues growing out of the equal protection and due process clauses is what is and what is not "state action."

The Supreme Court inspects closely whenever there is suspicion of state involvement in discriminatory conduct. For certain traditional sovereign functions exclusively reserved to governments, the Fourteenth Amendment applies regardless of who actually does the discriminating. Thus, if a state delegates responsibility for running elections, including primaries, to private associations such as political parties, the action of party officers is state action subject to constitutional restraint.[147] Similarly, if a state allows a private corporation to perform the municipal functions of running a company town, the action of company officials is state action.[148]

On the other side, the management of a private shopping center is not state action, nor is the action of a private warehouse operator, or a private utility, even though its franchise is given to it by a state.[149] A private school that specializes in dealing with students who have experienced difficulty completing public high schools because of behavior problems does not become subject either to the Fourteenth Amendment or to Section 1983—a provision permitting persons to sue public officials for depriving them of a constitutional right or a right secured by federal law—for purposes of determining whether it dismissed employees in violation of their First Amendment rights, even though its income is derived primarily from public sources and is regulated by public authorities. Providing an education, unlike holding elections, is not a function that has traditionally been "the *exclusive* prerogative of the State.[150] Congress has by law subjected such schools to equal protection like restraints. They cannot discriminate in their programs or employment practices because of race, and if they are organized as non-profit institutions they may lose certain tax advantages.

Covenants placed in deeds restricting the use of property to persons of particular races or religions by themselves are not state action (although they may violate federal and state laws), but no court or any other public official may help to enforce such covenants.[151] The receiving from the state of a liquor license does not make the discriminatory action of a private club state action,[152] but when a state leased space to a restaurant in a building designed to provide public parking, the action of the restaurant was no longer considered "purely private" and became subject to equal protection limitations.[153]

Sometimes when a state does nothing, or tries to do nothing, it may still be supporting, encouraging, or abetting discriminatory conduct. The mere repeal of race-related legislation or policies not required in the first place by the Constitution is not necessarily unconstitutional, but it may be. Take, for example, California's action when it adopted a constitutional amendment that repealed previously existing legislation forbidding racial discrimination in the private sale of houses and made such legislation unenforceable. It was argued that no state action was involved when individuals refused to sell property to blacks. But the Court concluded that when California amended its Constitution, it was not being neutral. Rather it was encouraging discrimination by making it more difficult for blacks than for whites to buy homes. This was state action forbidden by the Constitution.[154] And, as we have noted, Washington was ruled to have acted unconstitutionally when it took from school boards the power to order mandatory busing to overcome racial imbalance resulting from housing segregation (see page 236). In this instance Washington had allocated power in such a way as to impose a burden on the ability of blacks to enact legislation specifically designed to overcome prejudice and discrimination.[155] On the other hand, as we have also noted, California was ruled to have acted constitutionally neutral, when it repealed legislation encouraging judges to order busing and forbade them from doing so unless required to do so by the U.S. Constitution (see page 236).[156]

A closely divided Court found no violation by the state of the equal protection clause when a city closed its public swimming pools after being ordered by a court to operate them on a desegregated basis. Five members note that a city has no obligation to operate swimming pools, but only to make them available without respect to race if it does so. Four members argued that the city in closing the pools had used the power of the government to support and maintain segregation of the races as a way of life.[157]

In summary, "While the principle that private action is immune from the restrictions of the Fourteenth Amendment is well established and easily stated, the question whether particular conduct is 'private,' on the one hand, or 'state action' on the other, frequently admits of no easy answer."[158]

The conflict over whether a particular act is strictly that of a private individual, or is that of the state, at times shades into tension between the constitutionally protected rights of association and privacy on one side, and the rights to equal protection of the law on the other. Take the problem presented by the practices of Montgomery, Alabama. After it had been ordered in 1959 to desegregate its public parks, it first tried to avoid the impact of this ruling by turning control of the parks over to the local YMCA. Ten years later this was ruled to be state action and declared unconstitutional. Then the plaintiffs in the original action complained that the city was continuing to evade the decree by turning park facilities over to racially segregated schools and other segregated groups. The Supreme Court had no difficulty in concluding that to turn such facilities over to the exclusive use of a private group that discriminates is state action and violates the Constitution. However, if the city were merely to make its parks available to all comers without condition or reservation, it would not violate the Constitution to let groups that segregated use the facilities. In fact, the Court warned, "The exclusion of any person or group—all Negro, all oriental, or all white—from public facilities infringes upon the freedom of the individual to associate as he chooses. A person's membership in an organization that discriminates would not alone be grounds for his exclusion from public facilities."[159]

The Constitution precludes "government from interfering with private clubs or groups. The associational rights which our system honors permit all white, all black, all brown, and all yellow clubs to be established. Government may not tell a man or a woman who his or her associates must be. The individual may be selective as he desires."[160] But individuals may not use the power of government to impose their prejudices on others. "Although the Constitution does not prescribe private bias, it places no value on discrimination. . . . Invidious private discrimination may be characterized as a form of exercising freedom protected by the First Amendment, but it has never been accorded affirmative constitutional protections."[161]

While the right to discriminate in purely private matters is constitutionally protected, there is no constitutionally protected right to discriminate in public dealings with other persons. And what may not be a state action, and not forbidden by the Constitution, nonetheless today is often contrary to law. Thus an important question becomes, where is the line to be drawn between private associative behavior which however discriminatory is constitutionally protected and beyond government regulation, and public associative behavior which can be regulated by the state. As we have noted in *Roberts* v. *Jaycees,* the Supreme Court upheld the application of Minnesota public accommodations law to the Jaycees. It indicated that the Jaycees' actions with respect to admitting members fell on the public rather than private side of the line.[162] The same is true of a law partnership with respect to admission of partners.[163] When groups, associations, or businesses open their doors and invite in the public they may be compelled by the state to stop discriminating.

On the other side are such associations as families, social clubs, churches, and for certain purposes even political associations that have some constitutionally protected right to discriminate for certain purposes—let us say in deciding whom they will marry, whom they will admit to their club, their church, or political group. (If, however, the political association is a major party and is given governmental functions such as running a primary election to nominate its candidates for public office, it cannot discriminate because of race, sex, religion, national origin, or money. See page 248).

In addition to many state laws forbidding discrimination in places of public accommodation, today there are federal laws. Owners of places of public accommodation in business impinging on interstate commerce—and most businesses do—may not discriminate against blacks; employers in business affecting interstate commerce may not discriminate against persons because of race, sex, national origin, religion, or handicap. Private schools are not covered by the Fourteenth Amendment, but if they open their doors to the public they may not deny admissions to persons because of race, for this violates the Civil Rights Acts of 1866 and 1870 forbidding private persons to discriminate because of race in the making of contracts.[164] And any school, public or private, which receives federal funds—and most do—is subject to all kinds of limitations forbidding it to treat people differently because of race or sex or handicap.

There is no equal protection clause limiting the national government; however, just as the due process clause of the Fourteenth Amendment has been used to apply provisions of the Bill of Rights to the states, so has the due process clause of the Fifth Amendment been used to prevent national discriminatory legislation. Hence segregation in the public schools in the District of Columbia and the use of national courts to enforce racially restrictive covenants are also unconstitutional.[165] And a requirement of the District of Columbia that one must reside there for a year to be eligible for public assistance was held to be so "unjustifiable a discrimination against poor people as to be violative of the due process clause."[166]

Section 2

Representatives shall be apportioned among the several States according to their respective numbers, counting the whole number of persons in each State, excluding Indians not taxed.

This section supersedes Article I, Section 2, paragraph 3. Slaves were originally counted at three-fifths the number of free persons.

Section 2

[continued] But when the right to vote at any election for the choice of electors for President and Vice President of the United States, Representatives in Congress, the Executive and Judicial officers of a State, or the members of the Legislature thereof, is denied to any of the male inhabitants of such State, being twenty-one years of age, and citizens of the United States, or in any way abridged, except for participation in rebellion, or other crime, the basis of representation therein shall be reduced in the proportion which the number of such male citizens shall bear to the whole number of male citizens twenty-one years of age in such State.

This provision has never been enforced by Congress, and may today be regarded as obsolete through disuse and, also, possibly, through obvious disharmony with the Nineteenth and Twenty-sixth Amendments. In one of the few times this provision has even been mentioned by the Supreme Court, it was cited in support of a decision that a state suffrage regulation denying the vote to ex-felons is constitutional.[167]

Section 3

No person shall be a Senator or Representative in Congress, or elector of President and Vice President, or hold any office, civil or military, under the United States, or under any State, who, having previously taken an oath, as a member of Congress, or as an officer of the United States, or as a member of any State legislature, or as an executive or judicial officer of any State, to support the Constitution of the United States, shall have engaged in insurrection or rebellion against the same, or given aid or comfort to the enemies thereof. But Congress may by a vote of two-thirds of each House, remove such disability.

This section politically disabled those who led the southern states into the Confederacy. It was placed in the Fourteenth Amendment by the radical Republicans and was a factor in their struggle with President Johnson. It limited the President's power to pardon the leaders of the Confederacy and thus restore their political and civil rights. Congress removed this disability on June 6, 1898.

Section 4

The validity of the public debt of the United States, authorized by law, including debts incurred for payment of pensions and bounties for services in suppressing insurrection or rebellion, shall not be questioned. But neither the United States nor any State shall assume or pay any debt or obligation incurred in aid of insurrection or rebellion against the United States, or any claim for the loss or emancipation of any slave; but all such debts, obligations and claims shall be held illegal and void.

This section invalidated all the securities and other evidences of debt of the Confederacy and reaffirmed those of the Union.

The Congress shall have power to enforce, by appropriate legislation, the provisions of this article.

In the *Civil Rights Cases* (1883), the Supreme Court restricted the power of Congress under this section to the prevention or correction of state (including local) government action that abridges the privileges or immunities of a United States citizen, that deprives any persons of life, liberty, or property without due process, or that denies them the equal protection of the laws. The Supreme Court held that since the Fourteenth Amendment forbids only *state* action, Section 5 did not authorize Congress to make it a federal crime for innkeepers and other proprietors of public places to deny accommodations to persons because of race. Congress could adopt legislation under Section 5 only to prevent state discrimination, not abridgement of civil rights by private groups or persons.[168]

In view of the Supreme Court's holdings in the *Civil Rights Cases,* Congress relied on the commerce clause when it adopted the Civil Rights Act of 1964, which forbids discrimination by employers and by operators of places of public accommodation. If Congress had chosen to base the 1964 Act more directly on Section 5, the present Supreme Court would very likely have sustained it.

Even without any liberalization of either Section 5 of the Fourteenth Amendment or Section 2 of the Thirteenth Amendment, Congress clearly has authority under Section 5 to regulate the conduct of private individuals, as well as those who act under the color of law, who attempt to keep persons from securing the benefits of the Fourteenth Amendment. For example, persons violate federal law if they threaten children in order to keep them from attending a desegregated public school or if they coerce other persons in order to keep them from entering a state park. Congress has started to use its powers under Section 5; it has, for example, authorized the Department of Justice to initiate suits in federal courts to prevent public officials or *private* persons from depriving persons of the right not to have a *state* deny them equal protection of the laws.[169]

In 1966, the Supreme Court gave Section 5 a most interesting new significance. The Court held that Section 5 authorizes Congress to do whatever it thinks is necessary and proper in order to enforce the rights guaranteed by the Fourteenth Amendment, even to the extent of superseding state regulations that are not themselves an unconstitutional denial of Fourteenth Amendment rights! This ruling came about in a challenge to a section of the Voting Rights Act of 1965 that stipulates that no person who has had a sixth-grade education under the American flag shall be denied the right to vote because he is not literate in English. This section was adopted to set aside a literacy requirement of New York that was keeping many American citizens from Puerto Rico from voting. Even though the New York law was constitutional, the Court majority held, Congress is empowered by Section 5 to use its own judgment in determining what legislation is needed to keep states from denying persons equal protection of the laws. Justices Harlan and Stewart dissented on the grounds that

Congress was exercising judicial power. So long as a state is not denying any person the equal protection of the laws and is operating within its constitutional sphere, according to the dissenting justices, Congress has no power to act under Section 5.[170]

In his separate opinion in *Bakke* Justice Powell significantly noted, "We are not here presented with an occasion to review legislation by Congress pursuant to its powers under Paragraph 2 of the Thirteenth Amendment and Paragraph 5 of the Fourteenth Amendment to remedy the effects of prior discrimination. . . . We have previously recognized the special competence of Congress to make findings with respect to the effects of identified past discrimination and its discretionary authority to take appropriate remedial measures."[171] This language, with the other comments in the other *Bakke* opinions, makes it quite clear that when Congress authorizes racial classifications to provide remedial programs for blacks and other ethnic minorities, such programs are on stronger constitutional foundations than are similar programs adopted by trustees of universities, or other agencies, not empowered by Section 5 of the Fourteenth Amendment "to enforce, by appropriate legislation, the provisions of this article."

Independently of Section 5, Congress has ample constitutional authority to protect persons in the exercise of rights flowing from federal laws and directly from the Constitution, regardless of the source of the threat to these rights. For example, the right to travel freely in interstate commerce, the right to the privileges flowing from federal labor laws and from federal civil rights actions, and the right to not have the badges of slavery imposed are rights Congress can secure against abridgment by private citizens as well as by public officials.[172]

Following Reconstruction, the Supreme Court so narrowly interpreted the civil right statutes Congress had adopted to protect the recently freed slaves that for decades they were of little use in protecting civil rights of blacks or anyone else. In recent years, however, these statutes have become a major basis for a variety of suits against state officials. The Civil Rights Act of 1871, now known as 42 USC 1983, makes any person acting under color of law or custom of any state who subjects any other person to the deprivation of any right, privileges, or immunities secured by the Constitution, personally liable for damages. This statute is being broadly construed by the Court to permit persons to bring actions against public officials, including judges for any violation of any right protected by the Constitution or federal laws, not just those that stem from the Fourteenth Amendment. These suits are now an important part of the business of federal courts, creating what Justice Rehnquist has characterized as "staggering effect . . . upon the workload of the federal courts." In addition to paying compensatory damages to those whose rights they have interfered with officers are subject to punitive damages—designed to punish the offending officer—whenever it is shown that they have been motivated by evil intent or have acted with reckless or callous indifference to the federally protected rights of others. (Judges may not be sued for damages, but can be enjoined from future acts and can be required to pay rather substantial attorney's fees.) Municipalities, but not states, may also be subject to damage suits under 1983 suits but are subject only to compensatory damages.[173]

AMENDMENT XV: THE RIGHT TO VOTE

Section 1

The right of the citizens of the United States to vote shall not be denied or abridged by the United States or by any State on account of race, color, or previous condition of servitude.

This amendment was proposed February 26, 1869, and declared in force by the Secretary of State March 30, 1870.

"The Fifteenth Amendment nullifies sophisticated as well as simple-minded modes of discrimination."[1] Yet, for many decades, white southerners in charge of registration and voting readily circumvented the Fifteenth Amendment. They had an arsenal of discriminatory schemes. But at the end of World War II, the Supreme Court declared unconstitutional the devices used to keep blacks from registering and voting. The first to go was the white primary. Under the pretense that there was no state action involved, blacks were kept from voting in the Democratic party primaries, in many areas the only elections that really mattered. But in *Smith* v. *Allwright* (1944), the Supreme Court said, "When primaries become a part of the machinery for choosing officials . . . the same tests to determine the character of discrimination . . . would be applied to the primary as are applied to the general election."[2] The discriminatory use of understanding and good-character tests was also enjoined.[3] The Constitution has been amended to forbid the requirement of a poll tax payment as a condition for voting for presidential electors or for congress members, and the Constitution has been construed by the Supreme Court to forbid the requirement of a poll tax payment as a condition for voting in any public election. In lawsuit after lawsuit, the federal courts struck down one discriminatory scheme after another.

A unanimous Court in 1982 reinvigorated a 1875 precedent (*Minor* v. *Happersett*)[4] and reaffirmed a 1973 ruling (*San Antonio School District* v. *Rodriguez*)[5] to the effect that "the Constitution 'does not confer the right of suffrage upon any one,'" and "the right to vote, per se, is not a constitutionally protected right."[6] This holding has little significance for the Fifteenth Amendment, but removes the right to vote from among the fundamental rights especially protected by the equal protection clause of the Fourteenth Amendment.

Section 2

The Congress shall have power to enforce this article by appropriate legislation.

Until the Voting Rights Act of 1965, Congress used its powers under Section 2 very little, and the little it did use them was only to open federal courts for legal action against discriminatory state practices. This case-by-case litigation was inadequate to combat widespread and persistent discrimination because of the inordinate amount of time and energy required to overcome the obstructionist tactics invariably encountered in these lawsuits. Even after a lawsuit was won, there was no assurance that blacks would be permitted to vote. So, in 1965, Congress, using its authority under this section to do whatever is necessary and proper to ensure that no state shall deprive any person of the right to vote because of race, adopted a new approach.

By the Voting Rights Act of 1965—three times extended and strengthened by Congress, once in 1970, again in 1975, and most recently in 1982—Congress set aside literacy tests everywhere. In those states and counties, mostly but not exclusively in the South, that have had a persistent history of violating the Fifteenth Amendment, the Act forbids governments from adopting voting or electoral procedures, regardless of intent, that result in the dilution of black voting power. It authorizes the Attorney General to send federal officials to observe elections and if necessary to enroll voters in those states and counties covered by the Act. In those areas, if local election officials turn away any voter federal examiners find entitled to vote, the examiners may secure an order from a federal district court impounding all ballots until all persons entitled to vote are allowed to do so. The Attorney General may also appoint poll watchers to ensure that the votes of all qualified persons are properly counted. Furthermore, in order to keep states from constantly changing voting requirements and registration procedures, in the covered areas all new voting laws or practices that affect the electoral process are not effective unless approved by the Attorney General or by the United States District Court for the District of Columbia. A voting district may "bail out" from the prior clearance requirements for electoral changes only if it proves to the District Court for the District of Columbia that it has had a clean voting rights record for the preceding ten years.

The Act also provides some other protections in areas that contain more than ten percent of voting-age citizens belonging to language minorities—persons of Spanish heritage, Asian Americans, American Indians, and Alaskan natives. In these areas, bilingual election materials must be provided.

The Act also provides that any otherwise qualified persons be allowed to vote for presidential electors even if they fail to meet a state's residency requirements, orders states to keep registration for presidential elections open until thirty days before the election, and lowers from twenty-one to eighteen the voting age in all elections.

In *South Carolina* v. *Katzenbach,* the Supreme Court sustained the main provision of the Voting Rights Act of 1965. The Chief Justice said, "Congress may use any rational means to effectuate the constitutional prohibition of racial discrimination in voting."[7] The Court has also upheld all provisions of the Act except the one lowering the voting age to eighteen in order to vote for state and local officials (the Twenty-sixth Amendment governs the age requirement for voting in all elections for all officials).[8]

The Voting Rights Act goes considerably beyond the protections provided by the Fifteenth Amendment. Although that Amendment covers more than just the act of voting, electoral arrangements beyond those relating directly to the act of voting that are neutral on their face are not violations of the Fifteenth Amendment, even if they dilute the voting power of blacks, unless they are motivated by a discriminatory *purpose*. What does not violate the Fifteenth Amendment may violate the Voting Rights Act. Although that Act does not guarantee "members of a protected class a right to have members . . . elected in numbers equal to their proportion in the population," it does make it illegal for governments, subject to its provisions, to adopt or maintain procedures, regardless of intent, if such procedures result in the dilution of black voting power. Where blacks make up a substantial proportion of the population, the fact that few or none of them get elected is part of the "totality of circumstances" judges must take into account to determine whether there has been a violation of the Act.

When the Attorney General or the District Court for the District of Columbia reviews proposed changes in the electoral practices or procedures of units covered by the Act, in order to set them aside they do not have to show that the purpose of the change is to discriminate against blacks. It is sufficient to show that, if adopted, the proposed change would result in the dilution of the voting influence of a protected class. Thus, the Attorney General refused to allow Rome, Georgia, to alter its system of electing city council members and school boards from wards to a system in which they would be elected at large. This rather drastic intrusion into local matters was justified by the Court on the grounds that the Fifteenth Amendment was specifically designed as an expansion of federal powers: It gives Congress authority to adopt legislation to enforce its provisions, even if such legislation overrides principles of federalism that might otherwise be an obstacle to congressional authority.[9]

The Voting Rights Act even makes it easier for states to do some things when they act in response to the promptings of that Act. In *United Jewish Organization* v. *Carey,* the Court ruled that a state acting under provisions of the Voting Rights Act may draw district lines for the state legislature to ensure blacks will be in a majority in certain voting districts. "Where a plan presents no racial slur or stigma with respect to whites or any other race and does not deprive whites as a group of 'fair representation' " it is constitutional despite the fact that as a consequence of the plan, a Hasidic Jewish community was split into two voting districts and thereby had its voting strength diluted.[10]

As a result of the Voting Rights Act of 1965 and its amendments, for the first time in a hundred years the Fifteenth Amendment became an operating reality throughout the nation. By 1984 there were over 5000 blacks holding national, state, and local offices.

TWENTIETH-CENTURY AMENDMENTS
AMENDMENT XVI: INCOME TAXES

The Congress shall have the power to lay and collect taxes on incomes, from whatever source derived, without apportionment among the several States, and without regard to any census or enumeration.

This amendment was proposed July 12, 1909, and declared in force by the Secretary of State February 25, 1913.

During the Civil War, an income tax was levied as part of the war financing program. As was generally expected, the Supreme Court upheld the national government's right to levy such a tax. In 1894, the Wilson-Gorham Tariff levied a 2 percent tax on incomes over $4,000. The year following, after hearing the tax assailed as the opening wedge of "populism," "communism," and the like, the Supreme Court held, by a five-to-four decision, that a tax on income from property was tantamount to a tax on the property itself and hence a "direct tax" that had to be apportioned among the several states according to population (see Article I, Section 2, paragraph 3).[1] The levying of an income tax was thus rendered impracticable until the adoption of the Sixteenth Amendment in 1913.

AMENDMENT XVII: DIRECT ELECTION OF SENATORS

1. The Senate of the United States shall be composed of two Senators from each State, elected by the people thereof for six years; and each Senator shall have one vote. The electors in each State shall have the qualifications requisite for electors of the most numerous brand of the State legislatures.

This amendment was proposed May 13, 1912, and declared in force by the Secretary of State May 31, 1913.

The adoption of universal suffrage and the growing strength of the democratic spirit made it inevitable that United States senators should be chosen directly by the people. During the last half of the nineteenth century, dissident labor and farmer parties had called for direct election. The revelation of certain senators' great wealth and of their obligations to various large economic interests reinforced these demands. By the turn of the century, all the major parties supported proposals for direct election; the House of Representatives several times passed resolutions proposing an amendment to make the change. Finally, in 1912 the Senate capitulated. As a matter of fact, by that date the voters in half of the states had obtained the right to indicate their preference for senator in the party primaries; the state legislatures normally followed the wishes of the voters. The adoption of the Seventeenth Amendment merely rounded out a reform that had been long under way.

2. When vacancies happen in the representation of any State in the Senate, the executive authority of such State shall issue writs of election to fill such vacancies: Provided, That the legislature of any State may empower the executive thereof to make temporary appointments until the people fill the vacancies by election as the legislature may direct.

Most vacancies are filled by temporary appointments.

3. This amendment shall not be so construed as to affect the election or term of any Senator chosen before it becomes valid as part of the Constitution.

AMENDMENT XVIII: PROHIBITION

Section 1

After one year from the ratification of this article the manufacture, sale, or transportation of intoxicating liquors within, the importation thereof into, or the

exportation thereof from the United States and all territory subject to the jurisdiction thereof for beverage purposes is hereby prohibited.

This amendment was proposed December 18, 1917, and declared in force by the Acting Secretary of State January 29, 1919.

There have always been those who have have waged war upon demon rum As long ago as 1842 the state of Maine went dry, and the Prohibition Party has had a candidate on the ballot in at least a few states in every presidential election since 1872. But it was the Anti-Saloon League—a pressure group deluxe, formed in 1895—that gave the prohibition movement its greatest impetus. During World War I, the necessity of saving grain lent prohibition a guise of patriotism. Although the Eighteenth Amendment was ultimately ratified by all the states except Rhode Island and Connecticut, it always lacked the support of large groups of citizens, especially in the large cities. Bootlegging, lax enforcement, and general disregard for the amendment impaired respect for the entire Constitution. The "noble experiment," as it was called, demonstrated that it is almost impossible to regulate personal conduct by legal machinery when the law is contrary to the mores of large sections of the country. National prohibition was finally repealed in 1933 by the Twenty-first Amendment.

Section 2

The Congress and the several States shall have concurrent power to enforce this article by appropriate legislation.

The Volstead Act went into effect January 17, 1920. By 1929, three states *repealed* their enforcement acts; most states left it to the national government to implement this amendment.

Section 3

This article shall be inoperative unless it shall have been ratified as an amendment to the Constitution by the legislatures of the several States, as provided in the Constitution, within seven years from the date of the submission hereof to the States by the Congress.

AMENDMENT XIX: WOMAN SUFFRAGE

---

1. The right of citizens of the United States to vote shall not be denied or abridged by the United States or by any State on account of sex.

The Nineteenth Amendment was proposed June 4, 1919, and declared in force by the Secretary of State August 26, 1920.

This amendment was the culmination of a struggle that began in the 1840s. In 1890, women were admitted to full suffrage rights in Wyoming; by the time the amendment was adopted, fifteen states and Alaska had given them full suffrage, fourteen states had given them "presidential suffrage," and two states had given them the right to take part in the primaries. Many of the arguments advanced against women suffrage were ludicrous. Much of the opposition came from certain business groups (especially the liquor industry) who feared that women would vote for regulation.

---

2. Congress shall have power to enforce this article by appropriate legislation.

AMENDMENT XX: THE LAME-DUCK AMENDMENT

Section 1

The terms of the President and Vice President shall end at noon on the 20th day of January, and the terms of Senators and Representatives at noon on the 3d day of January, of the years in which such terms would have ended if this article had not been ratified; and the terms of their successors shall then begin.

This amendment was proposed March 3, 1932, and declared in force by the Secretary of State February 6, 1933.

This amendment was eventually ratified by all the states. Senator George W. Norris of Nebraska was the moving force behind the amendment, which sometimes bears his name. Its adoption brought to a close the Progressive Movement's contribution to constitutional reform, a movement that led to the Sixteenth through the Twentieth Amendments.

Before the adoption of the Twentieth Amendment, the President and congress members elected in November did not take office until the following March, and newly elected congress members did not (unless called into special session) actually begin their work until the following December—thirteen months after their election. Meanwhile, congress members defeated in the November election ("lame ducks") continued to serve until the following March 4 and, although repudiated at the polls, continued to represent their constituencies in the December-to-March session.

Section 2

The Congress shall assemble at least once in every year, and such meeting shall begin at noon on the 3d day of January, unless they shall by law appoint a different day.

This section supersedes Article I, Section 4, paragraph 2, which called for Congress to meet on the first Monday in December and so necessitated every other year a short, ineffective, December-to-March, "lame-duck" session. The Twentieth Amendment does away with this session, which was frequently marked in the Senate by filibusters.

Normally Congress meets on the constitutionally designated January 3 but in 1975 Congress exercised its option and convened the 94th Congress on January 14.

Section 3

If, at the time fixed for the beginning of the term of the President, the President elect shall have died, the Vice President elect shall become President. If a President shall not have been chosen before the time fixed for the beginning of his term, or if the President elect shall have failed to qualify, then the Vice President elect shall act as President until a President shall have qualified; and the Congress may by law provide for the case wherein neither a President elect nor a Vice President elect shall have qualified, declaring who shall then act as President, or the manner in which one who is to act shall be selected, and such person shall act accordingly until a President or Vice President shall have qualified.

It should be noted that within the meaning of the Constitution there is no President-elect or Vice-President-elect until the electoral votes have been counted by Congress or, in the event that no person has a majority of the electoral votes, until the House of Representatives and the Senate make their choice.

Congress has now made the same provision for succession in the event of the disability of disqualification of the President-elect and Vice-President-elect as in the case of the President and Vice-President (see page 266).

Section 4

The Congress may by law provide for the case of the death of any of the persons from whom the House of Representatives may choose a President whenever the right of choice shall have devolved upon them, and for the case of the death of any of the persons from whom the Senate may choose a Vice President whenever the right of choice shall have devolved upon them.

Congress has failed to act under this section, but see the Twenty-fifth Amendment.

Section 5

Sections 1 and 2 shall take effect on the 15th day of October following the ratification of this article.

Section 6

This article shall be inoperative unless it shall have been ratified as an amendment to the Constitution by the legislatures of three-fourths of the several States within seven years from the date of its submission.

AMENDMENT XXI: REPEAL OF PROHIBITION

Section 1

The eighteenth article of amendment to the Constitution of the United States is hereby repealed.

This amendment was proposed February 20, 1933, and declared in force by the Secretary of State December 5, 1933.

It soon became apparent that the Eighteenth Amendment failed to diminish the amount of liquor consumed; instead, it diverted taxes and profits from legitimate interests into the hands of bootleggers and criminals and was endangering respect for the Constitution and the laws of the land. The demand for repeal became insistent. In 1928, Alfred Smith, the Democratic candidate for President, advocated repeal; by 1932, the platforms of both major parties were, in the phrase of the day, "dripping wet."

Section 2

The transportation or importation into any State, Territory, or possession of the United States for delivery or use therein of intoxicating liquors, in violation of the laws thereof, is hereby prohibited.

This section gives states greater authority to regulate intoxicating beverages than any other item of interstate commerce. States may impose restrictions on the transportation or importation of intoxicating liquors and regulate their distribution or sale in ways that would be an unconstitutional interference with commerce among the states for any other commodity. Nonetheless state regulations may be set aside by Congress under the commerce clause and must be "reasonable" in the judgment of the Supreme Court. For example, in 1964, the Court set aside a Kentucky tax on each gallon of whiskey imported from Scotland as a violation of the export-import clause. Justice Black, in dissent, quipped, "Although I was brought up to believe that Scotch whiskey would need a tax preference to survive in competition with Kentucky bourbon, I never understood the Constitution to require a State to give such preference."[2]

The amendment has also been applied to allow a state greater authority than otherwise would be the case to ban certain kinds of entertainment in bars and taverns. The California Department of Alcoholic Beverage Control prohibited certain kinds of live and filmed sexual entertainment in places that serve alcohol. In sustaining this action, the Court majority recognized that some of the entertainment forbidden could not be deemed obscene, but that just as a state may forbid the sale of liquor where food is not served, where dancing is permitted, where gasoline is sold, and within so many feet of a church or a school, so because of the Twenty-first Amendment it may ban entertainment.[3]

"The Amendment does not license the States, [however] to ignore their obligations under other provisions of the Constitution."[4] Thus, as we have noted, a city cannot delegate to a church authority to decide whether a liquor license should be granted to a tavern in the church's neighborhood: This would violate the First Amendment. Nor does this amendment exempt states from the supremacy clause. If a state law purportedly authorized by the amendment, such as that of Oklahoma forbidding advertisements of wine on cable television, conflicts with a federal regulation, such as that of the FCC permitting such advertising, the Supreme Court will decide whether the state regulation is so closely related to the power reserved by the amendment to states to regulate the importation and use of intoxicating liquors within their borders so as to save the regulation from preemption. In the example given, the Court concluded that since Oklahoma permitted circulation of out-of-state advertisements of wine in newspapers and other publications sold in the state, its interests in discouraging consumption by forbidding cable television to advertise wine was not of the same stature as the FCC's interest in ensuring the widespread availability of cable television throughout the United States.[5] (It is doubtful that if Oklahoma had tried to ban within its boundaries all advertising of alcoholic beverages, it would have made any difference and that the state would have been allowed to do so.)

Section 3

This article shall be inoperative unless it shall have been ratified, as an amendment to the Constitution by conventions in the several States, as provided in the Constitution, within seven years from the date of submission hereof to the States by the Congress.

This is the only amendment Congress submitted to conventions in the several states for ratification rather than to the state legislature. Congress chose this method because it believed that the "drys" had more influence within some of the rural legislatures than they would have in special ratifying conventions.

Congress left it up to the judgment of each state legislature how to organize and hold the ratifying conventions. Delegates ran on "dry" and "wet" slates so that, in effect, the voters in each state made the decision and the conventions merely ratified the decisions of the voter.

AMENDMENT XXII: THE NUMBER OF PRESIDENTIAL TERMS

Section 1

No person shall be elected to the office of the President more than twice, and no person who has held the office of President, or acted as President, for more than two years of a term to which some other person was elected President shall be elected to the office of the President more than once. But this article shall not apply to any person holding the office of President when this Article was proposed by the Congress,

---

This amendment was proposed March 24, 1947, and certified as adopted by the Administrator of General Services March 1, 1951. It is one of the few, perhaps the only, amendment adopted since 1787 that, instead of expanding the power of the electorate, places direct curbs on it. It was adopted in reaction to Franklin D. Roosevelt's election to four terms in office.

The maximum period that a person could serve would be ten years—two years by elevation to the office through the death or disability of the elected President, and two elected terms of four years each; in some cases, it might be only six years, since elevation for two years and a day, through death, disability, or resignation of the elected President, would make a person eligible for only one elected term of four years.

Section 1

[continued] and shall not prevent any person who may be holding the office of President, or acting as President, during the term within which this Article becomes operative from holding the office of President or acting as President during the remainder of such term.

The person in office was Harry Truman, and if he had chosen to run again, which he did not, and had been re-elected his term would have extended beyond the ten years.

Section 2

This article shall be inoperative unless it shall have been ratified as an amendment to the Constitution by the legislatures of three-fourths of the several States within seven years from the date of its submission to the States by the Congress.

Within four years after submission, forty-one state legislatures ratified this amendment. There was very little discussion of its significance; in some instances, the legislators voted for ratification without debate.

What effect will the Twenty-second Amendment have on the influence of the President? When it was possible, even if unlikely, that the President might seek a third term, he had considerably more influence than when he made known his decision not to run again. Congress members, governors, and politicians were much less inclined to oppose the person who might be the head of their ticket than the person who was about to retire to the role of elder statesman. The adoption of this amendment has eliminated even the outside possibility of a second-term President's running again.

AMENDMENT XXIII: PRESIDENTIAL ELECTORS FOR THE DISTRICT OF COLUMBIA

Section 1

The District constituting the seat of Government of the United States shall appoint in such manner as the Congress may direct:

A number of electors of President and Vice President equal to the whole number of Senators and Representatives in Congress to which the District would be entitled if it were a State, but in no event more than the least populous State; they shall be in addition to those appointed by the States, but they shall be considered, for the purposes of the election of President and Vice President, to be electors appointed by a State; and they shall meet in the District and perform such duties as provided by the twelfth article of amendment.

This amendment, proposed on June 16, 1960, was ratified March 29, 1961. On August 22, 1978 (see page 270), Congress proposed another amendment which, if ratified, will repeal this one.

Congress set the usual seven-year time limit for ratification when it submitted the Twenty-third Amendment to the state legislatures, but it took only nine months to secure approval of the legislatures in three-fourths of the states. (Tennessee was the only southern state to ratify.)

Since the least populous state, Alaska, has only three electoral votes, that is all this amendment assigns to the District of Columbia.

Adoption of the new amendment would also give to the voters of the District a voice in the deliberations in the event a presidential election is thrown into the House of Representatives.

Section 2

The Congress shall have the power to enforce this article by appropriate legislation.

AMENDMENT XXIV: THE ANTI-POLL TAX AMENDMENT

Section 1

The right of citizens of the United States to vote in any primary or other election for President or Vice President, for electors for President or Vice President, or for Senator or Representative in Congress shall not be denied or abridged by the United States or any State by reason of failure to pay any poll tax or other tax.

Section 2

The Congress shall have power to enforce this article by appropriate legislation.

This amendment, proposed August 27, 1962, was readily ratified within the seven years stipulated by Congress and became part of the Constitution on January 23, 1964. At the time it was submitted, only five states imposed a poll tax as a requirement for voting.

The anti-poll tax amendment by its own terms forbids payment of a poll tax as a condition for voting for presidential electors and congress members. It was rendered superfluous by the Supreme Court decision of 1966, *Harper* v. *Virginia Board of Electors,* that the equal protection clause precludes a state from imposing a poll tax as a requirement to vote in *any* election.[6] Earlier, the Supreme Court had held that under the Twenty-fourth Amendment a state could not give voters the choice of either paying a poll tax or filing a certificate of residence six months prior to an election. Such a requirement erects an obstacle to voting for those who assert their constitutional exemption from the poll tax.[7]

AMENDMENT XXV: PRESIDENTIAL DISABILITY—VICE PRESIDENTIAL VACANCIES

Section 1

In the case of the removal of the President from office or of his death or resignation, the Vice President shall become President.

At the time Congress submitted this proposal, on July 6, 1965, it stipulated that ratification would have to take place within seven years to be effective. It was ratified February 10, 1967.

This section merely confirms what has been the consistent practice (see page 95) of the eight Vice-Presidents who acceded to the presidency on the death of the President. It also deals with an additional situation, resignation of a President. By making the Vice-President the President, not merely Acting President, after the incumbent resigns, the amendment precludes a person from resigning and then after doing so attempting to return to office.

The only incumbent ever to resign was Richard Nixon. The amendment does not deal with how a President submits his resignation. Nixon did so by sending a two-line letter to the Secretary of State. Thus the precedent has been established.

Section 2

Whenever there is a vacancy in the office of the Vice President, the President shall nominate a Vice President who shall take office upon confirmation by a majority vote of both Houses of Congress.

The vice-presidency has been vacant eighteen times. Fortunately, during these periods there has been no need to go on down the line of presidential succession that Congress has provided by law—Speaker of the House, President pro tempore of the Senate, and then members of the Cabinet in order of the creation of their departments.

The procedure provided by Section 2 has some resemblance to that normally followed in the original selection and election of a Vice-President. Once a party selects its presidential candidate by a vote of the delegates to its national convention, that candidate normally chooses a vice-presidential running mate who, subject to confirmation by the national convention and election along with the President, becomes Vice-President. Section 2 calls on Congress to serve in lieu of the electorate to confirm the presidential choice.

Section 2 received little attention at the time of the adoption of the amendment since congressional and public attention was focused on the problems of presidential disability dealt with in Section 3. It was generally assumed that Section 2 would be used after the death of a President had elevated into the White House the elected Vice-President, thereby creating a vacancy in the vice-presidency.

But the first time Section 2 was used was in the unanticipated set of circumstances created by the resignation of Vice-President Agnew to avoid federal criminal charges at the same time that President Nixon himself was under the cloud of suspicion created by the Watergate affair. President Nixon nominated Gerald Ford, Republican, then minority leader in the House. The Democratic Party controlled both chambers of Congress, but Congress, in keeping with the spirit of the Constitution, limited its investigation to questions of Ford's fitness and integrity, rather than probing issues like his policy attitudes, in order that the Vice-President might be a person reflecting, through the elected President, the wishes of the majority of the voters in the immediately preceding election.

During the interim between Ford's nomination by Nixon and his confirmation by Congress, some wondered what would happen if President Nixon resigned or were removed from office. The Speaker of the House would become Acting President. Would the Ford nomination for Vice-President still stand if the Speaker were to send to Congress another name? Would Congress have the right to choose between the two nominees? The fact that there are any open questions about presidential succession is, of course, dangerous, for there is nothing more threatening to a constitutional democracy than doubts about who has the legitimate right to govern. But except for these brief moments, the constitutional crisis passed and the amendment appeared to be working.

Very soon thereafter, President Nixon resigned to escape being impeached and Ford became President, once again creating a vacancy in the vice-presidency. President Ford nominated Nelson Rockefeller, former four-term governor of New York and a well-known public figure. After a long examination of Rockefeller's record, Congress finally confirmed the nomination.

Although for the first time in our history we had both a President and a Vice-President who had not been voted upon by the electorate, there was never any question about the rights of President Ford and Vice-President Rockefeller to exercise to the full the powers vested in their offices by the Constitution. Nonetheless, some outside and some inside Congress called for a reconsideration of Section 2. President Ford suggested that some time limit should be placed on congressional confirmation. Some in Congress argued that in the event of a vacancy in the Presidency with more than two years of a term still to expire, another election should be held. But the consensus seemed to be that if Section 2 worked under the circumstances in which it was first used, it is likely to work under less constitutionally trying conditions.

Section 3

Whenever the President transmits to the President pro tempore of the Senate and the Speaker of the House of Representatives his written delcaration that he is unable to discharge the powers and duties of his office, and until he transmits to them a written declaration to the contrary, such powers and duties shall be discharged by the Vice President as Acting President.

Until this amendment, Congress had never established procedures to determine how it should be judged whether or not the President is unable to discharge his duties. Six times in our history this question has caused difficulty. when President Garfield suffered a lingering death from an assassin's bullet; when President Wilson had a physical breakdown during the closing years of his second term; when there was concern about President Roosevelt's health prior to his fatal attack; when President Eisenhower was temporarily disabled, first by a heart attack and later by a serious operation; and when President Reagan was briefly disabled by a gunshot wound.

Section 4

Whenever the Vice President and a majority of either the principal officers of the executive departments or of such other body as Congress may by law provide, transmit to the President pro tempore of the Senate and the Speaker of the House of Representatives their written declaration that the President is unable to discharge the powers and duties of his office, the Vice President shall immediately assume the powers and duties of the office as Acting President.

Section 4 deals with the situation in which a President may be unable to declare his own inability to discharge his duties. The responsibility then vests in the Vice-President *and* the Cabinet to so declare. Upon such a declaration, the Vice-President would *immediately* become Acting President.

It is interesting to note that although the Constitution in Article II, Section 2, mentions "the principal officers of the executive departments," in other words the Cabinet, this section is the first to assign them a collective responsibility. Previously, the composition of the Cabinet has varied from President to President, and there has been no very precise definition of its membership. Vesting this constitutional responsibility in the Cabinet as an entity suggests the need for some more formal definition of its composition.

The declaration of presidential disability by a majority of the Cabinet is subject to a vice-presidential veto. However, whenever the Cabinet and the Vice-President believe the President is unable to discharge the powers and duties of his office, the Vice-President immediately assumes the powers and duties, but he is only the Acting President. The disabled President remains President, but at least for the next twenty-one days, the President is without authority to act.[8]

The only time since the adoption of this provision that it might have been brought into play was when President Reagan was disabled as the result of an attempted assassination in 1982 and for about twenty-four hours was out of commission in the emergency room of George Washington Hospital. His aides did not invoke the Twenty-fifth Amendment, and the Cabinet was not asked to consider the matter.

Section 4

[continued] Thereafter, when the President transmits to the President pro tempore of the Senate and the Speaker of the House of Representative his written declaration that no inability exists, he shall resume the powers and duties of his office unless the Vice President and a majority of either the principal officers of the executive departments or of such other body as Congress may by law provide, transmit within four days to the President pro tempore of the Senate and the Speaker of the House of Representatives their written declaration that the President is unable to discharge the powers and duties of his office. Thereupon Congress shall decide the issue, assembling within forty-eight hours for that purpose, if not in session. If the Congress, within twenty-one days after receipt of the latter written declaration, or, if Congress is not in session, within twenty-one days after Congress is required to assemble, determines by two-thirds vote of both Houses that the President is unable to discharge the powers and duties of his office, the Vice President shall continue to discharge the same as Acting President; otherwise, the President shall resume the powers and duties of his office.

In case of a conflict between the President, the Vice-President, and a majority of the Cabinet over the issue of the President's fitness to assume his duties, Congress decides. However, the advantage is in favor of the President; a two-thirds vote of both Houses is required to retain the Vice-President as Acting President in the face of a declaration by the President that he is able to resume his duties.

A contingency still not covered is a method to fill postelection vacancies caused by the death of the winners of the election before there is in a constitutional sense a President-elect or a Vice-President-elect.

AMENDMENT XXVI: EIGHTEEN-YEAR-OLD VOTE

Section 1

The right of citizens of the United States, who are eighteen years of age or older, to vote shall not be denied or abridged by the United States or by any state on account of age.

This amendment proposed on March 23, 1971, was ratified on June 30, 1971, after only five weeks—the fastest ratification of any amendment.

After the Supreme Court ruled that Congress lacked authority to set the voting age for state and local elections but could do so for national elections, Congress proposed this amendment. Ratification was swift, in large part because without it many states would have been faced with the costly and administratively difficult task of operating separate registration books, ballots, and voting apparatus for election of federal officers and for election of state and local officers.

Section 2

The Congress shall have the power to enforce this article by appropriate legislation.

PROPOSED AMENDMENT: VOTING RIGHTS FOR THE DISTRICT OF COLUMBIA

Section 1

For purposes of representation in Congress, election of the President and Vice-President, and Article V of this Constitution, the District constituting the seat of government of the United States shall be treated as though it were a state.

This amendment, proposed on August 22, 1978, if ratified, would give to the people of the District two voting senators, and based on its population, one voting representative, and therefore three electoral votes for President. At the moment the District has one nonvoting delegate in the House and three electoral votes for President and Vice-President.

The District would, under this proposed amendment, also participate in ratifying constitutional amendments. (This would not alter the required number of states necessary for approval since three-fourths of both fifty and fifty-one is thirty-eight.)

Section 2

The exercise of the rights and powers conferred under this article shall be by the people of the District constituting the seat of government, and as shall be provided by the Congress.

Presumably Congress would delegate to the City Council of the District the responsibility for deciding suffrage qualifications, how elections should be administered, how congressional district lines should be drawn, and how ratification of amendments referred to "state legislatures" would take place.

Section 3

The twenty-third article of amendment to the Constitution is hereby repealed.

The Twenty-third Amendment, which would be repealed if this proposed amendment were ratified, as we have noted, gives to the voters of the District three electoral votes for President and Vice-President, but no representation in Congress or right to participate in the amendatory ratification process.

Section 4

This article shall be inoperative, unless it shall have been ratified as an amendment to the Constitution by the legislatures of three-fourths of the several states within seven years from the date of its submission.

As noted, debate in Congress about this amendment took place while Congress was also considering extending the time for ratification of the Equal Rights Amendment. The inclusion of the time limit for ratification in the body of this proposed amendment, rather than placing it in a separate resolution, suggests that Congress did this to preclude the possibility of extending the time limit by a vote of a simple majority in both houses.

Since only sixteen states have ratified this amendment by the end of 1984, it is highly unlikely that it will receive the required three-fourths majority by August 22, 1985. In fact proponents of greater representation by the people of the District have turned their attention away from this proposed amendment in favor of a strategy of persuading Congress to admit the District of Columbia as a state. A small part of the District of Columbia would be retained as the seat of government as required by the Constitution, but the rest of it would be admitted as a state. Such action would give to the people of the District everything that this proposed amendment would—and more—and would require only the vote of a majority of both houses of Congress.

The District has in fact held a constitutional convention, adopted a proposed constitution for the proposed new state to be called New Columbia, and petitioned Congress for admission under the terms of Article IV, Section 3. The probability that Congress will act favorably are not good, especially as long as the Republicans control one chamber of the Congress (since admission of the District as a State would undoubtedly add two Democratic Senators and one Democratic member of the House).

EQUAL RIGHTS AMENDMENT

Although this amendment failed to be ratified, the probability that it will be resubmitted justifies a few words about it. As proposed on March 22, 1972 it read as follows:

Section 1

Equality of rights under the law shall not be denied or abridged by the United States or by Any State on account of sex.

Section 2

The Congress shall have power to enforce, by appropriate legislation on the provisions of this article.

Section 3

This amendment shall take effect two years after the date of ratification.

Three years after the Nineteenth Amendment—which does not affect laws dealing with ownership of property, jury service, marriage and divorce, labor regulations, and so forth—was ratified, the first equal rights amendment was introduced in Congress. Forty-nine years later, Congress finally proposed an Equal Rights Amendment and submitted it to the states.

ERA had overwhelming support in both houses of Congress. Soon after its submission many legislatures quickly ratified—sometimes without hearings—and by overwhelming majorities. By the end of 1972 twenty-two states had ratified the amendment. It appeared that ERA would soon become part of the Constitution. Then the opposition got organized, under the articulate leadership of Phyllis Schlafly.

ERA became controversial. Legislatures were forced to hold hearings, floor debates became heated, and "with increasing frequency, legislators sought refuge in legislature procedure to delay or avoid entirely a public decision on the now controversial amendment.[9] Opposition to ratification centered chiefly in the same cluster of southern states that had opposed ratification of the Nineteenth Amendment, and in states such as Illinois, where although a majority in each chamber voted for ratification, it failed to obtain the three-fifths required by the Illinois Constitution.

In the enabling resolution, Congress, submitting the amendment to the states for ratification, adopted the usual time limit requiring the amendment to be ratified by the necessary number of states within seven years if it were to be considered part of the Constitution—that is, by March 22, 1979. By the summer of 1978 it became clear that the amendment would probably fall short of the necessary ratifications. Only thirty-five states had voted to do so, and four of these had subsequently voted to rescind their prior ratification.

After a heated debate in October 1978, Congress extended the time limit for ratification until June 30, 1982, voting down amendments that would have authorized legislatures to rescind their prior approval.

By June 30, 1982, the necessary number of ratifications had still not been obtained, and ERA failed to become part of the Constitution. The failure to secure the required number of ratifications rendered moot a pending legal challenge to the authority of Congress by a majority vote to have the time for ratification extended.

Whether or not Congress should permit state legislatures, once they have ratified an amendment, to change their mind and rescind that ratification is another open issue. As we have noted, if past precedents are followed, Congress has counted as ratifying every state in which the legislature has once given its approval.

Although ERA I failed to be ratified, ERA is not a dead issue. Congress is very likely to submit ERA II in the near future. The question before the Congress is whether to submit it in its original form or perhaps with a modification that would allow Congress to exempt women from combat service in the military.

Whether or not ERA eventually becomes part of the Constitution is also going to be affected by how the Supreme Court interprets the equal protection clause of the Fourteenth Amendment.

Appendix

The Text of the Constitution

We the People of the United States, in Order to form a more perfect Union, establish Justice, insure domestic Tranquility, provide for the common defence, promote the general Welfare, and secure the Blessings of Liberty to ourselves and our Posterity, do ordain and establish this Constitution for the United States of America.

Article I

Section 1

All legislative Powers herein granted shall be vested in a Congress of the United States, which shall consist of a Senate and House of Representatives.

Section 2

The House of Representatives shall be composed of Members chosen every second Year by the People of the several States, and the Electors in each State shall have the Qualifications requisite for Electors of the most numerous Branch of the State Legislature.

No Person shall be a Representative who shall not have attained to the Age of twenty five Years, and been seven Years a Citizen of the United States, and who shall not, when elected, be an Inhabitant of the State in which he shall be chosen.

Representatives and direct Taxes shall be apportioned among the several States which may be included within this Union, according to their respective Numbers, which shall be determined by adding to the whole Number of free Persons, including those bound to Service for a Term of Years, and excluding Indians not taxed, three fifths of all other Persons. The actual Enumeration shall be made within three Years after the first Meeting of the Congress of the United States, and within every subsequent Term of ten Years, in such Manner as they shall by Law direct. The Number of Representatives shall not exceed one for every thirty Thousand, but each State shall have at Least one Representative; and until such enumeration shall be made, the State of New Hampshire shall be entitled to chuse three, Massachusetts eight, Rhode-Island and Providence Plantations one, Connecticut five, New-York six, New Jersey four, Pennsylvania eight, Delaware one, Maryland six, Virginia ten, North Carolina five, South Carolina five, and Georgia three.

When vacancies happen in the Representation from any State, the Executive Authority thereof shall issue Writs of Election to fill such Vacancies.

The House of Representatives shall chuse their speaker and other Officers; and shall have the sole Power of Impeachment.

Section 3

The Senate of the United States shall be composed of two Senators from each State, chosen by the Legislature thereof, for six Years; and each Senator shall have one Vote.

Immediately after they shall be assembled in Consequence of the first Election, they shall be divided as equally as may be into three Classes. The Seats of the Senators of the first Class shall be vacated at the Expiration of the second Year, of the second Class at the Expiration of the fourth Year, and of the third Class at the Expiration of the sixth Year, so that one third may be chosen every second Year; and if Vacancies happen by Resignation, or otherwise, during the Recess of the Legislature of any State, the Executive thereof may make temporary Appointments until the next Meeting of the Legislature, which shall then fill such Vacancies.

No Person shall be a Senator who shall not have attained to the Age of thirty Years, and been nine Years a Citizen of the United States, and who shall not, when elected, be an Inhabitant of that State for which he shall be chosen.

The Vice President of the United States shall be President of the Senate, but shall have no Vote, unless they be equally divided.

The Senate shall chuse their other Officers, and also a President pro tempore, in the Absence of the Vice President, or when he shall exercise the Office of President of the United States.

The Senate shall have the sole Power to try all Impeachments. When sitting for that Purpose, they shall be on Oath or Affirmation. When the President of the United States is tried, the Chief Justice shall preside: And no Person shall be convicted without the Concurrence of two thirds of the Members present.

Judgment in Cases of Impeachment shall not extend further than to removal from Office, and disqualification to hold and enjoy any Office of Honor, Trust or Profit under the United States: but the Party convicted shall nevertheless be liable and subject to Indictment, Trial, Judgment and Punishment, according to law.

Section 4

The Times, Places and Manner of holding Elections for Senators and Representatives, shall be prescribed in each State by the Legislature thereof; but the Congress may at any time by Law make or alter such Regulations, except as to the Places of chusing Senators.

The Congress shall assemble at least once in every Year, and such Meeting shall be on the first Monday in December, unless they shall by Law appoint a different Day.

Section 5

Each House shall be the Judge of the Elections, Returns and Qualifications of its own Members, and a Majority of each shall constitute a Quorum to do Business; but a smaller Number may adjourn from day to day, and may be authorized to compel the Attendance of absent Members, in such Manner, and under such Penalties as each House may provide.

Each House may determine the Rules of its Proceedings, punish its Members for disorderly Behaviour, and, with the Concurrence of two thirds, expel a Member.

Each House shall keep a Journal of its Proceedings, and from time to time publish the same, excepting such Parts as may in their Judgment require Secrecy; and the Yeas and Nays of the Members of either House on any question shall, at the Desire of one fifth of those Present, be entered on the Journal.

Neither House, during the Session of Congress, shall, without the Consent of the other, adjourn for more than three days, nor to any other Place than that in which the two Houses shall be sitting.

Section 6

The Senators and Representatives shall receive a Compensation for their Services, to be ascertained by Law, and paid out of the Treasury of the United States. They shall in all Cases, except Treason, Felony and Breach of the Peace, be privileged from Arrest during their Attendance at the Session of their respective Houses, and in going to and returning from the same; and for any Speech or Debate in either House, they shall not be questioned in any other Place.

No Senator or Representative shall, during the Time for which he was elected, be appointed to any Civil Office under the Authority of the United States, which shall have been created, or the Emoluments whereof shall have been encreased during such time; and no Person holding any Office under the United States, shall be a Member of either House during his Continuance in Office.

Section 7

All Bills for raising Revenue shall originate in the House of Representatives; but the Senate may propose or concur with Amendments as on other Bills.

Every Bill which shall have passed the House of Representatives and the Senate, shall, before it become a Law, be presented to the President of the United States; If he approve he shall sign it, but if not he shall return it, with his Objections to that House in which it shall have originated, who shall enter the Objections at large on their Journal, and proceed to reconsider it. If after such Reconsideration two thirds of that House shall agree to pass the Bill, it shall be sent, together with the Objections, to the other House, by which it shall likewise be reconsidered, and if approved by two thirds of that House, it shall become a Law. But in all such Cases the Votes of both Houses shall be determined by Yeas and Nays, and the Names of the Persons voting for and against the Bill shall be entered on the Journal of each House respectively. If any Bill shall not be returned by the President within ten Days (Sundays excepted) after it shall have been presented to him, the Same shall be a Law, in like Manner as if he had signed it, unless the Congress by their Adjournment prevent its Return, in which Case it shall not be a Law.

Every Order, Resolution, or Vote to which the Concurrence of the Senate and House of Representatives may be necessary (except on a question of Adjournment) shall be presented to the President of the United States; and before the Same shall take Effect, shall be approved by him, or being disapproved by him, shall be repassed by two thirds of the Senate and House of Representatives, according to the Rules and Limitations prescribed in the Case of a Bill.

Section 8

The Congress shall have Power To lay and collect Taxes, Duties, Imposts and Excises, to pay the Debts and provide for the common Defence and general Welfare of the United States; but all Duties, Imposts and Excises shall be uniform throughout the United States;

To borrow Money on the Credit of the United States;

To regulate Commerce with foreign Nations, and among the several States, and with the Indian Tribes;

To establish an uniform Rule of Naturalization, and uniform Laws on the subject of Bankruptcies throughout the United States;

To coin Money, regulate the Value thereof, and of foreign Coin, and fix the Standard of Weights and Measures;

To provide for the Punishment of counterfeiting the Securities and current Coin of the United States;

To establish Post Offices and post Roads;

To promote the Progress of Science and useful Arts, by securing for limited Times to Authors and Inventors the exclusive Right to their respective Writings and Discoveries;

To constitute Tribunals inferior to the supreme Court;

To define and punish Piracies and Felonies committed on the high Seas, and Offences against the Law of Nations;

To declare War, grant Letters of Marque and Reprisal, and make Rules concerning Captures on Land and Water;

To raise and support Armies, but no Appropriation of Money to that Use shall be for a longer Term than two years;

To provide and maintain a Navy;

To make Rules for the Government and Regulation of the land and naval Forces;

To provide for calling forth the Militia to execute the Laws of Union, suppress Insurrections and repel Invasions;

To provide for organizing, arming, and disciplining, the Militia, and for governing such Part of them as may be employed in the Service of the United States, reserving to the States respectively, the Appointment of the Officers, and the Authority of training the Militia according to the discipline prescribed by Congress;

To exercise exclusive Legislation in all Cases whatsoever, over such District (not exceeding ten Miles square) as may, by Cession of particular States, and the Acceptance of Congress, become the Seat of the Government of the United States, and to exercise the Authority over all Places purchased by the Consent of the Legislature of the State in which the Same shall be for the Erection of Forts, Magazines, Arsenals, dock-Yards, and other needful Buildings;—And

To make all Laws which shall be necessary and proper for carrying into Execution the foregoing Powers, and all other Powers vested by this Constitution in the Government of the United States, or in any Department or Officer thereof.

Section 9

The Migration or Importation of such Persons as any of the States now existing shall think proper to admit, shall not be prohibited by the Congress prior to the Year one thousand eight hundred and eight, but a Tax or duty may be imposed on such Importation, not exceeding ten dollars for each Person.

The Privilege of the Writ of Habeas Corpus shall not be suspended, unless when in Cases of Rebellion or Invasion the public Safety may require it.

No Bill of Attainder or ex post facto Law shall be passed.

No Capitation, or other direct, Tax shall be laid, unless in Proportion to the Census or Enumeration herein before directed to be taken.

No Tax or Duty shall be laid on Articles exported from any State.

No Preference shall be given by any Regulation of Commerce or Revenue to the Ports of one State over those of another: nor shall Vessels bound to, or from, on? State, be obliged to enter, clear, or pay Duties in another.

No Money shall be drawn from the Treasury, but in Consequence of Appropriations made by law; and a regular Statement and Account of the Receipts and Expenditures of all public Money shall be published from time to time.

No Title of Nobility shall be granted by the United States: And no Person holding any Office or Profit or Trust under them, shall, without the Consent of the Congress, accept of any present, Emolument, Office, or Title, of any kind whatever, from any King, Prince, or foreign State.

Section 10

No State shall enter into any Treaty, Alliance, or Confederation; grant Letters of Marque and Reprisal; coin Money; emit Bills of Credit; make any Thing but gold and silver Coin a Tender in Payment of Debts; pass any Bill of Attainder, ex post facto Law, or Law impairing the Obligation of Contracts, or grant any Title of Nobility.

No State shall, without the Consent of the Congress, lay any Imposts or Duties on Imports or Exports, except what may be absolutely necessary for executing its inspection Laws: and the net Produce of all Duties and Imposts, laid by any State on Imports or Exports, shall be for the Use of the Treasury of the United States; and all such Laws shall be subject to the Revision and Control of the Congress.

No state shall, without the Consent of Congress, lay any Duty of Tonnage, keep Troops, or Ships of War in time of Peace, enter into any Agreement or Compact with another State, or with a foreign Power, or engage in War, unless actually invaded, or in such imminent Danger as will not admit of delay.

Article II

Section 1

The executive Power shall be vested in a President of the United States of America. He shall hold his Office during the Term of four Years, and, together with the Vice President, chosen for the same term, be elected, as follows.

Each State shall appoint, in such Manner as the Legislature thereof may direct, a Number of Electors, equal to the whole Number of Senators and Representatives to which the State may be entitled in the Congress: but no Senator or Representative, or Person holding an Office of Trust or Profit under the United States, shall be appointed an Elector.

The Electors shall meet in their respective States, and vote by Ballot for two Persons, of whom one at least shall not be an Inhabitant of the same State with themselves. And they shall make a List of all the Persons voted for, and of the Number of Votes for each; which List they shall sign and certify, and transmit sealed to the Seat of the Government of the United States, directed to the President of the Senate. The President of the Senate shall, in the Presence of the Senate and House of Representatives, open all the Certificates, and the Votes shall then be counted. The person having the greatest Number of Votes shall be the President, if such Number be a Majority of the whole Number of Electors appointed; and if there be more than one who have such Majority, and have an equal Number of Votes, then the House of Representatives shall immediately chuse by Ballot one of them for President: and if no Person have a Majority, then from the five highest on the List the said House shall in like Manner chuse the President. But in chusing the President, the Votes shall be taken by States, the Representation from each State having one Vote; A quorum for this Purpose shall consist of a Member or Members from two thirds of the States, and a Majority of all the States shall be necessary to a Choice. In every Case, after the Choice of the President, the Person having the greatest Number of Votes of the Electors shall be the Vice President. But if there should remain two or more who have equal Votes, the Senate shall chuse from them by Ballot the Vice President.

The Congress may determine the Time of chusing the Electors, and the Day on which they shall give their Votes; which Day shall be the same throughout the United States.

No Person except a natural born Citizen, or a Citizen of the United States, at the time of the Adoption of this Constitution, shall be eligible to the Office of President; neither shall any Person be eligible to that Office who shall not have attained to the Age of thirty five Years, and been fourteen Years a Resident within the United States.

In Case of the Removal of the President from Office, or of his Death, Resignation, or Inability to discharge the Powers and Duties of the said Office, the Same shall devolve on the Vice President, and the Congress may by Law provide for the Case of Removal, Death, Resignation or Inability, both of the President and Vice President, declaring what Officer shall then act as President, and such Officer shall act accordingly, until the Disability be removed, or a President shall be elected.

The President shall, at stated Times, receive for his Services, a Compensation, which shall neither be encreased nor diminished during the Period for which he shall have been elected, and he shall not receive within that Period any other Emolument from the United States, or any of them.

Before he enter on the Execution of his Office, he shall take the following Oath or Affirmation:—"I do solemnly swear (or affirm) that I will faithfully execute the Office of the President of the United States, and will to the best of my Ability, preserve, protect and defend the Constitution of the United States."

Section 2

The President shall be Commander in Chief of the Army and Navy of the United States, and of the Militia of the several States, when called into the actual Service of the United States; he may require the Opinion, in writing, of the principal Officer in each of the executive Departments, upon any Subject relating to the Duties of their respective Offices, and he shall have Power to grant Reprieves and Pardons for Offences against the United States, except in Cases of Impeachment.

He shall have Power, by and with the Advice and Consent of the Senate, to make Treaties, provided two thirds of the Senators present concur; and he shall nominate, and by and with the Advice and Consent of the Senate, shall appoint Ambassadors, other public Ministers and Consuls, Judges of the supreme Court, and all other Officers of the United States, whose Appointments are not herein otherwise provided for, and which shall be established by Law: but the Congress may be Law vest the Appointment of such inferior Officers, as they think proper, in the President alone, in the Courts of Law, or in the Heads of Departments.

The President shall have Power to fill up all Vacancies that may happen during the Recess of the Senate, by granting Commissions which shall expire at the end of their next Session.

Section 3

He shall from time to time give to the Congress Information of the State of the Union, and recommend to their Consideration such Measures as he shall judge necessary and expedient; he may, on extraordinary Occasions, convene both Houses, or either of them, and in Case of Disagreement between them, with Respect to the Time of Adjournment, he may adjourn them to such Time as he shall think proper; he shall receive Ambassadors and other public Ministers; he shall take Care that the Laws be faithfully executed, and shall Commission all Officers of the United States.

Section 4

The President, Vice President and all civil Officers of the United States, shall be removed from Office on Impeachment for, and Conviction of, Treason, Bribery, or other High Crimes and Misdemeanors.

Article III

Section 1

The judicial Power of the United States, shall be vested in one supreme Court, and in such inferior Courts as the Congress may from time to time ordain and establish. The Judges, both of the supreme and inferior Courts, shall hold their Offices during good Behaviour, and shall, at stated Times, receive for their Services, a Compensation, which shall not be diminished during their Continuance in Office.

Section 2

The judicial Power shall extend to all Cases, in Law and Equity, arising under this Constitution, the Laws of the United States, and Treaties made, or which shall be made, under their Authority;—to all Cases affecting Ambassadors, other public Ministers and Consuls;—to all Cases of admiralty and maritime Jurisdiction;—to Controversies to which the United States shall be a Party;—to Controversies between two or more States; between a State and Citizens of another State;—between Citizens of different States;—between Citizens of the same State claiming Lands under Grants of different States, and between a State, or the Citizens thereof, and foreign States, Citizens or Subjects.

In all Cases affecting Ambassadors, other public Ministers and Consuls, and those in which a State shall be Party, the supreme Court shall have original jurisdiction. In all the other cases before mentioned, the supreme Court shall have appellate Jurisdiction, both as to Law and Fact, with such Exceptions, and under such Regulations as the Congress shall make.

The Trial of all Crimes, except in Cases of Impeachment, shall be by Jury; and such Trial shall be held in the State where the said Crimes shall have been committed; but when not committed within any State, the Trial shall be at such Place or Places as the Congress may by Law have directed.

Section 3

Treason against the United States, shall consist only in levying War against them, or in adhering to their Enemies, giving them Aid and Comfort. No Person shall be convicted of Treason unless on the Testimony of two Witnesses to the same overt Act, or on Confession in open Court.

The Congress shall have Power to declare the Punishment of Treason, but no Attainder of Treason shall work Corruption of Blood, or Forfeiture except during the Life of the Person attained.

Article IV

Section 1

Full Faith and Credit shall be given in each State to the public Acts, Records, and judicial Proceedings of every other State. And the Congress may by general Laws prescribe the Manner in which such Acts, Records and Proceedings shall be proven, and the Effect thereof.

Section 2

The Citizens of each State shall be entitled to all Privileges and Immunities of Citizens in the several States.

A Person charged in any State with Treason, Felony, or other Crime, who shall flee from Justice, and be found in another State, shall on Demand of the executive Authority of the State from which he fled, be delivered up, to be removed to the State having Jurisdiction of the Crime.

No person held to Service or Labour in one State, under the Laws thereof, escaping into another, shall, in Consequence of any Law or Regulation therein, be discharged from such Service or Labour, but shall be delivered up on Claim of the Party to whom such Service or Labour may be due.

Section 3

New States may be admitted by the Congress into this Union; but no new State shall be formed or erected within the Jurisdiction of any other State; nor any State be formed by the Junction of two or more States, or Parts of States, without the Consent of the Legislatures of the States concerned as well as of the Congress.

The Congress shall have Power to dispose of and make all needful Rules and Regulations respecting the Territory or other Property belonging to the United States; and nothing in this Constitution shall be so construed as to Prejudice any Claims of the United States, or of any particular State.

Section 4

The United States shall guarantee to every State in this Union a Republican Form of Government, and shall protect each of them against Invasion; and on Application of the Legislature, or of the Executive (when the Legislature cannot be convened) against domestic Violence.

Article V

The Congress, whenever two thirds of both Houses shall deem it necessary, shall propose Amendments to this Constitution, or, on the Application of the Legislatures of two thirds of the several States, shall call a Convention for proposing Amendments, which, in either Case, shall be valid to all Intents and Purposes, as Part of this Constitution, when ratified by the Legislatures of three fourths of the several States, or by Conventions in three fourths thereof, as the one or the other Mode of Ratification may be proposed by the Congress; Provided that no Amendment which may be made prior to the Year One thousand eight hundred and eight shall in any Manner affect the first and fourth Clauses in the Ninth Section of the first Article; and that no State, without its Consent, shall be deprived of its equal Suffrage in the Senate.

Article VI

All Debts contracted and Engagements entered into, before the Adoption of this Constitution, shall be as valid against the United States under this Constitution, as under the Confederation.

This Constitution, and the Laws of the United States which shall be made in Pursuance thereof; and all Treaties made, or which shall be made, under the Authority of the United States, shall be the supreme Law of the Land; and the judges in every State shall be bounded thereby, any Thing in the Constitution of Laws of any State to the Contrary notwithstanding.

The Senators and Representatives before mentioned, and the Members of the Several State Legislatures, and all executive and judicial Officers, both of the United States and of the several States, shall be bound by Oath or Affirmation, to support this Constitution; but no religious Test shall ever be required as a Qualification to any Office or public Trust under the United States.

Article VII

The Ratification of the Conventions of nine States, shall be sufficient for the Establishment of this Constitution between the States so ratifying the Same.

Done in Convention by the Unanimous Consent of the States present the Seventeenth Day of September in the Year of our Lord one thousand seven hundred and Eighty seven and of the Independence of the United States of America the Twelfth. In Witness whereof We have hereunto subscribed our Names,

Gº WASHINGTON—Presidᵀ
and deputy from Virginia

New Hampshire	{ JOHN LANGDON NICHOLAS GILMAN
Massachusetts	{ NATHANIEL GORHAM RUFUS KING
Connecticut	{ Wᴹ Samᴸ JOHNSON ROGER SHERMAN
New York	ALEXANDER HAMILTON
New Jersey	{ WIL: LIVINGSTON DAVID BREARLEY. Wᴹ PATERSON. JONA: DAYTON
Pennsylvania	{ B FRANKLIN THOMAS MIFFLIN ROBTᵀ MORRIS GEO. CLYMER THOˢ FITZSIMONS JARED INGERSOLL JAMES WILSON GOUV MORRIS

Delaware	{ GEO: READ GUNNING BEDFORD JUN JOHN DICKINSON RICHARD BASSETT JACO: BROOM
Maryland	{ JAMES MᶜHENRY DAN OF Sᵀ THOˢ JENIFER DANᴸ CARROLL
Virginia	{ JOHN BLAIR— JAMES MADISON JR.
North Carolina	{ Wᴹ BLOUNT RICHᴰ DOBBS SPAIGHT. HU WILLIAMSON
South Carolina	{ J. RUTLEDGE CHARLES COTESWORTH PINCKNEY CHARLES PINCKNEY PIERCE BUTLER.
Georgia	{ WILLIAM FEW ABR BALDWIN

Amendments to the Constitution

The first ten Amendments were ratified December 15, 1791, and form what is known as the "Bill of Rights."

Amendment I

Congress shall make no law respecting an establishment of religion, or prohibiting the free exercise thereof; or abridging the freedom of speech, or of the press; or the right of the people peaceably to assemble, and to petition the Government for a redress of grievances.

Amendment II

A well regulated Militia, being necessary to the security of a free State, the right of the people to keep and bear Arms, shall not be infringed.

Amendment III

No Soldier shall, in time of peace be quartered in any house, without the consent of the Owner, nor in time of war, but in a manner to be prescribed by law.

Amendment IV

The right of the people to be secure in their persons, houses, papers, and effects, against unreasonable searches and seizures, shall not be violated, and no Warrants shall issue, but upon probable cause, supported by Oath or affirmation, and particularly describing the place to be searched, and the persons or things to be seized.

Amendment V

No person shall be held to answer for a capital, or otherwise infamous crime, unless on a presentment or indictment of a Grand Jury, except in cases arising in the land or naval forces, or in the Militia, when in actual service in time of War or public danger; nor shall any person be subject for the same offence to be twice put in jeopardy of life or limb; nor shall be compelled in any criminal case to be a witness against himself, nor be deprived of life, liberty, or property, without due process of law; nor shall private property be taken for public use, without just compensation.

Amendment VI

In all criminal prosecutions, the accused shall enjoy the right to a speedy and public trial, by an impartial jury of the State and district wherein the crime shall have been committed, which district shall have been previously ascertained by law, and to be informed of the nature and cause of the accusation; to be confronted with the witnesses against him; to have compulsory process for obtaining witnesses in his favor, and to have the Assistance of Counsel for his defence.

Amendment VII

In Suits at common law, where the value in controversy shall exceed twenty dollars, the right of trial by jury shall be preserved, and no fact tried by a jury, shall be otherwise re-examined in any Court of the United States, than according to the rules of the common law.

Amendment VIII

Excessive bail shall not be required, nor excessive fines imposed, nor cruel and unusual punishments inflicted.

Amendment IX

The enumeration in the Constitution, of certain rights, shall not be construed to deny or disparage others retained by the people.

Amendment X

The powers not delegated to the United States by the Constitution, nor prohibited by it to the States, are reserved to the States respectively, or to the people.

Amendment XI

The Judicial power of the United States shall not be construed to extend to any suit in law or equity, commenced or prosecuted against one of the United States by Citizens of another State, or by Citizens or Subjects of any Foreign State.

Amendment XII

The Electors shall meet in their respective states and vote by ballot for President and Vice President, one of whom, at least, shall not be an inhabitant of the same state with themselves; they shall name in their ballots the person voted for as President, and in distinct ballots the person voted for as Vice President, and they shall make distinct lists of all persons voted for as President, and of all persons voted for as Vice President, and of the number of votes for each, which lists they shall sign and certify, and transmit sealed to the seat of the government of the United States, directed to the President of the Senate;—The President of the Senate shall, in the presence of the Senate and House of Representatives, open all the certificates and the votes shall then be counted;—The person having the greatest number of votes for President, shall be the President, if such number is a majority of the whole number of Electors appointed; and if no person have such majority, then from the persons having the highest numbers not exceeding three on the list of those voted for as President, the House of Representatives shall choose immediately, by ballot, the President. But in choosing the President, the votes shall be taken by states, the representation from each state having one vote; a quorum for this purpose shall consist of a member or members from two-thirds of the states, and a majority of all the states shall be necessary to a choice. And if the House of Representatives shall not choose a President whenever the right of choice shall devolve upon them, before the fourth day of March next following, then the Vice President shall act as President, as in the case of the death or other constitutional disability of the President.—The person having the greatest number of votes as Vice President, shall be the Vice President, if such number be a majority of the whole number of Electors appointed, and if no person have a majority, then from the two highest numbers on the list, the Senate shall choose the Vice President; a quorum for the purpose shall consist of two-thirds of the whole number of Senators, and a majority of the whole number shall be necessary to a choice. But no person constitutionally ineligible to the office of President shall be eligible to that of Vice President of the United States.

Amendment XIII

Section 1

Neither slavery nor involuntry servitude, except as a punishment for crime whereof the party shall have been duly convicted, shall exist within the United States, or any place subject to their jurisdiction.

Section 2

Congress shall have power to enforce this article by appropriate legislation.

Amendment XIV

Section 1

All persons born or naturalized in the United States, and subject to the jurisdiction thereof, are citizens of the United States and of the State wherein they reside. No State shall make or enforce any law which shall abridge the privileges or immunities of citizens of the United States; nor shall any State deprive any person of life, liberty, or property, without due process of law; nor deny to any person within its jurisdiction the equal protection of the laws.

Section 2

Representatives shall be apportioned among the several States according to their respective numbers, counting the whole number of persons in each State, excluding Indians not taxed. But when the right to vote at any election for the choice of electors for President and Vice President of the United States, Representatives in Congress, the Executive and Judicial officers of a State, or the members of the Legislature thereof, is denied to any of the male inhabitants of such State, being twenty-one years of age, and citizens of the United States, or in any way abridged, except for participation in rebellion, or other crime, the basis of representation therein shall be reduced in the proportion which the number of such male citizens shall bear to the whole number of male citizens twenty-one years of age in such state.

Section 3

No person shall be a Senator or Representative in Congress, or elector of President and Vice President, or hold any office, civil or military, under the United States, or under any State, who, having previously taken an oath, as a member of Congress, or as an officer of the United States, or as a member of any State legislature, or as an executive or judicial officer of any State, to support the Constitution of the United States, shall have engaged in insurrection or rebellion against the same, or given aid or comfort to the enemies thereof. But Congress may be a vote of two-thirds of each House, remove such disability.

Section 4

The validity of the public debt of the United States, authorized by law, including debts incurred for payment of pensions and bounties for services in suppressing insurrection or rebellion, shall not be questioned. But neither the United States nor any State shall assume or pay any debt or obligation incurred in aid of insurrection or rebellion against the United States, or any claim for the loss of emancipation of any slave; but all such debts, obligations and claims shall be held illegal and void.

Section 5

The Congress shall have power to enforce by appropriate legislation the provisions of this article.

Amendment XV

The right of citizens of the United States to vote shall not be denied or abridged by the United States or by any State on account of race, color, or previous condition of servitude.

Section 2

The Congress shall have power to enforce this article by appropriate legislation.

Amendment XVI

The Congress shall have power to lay and collect taxes on incomes, from whatever source derived, without apportionment among the several States, and without regard to any census or enumeration.

Amendment XVII

The Senate of the United States shall be composed of two Senators from each State, elected by the people thereof for six years; and each Senator shall have one vote. The electors in each State shall have the qualifications requisite for electors of the most numerous branch of the State legislatures.

When vacancies happen in the representation of any State in the Senate, the executive authority of such State shall issue writs of election to fill such vacancies: *Provided,* That the legislature of any State may empower the executive thereof to make temporary appointments until the people fill the vacancies by election as the legislature may direct.

This amendment shall not be so construed as to affect the election or term of any Senator chosen before it becomes valid as part of the Constitution.

Amendment XVIII

Section 1
After one year from the ratification of this article the manufacture, sale, or transportation of intoxicating liquors within, the importation thereof into, or the exportation thereof from the United States and all territory subject to the jurisdiction thereof for beverage purposes is hereby prohibited.

Section 2
The Congress and the several States shall have concurrent power to enforce this article by appropriate legislation.

Section 3
This article shall be inoperative unless it shall have been ratified as an amendment to the Constitution by the legislatures of the several States, as provided in the Constitution, within seven years from the date of the submission hereof to the States by the Congress.

Amendment XIX

The right of citizens of the United States to vote shall not be denied or abridged by the United States or by any State on account of sex.

Congress shall have power to enforce this article by appropriate legislation.

Amendment XX

Section 1
The terms of the President and Vice President shall end at noon on the 20th day of January, and the terms of Senators and Representatives at noon on the 3d day of

January, of the years in which such terms would have ended if this article had not been ratified; and the terms of their successors shall then begin.

Section 2

The Congress shall assemble at least once in every year, and such meeting shall begin at noon on the 3d day of January, unless they shall by law appoint a different day.

Section 3

If, at the time fixed for the beginning of the term of the President, the President elect shall have died, the Vice President elect shall become President. If a President shall not have been chosen before the time fixed for the beginning of his term, or if the President elect shall have failed to qualify, then the Vice President elect shall act as President until a President shall have qualified; and the Congress may by law provide for the case wherein neither a President elect nor a Vice President elect shall have qualified, declaring who shall then act as President, or the manner in which one who is to act shall be selected, and such person shall act accordingly until a President or Vice President shall have qualified.

Section 4

The Congress may by law provide for the case of the death of any of the persons from whom the House of Representatives may choose a President whenever the right of choice shall have devolved upon them, and for the case of the death of any of the persons from whom the Senate may choose a Vice President whenever the right of choice shall have devolved upon them.

Section 5

Sections 1 and 2 shall take effect on the 15th day of October following the ratification of this article.

Section 6

This article shall be inoperative unless it shall have been ratified as an amendment to the Constitution by the legislatures of three-fourths of the several States within seven years from the date of its submission.

Amendment XXI

Section 1

The eighteenth article of amendment to the Constitution of the United States is hereby repealed.

Section 2

The transportation or importation into any State, Territory, or possession of the United States for delivery or use therein of intoxicating liquors, in violation of the laws thereof, is hereby prohibited.

Section 3

This article shall be inoperative unless it shall have been ratified as an amendment to the Constitution by conventions in the several States, as provided in the Constitution, within seven years from the date of the submission hereof to the States by the Congress.

Amendment XXII

Section 1

No person shall be elected to the office of the President more than twice, and no person who has held the office of President, or acted as President, for more than two years of a term to which some other person was elected President shall be elected to the office of the President more than once. But this Article shall not apply to any person holding the office of President when this Article was proposed by the Congress, and shall not prevent any person who may be holding the office of President, or acting as President, during the term within which this Article becomes operative from holding the office of President or acting as President during the remainder of such term.

Section 2

This article shall be inoperative unless it shall have been ratified as an amendment to the Constitution by the legislatures of three-fourths of the several States within seven years from the date of its submission to the States by the Congress.

Amendment XXIII

Section 1

The District constituting the seat of Government of the United States shall appoint in such manner as the Congress may direct:

A number of electors of President and Vice President equal to the whole number of Senators and Representatives in Congress to which the District would be entitled if it were a State, but in no event more than the least populous State; they shall be in addition to those appointed by the States, but they shall be considered, for the purposes of the election of President and Vice President, to be electors appointed by a State; and they shall meet in the District and perform such duties as provided by the twelfth article of amendment.

Section 2

The Congress shall have power to enforce this article by appropriate legislation.

Amendment XXIV

Section 1

The right of citizens of the United States to vote in any primary or other election for President or Vice-President, for electors for President or Vice-President, or for Senator or Representative in Congress shall not be denied or abridged by the United States or any State by reason of failure to pay any poll tax or other tax.

Section 2

The Congress shall have power to enforce this article by appropriate legislation.

Amendment XXV

Section 1

In the case of the removal of President from office or of his death or resignation, the Vice President shall become President.

Section 2

Whenever there is a vacancy in the office of the Vice President, the President shall nominate a Vice President who shall take office upon confirmation by a majority vote of both Houses of Congress.

Section 3

Whenever the President transmits to the President pro tempore of the Senate and the Speaker of the House of Representatives his written declaration that he is unable to discharge the powers and duties of his office, and until he transmits to them a written declaration to the contrary, such powers and duties shall be discharged by the Vice President as Acting President.

Section 4

Whenever the Vice President and a majority of either the principal officers of the executive departments or of such other body of Congress may by law provide, transmit to the President pro tempore of the Senate and the Speaker of the House of Representatives their written declaration that the President is unable to discharge the powers and duties of his office, the Vice President shall immediately assume the powers and duties of the office as Acting President. Thereafter, when the President transmits to the President pro tempore of the Senate and the Speaker of the House of Representatives his written declaration that no inability exists, he shall resume the powers and duties of his office unless the Vice President and a majority of either the Principal officers of the executive departments or of such other body as Congress may by law provide, transmit within four days to the President pro tempore of the Senate and the Speaker of the House of Representatives their written declaration that the President is unable to discharge the powers and duties of his office. Thereupon Congress shall decide the issue, assembling within forty-eight hours for that purpose, if not in session. If the Congress, within twenty-one days after receipt of the latter written declaration, or, if Congress is not in session, within twenty-one days after Congress is required to assemble, determines by two-thirds vote of both Houses that the President is unable to discharge the powers and duties of his office, the Vice President shall continue to discharge the same as Acting President; otherwise, the President shall resume the powers and duties of his office.

Amendment XXVI

Section 1

The right of citizens of the United States, who are eighteen years of age or older, to vote shall not be denied or abridged by the United States or by any State on account of age.

Section 2

The Congress shall have the power to enforce this article by appropriate legislation.

Proposed Amendment

Section 1

For purposes of representation in Congress, election of the President and Vice President, and Article V of this Constitution, the District constituting the seat of government of the United States shall be treated as though it were a state.

Section 2
The exercise of the rights and powers conferred under this article shall be by the people of the District constituting the seat of government, and as shall be provided by Congress.

Section 3
The twenty-third article of amendment to the Constitution is hereby repealed.

Section 4
This article shall be inoperative, unless it shall have been ratified as an amendment to the Constitution by the legislatures of three-fourths of the several states within seven years from the date of its submission.

Notes

BACKGROUND OF THE CONSTITUTION

1. Edward Dumbauld, *The Declaration of Independence and What It Means Today* (Norman, Okla.: University of Oklahoma Press, 1950), p. 27.
2. Letter of May 8, 1825, to Henry Lee, from *The Writings of Thomas Jefferson*, ed. P. L. Ford (10 vols., 1892–1899), X, 343.
3. Letter to John Taylor, 1814, quoted in Adrienne Koch, *The American Enlightenment* (New York: George Braziller, 1965), p. 222.

BASIC FEATURES OF THE CONSTITUTION

1. *National League of Cities* v. *Usery,* 426 U.S. 833 (1976).
2. *McCulloch* v. *Maryland,* 4 Wheaton 316 (1819).
3. *Hodel* v. *Virginia Surface Min. & Recl. Assn,* 452 U.S. 264 (1981).
4. *FPC* v. *New England Power Co.,* 415 U.S. 345 (1974).
5. *National Cable Television Assn.* v. *United States,* 415 U.S. 336 (1974).
6. *Industrial Union Department* v. *American Petroleum Institute,* 448 U.S. 607 (1980); *American Textile Mfrs. Inst.* v. *Donovan,* 452 U.S. 490 (1981).
7. *California Bankers Assn.* v. *Schultz,* 416 U.S. 21 (1974).
8. *Schechter Poultry Corp.* v. *United States,* 295 U.S. 495 (1981).
9. *Nixon* v. *Administrator of General Services,* 433 U.S. 425 (1977).
10. 1 Cr. 137 (1803).
11. Oliver Wendell Holmes, *Collected Legal Papers* (New York: Harcourt, Brace & World, 1920), pp. 295–296.
12. Judge Bork quoted by Justice O'Connor writing for the Court in *Allen* v. *Wright,* 82 L Ed 2d 556 (1984).
13. *Sierra Club* v. *Morton,* 405 U.S. 727 (1972).
14. *Baker* v. *Carr,* 369 U.S. 186 (1962).
15. Justice Powell concurring in *United States* v. *Richardson,* 418 U.S. 166 (1974).
16. *Association of Data Processing Service Organizations, Inc.* v. *Camp,* 397 U.S. 150 (1970); *Barlow* v. *Collins,* 397 U.S. 159 (1970).
17. *United States* v. *SCRAP,* 413 U.S. 669 (1973).

18. *Havens Realty Corp.* v. *Coleman,* 455 U.S. 363 (1982).

19. *United States* v. *SCRAP,* 413 U.S. 669 (1973).

20. *City Council* v. *Taxpayers for Vincent,* 80 L Ed 2d 772 (1984).

21. *Warth* v. *Seldin,* 422 U.S. 490 (1975).

22. *Los Angeles* v. *Lyons,* 75 L Ed 2d 675 (1983).

23. *Allen* v. *Wright,* 82 L Ed 2d 556 (1984).

24. *Allen* v. *Wright,* 82 L Ed 2d 556 (1984).

25. Dissenting in *United States* v. *SCRAP,* 412 U.S. 669 (1973).

26. *United States* v. *Richardson,* 418 U.S. 166 (1974).

27. *Baker* v. *Carr,* 369 U.S. 186 (1962).

28. *Luther* v. *Borden,* 7 Howard 1 (1849); *Colegrove* v. *Green,* 328 U.S. 549 (1946).

29. *Baker* v. *Carr,* 369 U.S. 186 (1962).

30. *Wesberry* v. *Sanders,* 376 U.S. 1 (1964).

31. *Gray* v. *Sanders,* 372 U.S. 368 (1963).

32. *Avery* v. *Midland County,* 390 U.S. 474 (1968).

33. Justice Brandeis concurring in *Ashwander* v. *TVA,* 297 U.S. 288 (1936).

34. *Myers* v. *United States,* 272 U.S. 52 (1926).

35. *Powell* v. *McCormack,* 395 U.S. 486 (1969).

36. *United States* v. *Nixon,* 418 U.S. 683 (1974).

37. *Rostker* v. *Goldberg,* 453 U.S. 57.

38. J.W. Peltason, *Federal Courts in the Political Process,* (New York: Random House, 1955).

39. Stuart Taylor, Jr., "The One-Pronged Test for Federal Judges. Reagan Puts Ideology First," *The New York Times,* April 22, 1984, p.E, 5.

40. 77 L Ed 2d 317 (1983).

41. *United States* v. *United States District Court,* 407 U.S. 297 (1972).

42. *United States* v. *Nixon,* 418 U.S. 683 (1974).

43. Stephen Wermeil, "Justices' Tenure Is Campaign Issue," *The Wall Street Journal,* February 8, 1984, p. 62.

THE CONSTITUTION OF THE UNITED STATES

The Preamble; Article I; The Legislative Article

1. *Jacobson* v. *Massachusetts,* 197 U.S. 11 (1905).

2. *McCulloch* v. *Maryland,* 4 Wheaton 316 (1819).

3. Constitution of Massachusetts, Part the First, Article XXX.

4. *United States* v. *Curtiss-Wright Export Corp.,* 299 U.S. 304 (1936).

5. *Wesberry* v. *Sanders,* 376 U.S. 1 (1964).

6. *Karcher* v. *Dagett,* 77 L Ed 2d 133 (1983).

7. *Kirkpatrick* v. *Preisler,* 394 U.S. 526 (1969); *Karcher* v. *Dagett,* 77 L Ed 2d 133 (1983).

8. *Brown* v. *Thomson*, 77 L Ed 2d 214 (1983).

9. *Ex parte Yarbrough*, 110 U.S. 651 (1884).

10. *Pollock* v. *Farmers' Loan & Trust Co.*, 157 U.S. 429 (1895).

11. *Eastland* v. *United States Servicemen's Fund*, 421 U.S. 491 (1975).

12. *Nixon* v. *Fitzgerald*, 457 U.S. 731 (1982).

13. *Ibid.*

14. *Smiley* v. *Holm*, 285 U.S. 355 (1932).

15. *United States* v. *Classic*, 313 U.S. 299 (1941).

16. *Oregon* v. *Mitchell*, 400 U.S. 112 (1970).

17. *Powell* v. *McCormack*, 395 U.S. 486 (1969).

18. *Roudebush* v. *Hartke*, 405 U.S. 15 (1972).

19. *Gravel* v. *United States*, 408 U.S. 606 (1980).

20. *United States* v. *Gillock*, 445 U.S. 360 (1980).

21. *United States* v. *Helstoski*, 442 U.S. 477 (1979).

22. *United States* v. *Johnson*, 383 U.S. 169 (1966).

23. *United States* v. *Helstoski*, 442 U.S. 477 (1979); *United States* v. *Brewster*, 408 U.S. 501 (1972).

24. *Gravel* v. *United States*, 408 U.S. 606 (1972).

25. *Hutchinson* v. *Proxmire*, 443 U.S. 111 (1979).

26. *Doe* v. *McMillian*, 412 306 (1973).

27. *Ex parte Levitt*, 302 U.S. 633 (1937).

28. *McClure* v. *Regan*, 454 U.S. 1025 (1981); these materials are taken from Stephen L. Wasby, *The Supreme Court in the Federal Judicial System*, (New York: Holt, Rinehart and Winston, 2nd ed., 1984), p. 84.

29. *Schlesinger* v. *Reservists to Stop the War*, 418 U.S. 206 (1974).

30. *INS* v. *Chadha*, 77 L Ed 2d 317 (1983).

31. Justice White dissenting in *INS* v. *Chadha*.

32. *McCulloch* v. *Maryland*, 4 Wheaton, 316 (1819).

33. *Pennhurst* v. *Halderman*, 451 U.S. 1 (1981).

34. *Massachusetts* v. *Mellon*, 262 U.S. 447 (1923).

35. *Frothingham* v. *Mellon*, 262 U.S. 447 (1923).

36. *Flast* v. *Cohen*, 392 U.S. 83 (1968).

37. *Valley Forge Christian College* v. *Americans United for Separation of Church & States*, 454 U.S. 464 (1982).

38. *United States* v. *Richardson*, 418 U.S. 166 (1974).

39. *Marchetti* v. *United States*, 390 U.S. 39 (1968); *Haynes* v. *United States*, 390 U.S. 85 (1968); *Leary* v. *United States*, 395 U.S. 6 (1969).

40. *United States* v. *Ptasynski*, 76 L Ed 2d 427 (1983).

41. *Japan Line, Ltd.* v. *County of Los Angeles*, 441 U.S. 434 (1979).

42. *Ibid.*

43. *Container Corp.* v. *Franchise Tax Board*, 77 L Ed 2d 545 (1983).

44. *Gibbons* v. *Ogden,* 9 Wheaton 1 (1824).

45. *United States* v. *Darby,* 312 U.S. 100 (1941).

46. *Hodel* v. *Virginia Surface Min. & Recl. Assn.,* 452 U.S. 264 (1981).

47. *Heart of Atlanta Motel* v. *United States,* 379 U.S. 241 (1964).

48. *Daniel* v. *Paul,* 395 U.S. 298 (1969).

49. Concurring in *Hodel* v. *Virginia Surface Min. & Recl. Assn.*

50. *FERC* v. *Mississippi,* 456 U.S. 742 (1982).

51. *McLain* v. *Real Estate Board of New Orleans,* 444 U.S. 232 (1980); *Goldfarb* v. *Virginia State Board,* 421 U.S. 733 (1975); *Hodel* v. *Virginia Surface Min. & Recl. Assn.*

52. *United States* v. *Appalachian Electric Power Co.,* 311 U.S. 377 (1940).

53. *Lewis* v. *Bt. Investment Managers, Inc.,* 447 U.S. 27 (1980).

54. *Minnesota* v. *Clover Leaf Creamery Co.,* 449 U.S. 456 (1981).

55. *Western & Southern L.I. Co.,* v. *Board of Equalization of California,* 451 U.S. 648 (1981).

56. *White* v. *Massachusetts Council of Construction Employers,* 77 L Ed 2d (1983); *Hughes* v. *Alexandria Scrap Corp.,* 426 U.S. 794 (1976); *Reeves* v. *Stake,* 447 U.S. 429 (1980).

57. *Lewis* v. *Bt. Investment Managers, Inc.,* 447 U.S. 27 (1980).

58. *Southern Pacific Co.* v. *Arizona,* 325 U.S. 761 (1945); *Fireman* v. *Chicago, Rock Island and Pacific R.R. Co.,* 393 U.S. 129 (1968).

59. *Minnesota* v. *Clover Leaf Creamery Co.,* 449 U.S. 456 (1981).

60. *Bibb* v. *Navajo Freight Lines,* 359 U.S. 520 (1959).

61. *Kassel* v. *Consolidated Freightways Corp.,* 450 U.S. 662 (1981).

62. *Ray* v. *Atlantic Richfield Co.,* 435 U.S. 151 (1978).

63. *Philadelphia* v. *New Jersey,* 437 U.S. 617 (1978).

64. *Pike* v. *Bruce Church, Inc.,* 397 U.S. 137 (1970).

65. *Hunt* v. *Washington State Apple Advertising Commission,* 432 U.S. 333 (1977).

66. *Exxon Corporation* v. *Governor of Maryland,* 437 U.S. 117 (1978).

67. *Edgar* v. *Mite Corp.,* 457 U.S. 624 (1982).

68. *Ark. Elec. Coop.* v. *Ark. Public Ser. Commission,* 76 L Ed 2d 1 (1983).

69. *Hughes* v. *Oklahoma,* 441 U.S. 322 (1979).

70. Justice Powell dissenting in *Reeves, Inc.* v. *Stake,* 447 U.S. 429 (1980).

71. *Reeves, Inc.* v. *Stake,* 447 U.S. 429 (1980).

72. 430 U.S. 274 (1977); *Mobil Oil Corp.* v. *Commissioner of Taxes,* 445 U.S. 425 (1980); *Exxon Corp.* v. *Wisconsin Dept. of Revenue,* 447 U.S. 207 (1980).

73. *Container Corporation* v. *Franchise Tax Bd.,* 77 L Ed 2d 545 (1983).

74. *Maryland* v. *Louisiana,* 451 U.S. 725 (1981).

75. *Armco* v. *Hardesty,* 81 L Ed 2d 540 (1984).

76. *Commonwealth Edison Company* v. *Montana,* 453 U.S. 609 (1981).

77. *National Bellas Hess* v. *Dept. of Revenue,* 386 U.S. 753 (1967).

78. *National Geographic Society* v. *California Equalization Board,* 430 U.S. 551 (1977).

79. *Dunbar-Stanley Studios* v. *Alabama,* 393 U.S. 537 (1969).

80. *The Minnesota Rate Cases,* 230 U.S. 537 (1913).

81. *Morton* v. *Mancari,* 417 U.S. 535 (1974).

82. *Ibid.*

83. *Ramah Navajo Sch. Bd.* v. *Bureau of Revenue,* 458 U.S. 833 (1982).

84. *Antoine* v. *Washington,* 420 U.S. 194 (1975); *Mescalero Apache Tribe* v. *Jones,* 411 U.S. 145 (1973); *New Mexico* v. *Mescalero Apache Tribe,* 76 L Ed 2d 611 (1983).

85. *United States* v. *Mazurie,* 419 U.S. 544 (1975).

86. *Rice* v. *Rehner,* 77 L Ed 2d 961 (1983).

87. *Washington* v. *Confederated Tribes,* 447 U.S. 134 (1980).

88. *McClanahan* v. *Arizona,* 411 U.S. 164 (1973); *White Mountain Apache Tribe* v. *Bracker,* 448 U.S. 136 (1980); *Central Machinery Co.* v. *Arizona Tax Comm.,* 448 U.S. 160 (1980).

89. *Ramah Navajo School Board; United States* v. *New Mexico,* 455 U.S. 720 (1982).

90. *Mescalero Apache Tribe* v. *Jones,* 411 U.S. 145 (1973).

91. *Montana* v. *United States,* 450 U.S. 544 (1981); *Oliphant* v. *Suquamis Indian Tribe,* 435 U.S. 1911 (1979); *Merrion* v. *Jicarilla Apache Tribe,* 455 U.S. 130 (1982).

92. *Santa Clara Pueblo* v. *Martinez,* 436 U.S. 49 (1978).

93. *Fong Yue Ting* v. *United States,* 149 U.S. 698 (1893); reaffirmed in *Kleindienst* v. *Mandel,* 408 U.S. 753 (1972).

94. *Graham* v. *Richardson,* 403 U.S. 365 (1971).

95. *Perez* v. *Campbell,* 402 U.S. 637 (1971).

96. *United States* v. *Security Industrial Park,* 74 L Ed 2d 235 (1983).

97. *Regional Rail Reorganization Act Cases,* 419 U.S. 102 (1974).

98. *Railroad Labor Executives' Association* v. *Gibbons,* 445 U.S. 457 (1982).

99. *Regan* v. *Time, Inc.,* 82 L Ed 2d 487 (1984).

100. *Sony Corp.* v. *Universal City Studios,* 78 L Ed 2d 574 (1984).

101. *Diamond* v. *Chakrabarty,* 447 U.S. 303 (1980).

102. *Graham* v. *John Deere Co.,* 383 U.S. 1 (1966).

103. *Goldstein* v. *California,* 421 U.S. 546 (1973).

104. *Kewanee Oil Co.* v. *Bicron Corp.,* 416 U.S. 470 (1974).

105. Charles Evans Hughes, "War Powers under the Constitution," 42 *Reports of the American Bar Association,* September 5, 1971.

106. *Rostker* v. *Goldberg,* 453 U.S. 57 (1981).

107. *Parker* v. *Levy,* 417 U.S. 733 (1974); *Secretary of the Navy* v. *Avrech,* 418 U.S. 676 (1974).

108. *McGrain* v. *Daugherty,* 272 U.S. 135 (1927).

109. *Watkins* v. *United States,* 354 U.S. 178 (1957); *Barenblatt* v. *United States,* 360 U.S. 109 (1959).

110. *Yellin* v. *United States,* 374 U.S. 109 (1957).

111. *Gojack* v. *United States,* 384 U.S. 702 (1966); *Russell* v. *United States,* 369 U.S. 749 (1962).

112. *Wainwright* v. *Sykes,* 433 U.S. 72 (1977).

113. Chief Justice Burger quoting Justice Friendly in *Swain* v. *Pressley,* 430 U.S. 372 (1977).

114. *Stone* v. *Powell,* 428 U.S. 465 (1976); *Caldwell* v. *Taylor,* 76 L Ed 2d 333 (1983).

115. *Engle* v. *Isaac,* 456 U.S. 107 (1982); *Wainwright* v. *Sykes,* 433 U.S. 72 (1977).

116. *United States* v. *Lovett,* 328 U.S. 303 (1946).

117. *United States* v. *Brown,* 381 U.S. 437 (1965).

118. *Nixon* v. *Administrator of General Services,* 433 U.S. 425 (1977).

119. *Selective Service System et al.* v. *Minnesota Public Interest Research Group et al.,* 82 L Ed 2d 632 (1984).

120. *Weaver* v. *Graham,* 450 U.S. 24 (1981).

121. *Dobbert* v. *Florida,* 432 U.S. 282 (1977).

122. *United States* v. *Darusmont,* 449 U.S. 292 (1981).

123. *Kring* v. *Missouri,* 107 U.S. 221 (1883). For due process considerations with respect to retroactive civil laws see, *Pension Benefit Guaranty Corp.* v. *R.A. Gray & Co.,* 81 L Ed 2d 601 (1984).

124. *United States* v. *Richardson,* 418 U.S. 166 (1974).

125. *Zschering* v. *Miller,* 389 U.S. 429 (1968).

126. *Fletcher* v. *Peck,* 6 Cranch 87 (1810); *Dartmouth College* v. *Woodward,* 4 Wheaton 518 (1819); *Sturges* v. *Crowninshield,* 4 Wheaton 122 (1819).

127. *Charles River Bridge Co.* v. *Warren Bridge,* 11 Peters 420 (1837); *Stone* v. *Mississippi,* 101 U.S. 814 (1880).

128. *United States Trust Co.* v. *New Jersey,* 431 U.S. 1 (1977).

129. *Allied Structural Steel Company* v. *Spannaus,* 438 U.S. 234 (1978).

130. *Exxon Corp.* v. *Eagerton,* 76 L Ed 2d 67 (1983).

131. *Energy Reserves* v. *Kansas Power & Light,* 74 L Ed 2d 569 (1983).

132. *Michelin Tire Corp.* v. *Wages,* 423 U.S. 276 (1976).

133. *Washington Revenue Department* v. *Stevedoring Association,* 435 U.S. 734 (1978).

134. *U.S. Steel Corp.* v. *Multistate Tax Commission,* 434 U.S. 452 (1978); *Virginia* v. *Tennessee,* 148 U.S. 503 (1893).

135. *New Hampshire* v. *Maine,* 426 U.S. 363 (1976).

136. *U.S. Steel Corp.* v. *Multistate Tax Commission,* 434 U.S. 452 (1978); *Virginia* v. *Tennessee,* 148 U.S. 503 (1893).

137. *Cuyler* v. *Adams,* 449 U.S. 433 (1981).

138. *West Virginia ex rel Dyer* v. *Sims,* 341 U.S. 22 (1951); *Nebraska* v. *Iowa,* 406 U.S. 117 (1972).

Article II: The Executive Article

1. John Locke, *Second Treatise of Civil Government,* ed. Charles L. Sherman (New York: D. Appleton-Century Co., 1937), p. 109.

2. Justice Rehnquist for the Court in *Dames & Moore* v. *Regan* 453 U.S. 654 (1981) quoting Justice Jackson concurring in *Youngstown Sheet & Tube Co.* v. *Sawyer,* 343 U.S. 579 (1952).

3. *Youngstown Sheet & Tube Co.* v. *Sawyer,* 343 U.S. 579 (1952).

4. *New York Times Company* v. *United States,* 403 U.S. 713 (1971).

5. *United States* v. *United States District Court,* 407 U.S. 297 (1972).

6. *United States* v. *Nixon,* 418 U.S. 683 (1974).

7. *Dames & Moore* v. *Regan,* 453 U.S. 654 (1981).

8. *Williams* v. *Rhodes,* 393 U.S. 23 (1968).

9. *Moore* v. *Ogilvie,* 394 U.S. 814 (1969).

10. *Anderson* v. *Celebrezze,* 75 L Ed 2d 547 (1983).

11. James Madison, *The Records of the Federal Convention of 1787,* ed. MacFarrand (New Haven: Yale University Press, 1937), II, 110.

12. George Mason, *Ibid.,* II, 31.

13. *Ray* v. *Blair,* 343 U.S. 214 (1952).

14. *Korematsu* v. *United States,* 323 U.S. 214 (1944).

15. *Duncan* v. *Kahanamoku,* 32 U.S. 304 (1946).

16. *Schick* v. *Reed,* 419 U.S. 256 (1974).

17. David C. Stephenson, Acting U.S. Pardon Attorney in Pete Earley, "Presidents Set Own Rules Granting Clemency," *The Washington Post,* March 19, 1984, p. A17.

18. *Goldwater et al.* v. *Carter, President of the United States,* 444 U.S. 996 (1979).

19. *Buckley* v. *Valeo,* 424 U.S. 1 (1976).

20. Wallace Turner, "Judge's Decisions Are Now in Doubt," *The New York Times,* January 22, 1984, p. 19.

21. *Wiener* v. *United States,* 357 U.S. 349 (1958); *Myers* v. *United States,* 272 U.S. 52 (1926); *Humphrey's Executor* v. *United States,* 295 U.S. 602 (1935).

Article III: The Judicial Article

1. *Brown Transport Corp.* v. *Acton,* 439 U.S. 1014 (1978).

2. Justice White dissenting in *Northern Pipeline Co.* v. *Marathon Pipe Line Co.,* 458 U.S. 50 (1982).

3. *Northern Pipeline Construction Co.* v. *Marathon Pipe Line Co.*

4. *Chandler* v. *Judicial Council,* 382 U.S. 1003 (1966).

5. Larry C. Berkson and Irene A. Tesitor, "Holding Federal Judges Accountable," *Judicature* 61, no 10 (May 1978): 455.

6. *United States* v. *Raddatz,* 447 U.S. 667 (1980).

7. *O'Malley* v. *Woodrough,* 307 U.S. 277 (1939).

8. *United States* v. *Will,* 449 U.S. 200 (1981).

9. *Osborn* v. *Bank of the United States,* 9 Wheaton 738 (1824).

10. *Verlinden B.V.* v. *Central Bank of Nigeria,* 76 L Ed 2d 81 (1983).

11. *Maine* v. *Thiboutot,* 448 U.S. 1 (1980).

12. *Gutierrez* v. *Waterman S.S. Corp.,* 373 U.S. 206 (1963).

13. *Foremost Ins. Co.* v. *Richardson,* 452 U.S. 668 (1982).
14. *Victory Carriers, Inc.* v. *Law,* 404 U.S. 249 (1972).
15. *Executive Jet Aviation* v. *Cleveland,* 409 U.S. 249 (1972).
16. *California* v. *Arizona,* 440 U.S. 59 (1979).
17. Justice Rehnquist dissenting in *Maryland* v. *Louisiana,* 451 U.S. 725 (1981).
18. *Illinois* v. *Michigan,* 409 U.S. 36 (1972).
19. Justice Rehnquist dissenting in *Maryland et al.* v. *Louisiana.*
20. *Vermont* v. *New York,* 417 U.S. 270 (1974).
21. *Ex parte McCardle,* 6 Wallace 318 (1868); *Ex parte McCardle,* 7 Wallace 506 (1869).
22. *Key* v. *Doyle,* 434 U.S. 59 (1978).
23. *Hicks* v. *Miranda,* 422 U.S. 332 (1975).

Article IV: States' Relations

1. *Williams* v. *North Carolina,* 325 U.S. 226 (1945).
2. *Johnson* v. *Muelberger,* 340 U.S. 581 (1951).
3. *Nevada* v. *Hall,* 400 U.S. 410 (1979).
4. *Allstate Insurance Co.* v. *Hague,* 449 U.S. 302 (1981).
5. *Baldwin* v. *Montana Fish and Game Commission,* 436 U.S. 371 (1978).
6. *Martinez* v. *Bynum,* 76 L Ed 2d 879 (1983).
7. *United Bldg. & Construction Trades* v. *Mayor,* 79 L Ed 2d 249 (1984).
8. *Austin* v. *New Hampshire,* 420 U.S. 656 (1975).
9. *Toomer* v. *Witsell,* 334 U.S. 385 (1948).
10. *Hicklin* v. *Orbeck,* 437 U.S. 518 (1978).
11. *Baldwin* v. *Montana Fish and Games Commission,* 436 U.S. 371 (1978).
12. *Hicklin* v. *Orbeck,* 437 U.S. 518 (1978).
13. *Shapiro* v. *Thompson,* 394 U.S. 618 (1969).
14. *Dunn* v. *Blumstein,* 405 U.S. 331 (1972).
15. *Sosna* v. *Iowa,* 419 U.S. 393 (1975).
16. *Vlandis* v. *Kline,* 412 U.S. 441 (1973).
17. Bill Richards, "Governors' Decisions in Extradition Cases Vary All Over the Map," *The Wall Street Journal,* May 27, 1984, p. 1.
18. *Michigan* v. *Doran,* 439 U.S. 282 (1978); *Pacileo* v. *Walker,* 449 U.S. 86 (1980).
19. Compare *Stearns* v. *Minnesota,* 179 U.S. 223 (1900), with *Coyle* v. *Smith,* 221 U.S. 559 (1911).
20. *Texas* v. *White,* 7 Wallace 700 (1869).
21. *Hawaii* v. *Mankichi,* 190 U.S. 197 (1903), and *Balzac* v. *Puerto Rico,* 258 U.S. 298 (1922).
22. *Rodriguez* v. *Popular Democratic Party,* 407 U.S. 1 (1982).
23. *Harris* v. *Rosario,* 446 U.S. 651 (1980).
24. *Pacific States Tel. & Tel. Co.* v. *Oregon,* 223 U.S. 118 (1912); *Colegrove* v. *Green,* 328 U.S. 549 (1946). See also *Baker* v. *Carr,* 369 U.S. 186 (1962)

25. The quotes from Adams and Sumner on page 124 come from C. Gordon Post's review of William M. Wiececk, *The Guarantee Clause of the U.S. Constitution (Ithaca, N.Y.: Cornell University Press, 1972) in* Annals of the American Academy of Political and Social Science, vol. 402, July 1972, pp. 169–170.
26. *Luther* v. *Borden,* 7 Howard 1 (1849).
27. In re *Debs,* 158 U.S. 464 (1895).

Article V: The Amending Power

1. Larry Green, "Cries Grow for Balanced U.S. Budget," *Los Angeles Times,* February 18, 1984, p. 1, 25.
2. *Coleman* v. *Miller,* 307 U.S. 433 (1939), concurring opinion.
3. Walter Dellinger, "The Legitimacy of Constitutional Change: Rethinking the Amendment Process," *The Harvard Law Review,* vol. 92, December 1983, pp. 386–432.
4. *Hammer* v. *Dagenhart,* 247 U.S. 251 (1918).
5. *United States* v. *Darby,* 312 U.S. 11 (1941).

Article VI: The Supremacy Article

1. *Pennsylvania* v. *Nelson,* 350 U.S. 497 (1956); *Uphaus* v. *Wyman,* 360 U.S. 72 (1959).
2. *Pacific Gas & Electric* v. *Energy Res. Comm'n.,* 75 L ed 2d 752 (1983).
3. *Ibid.*
4. *Fidelity Federal S & L Assn.* v. *De la Cuesta,* 458 U.S. 141 (1982).
5. *Reid* v. *Covert,* 354 U.S. 1 (1957).
6. *Missouri* v. *Holland,* 252 U.S. 416 (1920).
7. *National League of Cities* v. *Usery,* 426 U.S. 833 (1976).
8. *Hodel* v. *Virginia Surface Min. & Recl. Assn.,* 452 U.S. 264 (1981).
9. *United Transportation Union* v. *Long Island Railroad Co.* 455 U.S. 678 (1982).
10. *FERC* v. *Mississippi,* 72 L Ed 2d 532 (1983).
11. *EEOC* v. *Wyoming,* 75 L Ed 18 (1983).
12. *FERC* v. *Mississippi,* 72 L Ed 2d 532 (1983).
13. *Ibid.*
14. *Fitzpatrick* v. *Bitzer,* 427 U.S. 445 (1976).
15. *Torcaso* v. *Watkins,* 367 U.S. 488 (1961).

AMENDMENTS TO THE CONSTITUTION

The Bill of Rights; Amendment I: Religion, Speech, Assembly, and Petition

1. Alexander Hamilton, No. 84, *The Federalist.*
2. *Barron* v. *Baltimore,* 7 Peters (1833).
3. *Gitlow* v. *New York,* 268 U.S. 652 (1925).

4. *Palko* v. *Connecticut,* 302 U.S. 319 (1937).

5. *Duncan* v. *Louisiana,* 391 U.S. 145 (1968).

6. *Chapman* v. *California,* 386 U.S. 18 (1967).

7. *Schneble* v. *Florida,* 405 U.S. 427 (1972).

8. *Gideon* v. *Wainwright,* 372 U.S. 335 (1963).

9. *Duncan* v. *Louisiana,* 391 U.S. 145 (1968).

10. *Harvard Civil Rights-Civil Liberties Law Review,* 1973 quoted by Robert Welsh and Ronald K. L. Collins, *The Center Magazine,* vol. XIV (September–October 1981), p. 6.

11. Justice Stanley Mosk of the California Supreme Court quoted by Fred Barbash, "State Courts Expanding Individual's Rights: Role Reversal in Judicial System," *The Washington Post,* April 2, 1984, p. A1.

12. "Developments in the Law—The Interpretation of State Constitutional Rights," *Harvard Law Review,* vol. 95 (April 1982), p. 1493.

13. Justice Jackson concurring in *Illinois ex rel McCollum* v. *Board of Education,* 333 U.S. 203 (1948).

14. *Lynch* v. *Donnelly,* 79 L Ed 2d 604 (1984).

15. *Jones* v. *Wolf,* 443 U.S. 595 (1979).

16. *Abington School District* v. *Schempp,* 374 U.S. 203 (1963); *Engel* v. *Vitale,* 370 U.S. 421 (1962).

17. *Lemon* v. *Kurtzman,* 403 U.S. 602 (1971).

18. *Lynch* v. *Donnelly,* 79 L Ed 2d 604 (1984).

19. *Ibid.*

20. Justice Brennan dissenting opinion, joined by Justices Marshall, Blackmun, and Stevens, in *Lynch* v. *Donnelly.*

21. *Abington School District* v. *Schempp,* 374 U.S. 203 (1963); *Engel* v. *Vitale,* 370 U.S. 421 (1962); *Stone* v. *Graham,* 449 U.S. 39 (1980).

22. *Widmar* v. *Vincent,* 454 U.S. 263 (1981).

23. *Epperson* v. *Arkansas,* 393 U.S. 97 (1968).

24. *Illinois ex rel McCollum* v. *Board of Education,* 333 U.S. 203 (1948).

25. *Zorach* v. *Clauson,* 343 U.S. 306 (1952); *Abington* v. *Schempp,* 377 U.S. 203 (1963).

26. *Tilton* v. *Richardson,* 403 U.S. 672 (1971); *Hunt* v. *McNair,* 413 U.S. 734 (1973); *Roemer* v. *Board of Public Works of Maryland,* 426 U.S. 736 (1976).

27. *Ibid.*

28. *Norwood* v. *Harrison,* 413 U.S. 455 (1973).

29. *Board of Education* v. *Allen,* 392 U.S. 236 (1968); *Wolman* v. *Walter,* 433 U.S. 229 (1977).

30. *Cochran* v. *Board of Education,* 281 U.S. 370 (1930); *Everson* v. *Board of Education,* 330 U.S. 1 (1947); *Board of Education* v. *Allen,* 392 U.S. 236 (1968); *Meek* v. *Pittenger,* 421 U.S. 349 (1975).

31. *Wolman* v. *Walter,* 433 U.S. 229 (1977); *Meek* v. *Pittenger,* 421 U.S. 349 (1975).

32. *Committee for Public Education* v. *Regan,* 444 U.S. 646 (1980).

33. *Mueller* v. *Allen,* 77 L Ed 2d 721 (1983).

34. *Committee for Public Education* v. *Nyquist,* 413 U.S. 756 (1973).

35. *Wolman* v. *Walter,* 433 U.S. 229 (1977).

36. *Committee for Public Education* v. *Nyquist,* 413 U.S. 756 (1973); *Sloan* v. *Lemon,* 413 U.S. 825 (1973).

37. *Levitt* v. *Committee for Public Education,* 413 U.S. 472 (1973).

38. *Ibid.*

39. *Wolman* v. *Walter,* 433 U.S. 229 (1977); *Meek* v. *Pittenger,* 421 U.S. 349 (1975).

40. *Ibid.*

41. *McGowan* v. *Maryland,* 366 U.S. 420 (1961).

42. *Walz* v. *Tax Commission,* 397 U.S. 664 (1970); *Diffenderfer* v. *Central Baptist Church,* 404 U.S. 412 (1972).

43. *Lynch* v. *Donnelly,* 79 L Ed 2d 604 (1984).

44. *Larkin* v. *Grendel's Den,* 459 U.S. 116 (1982).

45. *Larson* v. *Valente,* 456 U.S. 228 (1982).

46. *Marsh* v. *Chambers,* 77 L Ed 2d 1019 (1983).

47. *Walz* v. *Tax Commission,* 397 U.S. 664 (1970).

48. *Welsh* v. *United States,* 398 U.S. 333 (1970); *Gillette* v. *United States,* 401 U.S. 437 (1971).

49. *McDaniel* v. *Paty,* 435 U.S. 618 (1978).

50. *Braunfeld* v. *Brown,* 366 U.S. 599 (1961).

51. *Jacobson* v. *Massachusetts,* 197 U.S. 11 (1905).

52. *Heffron* v. *International Society for Krishna Consciousness, Inc.,* 452 U.S. 640 (1981).

53. *United States* v. *Lee,* 455 U.S. 252 (1982).

54. *Bob Jones University* v. *United States,* 76 L Ed 2d 157 (1983).

55. *Wisconsin* v. *Yoder,* 406 U.S. 205 (1972).

56. *Bob Jones University* v. *United States,* 76 L Ed 2d 157 (1983).

57. *West Virginia State Board of Education* v. *Barnette,* 319 U.S. 624 (1943); *Wooley* v. *Maynard,* 430 U.S. 705 (1977).

58. *Wisconsin* v. *Yoder,* 406 U.S. 205 (1972).

59. *Pierce* v. *Society of Sisters,* 268 U.S. 510 (1925).

60. *Sherbert* v. *Verner,* 374 U.S. 398 (1963); *Thomas* v. *Review Board,* 450 U.S. 707 (1981).

61. *Ibid.*

62. *Ibid.*

63. *Bose Corporation* v. *Consumers Union,* 80 L Ed 2d 502 (1984).

64. *Cohen* v. *California,* 403 U.S. 15 (1971); *Gooding* v. *Wilson,* 405 U.S. 518 (1972).

65. David O'Brien, *The Public's Right to Know: The Supreme Court and the First Amendment,* (New York: Praeger Publishers, 1981), p. 97, quoting from John Hart Ely, "Flag Desecration," *Harvard Law Review* 88 (1975): 1493.

66. *NAACP* v. *Claiborne Hardware Co.,* 458 U.S. 886 (1982).

67. *New York Times* v. *Sullivan,* 376 U.S. 254 (1964); *Rosenbloom* v. *Metromedia,* 403 U.S. 29 (1971); *Gertz* v. *Welch,* 418 U.S. 323 (1974); *Cantrell* v. *Forest City Publishing Co.,* 419 U.S. 245 (1974).

68. *Herbert* v. *Lando,* 441 U.S. 153 (1979).

69. *Wolston* v. *Reader's Digest Association,* 443 U.S. 157 (1979).

70. *Calder* v. *Jones,* 79 L Ed 2d 804 (1984); *Keeton* v. *Hustler Magazine, Inc.,* 79 L Ed 2d 790 (1984).

71. *Bose Corporation* v. *Consumers Union,* 80 L Ed 2d 502 (1984).

72. *Stanley* v. *Georgia,* 394 U.S. 557 (1969).

73. *Paris Adult Theatre I* v. *Slaton,* 413 U.S. 49 (1973).

74. *Miller* v. *California,* 415 U.S. 15 (1973).

75. *Memoirs* v. *Massachusetts,* 383 U.S. 413 (1966); *Roth* v. *United States,* 354 U.S. 476 (1957).

76. *Hamling* v. *United States,* 418 U.S. 87 (1974).

77. *Pinkus* v. *United States,* 436 U.S. 293 (1978).

78. *Splawn* v. *California,* 431 U.S. 595 (1977).

79. *Cooper* v. *Mitchell Brothers,* 454 U.S. 90 (1981).

80. *Jenkins* v. *Georgia,* 418 U.S. 153 (1974).

81. *Miller* v. *California,* 413 U.S 15 (1973); *Paris Adult Theatre I.* v. *Slaton,* 413 U.S. 49 (1973).

82. *Young* v. *American Mini Theatres,* 427 U.S. 50 (1976).

83. *Ibid.*

84. *Schad* v. *Mt. Ephraim,* 452 U.S. 61 (1981).

85. *New York* v. *Ferber,* 458 U.S. 747 (1982); *Ginsberg* v. *New York,* 390 U.S. 629 (1968).

86. *Friedman* v. *Rogers,* 440 U.S. 1 (1979).

87. *Central Hudson Gas & Electric Corporation* v. *Public Service Commission of New York,* 447 U.S. 557 (1980).

88. Justice Stewart concurring in *Virginia Pharmacy Board* v. *Virginia Consumer Council,* 425 U.S. 748 (1976).

89. *In Re R.M.J.,* 455 U.S. 191 (1982).

90. *Friedman* v. *Rogers,* 440 U.S. 1 (1979).

91. *Pittsburgh Press Co.* v. *Human Relations Commission,* 413 U.S. 376 (1973)

92. *Virginia Pharmacy Board* v. *Virginia Consumer Council,* 452 U.S. 746 (1976); *Bates* v. *State Bar of Arizona,* 433 U.S. 530 (1977); *In re R.M.J.,* 455 U.S. 191 (1982).

93. *Linmark Associates, Inc.* v. *Township of Willingboro,* 431 U.S. 85 (1977).

94. *Carey* v. *Population Services International,* 431 U.S. 678 (1977).

95. *First National Bank of Boston* v. *Bellotti,* 435 U.S. 765 (1978); *Central Hudson Gas* v. *Public Service Commission,* 447 U.S. 557 (1980); *Consolidated Edison* v. *Public Service Commission,* 447 U.S. 530 (1980).

96. *Dennis* v. *United States,* 341 U.S. 494 (1951).

97. *Yates* v. *United States,* 354 U.S. 298 (1957); *Brandenburg* v. *Ohio,* 395 U.S. 444 (1969).

98. *Organization for a Better Austin* v. *Keefe,* 402 U.S. 415 (1971).

99. *New York Times Company* v. *United States,* 403 U.S. 713 (1971).

100. *United States* v. *The Progressive, Inc.,* 467 F. Supp. 990 (1979); *Moreland* v. *Sprecher,* 443 U.S. 709 (1979).

101. *Greer* v. *Spock,* 424 U.S. 828 (1976); *Brown* v. *Glines,* 444 U.S. 620 (1980); *Secretary of Navy* v. *Huff,* 444 U.S. 507 (1980).

102. *Snepp* v. *United States,* 444 U.S. 507 (1980).

103. *Seattle Times Co.* v. *Rhinehart,* 81 L Ed 2d 17 (1984).

104. *Consolidated Edison Company* v. *Public Service Commission of New York,* 447 U.S. 530 (1980).

105. *NAACP* v. *Button,* 371 U.S. 415 (1963).

106. *Schuamburg* v. *Citizens for Better Environment,* 444 U.S. 620 (1980).

107. *Secretary of State of Maryland* v. *Munson Co.,* 81 L Ed 2d 786 (1984).

108. *Erznoznik* v. *City of Jacksonville,* 422 U.S. 205 (1975).

109. *Burstyn* v. *Wilson,* 343 U.S. 495 (1952); *Winters* v. *New York,* 333 U.S. 507 (1948).

110. *Lewis* v. *City of New Orleans,* 415 U.S. 130 (1974).

111. *Plummer* v. *City of Columbus,* 414 U.S. 2 (1973).

112. *Papish* v. *Board of Curators,* 410 U.S. 667 (1973).

113. *Bond* v. *Floyd,* 385 U.S. 116 (1966).

114. *Landmark Communications* v. *Virginia,* 435 U.S. 829 (1978).

115. *United States* v. *O'Brien,* 391 U.S. 367 (1968).

116. *Paris Adult Theatre I* v. *Slaton,* 413 U.S. 49 (1973).

117. *Haig* v. *Agee,* 453 U.S. 280 (1981).

118. Justice Black concurring, *Gregory* v. *Chicago,* 394 U.S. 111 (1969).

119. *Tinker* v. *Des Moines School District,* 391 U.S. 367 (1968).

120. *United States* v. *O'Brien,* 391 U.S. 367 (1968).

121. *Ohralik* v. *Ohio State Bar Association,* 436 U.S. 447 (1978).

122. *In re Primus,* 436 U.S. 412 (1978).

123. *Buckley* v. *Valeo,* 424 U.S. 1 (1976); *California Medical Association* v. *Federal Election Commission,* 453 U.S. 182 (1981).

124. *Citizens Against Rent Control* v. *Berkeley,* 454 U.S. 290 (1981).

125. *FEC* v. *National Right to Work Committee,* 459 U.S. 197 (1984).

126. *Board of Education* v. *Pic,* 457 U.S. 853 (1982).

127. *Lloyd* v. *Corporation* v. *Tanner,* 407 U.S. 551 (1972).

128. *PruneYard Shopping Center* v. *Robins,* 407 U.S. 551 (1972).

129. *Houchins* v. *KQED,* 438 U.S. 1 (1978).

130. *First National Bank of Boston* v. *Bellotti,* 435 U.S. 765 (1978).

131. *Grosjean* v. *American Press Co.,* 297 U.S. 233 (1936).

132. *Minneapolis Star* v. *Minnesota Comm. of Rev.,* 75 L Ed 2d 295 (1983).

133. *Seattle Times Co.* v. *Rhinehart,* 81 L Ed 2d 17 (1984).

134. *Saxbe* v. *Washington Post,* 417 U.S. 843 (1974); *Pell* v. *Procunier,* 417 U.S. 817 (1974); *Houchins* v. *KQED,* 438 U.S. 1 (1978).

135. 448 U.S. 555 (1980).
136. *Globe Newspaper Co.* v. *Superior Court,* 457 U.S. 596 (1982).
137. *Ibid.*
138. *Press Enterprise Co.* v. *Superior Court,* 78 L Ed 2d 629 (1984).
139. *Miami Herald Publishing Co.* v. *Tornillo,* 418 U.S. 241 (1974).
140. *CBS, Inc.* v. *Federal Communications Commission,* 453 U.S. 775 (1978).
141. *Branzburg* v. *Hayes,* 408 U.S. 665 (1972).
142. *Zurcher* v. *Stanford Daily,* 436 U.S. 547 (1978).
143. *Metromedia, Inc.* v. *San Diego,* 453 U.S. 490 (1981).
144. *Milwaukee Pub. Co.* v. *Burleson,* 255 U.S. 407 (1921).
145. *Lamont* v. *Postmaster General,* 381 U.S. 301 (1965).
146. *Blount* v. *Rizzi,* 400 U.S. 410 (1971).
147. *United States* v. *Thirty-seven Photographs,* 402 U.S. 363 (1971); *United States* v. *12-200-Ft Reels of Film,* 413 U.S. 123 (1973).
148. *Rowan* v. *Post Office Department,* 397 U.S. 728 (1970).
149. *Ibid.*
150. *United States Postal Service* v. *Greenburgh Civic Association,* 453 U.S. 114 (1981).
151. *Hamling* v. *United States,* 418 U.S. 87 (1974); *United States* v. *Reidel,* 402 U.S. 351 (1971).
152. *United States* v. *Orito,* 413 U.S. 139 (1973).
153. *Federal Communications Commission* v. *Pacifica Foundation,* 438 U.S. 726 (1978).
154. *Red Lion Broadcasting Co.* v. *Federal Communications Commission,* 395 U.S. 367 (1969).
155. *FCC* v. *League of Women Voters of California,* 82 L Ed 2d 278 (1984).
156. *Ibid.*
157. *Federal Communications Commission* v. *National Citizens Committee for Broadcasting,* 436 U.S. 775 (1978).
158. *Federal Communications Commission* v. *Pacifica Foundation,* 438 U.S. 726 (1978).
159. *Times Film Corp.* v. *Chicago,* 356 U.S. 43 (1961).
160. *Teitel Film Corp.* v. *Cusak,* 390 U.S. 139 (1968); *Freedman* v. *Maryland,* 380 U.S. 51 (1965).
161. *Burstyn* v. *Wilson,* 343 U.S. 495 (1952); *Superior Films* v. *Department of Education,* 346 U.S. 587 (1954); *Kingsley Corp.* v. *Regents,* 360 U.S. 684 (1959).
162. *Southeastern Promotions Ltd.* v. *Conrad,* 420 U.S. 546 (1975).
163. *California* v. *LaRue,* 409 U.S. 109 (1972).
164. *Amalgamated Food Employees Local 590* v. *Logan Valley Plaza, Inc.,* 391 U.S. 308 (1968).
165. *Building Serv. Employees Union* v. *Gazzam,* 339 U.S. 532 (1950).
166. *Carey* v. *Brown,* 447 U.S. 455 (1980).
167. *Ibid.*
168. *Talley* v. *California,* 362 U.S. 60 (1960).
169. *United States Postal Service* v. *Greenburgh Civic Assn.,* 453 U.S. 114 (1981).

170. *Kovacs* v. *Cooper*, 336 U.S. 77 (1949).

171. *Los Angeles City Council* v. *Taxpayers for Vincent*, 80 L Ed 2d 772 (1984).

172. *Metromedia* v. *San Diego*, 453 U.S. 490 (1981).

173. *Adderley* v. *Florida*, 385 U.S. 39 (1966).

174. *Cox* v. *Louisiana*, 379 U.S. 559 (1965).

175. *Cox* v. *Louisiana*, 379 U.S. 536 (1965).

176. *United States* v. *Grace*, 461 U.S. 171 (1983).

177. *Hague* v. *CIO*, 307 U.S. 496 (1939).

178. *Perry Ed. Assn.* v. *Perry Local Ed. Assn.*, 74 L Ed 2d 794 (1983).

179. *Clark* v. *Community for Creative Non-Violence*, 82 L Ed 2d 221 (1984).

180. *Perry Ed Assn.* v. *Perry Local Ed. Assn.*, 74 L Ed 2d 794 (1983).

181. *Ibid.*

182. *Feiner* v. *New York*, 340 U.S. 315 (1951).

183. *Edwards* v. *South Carolina*, 372 U.S. 229 (1963).

184. *Gregory* v. *Chicago*, 394 U.S. 111 (1969).

185. *Coates* v. *Cincinnati*, 402 U.S. 611 (1971).

186. *Grayned* v. *Rockford*, 408 U.S. 104 (1972).

187. *Brown* v. *Louisiana*, 383 U.S. 131 (1966).

188. *Grayned* v. *Rockford*, 408 U.S. 104 (1972).

189. *Adderley* v. *Florida*, 385 U.S. 39 (1966).

190. *Healy* v. *James*, 408 U.S. 169 (1972).

191. *Roberts* v. *United States Jaycees*, 82 L Ed 2d 462 (1984).

192. *Healy* v. *James*, 408 U.S. 169 (1972).

193. *Gibson* v. *Legislative Investigation Commission*, 372 U.S. 539 (1963) and cases cited therein.

194. *Buckley* v. *Valeo*, 424 U.S. 1 (1976).

195. *Brown* v. *Socialist Workers*, 459 U.S. 87 (1983).

196. *Hishon* v. *King & Spalding*, 81 L Ed 2d 59 (1984).

197. *Roberts* v. *United States Jaycees*, 82 L Ed 2d 462 (1984).

198. *Cousins* v. *Wigoda*, 419 U.S. 477 (1977).

199. *Democratic Party of the United States* v. *LaFollette*, 450 U.S. 107 (1981).

200. *Regan* v. *Taxation with Representation*, 76 L Ed 2d 129 (1984).

201. *Bill Johnson's Restaurants* v. *NLRB*, 76 L Ed 2d 277 (1983).

202. *NAACP* v. *Claiborne Hardware*, 73 L Ed 1215 (1982).

203. *International Longshoremen's Association* v. *Allied International*, 456 U.S. 212 (1982).

204. *International Association of Machinists* v. *Street*, 367 U.S. 74 (1961); *Abood* v. *Detroit Board of Education*, 431 U.S. 209 (1977).

205. *Ellis* v. *Railway Clerks*, 80 L Ed 2d 428 (1984).

206. *Minnesota Board for Community Colleges* v. *Knight*, 79 L Ed 2d 299 (1984).

207. *Elfbrandt* v. *Russell*, 384 U.S. 11 (1966); *Connell* v. *Higginbotham*, 403 U.S. 207 (1971).

208. *McAuliffe* v. *Mayor of New Bedford,* 155 Mass. 216 (1892).
209. *Connick* v. *Myers,* 461 U.S. 138 (1983).
210. *Connick* v. *Myers; Pickering* v. *Board of Education,* 391 U.S. 563 (1968).
211. *United Public Workers* v. *Mitchell,* 330 U.S. 75 (1947); *Civil Service Commission* v. *Letter Carriers,* 413 U.S. 548 (1973); *Broadrick* v. *Oklahoma,* 413 U.S. 601 (1973).
212 *Clements* v. *Fashing,* 457 U.S. 957 (1982).
213 *Branti* v *Finkel,* 445 U.S 507 (1980); *Elrod* v. *Burns,* 427 U.S 347 (1976)

Amendment II: Militia and the Right to Bear Arms

1. *United States* v. *Miller,* 307 U.S 174 (1939)
2. *Lewis* v. *United States,* 445 U.S. 55 (1980)
3. *Adams* v. *Williams,* 407 U.S. 143 (1972).

Amendment III: Quartering of Soldiers

1. Justice Samuel F. Miller, *The Constitution* (1893), p. 646, quoted in *The Constitution Annotated,* 1964 ed., p. 923.

Amendment IV: Searches and Seizures

1. *Schneckloth* v. *Bustamonte,* 412 U.S. 218 (1973), and quoting from Justice Harlan in *Ker* v. *California,* 374 U.S. 23 (1963).
2. *Chimel* v. *California,* 395 U.S. 752 (1969); *United States* v. *Harris,* 403 U.S. 573 (1971).
3. *United States* v. *Edwards,* 415 U.S. 800 (1974).
4. *United States* v. *Cortez,* 449 U.S. 411 (1981).
5. *Kolender* v. *Larson,* 461 U.S. 352 (1983).
6. *Payton* v. *New York,* 445 U.S. 573 (1980).
7. *Steagald* v. *United States,* 451 U.S. 204 (1981).
8. *Welsh* v. *Wisconsin,* 80 L Ed 2d 732 (1984).
9. *Michigan* v. *Summers,* 452 U.S. 693 (1981).
10. *Florida* v. *Royer,* 75 L Ed 2d 229 (1983).
11. *INS* v. *Delgado,* 80 L Ed 2d 247 (1984); *United States* v. *Mendenhall,* 446 U.S. 544 (1980).
12. *INS* v. *Delgado,* 80 L Ed 2d 247 (1984).
13. *Mincey* v. *Arizona,* 437 U.S. 385 (1970).
14. Justice Powell concurring in *Robbins* v. *California,* 453 U.S. 420 (1981).
15. *Michigan* v. *Thomas,* 458 U.S. 259 (1982).
16. *United States* v. *Ross,* 456 U.S. 798 (1982).
17. *Terry* v. *Ohio,* 392 U.S. 1 (1968).
18. *Chimel* v. *California,* 395 U.S. 752 (1969); *United States* v. *Edwards,* 415 U.S. 800 (1974); *Illinois* v. *Lafayette,* 77 L Ed 2d 65 (1983).

19. *Adams* v. *Williams,* 407 U.S. 143 (1972).

20. *Cupp* v. *Murphy,* 412 U.S. 291 (1973).

21. *Schneckloth* v. *Bustamonte,* 412 U.S. 218 (1973); *United States* v. *Matlock,* 415 U.S. 164 (1974).

22. *Almeida-Sanchez* v. *United States,* 413 U.S. 266 (1973); *United States* v. *Ortiz,* 422 U.S. 891 (1975).

23. *United States* v. *Ramsey,* 431 U.S. 606 (1977).

24. *Torres* v. *Puerto Rico,* 442 U.S. 465 (1979).

25. *Coolidge* v. *New Hampshire,* 403 U.S. 443 (1971); *Texas* v. *Brown,* 75 L Ed 2d 502 (1983).

26. *Michigan* v. *Taylor,* 436 U.S. 499 (1978); *Mincey* v. *Arizona,* 437 U.S. 385 (1978).

27. *Rakas* v. *Illinois,* 439 U.S. 128 (1978); *Rawlings* v. *Kentucky,* 448 U.S. 98 (1980).

28. *United States* v. *Chadwick,* 433 U.S. 1 (1977) quoting *Katz* v. *United States,* 389 U.S. 347 (1967).

29. *Oliver* v. *United States,* 80 L Ed 2d 214 (1984).

30. *Walter* v. *United States,* 447 U.S. 649 (1980).

31. *United States* v. *Salvucci,* 448 U.S. 83 (1980).

32. *Hudson* v. *Palmer,* 82 L Ed 2d 393 (1984).

33. *Oliver* v. *United States,* 80 L Ed 2d 214 (1984).

34. Taylor, "Two Studies on Constitutional Interpretation," quoted by Justice Stevens dissenting in *Marshall* v. *Barlow's,* 436 U.S. 307 (1978).

35. *Marshall* v. *Barlow's,* 436 U.S. 307 (1978).

36. *Franks* v. *Delaware,* 438 U.S. 154 (1978).

37. *Shadwick* v. *Tampa,* 407 U.S. 345 (1972); *Coolidge* v. *New Hampshire,* 403 U.S. 433 (1971); *Connally* v. *Georgia,* 429 U.S. 245 (1977).

38. *Aguilar* v. *Texas,* 378 U.S. 108 (1964).

39. *Lo-Ji Sales, Inc.* v. *New York,* 442 U.S. 319 (1979).

40. *Illinois* v. *Gates,* 76 L Ed 2d 527 (1983).

41. *Ybarra* v. *Illinois,* 444 U.S. 85 (1979).

42 *Zurcher* v. *Stanford Daily,* 436 U.S. 547 (1978).

43. *Marshall* v. *Barlow's,* 436 U.S. 307 (1978); *See* v. *City of Seattle,* 387 U.S. 541 (1967); *Camara* v. *Municipal Court,* 387 U.S. 523 (1967).

44. *Colonnade Catering Corp.* v. *United States,* 397 U.S. 72 (1970); *United States* v. *Biswell,* 406 U.S. 311 (1972).

45. *Donovan* v. *Dewey,* 452 U.S. 594 (1981).

46. *Air Pollution Variance Board of Colorado* v. *Western Alfalfa Corp.,* 416 U.S. 86[1] (1974).

47. *Wyman* v. *James,* 400 U.S. 309 (1971).

48. *Donovan* v. *Lone Steer,* 78 L Ed 2d 567 (1984).

49. *Olmstead* v. *United States,* 277 U.S. 438 (1928).

50. *Katz* v. *United States,* 389 U.S. 347 (1967).

51. *United States* v. *Giordano,* 416 U.S. 505 (1974).

52. *United States* v. *United States District Court*, 407 U.S. 297 (1972).
53. *Congressional Quarterly*, October 15, 1978, p. 2966; *The Washington Post*, June 24, 1981.
54. *United States* v. *Raymond J. Place*, 77 L Ed 2d 110 (1983).
55. *On Lee* v. *United States*, 343 U.S. 747 (1952); *Hoffa* v. *United States*, 385 U.S. 293 (1966); *United States* v. *White*, 401 U.S. 745 (1971).
56. *United States* v. *Knotts*, 460 U.S. 276 (1983).
57. *United States* v. *Karo*, 82 L Ed 2d 530 (1984).
58. *Bivens* v. *Six Unknown Named Agents of the Bureau of Narcotics*, 403 U.S. 388 (1971).
59. *Weeks* v. *United States*, 232 U.S. 383 (1914); *Mapp* v. *Ohio*, 367 U.S. 643 (1961).
60. *Alderman* v. *United States*, 394 U.S. 165 (1969).
61. Justice Powell concurring in *Brown* v. *Illinois*, 422 U.S. 590 (1975).
62. *People* v. *Defore*, 242 N.Y. 13 (1926).
63. Justice Brennan dissenting in *United States* v. *Leon*, 83 L Ed 2d 677 (1984).
64. *Harris* v. *New York*, 401 U.S. 222 (1971); *United States* v. *Havens*, 446 U.S. 620 (1976).
65. *Stone* v. *Powell*, 428 U.S. 465 (1976).
66. *Nix* v. *Williams*, 81 L Ed 2d 377 (1984).
67. *Segura* v. *United States*, 82 L Ed 2d 599 (1984).
68. *Illinois* v. *Gates*, 76 L Ed 2d 528 (1983).
69. *United States* v. *Leon*, 82 L Ed 2d 677 (1984).
70. *Massachusetts* v. *Sheppard*, 82 L Ed 2d 737 (1984).
71. Dissenting in *United States* v. *Leon*.
72. Dissenting along with Justice Brennan and Marshall in *New Jersey* v. *T.L.O.*, 82 L Ed 2d 881 (1984).
73. *United States* v. *Payner*, 447 U.S. 727 (1980).
74. *United States* v. *Calandra*, 414 U.S. 338 (1974).
75. *INS* v. *Lopez-Mendoza*, 82 L Ed 2d 778 (1984).

Amendment V: Grand Juries, Double Jeopardy, Self-Incrimination, Due Process, and Eminent Domain

1. *Hobby* v. *United States*, 82 L Ed 260 (1984).
2. Marvin E. Frankel and G. P. Naftalis, *The Grand Jury: An Institution on Trial*, (New York: Shill & Way, 1977), pp. 18–19.
3. *Gerstein* v. *Pugh*, 420 U.S. 103 (1975).
4. *Kinsella* v. *Singleton*, 361 U.S. 234 (1960), and companion cases.
5. *Toth* v. *Quarles*, 350 U.S. 11 (1955).
6. *O'Callahan* v. *Parker*, 395 U.S. 258 (1969); *Relford* v. *Commandant*, 401 U.S. 355 (1971).
7. *McLucas* v. *De Champlain*, 421 U.S. 21 (1975).
8. *Breed* v. *Jones*, 421 U.S. 519 (1975).

9. *North Carolina* v. *Pearce*, 395 U.S. 711 (1969).

10. *Whalen* v. *United States*, 445 U.S. 684 (1980).

11. *Ibid.*

12. *Crist* v. *Bretz*, 437 U.S. 28 (1979).

13. *Albernaz* v. *United States*, 450 U.S. 333 (1981).

14. *Justices of Boston Municipal Court* v. *Lydon*, 80 L Ed 2d 311 (1984).

15. *Tibbs* v. *Florida*, 457 U.S. 31 (1982).

16. *Ibid.*

17. *Hudson* v. *Louisiana*, 450 U.S. 40 (1981); *Burks* v. *United States*, 437 U.S. 1 (1978).

18. *Oregon* v. *Kennedy*, 456 U.S. 667 (1982).

19. *Oregon* v. *Kennedy; United States* v. *Scott*, 437 U.S. 82 (1978); *Arizona* v. *Washington*, 434 U.S. 497 (1978); *United States* v. *Martin Linen*, 430 U.S. 564 (1977).

20. *Bullington* v. *Missouri*, 451 U.S. 430 (1981); *North Carolina* v. *Pearce*, 395 U.S. 711 (1969).

21. *Bullington* v. *Missouri*, 451 U.S. 430 (1981); *Arizona* v. *Rumsey*, 81 L Ed 2d 164 (1984).

22. *United States* v. *DiFrancesco*, 449 U.S. 117 (1980).

23. *Albernaz* v. *United States*, 450 U.S. 333 (1981).

24. *Brown* v. *Ohio*, 432 U.S. 161 (1977).

25. *Ashe* v. *Swenson*, 397 U.S. 436 (1970).

26. *Ohio* v. *Johnson*, 81 L Ed 2d 425 (1984).

27. *Missouri* v. *Hunter*, 74 L Ed 2d 535 (1983).

28. *Iannelli* v. *United States*, 420 U.S. 770 (1975).

29. *United States* v. *One Assortment of Firearms*, 79 L Ed 2d 361 (1984).

30. *One Lot Emerald Cut Stones and One Right* v. *United States*, 409 U.S. 232 (1972).

31. *United States* v. *One Assortment of Firearms*, 79 L Ed 2d 361 (1984).

32. *Breed* v. *Jones*, 421 U.S. 519 (1975).

33. *Benton* v. *Maryland*, 395 U.S. 784 (1969); *Bartkus* v. *Illinois*, 359 U.S. 121 (1972).

34. *Rinaldi* v. *United States*, 434 U.S. 22 (1977); *Petite* v. *United States*, 361 U.S. 529 (1960).

35. *United States* v. *Wheeler*, 435 U.S. 313 (1978).

36. *Waller* v. *Florida*, 397 U.S. 387 (1970).

37. *Malloy* v. *Hogan*, 378 U.S. 1 (1964).

38. *Murphy* v. *Waterfront Commission*, 378 U.S. 52 (1964).

39. *Marchetti* v. *United States*, 390 U.S. 39 (1968); *Haynes* v. *United States*, 390 U.S. 85 (1968); *Leary* v. *United States*, 395 U.S. 6 (1969).

40. *California* v. *Byers*, 402 U.S. 424 (1971).

41. *United States* v. *Freed*, 401 U.S. 601 (1971).

42. *United States* v. *Ward*, 448 U.S. 242 (1980).

43. *Selective Service System* v. *Minnesota Public Service Research Group*, 82 L Ed 2d 632 (1984).

44. *Ibid.*

45. *Schmerber* v. *California*, 384 U.S. 757 (1966); *South Dakota* v. *Neville*, 74 L Ed 2d 748 (1983).

46. *Couch* v. *United States,* 409 U.S. 322 (1973).
47. Concurring in *United States* v. *Doe,* 79 L Ed 2d 552 (1984).
48. *United States* v. *Apfelbaum,* 445 U.S. 115 (1980).
49. *Pillsbury* v. *Conboy,* 459 U.S. 248 (1983).
50. *Garrity* v. *New Jersey,* 385 U.S. 493 (1967); *Spevack* v. *Klein,* 385 U.S. 511 (1967); *Gardner* v. *Broderick,* 392 U.S. 273 (1968); *Sanitation Men* v. *Sanitation Comm.,* 392 U.S. 281 (1968); *Lefkowtiz* v. *Turley,* 414 U.S. 70 (1973).
51. *Griffin* v. *California,* 380 U.S. 609 (1965); *Bruno* v. *United States,* 308 U.S. 287 (1939); *Carter* v. *Kentucky,* 450 U.S. 288 (1981); *James* v. *Kentucky,* 80 L Ed 2d 346 (1984).
52. *Haynes* v. *Washington,* 373 U.S. 503 (1963); *Lego* v. *Twomey,* 404 U.S. 477 (1972).
53. *Mincey* v. *Arizona,* 437 U.S. 385 (1978).
54. *Miranda* v. *Arizona,* 384 U.S. 436 (1966).
55. *Berkemer* v. *McCarty,* 82 L Ed 2d 317 (1984); *Mathis* v. *United States,* 391 U.S. 1 (1968); *Orozco* v. *Texas,* 394 U.S. 324 (1969).
56. *California* v. *Beheler,* 463 U.S. 1121 (1983).
57. *Oregon* v. *Mathiason,* 429 U.S. 492 (1977); *California* v. *Beheler,* 77 L Ed 2d 1275 (1983).
58. *Berkemer* v. *McCarty,* 82 L Ed 2d 317 (1984).
59. *Minnesota* v. *Murphy,* 79 L Ed 2d 409 (1984).
60. *New York* v. *Quarles,* 81 L Ed 2d 550 (1984).
61. *Rhode Island* v. *Innis,* 446 U.S. 291 (1980); *Edwards* v. *Arizona,* 451 U.S. 477 (1981).
62. *Estelle* v. *Smith,* 451 U.S. 454 (1981).
63. *Harris* v. *New York,* 401 U.S. 222 (1971).
64. Quoted in *Blackledge* v. *Allison,* 432 U.S. 63 (1977); *Bordenkircher* v. *Hayes,* 434 U.S. 357 (1978).
65. *Brady* v. *United States,* 397 U.S. 742 (1970).
66. *Marby* v. *Johnson,* 81 L Ed 2d 437 (1984).
67. *Davidson* v. *New Orleans,* 96 U.S. 97 (1878).
68. *Bolling* v. *Sharpe,* 347 U.S. 497 (1954).
69. *Blum* v. *Yaretsky,* 457 U.S. 991 (1982).
70. *Lugar* v. *Edmonson Oil Co.,* 457 U.S. 922 (1983).
71. *Meyer* v. *Nebraska,* 262 U.S. 390 (1923).
72. *Bounds* v. *Smith,* 430 U.S. 817 (1978).
73. *Lochner* v. *New York,* 198 U.S. 45 (1905); *Muller* v. *Oregon,* 208 U.S. 424 (1908); *West Coast Hotel* v. *Parrish,* 300 U.S. 379 (1937).
74. *Leis* v. *Flynt,* 439 U.S. 438 (1979).
75. *Meachum* v. *Fano,* 427 U.S. 215 (1976); *Jago* v. *Van Curen,* 445 U.S. 14 (1981).
76. *Board of Regents* v. *Roth,* 408 U.S. 564 (1972).
77. *Block* v. *Rutherford,* 82 L Ed 2d 438 (1984).
78. *Meachum* v. *Fano; Olim* v. *Wakinekona,* 75 L Ed 2d 813 (1983).
79. *Block* v. *Rutherford,* 82 L Ed 2d 438 (1984).

80. *Givhan* v. *Western Line Consolidated School District,* 439 U.S. 410 (1979).

81. *Bishop* v. *Wood,* 426 U.S. 341 (1976).

82. *Smith* v. *Foster Families,* 431 U.S. 816 (1977).

83. *Leis* v. *Flynt,* 439 U.S. 438 (1978).

84. *New Motor Board of California* v. *Orrin W. Fox Co.,* 439 U.S. 96 (1978).

85. *O'Bannon* v. *Town Court Nursing Center,* 447 U.S. 773 (1980).

86. *Greenholtz* v. *Nebraska Penal Inmates,* 442 U.S. 1 (1979); *Connecticut Board of Pardons* v. *Dumschat,* 452 U.S. 458 (1981).

87. *Morrissey* v. *Brewer,* 408 U.S. 471 (1972).

88. *Connally* v. *General Construction Co.,* 269 U.S. 385 (1926).

89. *Grayned* v. *Rockford,* 408 U.S. 104 (1972).

90. *Kolender* v. *Lawson,* 461 U.S. 352 (1983).

91. *Palmer* v. *City of Euclid, Ohio,* 402 U.S. 544 (1972).

92. *Kolender* v. *Lawson,* 461 U.S. 352 (1983).

93. *Papachristou* v. *City of Jacksonville,* 405 U.S. 156 (1972).

94. *Colautti* v. *Franklin,* 439 U.S. 379 (1979).

95. *Hoffman Estates* v. *Flipside Hoffman Estates,* 455 U.S. 489 (1982).

96. *City of Mesquite* v. *Aladdin's Castle,* 455 U.S. 283 (1983).

97. In re *Winship,* 397 U.S. 358 (1970); *Estelle* v. *Williams,* 425 U.S. 501 (1976); *Taylor* v. *Kentucky,* 436 U.S. 478 (1978); *Kentucky* v. *Whorton,* 441 U.S. 786 (1979).

98. *Ulster County Court* v. *Allen,* 442 U.S. 140 (1979).

99. *Tot* v. *United States,* 319 U.S. 463 (1943).

100. *Leary* v. *United States,* 395 U.S. 6 (1969).

101. *Turner* v. *United States,* 396 U.S. 398 (1970).

102. *Barnes* v. *United States,* 412 U.S. 837 (1973).

103. *Bell* v. *Burson,* 402 U.S. 535 (1971).

104. *Dixon* v. *Love,* 431 U.S. 105 (1977).

105. *Wisconsin* v. *Constantineau,* 400 U.S. 433 (1971).

106. *Stanley* v. *Illinois,* 405 U.S. 645 (1972).

107. *Ward* v. *Village of Monroeville,* 409 U.S. 57 (1972).

108. *Drope* v. *Missouri,* 420 U.S. 162 (1975).

109. *Gerstein* v. *Pugh,* 420 U.S. 103 (1975).

110. *Schall* v. *Martin,* 81 L Ed 2d 207 (1984).

111. *Morrissey* v. *Brewer,* 408 U.S. 471 (1972).

112. *Gagnon* v. *Scarpelli,* 411 U.S. 778 (1973).

113. *Hewitt* v. *Helms,* 74 L Ed 2d 675 (1983).

114. *Wolff* v. *McDonnell,* 418 U.S. 539 (1974).

115. *Block* v. *Rutherford,* 82 L Ed 2d 438 (1984); *Hudson* v. *Palmer,* 82 L Ed 2d 393 (1984).

116. *Groppi* v. *Leslie,* 404 U.S. 496 (1972); *Goldberg* v. *Kelly,* 397 U.S. 254 (1970); In re *Gault,* 387 U.S. 1 (1967); *Thorpe* v. *Housing Authority,* 393 U.S. 268 (1969).

117. *Mathews* v. *Eldridge,* 424 U.S. 319 (1976).

118. *Hodel* v. *Virginia Surface Min. & Recl. Assn.*, 452 U.S. 264 (1981); *Haig* v. *Agee*, 453 U.S. 280 (1981).

119. *Goss* v. *Lopez*, 419 U.S. 565 (1975).

120. *Board of Curators, University of Missouri* v. *Horowitz*, 435 U.S. 78 (1978).

121. *Memphis Light, Gas & Water Division* v. *Craft*, 436 U.S. 1 (1978).

122. *Schweiker* v. *McClure*, 456 U.S. 188 (1982).

123. *Santosky* v. *Kramer*, 455 U.S. 745 (1982).

124. *Lassiter* v. *Department of Social Services*, 452 U.S. 18 (1981).

125. *Parham* v. *J.R.*, 442 U.S. 584 (1979).

126. *Vitek* v. *Jones*, 445 U.S. 480 (1980).

127. *Sniadach* v. *Family Finance Corp.*, 359 U.S. 337 (1969).

128. *Fuentes* v. *Shevin*, 407 U.S. 67 (1972).

129. *Mitchell* v. *W.T. Grant*, 416 U.S. 600 (1975).

130. *North Georgia Finish, Inc.* v. *Di-Chem, Inc.*, 419 U.S. 601 (1975).

131. *United States* v. *Eight Thousand Eight Hundred and Fifty Dollars*, 76 L Ed 2d 143 (1983).

132. *West Coast Hotel* v. *Parrish*, 300 U.S. 379 (1937).

133. *Hodel* v. *Virginia Surface Min. & Recl. Assn.*, 452 U.S. 264 (1981); *Exxon* v. *Maryland*, 437 U.S. 117 (1978).

134. *U.S. Dept. of Agriculture* v. *Murry*, 413 U.S. 508 (1973).

135. *U.S. Dept. of Agriculture* v. *Moreno*, 413 U.S. 528 (1973).

136. *Cleveland Board of Education* v. *LaFleur*, 414 U.S. 632 (1974).

137. *Weinberger* v. *Salfi*, 422 U.S. 749 (1975).

138. *Jones* v. *United States*, 77 L Ed 2d 694 (1983).

139. *O'Connor* v. *Donaldson*, 422 U.S. 563 (1975).

140. *Moore* v. *East Cleveland*, 431 U.S. 494 (1977).

141. *Roe* v. *Wade*, 410 U.S. 113 (1973).

142. *Bellotti* v. *Baird*, 43 U.S. 622 (1969); *H. L. Matheson*, 450 U.S. 398 (1981).

143. *Maher* v. *Roe*, 432 U.S. 464 (1977).

144. *Akron* v. *Akron Center for Reproductive Health*, 76 L Ed 2d 687 (1983).

145. *Kelley* v. *Johnson*, 425 U.S. 238 (1976); *Harrah Independent School District* v. *Martin*, 440 U.S. 194 (1979).

146. *Chicago, Milwaukee & St. Paul Ry.* v. *Minnesota*, 134 U.S. 418 (1890).

147. *Thompson* v. *Consolidated Gas Corp.*, 300 U.S. 55 (1937).

148. *Hawaii Housing Authority et al.* v. *Midkiff*, 81 L Ed 2d 186 (1984).

149. *Penn Central Transportation Co.* v. *City of New York*, 438 U.S. 104 (1978).

150. *Pittsburgh* v. *Alco Parking Corp.*, 417 U.S. 369 (1974).

151. *YMCA* v. *United States*, 395 U.S. 841 (1962).

152. *Agins* v. *Tiburon*, 447 U.S. 255 (1980).

153. *Penn Central Transportation Co.* v. *City of New York*, 438 U.S. 104 (1978).

154. *United States* v. *Causby*, 328 U.S. 256 (1946).

155. *Regional Rail Reorganization Act Cases*, 419 U.S. 102 (1974).

156. *Kaiser Aetna* v. *United States,* 44 U.S. 164 (1979).

157. *United States* v. *564.54 Acres of Land,* 441 U.S. 506 (1979).

158. *United States* v. *Sioux Nation of Indians,* 448 U.S. 371 (1980).

Amendment VI: Criminal Court Procedures

1. *United States* v. *Ewell,* 383 U.S. 116 (1966).

2. *Strunk* v. *United States,* 412 U.S. 434 (1973).

3. *United States* v. *MacDonald,* 456 U.S. 1 (1982).

4. *United States* v. *Marion,* 404 U.S. 307 (1971).

5. *United States* v. *Lovasco,* 431 U.S. 783 (1977).

6. *Barker* v. *Wingo,* 407 U.S. 514 (1972).

7. *United States* v. *Ewell,* 383 U.S. 116 (1966).

8. *Smith* v. *Hooey,* 393 U.S. 374 (1969).

9. *In re Oliver,* 333 U.S. 257 (1948).

10. *Nixon* v. *Warner Communications,* 435 U.S. 589 (1978).

11. *Gannett Co.* v. *De Pasquale,* 443 U.S. 368 (1979).

12. *Press-Enterprise Co.* v. *Superior Court,* 464 U.S. ___ (1984); *Waller* v. *Georgia,* 81 L Ed 2d 31 (1984).

13. *Estes* v. *Texas,* 381 U.S. 532 (1965).

14. *Chandler* v. *Florida,* 449 U.S. 560 (1981).

15. *Sheppard* v. *Maxwell,* 384 U.S. 333 (1966).

16. *Duncan* v. *Louisiana,* 391 U.S. 145 (1968).

17. *Dyke* v. *Taylor Implement Manufacturing Co.,* 391 U.S. 216 (1968).

18. *Bloom* v. *Illinois,* 391 U.S. 194 (1968); *Frank* v. *United States,* 395 U.S. 147 (1969).

19. *Williams* v. *Florida,* 399 U.S. 78 (1970).

20. *Ballew* v. *Georgia,* 435 U.S. 223 (1978).

21. *Apodaca* v. *Oregon,* 406 U.S. 404 (1972); *Johnson* v. *Louisiana,* 406 U.S. 356 (1972).

22. *Burch* v. *Louisiana,* 419 U.S. 522 (1975).

23. *Singer* v. *United States,* 380 U.S. 24 (1965).

24. *Taylor* v. *Louisiana,* 419 U.S. 522 (1975).

25. *Duren* v. *Missouri,* 439 U.S. 357 (1979).

26. *Rosales* v. *Lopez,* 451 U.S. 182 (1981).

27. *Ham* v. *South Carolina,* 409 U.S. 524 (1973).

28. *Witherspoon* v. *Illinois,* 391 U.S. 510 (1968); *Adams* v. *Texas,* 448 U.S. 38 (1980).

29. *Dutton* v. *Evans,* 400 U.S. 74 (1970).

30. *Ohio* v. *Roberts,* 448 U.S. 56 (1980).

31. *Mancusi* v. *Stubbs,* 408 U.S. 204 (1972).

32. *Illinois* v. *Allen,* 397 U.S. 337 (1970); *Taylor* v. *United States,* 414 U.S. 17 (1973).

33. *Bruton* v. *United States,* 391 U.S. 123 (1968); *Parker* v. *Randolph,* 442 U.S. 62 (1979).

34. *Davis* v. *Alaska,* 415 U.S. 308 (1974).

35. *Rosen* v. *United States,* 245 U.S. 476 (1918).

36. *Washington* v. *Texas,* 388 U.S. 14 (1967).
37. *United States* v. *Valenzuela-Bernal,* 458 U.S. 866 (1982)
38. *Trammel* v. *United States,* 445 U.S. 40 (1980).
39. *Barber* v. *Page,* 390 U.S. 719 (1968).
40. *Johnson* v. *Zerbst,* 304 U.S. 458 (1938); *Miranda* v. *Arizona,* 384 U.S. 436 (1966).
41. *Fuller* v. *Oregon,* 417 U.S. 40 (1974).
42. *Gideon* v. *Wainwright,* 372 335 (1963); *Faretta* v. *California,* 422 U.S. 806 (1975).
43. *McKaskle* v. *Wiggins,* 79 L Ed 2d 122 (1984).
44. *United States* v. *Gouveia,* 81 L Ed 2d 146 (1984).
45. *Herring* v. *New York,* 422 U.S. 853 (1975); *Kirby* v. *Illinois,* 406 U.S. 682 (1972); *United States* v. *Wade,* 388 U.S. 218 (1967); *Moore* v. *Illinois,* 434 U.S. 220 (1977)
46. *Ross* v. *Moffit,* 417 U.S. 600 (1974).
47. *Morris* v. *Slappy,* 75 L Ed 2d 610 (1983).
48. *United States* v. *Cronic,* 80 L Ed 2d (1984); *Strickland* v. *Washington,* 80 L Ed 2d 674 (1984).
49. *Massiah* v. *United States,* 377 U.S. 201 (1964); *United States* v. *Henry,* 447 U.S. 264 (1980).
50. *Brewer* v. *Williams,* 430 U.S. 387 (1977).
51. *Segura* v. *United States,* 82 L Ed 2d 599 (1984).
52. *Argersinger* v. *Hamlin,* 407 U.S. 25 (1972).
53. *Scott* v. *Illinois,* 440 U.S. 367 (1979).

Amendment VII: Trial by Jury in Common-Law Cases

1. *Lorillard* v. *Pons,* 434 U.S. 575 (1978); *Curtis* v. *Loether,* 415 U.S. 189 (1974).
2. *Colegrove* v. *Battin,* 413 U.S. 149 (1973).
3. Edward N. Beiser and Rene Varrin, "Six-Member Juries in the Federal Courts," *Judicature,* vol. 58 (April 1975), p. 425.

Amendment VIII: Bail and Cruel and Unusual Punishments

1. *Stack* v. *Boyle,* 342 U.S. 1 (1951); *Schlib* v. *Kuebel,* 404 U.S. 357 (1971).
2. *Schall* v. *Martin,* 81 L Ed 2d 207 (1984).
3. *Rhodes* v. *Gamble,* 429 U.S. 97 (1972).
4. *Estelle* v. *Gamble,* 429 U.S. 97 (1972).
5. *Coker* v. *Georgia,* 433 U.S. 588 (1977); *Hutto* v. *Finney,* 437 U.S. 678 (1978).
6. *Rummel* v. *Estelle,* 445 U.S. 263 (1980).
7. *Hutto* v. *Davis,* 454 U.S. 370 (1982).
8. *Solem* v. *Helm,* 77 L Ed 2d 637 (1983).
9. *Robinson* v. *California,* 370 U.S. 660 (1962).
10. *Powell* v. *Texas,* 392 U.S. 514 (1968).
11. *Ingraham* v. *Wright,* 430 U.S. 651 (1977).

12. *Gardner* v. *Florida,* 430 U S. 349 (1977); *Woodson* v. *North Carolina,* 428 U.S. 280 (1976).
13. *Roberts* v. *Louisiana,* 431 U.S. 663 (1977).
14. *Lockett* v. *Ohio,* 428 U.S. 586 (1978).
15. Justice Brennan concurring in *Adams* v. *Texas,* 448 U.S. 38 (1980).
16. *Godfrey* v. *Georgia,* 446 U.S. 420 (1980).
17. *Spaziano* v. *Florida,* 82 L Ed 2d 340 (1984).
18. Chief Justice Burger in *Coker* v. *Georgia,* 433 U.S. 584 (1977).
19. *Godfrey* v. *Georgia,* 446 U.S. 420 (1980); *Edmund* v. *Florida,* 73 L Ed 2d 1140 (1983).
20. *Pulley* v. *Harris,* 79 L Ed 2d 29 (1984).

Amendment IX: Rights Retained by the People

1. *United Public Workers* v. *Mitchell,* 330 U.S. 75 (1947).
2. *Griswold* v. *Connecticut,* 381 U.S. 479 (1965).
3. *Richmond Newspapers Inc.* v. *Virginia,* 448 U.S. 555 (1980).

Amendment X: Reserved Powers of the States

1. *United States* v. *Butler,* 297 U.S. 1 (1936).
2. *Hodel* v. *Virginia Surface Mining & Recl. Assn.,* 452 U.S. 264 (1981).
3. *United States* v. *Butler,* 297 U.S. 1 (1936).
4. *Hammer* v. *Dagenhart,* 247 U.S. 251 (1918); *Child Labor Tax Cases,* 259 U.S. 20 (1922).
5. *Fry* v. *United States,* 421 U.S. 542 (1975).
6. *National League of Cities* v. *Usery,* 426 U.S. 833 (1976).
7. *United States* v. *Tax Commission of Mississippi,* 421 U.S. 599 (1975).
8. *Massachusetts* v. *United States,* 435 U.S. 444 (1978); *New York Gaslight Club* v. *Carey,* 447 U.S. 54 (1980).

Amendment XI: Suits Against States

1. *Chisholm* v. *Georgia,* 2 Dallas 419 (1793).
2. *Hans* v. *Louisiana,* 134 U.S. 1 (1890).
3. *Lake Country Estates* v. *Tahoe Regional Planning Agency,* 440 U.S. 391 (1979); *Mt. Healthy City Board of Education* v. *Doyle,* 429 U.S. 274 (1977).
4. *Edelman* v. *Jordan,* 415 U.S. 651 (1974); *Florida Department of Health* v. *Florida Nursing Home Association,* 450 U.S. 147 (1980).
5. *Florida Department of State* v. *Treasurer Salvors,* 458 U.S. 670 (1982).
6. *Ibid.*
7. *Nevada* v. *Hall,* 440 U.S. 410 (1979).
8. *Parden* v. *Terminal Ry. Co.,* 377 U.S. 184 (1964).
9. *Employees* v. *Missouri Health Department,* 411 U.S. 279 (1973).
10. *Fitzpatrick* v. *Bitzer,* 427 U.S. 445 (1976).

11. *Milliken* v. *Bradley,* 433 U.S. 267 (1977).
12. *Ex parte Young,* 209 U.S. 123 (1908).
13. *Scheuer* v. *Rhodes,* 416 U.S. 233 (1974); *Wood* v. *Strickland,* 420 U.S. 308 (1975); *Monroe* v. *Pape,* 365 U.S. 167 (1961).
14. *Monell* v. *New York City Dept. of Social Services,* 436 U.S. 658 (1978); *Owen* v. *City of Independence,* 445 U.S. 622 (1980); *Newport* v. *Fact Concerts, Inc.,* 453 U.S. 247 (1981).
15. *Hutto* v. *Finney,* 437 U.S. 678 (1978); *Maher* v. *Gagne,* 448 U.S. 122 (1980).
16. *Stump* v. *Sparkman,* 435 U.S. 349 (1978); *Imbler* v. *Pachtman,* 424 U.S. 409 (1976).
17. *Pullman* v. *Allen,* 80 L Ed 2d 565 (1984).
18. *Pennhurst State School & Hosp.* v. *Halderman,* 79 L Ed 2d 67 (1984).

Amendment XII: Election of the President

1. Stephen Hess, "Good Fixes for the Constitution," *Washington Star,* May 28, 1978, p. D–4.

Amendment XIII: Slavery

1. *The Slaughter House Cases,* 16 Wallace 36 (1873).
2. *Pollock* v. *Williams,* 322 U.S. 4 (1944).
3. *General Building Contractors* v. *Pennsylvania,* 458 U.S. 375 (1982).
4. *Jones* v. *Alfred H. Mayer Co.,* 392 U.S. 409 (1968); *Memphis* v. *Greene,* 451 U.S. 100 (1981).
5. *The Civil Rights Cases,* 109 U.S. 3 (1883).
6. *Jones* v. *Alfred H. Mayer Co.,* 392 U.S. 409 (1968).
7. *McDonald* v. *Santa Fe Trail Transportation Co.,* 427 U.S. 273 (1976); *Runyon* v. *McCrary,* 427 U.S. 160 (1976); *Tillman* v. *Wheaton-Haven Recreation Association,* 410 U.S. 431 (1973); *Sullivan* v. *Little Hunt Park,* 376 U.S. 226 (1969).

Amendment XIV: Citizenship, Privileges and Immunities of United States Citizenship, Due Process, and Equal Protection of the Laws

1. *Scott* v. *Sandford,* 19 Howard 393 (1857).
2. *Vance* v. *Terrazas,* 444 U.S. 252 (1980); *Trop* v. *Dulles,* 356 U.S. 86 (1958); *Kennedy* v. *Mendoza-Martinez,* 372 U.S. 144 (1963); *Schneider* v. *Rusk,* 377 U.S. 163 (1964); *Afroyim* v. *Rusk,* 387 U.S. 253 (1967).
3. *Vance* v. *Terrazas,* 444 U.S. 252 (1980).
4. *Rogers* v. *Bellei,* 401 U.S. 815 (1971).
5. *The Slaughter House Cases,* 16 Wallace 36 (1873).
6. *Twining* v. *New Jersey,* 211 U.S. 78 (1908).
7. *Dandridge* v. *Williams,* 397 U.S. 471 (1970); *Jefferson* v. *Hackney,* 406 U.S. 535 (1972).

8. *Ibid.*

9. *Hodel* v. *Virginia Surface Min. & Recl. Assn.,* 452 U.S. 264 (1981)

10. *Califano* v. *Jobst,* 434 U.S. 47 (1977).

11. *Schweiker* v. *Wilson,* 450 U.S. 221 (1981).

12. *United States Railroad Retirement Board* v. *Fritz,* 449 U.S. 166 (1980).

13. *Dunn* v. *Blumstein,* 405 U.S. 330 (1972).

14. *Craig* v. *Borden,* 429 U.S. 190 (1976).

15. *San Antonio School District* v. *Rodriguez,* 411 U.S. 1 (1973); *Roe* v. *Wade,* 410 U.S. 113 (1973); *Beal* v. *Doe,* 432 U.S. 464 (1965); *Jones* v. *Helms,* 452 U.S. 412 (1981); *Haig* v. *Agee,* 453 U.S. 280 (1981); *Califano* v. *Aznarorian,* 439 U.S. 179 (1978); *Illinois Elections Board* v. *Socialist Workers Party,* 440 U.S. 173 (1979).

16. *San Antonio School District* v. *Rodriguez,* 411 U.S. 1 (1973).

17. *Nyquist* v. *Mauclet,* 432 U.S. 1 (1977); *Graham* v. *Richardson,* 403 U.S. 365 (1971); *Fiallo* v. *Bell,* 430 U.S. 787 (1977).

18. *Trimble* v. *Gordon,* 430 U.S. 762 (1977); *Matthews* v. *Lucas,* 427 U.S. 495 (1976).

19. *Ibid.*

20. *Lenhausen* v. *Lake Shore Auto Parts Co.,* 410 U.S. 356 (1973).

21. *Ohio Bureau of Employment Services* v. *Hodory,* 431 U.S. 471 (1977).

22. *San Antonio School District* v. *Rodriguez,* 411 U.S. 1 (1973).

23. *Village of Belle Terre* v. *Boraas,* 416 U.S. 1 (1974).

24. *Idaho Employment* v. *Smith,* 434 U.S. 100 (1977).

25. *Ballew* v. *Georgia,* 435 U.S. 223 (1978).

26. *Barry* v. *Barchi,* 443 U.S. 55 (1979).

27. *Minnesota* v. *Clover Leaf Creamery Co.,* 449 U.S. 456 (1981).

28. *United States Railroad Retirement Board* v. *Fritz,* 449 U.S. 166 (1980).

29. *California* v. *Boles,* 443 U.S. 282 (1980).

30. *Regan* v. *Taxation with Representation,* 76 L Ed 2d 129 (1983).

31. *Zobel* v. *Williams,* 457 U.S. 55 (1982).

32. Chief Justice Burger dissenting in *Plyler* v. *Doe,* 457 U.S. 202 (1982).

33. *Plyler* v. *Doe,* 457 U.S. 202 (1982).

34. *Burns* v. *Fortson,* 410 U.S. 686 (1973); *Dunn* v. *Blumstein,* 405 U.S. 330 (1972); *Memorial Hospital* v. *Maricopa County,* 415 U.S. 250 (1974).

35. *Vlandis* v. *Kline,* 412 U.S. 441 (1973).

36. *Califano* v. *Torres,* 435 U.S. 1 (1978).

37. *Jones* v. *Helms,* 452 U.S. 412 (1981).

38. *Evans* v. *Cornman,* 398 U.S. 419 (1970); *Carrington* v. *Rash,* 380 U.S. 89 (1965).

39. *Turner* v. *Fouche,* 396 U.S. 346 (1970).

40. *Hill* v. *Stone,* 421 U.S. 289 (1975).

41. *Cipriano* v. *Houma,* 395 U.S. 701 (1969); *City of Phoenix* v. *Kolodziejski,* 399 U.S. 204 (1970).

42. *Kramer* v. *Union Free School District,* 395 U.S. 621 (1969).

43. *Eisenstadt* v. *Baird,* 405 U.S. 438 (1972).

44. *Stanley* v. *Illinois,* 405 U.S. 645 (1972)

45. *Williams* v. *Illinois,* 399 U.S 235 (1970).

46. *Cruz* v. *Beto,* 405 U.S. 319 (1972).

47. *Bullock* v. *Carter,* 405 U.S. 134 (1972).

48. *Carrington* v. *Rush,* 380 U.S. 89 (1965).

49. *Moore* v. *Ogilvie,* 394 U.S. 814 (1969).

50. *Williams* v. *Rhodes,* 393 U.S. 23 (1968); *Jenness* v. *Fortson,* 403 U.S. 431 (1971).

51. *Zablocki* v. *Redhail,* 434 U.S. 374 (1978).

52. *Palmore* v. *Sidoti,* 80 L Ed 2d 421 (1984).

53. *San Antonio School District* v. *Rodriguez,* 411 U.S. 1 (1973).

54. *Plessy* v. *Ferguson,* 163 U.S. 537 (1896).

55. *Brown* v. *Board of Education,* 347 U.S. 483 (1954).

56. *Brown* v. *Board of Education,* 349 U.S. 294 (1955).

57. *Alexander* v. *Board of Education,* 396 U.S. 19 (1969).

58. *Swann* v. *Charlotte-Mecklenburg Board of Education,* 402 U.S. 1 (1971). *See also* Chief Justice Burger's further elaboration in *Winston-Salem/Forsythe Board of Education* v. *Scott,* 404 U.S. 122 (1971).

59. *Milliken* v. *Bradley,* 433 U.S. 267 (1977).

60. *Swann* v. *Charlotte-Mecklenburg Board of Education,* 402 U.S. 1 (1971); *Milliken* v. *Bradley,* 433 U.S. 267 (1977).

61. *Milliken* v. *Bradley,* 418 U.S. 717 (1974).

62. *Estes* v. *Metropolitan Branches, Dallas NAACP,* 444 U.S. 437 (1980).

63. *Columbus Board of Education* v. *Penick,* 443 U.S. 449 (1979).

64. *Washington* v. *Seattle School District No. 1,* 458 U.S. 457 (1982).

65. *Crawford* v. *Los Angeles Board of Education,* 458 U.S. 527 (1982).

66. *Mayor* v. *Dawson,* 350 U.S. 877 (1956); *Gayle* v. *Browder,* 352 U.S. 903 (1956).

67. *Loring* v. *Virginia,* 388 U.S. 1 (1967).

68. *Palmore* v. *Sidoti,* 80 L Ed 2d 421 (1984).

69. *Washington* v. *Davis,* 426 U.S. 229 (1976); *Mobile* v. *Bloden,* 446 U.S. 55 (1979); *Arlington Heights* v. *Metro Housing Corp.,* 429 U.S. 252 (1977).

70. *Dothard* v. *Rawlingson,* 433 U.S. 321 (1977).

71. *Mobile* v. *Bloden,* 446 U.S. 55 (1980).

72. *Rogers* v. *Lodge,* 458 U.S. 613 (1982).

73. *Board of Education of New York* v. *Harris,* 444 U.S. 130 (1979): *Texas Department of Community Affairs* v. *Burdine,* 450 U.S. 248 (1981); *Griggs* v. *Duke Power Co.,* 401 U.S. 424 (1971).

74. *General Building Contractors* v. *Pennsylvania,* 458 U.S. 375 (1983).

75. *Regents of the University of California* v. *Bakke,* 438 U.S. 265 (1978).

76. 443 U.S. 193 (1979).

77. 448 U.S. 448 (1980).

78. *Firefighters* v. *Stotts,* 81 L Ed 2d 483 (1984).

79. *Regents of the University of California* v. *Bakke,* 438 U.S. 265 (1978); *Fullilove* v. *Klutznick,* 448 U.S. 448 (1980).

80. *Minnick* v. *California Department of Corrections,* 452 U.S. 105 (1981).

81. Justice Marshall in *Fullilove* v. *Klutznick*

82. *Ambach* v. *Norwich,* 441 U.S. 68 (1979).

83. *Cabell* v. *Chavez-Salido,* 454 U.S. 432 (1982).

84. *Bernal* v. *Fainter,* 81 L Ed 2d 175 (1984); *Graham* v. *Richardson,* 403 U.S. 365 (1971); *Nyquist* v. *Mauclet* 432 U.S. 1 (1977).

85. *Foley* v. *Connelie,* 435 U.S. 291 (1978); *Ambach* v. *Norwich,* 441 U.S. 68 (1979)

86. *Toll* v. *Moreno,* 441 U.S. 458 (1979), quoting *DeCana* v. *Bica,* 424 U.S. 351 (1976).

87. *Toll* v. *Moreno.*

88. *Bernal* v. *Fainter,* 81 L Ed 2d 175 (1984).

89. *Pickett* v. *Brown,* 76 L Ed 2d 372 (1983).

90. *Pickett* v. *Brown,* 76 L Ed 372 (1983); *Mills* v. *Habluetzel,* 456 U.S. 96 (1982) and cases cited therein.

91. *Harris* v. *McRae,* 448 U.S. 297 (1980); *Maher* v. *Roe,* 432 U.S. 464 (1977).

92. *San Antonio School District* v. *Rodriguez,* 411 U.S. 1 (1973).

93. *United States* v. *Kras,* 409 U.S. 434 (1973); *Boddie* v. *Connecticut,* 401 U.S. 371 (1971).

94. Justice Rehnquist, plurality in *Clements* v. *Fashing,* 457 U.S. 957 (1982).

95. *Griffin* v. *Illinois,* 351 U.S. 12 (1956); *Douglas* v. *California,* 372 U.S. 353 (1963); *Meyer* v. *City of Chicago,* 404 U.S. 189 (1971).

96. *Ross* v. *Moffit,* 417 U.S. 600 (1974).

97. *Brearden* v. *Georgia,* 76 L Ed 2d 221 (1983).

98. *Boddie* v. *Connecticut,* 401 U.S. 371 (1971).

99. *United States* v. *Kras,* 409 U.S. 434 (1973).

100. *Ortwein* v. *Schwab,* 410 U.S. 656 (1973).

101. *Little* v. *Streater,* 452 U.S. 1 (1981).

102. *Harper* v. *Board of Elections,* 338 U.S. 663 (1966).

103. *Massachusetts Board of Retirement* v. *Murgia,* 427 U.S. 307 (1976); *Vance* v. *Bradley,* 440 U.S. 93 (1979).

104. *Schweiker* v. *Wilson,* 450 U.S. 221 (1981).

105. *Goesaert* v. *Cleary,* 335 U.S. 464 (1948).

106. *Phillips* v. *Martin Marietta Corp.,* 400 U.S. 542 (1971).

107. *Reed* v. *Reed,* 404 U.S. 71 (1971).

108. *Frontiero* v. *Richardson,* 411 U.S. 677 (1973).

109. *Stanton* v. *Stanton,* 421 U.S. 7 (1976).

110. *Taylor* v. *Louisiana,* 419 U.S. 522 (1975).

111. *Califano* v. *Goldfarb,* 430 U.S. 199 (1977).

112. *Craig* v. *Borden,* 429 U.S. 190 (1976).

113. *Kirchberg* v. *Feenstra,* 450 U.S. 455 (1981).

114. *Orr* v. *Orr,* 440 U.S. 268 (1979).

115. *Caban* v. *Mohammed,* 441 U.S. 380 (1979).

116. *Califano* v. *Westcott,* 443 U.S. 76 (1979).

117. *Wengler* v. *Druggists Mutual Insurance Co.,* 446 U.S. 142 (1980).

118. *Mississippi University for Women* v. *Hogan,* 458 U.S. 718 (1982).

119. *Davis* v. *Passman,* 442 U.S. 228 (1979).

120. *Kahan* v. *Shevin,* 416 U.S. 351 (1974).

121. *Schlesinger* v. *Ballard,* 419 U.S. 498 (1975).

122. *Califano* v. *Webster,* 430 U.S. 313 (1977).

123. *Fiallo* v. *Bell,* 430 U.S. 787 (1977).

124. *Lehr* v. *Robertson,* 77 L Ed 2d 614 (1983).

125. *Geduldig* v. *Aiello,* 417 U.S. 484 (1974); *Califano* v. *Webster,* 430 U.S. 313 (1977).

126. *Michael M.* v. *Superior Court of Sonoma County,* 450 U.S. 464 (1981).

127. *Personnel Administrator of Massachusetts* v. *Feeney,* 442 U.S. 256 (1979).

128. *Rostker* v. *Goldberg,* 453 U.S. 57 (1981).

129. *Califano* v. *Webster,* 430 U.S. 313 (1977) and cases cited therein.

130. *Dothard* v. *Rawlinson,* 433 U.S. 321 (1977).

131. *Los Angeles Department of Water and Power* v. *Manhart,* 435 U.S. 702 (1978); *General Electric Co.* v. *Gilbert,* 429 U.S. 125 (1976).

132. *Ibid.*

133. *Regents of the University of California* v. *Bakke,* 438 U.S. 265 (1978).

134. *Trimble* v. *Gordon,* 430 U.S. 762 (1977).

135. *Beal* v. *Doe,* 432 U.S. 438 (1977).

136. *Illinois Elections Bd.* v. *Socialist Workers Party,* 440 U.S. 173 (1979).

137. *Gray* v. *Sanders,* 372 U.S. 368 (1963).

138. *Moore* v. *Ogilvie,* 394 U.S. 814 (1969).

139. *Sayler Land Co.* v. *Tulare Lake Basin Water Storage District,* 410 U.S. 719 (1973); *Associated Enterprises, Inc.* v. *Toltec District,* 410 U.S. 743 (1973); *Ball* v. *James,* 455 U.S. 355 (1981).

140. *Wells* v. *Edwards,* 409 U.S. 1095 (1973).

141. *Wells* v. *Rockefeller,* 394 U.S. 542 (1969); *Kirkpatrick* v. *Preisler,* 394 U.S. 526 (1969).

142. *Reynolds* v. *Simms,* 377 U.S. 533 (1964) and companion cases.

143. *Avery* v. *Midland County,* 390 U.S. 474 (1968).

144. *Hadley* v. *Junior College District of Kansas City,* 397 U.S. 50 (1972).

145. *Abate* v. *Mundt,* 403 U.S. 182 (1971); *Connor* v. *Williams,* 404 U.S. 549 (1970); *Mahan* v. *Howell,* 410 U.S. 315 (1973).

146. *Chapman* v. *Meier,* 420 U.S. 1 (1975); *Connor* v. *Finch,* 431 U.S. 407 (1977).

147. *Terry* v. *Adams,* 345 U.S. 461 (1953).

148. *Marsh* v. *Alabama,* 326 U.S. 501 (1946).

149. *Flagg Brothers, Inc.* v. *Brooks,* 436 U.S. 14 (1978) and cases cited therein.

150. *Rendell-Baker* v. *Kohn,* 457 U.S. 830 (1982).
151. *Shelley* v. *Kraemer,* 344 U.S. 1 (1948); *Barrows* v. *Jackson,* 346 U.S. 249 (1953).
152. *Moose Lodge No. 107* v. *Irvis,* 407 U.S. 163 (1972).
153. *Burton* v. *Wilmington Parking Authority,* 365 U.S. 715 (1961).
154. *Reitman* v. *Mulkey et al.,* 387 U.S. 369 (1967).
155. *Washington* v. *Seattle School District No. 1,* 458 U.S. 457 (1982).
156. *Crawford* v. *Los Angeles Board of Education,* 458 U.S. 527 (1982).
157. *Palmer* v. *Thompson,* 403 U.S. 217 (1971); *Bolling* v. *Sharpe,* 347 U.S. 497 (1953); *McGhee* v. *Sipes,* 334 U.S. 1 (1948).
158. *Jackson* v. *Metropolitan Edison Co.,* 419 U.S. 345 (1974).
159. *Gilmore* v. *City of Montgomery,* 417 U.S. 556 (1974).
160. *Moose Lodge No. 107* v. *Irvis,* 407 U.S. 163 (1972).
161. *Norwood* v. *Harrison,* 413 U.S. 455 (1973); *Hishon* v. *King & Spalding,* 81 L Ed 2d 59 (1984).
162. *Roberts* v. *Jaycees,* 82 L Ed 2d 462 (1984).
163. *Hishon* v. *King & Spaulding,* 81 L Ed 2d 59 (1984).
164. *Runyon* v. *McCrary,* 427 U.S. 160 (1976).
165. *Bolling* v. *Sharpe,* 347 U.S. 497 (1976).
166. *Washington* v. *Legrant,* 394 U.S. 618 (1969); *Richardson* v. *Belcher,* 404 U.S. 78 (1971).
167. *Richardson* v. *Ramirez,* 418 U.S. 24 (1974).
168. *The Civil Rights Cases,* 109 U.S. 3 (1883).
169. *Adickes* v. *S.H. Kress Co.,* 398 U.S. 144 (1970); *United States* v. *Guest,* 383 U.S. 745 (1966).
170. *Katzenbach* v. *Morgan,* 384 U.S. 641 (1966).
171. *Regents of the University of California* v. *Bakke,* 438 U.S. 256 (1978).
172. *United States* v. *Guest,* 383 U.S. 745 (1966); *Jones* v. *Alfred Mayer,* 392 U.S. 409 (1969); *United States* v. *Johnson,* 390 U.S. 563 (1968).
173. *Smith* v. *Wade,* 75 L Ed 2d 643 (1983).

Amendment XV: The Right to Vote

1. *Lane* v. *Wilson,* 307 U.S. 368 (1939).
2. *Smith* v. *Allwright,* 321 U.S. 649 (1944); *Terry* v. *Adams,* 345 U.S. 461 (1953).
3. *United States* v. *Mississippi,* 380 U.S. 128 (1965); *Louisiana* v. *United States,* 380 U.S. 145 (1965).
4. *Minor* v. *Happersett,* 21 Wallace 162
5. *San Antonio School District* v. *Rodriguez,* 411 U.S. 1 (1973).
6. *Rodriguez* v. *Popular Democratic Party,* 457 U.S. 1 (1982).
7. *South Carolina* v. *Katzenbach,* 383 U.S. 301 (1966).
8. *Mobile* v. *Bolden,* 446 U.S. 55 (1980).
9. *Rome* v. *United States,* 446 U.S. 156 (1980).
10. *United Jewish Organizations* v. *Carey,* 430 U.S. 144 (1977).

Twentieth-Century Amendments

1. *Pollock* v. *Farmers Loan & Trust Co.,* 158 U.S. 601 (1895).
2. *Dept. of Revenue* v. *James Beam Co.,* 377 U.S. 341 (1964)
3. *California* v. *LaRue,* 409 U.S. 109 (1972); *New York State Liquor Authority* v. *Belanca,* 452 U.S. 714 (1981).
4. *Capital Cities Cable, Inc.* v. *Crisp,* 81 L Ed 2d 580 (1984).
5. *Ibid.*
6. *Harper* v. *Virginia Board of Elections,* 383 U.S. 663 (1966).
7. *Harman* v. *Forssenius,* 380 U.S. 529 (1965).
8. See William Safire, *Full Disclosure* (Garden City, N.Y.) Doubleday & Company, for a political novel dealing with the ramifications of the Twenty-fifth Amendment.
9. Janet K. Boles, *The Politics of the Equal Rights Amendment* (Longmans, 1979), pp. 181–182.

Index